THE PHILOSOPHICAL PHILOSOPHER PRESENTS

THE KING BUSINESS

THE BOSS PLAYER ASSOCIATION

MACKOLOGY 2ND EDITION
TURNING DREAMS TO REALITY
AUGUST 3RD, 1981 EDITION

WRITTEN BY
a king named Mr. Mack Millon

authorHOUSE®

AuthorHouse™
1663 Liberty Drive
Bloomington, IN 47403
www.authorhouse.com
Phone: 833-262-8899

Published by AuthorHouse 07/28/2021

ISBN: 978-1-6655-3336-2 (sc)
ISBN: 978-1-6655-3334-8 (hc)
ISBN: 978-1-6655-3335-5 (e)

Library of Congress Control Number: 2021915306

Print information available on the last page.

Any people depicted in stock imagery provided by Getty Images are models, and such images are being used for illustrative purposes only. Certain stock imagery © Getty Images.

This book is printed on acid-free paper.

CONTENTS

FACTS OF LIFE

Respect to crime boss, he got an historic song called, "that's how the story goes,"royalty said, "cover all angles, & then connect game.

Elamites favorite chilling spot is susa, shishak & tirhaquah taharka soul people in the basic instructions before leaving earth, eshmunuzar Ii is the phoenixan has ancient soulful history, which name is more important, Ganges, or chilaros, lush is refer named after ancient civilization named Cush, what does ixtlilton mean in Mexico, who is bapsiste pointe de saible in Chicagoans truth beyond belief, is-em-hoteplife story has been applied to who made up life story, you know who it is, but you don't know who life story it dirived from, respect to soulful Hannibal the elephant king, it's a book called, "the white slave trade," written by James O'Neal possibly.

I'm watching the 2021 home run derby in Denver, I just was In Denver shaking hands with Damien Marley, Denver downtown is nice big to, coyote ugly bar was cool, went with Jim from Jacksonville Florida, true player Jim was, never watched the mlb all star weekend, stars Is Pete Alonso Trevor story & shohei ohtani.

THE GAME OF LIFE SCRIPTURES

1.

Playing the game of life is knowing how to roll it, live to give, give to live, the game of life has always been about unity, team work works, it's a proven fact that teams have won championships, everybody need everybody, cross country living will explain precisely, exactly, specifically what the game of life scriptures is all about.

Three things you guarantee to see, is somebody in your day, or night, that will show signs of being mad, sad, or glad.

Everybody route through the game of life, it is not the same, Don't be bait for the bait, Those who survived the pinky ring street king lifestyle, can live to talk about it, If you know the game of life, why stay & play in it forever, especially if you know the facts of life, that the whole lifestyle of short cut living, is setup to be a permanent losing game, specifically for those who get caught slippin'."

Crucial conflict said, "don't let it go to your head," Pimpin is survival, might be different spellings, but both have the exact same meaning.

The young player in the neighborhood said, "You told me what to do, but I got to deal with what I did, or do, not the one who told me what to do, see, most people gone cover their end of what situation they lost in, possibly by saying, "i didn't make you do it," so then props get dropped, next you will see the sight of respect leaving the spotlight you in.

If you mad, read the best book you can find, go sit by a Solaris See-Through Glass Fireplace if you sad, if you feeling lost, go to the Atlantic ocean, & watch everything fall into place.

2021 BEST SELLING BOOK

This title describes the intriguing author twice, philosophical philosopher, street life philosophy means no college degree, which mean self educated from higher learning, kemetic sent intelligence, with prosperous progressive simply remarkable unbelievable Champagne brilliant Chicago home schooling.

The game of Life scriptures, lifeology is the study of Life it self, on all of the most important unique classified confidential levels in the game of life, important titles that's still being misunderstood in the game of life will be explained in the most incredible INTELLECTUAL WAY, BY AN INTELLECTUAL MAGNIFICENT UNIQUE INDIVIDUAL, specifically inside this intriguing intellectual magnificent book.

The last mack standing scriptures is a story that took years to write, with names of historic powerful indigenous people, a story with unbreakable love, unforgettable betrayal, mandatory dedication, embraced unity, & one out of many indigenous royal families is in the last mack standing scriptures storyline.

This unique book I present to you, it is the 2021 brilliantly wrote street life exciting historic book, Webster dictionary is needed while you get better acquainted with this spectacular book.

This is High intelligent intellectual Philosophy in a way you have never known before now, inside is the most anticipated history in the making of a storyline, lifeology gives you an highly anticipated game of life type of a book, read this book, & see life in a perspective, a perspective you never thought was possible to see from in this lifetime.

This book will make the sad happy, it will humble the angriest person in the world, it will bring truth to lies, it's truth beyond belief, true game, solid gold ism, today anything is everything, this book will help you understand everybody, this book creates solutions to permanent problems, this book answers forbidden questions.

This book is every book that has ever been written in this lifetime, past present future, every book combined in one book, it is this brilliant book..

The philosophical philosopher describes the author writing style's personality, with not even a piece of college degree, he presents street life philosophy from an intellectual, individual, spectacular, powerful perspective created in the projects, during childhood, in chicago to Milwaukee, same game of life systematic upbringing we all was born in, land to your land, to everybody else land, indigenous intelligence to brilliance is mandatory in the most important way possible, 39 year old notes put In book format, from birth to earth, childhood to adulthood, ocean floor deep, & so precisely correct, a 6 year old can understand this gigantic book meaning, & purpose.

I'm speed editing this intriguing book, due to working, simply to take care of family, so Mackology 3rd edition will be wrote during retirement, simply so Mackology 3rd edition book can be precisely correct, sit back relax enjoy the show, Im watching bishop and friends podcast minister seamore, p thuggin, honey haze, Sophia ruby, queen, aka gorgeous, they speaking on recent Miami condo left side of condo collapsed, bodies still being found.

THE LAST MACK STANDING SCRIPTURES

1.

Step in smooth to lay It down thick, straight grinding, just like indigenous people do in Little Rock Arkansas, got to learn how to live, then learn how to earn, then learn how to make money work for you, then learn how to pull up shining brand new, like they say In Memphis, "this what game plus money do for you," if you learn how to direct traffic, Memphis know the business, on some project pat type stuff, It's all about getting life right, wealthy comfortable with longevity, and spirituality.

I'm in country knolls New York watching New York Mets play New York Yankees on spectrum, the Mets is up 8 to 1 In the bottom of the 6 Inning, the grandfather loved the white socks when giant frank Thomas was playing for Chicago white socks.

ABOUT THE AUTHOR

The lovely sounds of Milwaukee police sirens is screaming through the air around me, all type of cars speeding through stop lights, all of which is saying to me, "welcome back home King, where you been at, wait till we show you what you missed sense you been gone."

Lightening hit the ground, & this unbelievable book was stuck inside the cracked up, stainless steel hard cement, it was stuck sizzling when the smoke cleared, a hardcover book, it's called, "the king business Mackology 2nd edition," it was in my arm reach, if you don't believe me, ask three 6 mafia what happened when the smoke cleared.

Once I picked up this unbelievable book, I decided to work a deal out with authorhouse book publishing company, to distribute copies of this book globally, for global intelligence reasons, which will be understood once you read this whole book, in one pimpin gangster player hustler day, which Is today, right now.

So do just that, stick to the script, remain true to the game, at the present moment I'm leaning back in Appleton Wisconsin, looking through this highly anticipated game tight book, reading this book is identical to walking down energy cities roads, with halls full of game, with worldwide indigenous people pictures on them walls, & ancient statues in these halls, it's like going through Atlanta airport, statues, & pictures of Indigenous people everywhere, Atlanta airport look like soul plane airport, it's something to see.

This Is what this unique book has to offer: the game of life scriptures, street life philosophy, mackology, currency lifestyle, the last mack standing scriptures, from birth to earth, journey wealthy longevity Scriptures, third eye watching, prayer was made for the boss player, the pinky ring street

King, everywhere specialize in some part of life differently than other places, all of that combined.

My name spit game, I sip dip luxury live, I floss toss money in the air, I switch lanes sipping Champagne, I'm in it to the finish, I don't write to excite, I write to educate & motivate, you could have been anywhere in the world, but you here with me, the floor mat in front of this King's castle, it says, "welcome to the mack moon," now keep in mind, I didn't say I own land, I didn't say buy property, or own your own business, so as the book go on, let's see if statements like that will start being made, also see if progress is being made during city to city traveling statements in some chapters.

JOURNEY WEALTHY LONGEVITY SCRIPTURES

1.

Everywhere you go, be on the prowl to see if that city got benefits for you on the business tip, vehicles, homes, a new crew, or new members bringing something to the table, showing a down for life mentality, simply to be in the royal family, to help the royal family get wealthy on the journey to longevity.

I'm in Topeka Kansas right now, I'm just editing this mysterious book, I'm watching pastor tony smith, I'm reading Egyptian proverbs written by Dr. Muata ashby, it's around 40 degrees here in January, it's the state capitol, but why, not much to see here in plain sight far as royalty eyes can see.

Don't be here to entertain, be here to maintain, Cross country living is nice, but like coo coo cal told dorthy and toe-doe, "there's no place like home," on some 227 type stuff, Thug life is the young man game, gangster lifestyle is the grown man business, so when you see grown men talking, like pretty tony said, "shut the truck up," & get out the way respectfully, until you become a grown man, no disrespect, just saying, "grow, develop from boys to men, here at the boss player association, we love all y'all, know that.

RED ROOF INN TOLEDO OHIO

Ok let me say this quick, if you hear somebody say something in this boss player book, with quotes on what they saying inside this specific book, that's exactly who said it, I'm noticing my phrases in this book, randomly being spoken on television, If you hear anything in this book you heard spoken before, it's because of cross country word of mouth, which will travel in the air globally, especially if it's longevity game phrases, or you gone hear words spoken straight from my mouth, that which you will read inside my chapters.

I just want to say, when you yourself, or anybody you know, or will meet, before y'all hit queen khalifa California border line, turn on some indigenous historic music, like Toni tony tone, it will instantly give you that I'm in California feeling, hit los Angeles, play that song that says, "it never rain in southern california," music.

whoever controls music will rule the world, Picking soulful soul food music is very important to know how to do, music is everything the definition of important is, (respect to sinful the p how he say everything the definition of a word is), in this world of words, music is meant to be studied, on the strength that it is mandatory, to understand what is required to be understood from what we listen to, far as music go, I recommend listening to Lauryn hill words grouped in the classic song, it's called, "ex-factor," a woman has to read, write daily, consistently, to know how to get her point across like lauryn hill did in this song, talking is something in your life that is mandatory to master, we all get taught basic verbal communication skills throughout our childhood, conversation rule the nation, is what indigenous people will recite multiple times every year, study how indigenous queens recognize indigenous kings, then analyze how indigenous kings recognize indigenous queens, it's a truly remarkable sight to see, it's then that you will come to realize, that figuring out the importance of communication is required 24 hours a day, everywhere indigenous people walk the earth at, this is what you soon will refer to as, "the game of life being philosophically broke down in fractions in the form of street life philosophy," I'm listening to Houston king z-to song, it's called, "25 lighters freestyle," I like that trae the truth cartoon to, Houston be making major moves, you hear me.

THE GAME OF LIFE SCRIPTURES

2.

Playing the game of life is knowing how to roll it, live to give, give to live, the game of life has always been about unity, team work works, it's a proven fact teams have won championships, everybody need everybody, cross country living will explain precisely, exactly, specifically what the game of life scriptures is all about.

I'm in pine bluff Arkansas editing this part of this fascinating intriguing exuberayting book, I'm listening to leroy hutson song, it's called, "when you smile," pine bluff had cool people there, stores sold everything you need, from everything to everything.

INTELLIGENT TO BRILLIANT
THINKING PROCESS

All Royalty got is royalty hands on money, capital game, beneficial plans, it's the game of life, & everybody play it the way they experienced it, how the game of life was introduced to them, peep each other styles, it shows your native land behavior, you a representative of what land you indigenous to, by your overall performance when you in other indigenous people land, also the game develops how they perceive it to be setup to be played, by themselves, or either its natural instinct to do what they born to do, I mean its just like a fish takes to water, it be like that for some, I mean if game falling like rain on you, all your life, some of that good game comes from people who survived the seventies, and others who pimped in the 70s to 80s, also original gangsters, extra ordinary boss players, supreme hustlers who made it out them decades to now, hear what they got to say, it's solid, & polished like a new diamond pinky ring from paks, I mean wisdom from elders 70 years, and older, I mean, what you expect to come next, I mean it's the game of life, if you didn't know, I welcome the real world to you right now, with this gigantic book, if you knew then what you know now, how would you have played the game of life?

This is what you will soon call chopping up game, in the most highly intellectual street life philosphical way, with true boss player king philosophy chapters.

Starving for great game in an indigenous Childhood, to mastermind indigenous adulthood, if game was raining on you from childhood to adulthood, then you most likely lived life in the fast lane, your lifestyle is all About thinking quick, you obligated to living life comfortable, your daily focus is all about moving around the world enjoying life, surviving in the most memorable way possible, so with that being said, living life being on the ground floor, instantaneously starts to become unacceptable, & uncomfortable in the worst way possible.

we gone start right there, if your life transpired identical to what was just spoke on, then your mindset is full speed ahead, no breaks, no day off, just serious survival with a successful perspective, if you slip, or fall, get back up like king boo said, bounce back like juvenile, play to win like kobe Bryant, live longevity long like Fillmore slim doing at this present moment.

these is the type of indigenous individuals, who pinky ring street kings consider to be in it to the finish, these indigenous individuals is dedicated to living life being stupendous, & they consistently cross country is being known for that.

far as I know, that's what giants call longevity in the game of life, professional paid lifestyle in the fast lane, respect to king Fillmore slim, that's my respect to a macknificent king, one of the game of life survivalist experts, I would say he 80 plus years still ticking, that's a great book title, "journey wealthy longevity."

The average boss player giants would say, "if you made numerous fool moves, slipped off the throne, but through age plus experience, & figured out what to do next, that's normal in the game of life, its normal to know mistakes make you brilliant, that is, if you learning everyday to avoid making mistakes."

right on for darkness is what Curtis Mayfield once said, that's game if you can recognize what he tum bout, back to the breakdown, so then you fix everything up every chance you get, then master how to be gone with the wind like Clarke gable, as top ladies Referred to him as, "tall dark handsome Clarke gable," gone with the wind mean just getting to the mastermind level, & then you will simultaneously find yourself moving up to the upper class, like George Jefferson did, ask eloise gwendolyn sanford from harlem New York what I'm tum bout.

It's mandatory to know full dedication, combined with cooperation, is most definitely a characteristic trait Every queen bee flying around you must posses, all year round consistently daily, or however the game is able to be played by you, it's most definitely good to get the automatic best female boss players, from every city you touch your feet down in, every city you hit consistently, that's how you connect the dots meaning cities, now your money route income is multiplied, like they say in New York the concrete jungle, "straight like that."

This to, if you been around sense back in the beginning of the game of life, or before the 80s, the boss player Association says congratulations on making it past 18 years old.

Because that's proof you here for a reason, and if you know what um tum bout, that mean game recognize game, the ancestors been putting the truth in the air like that, for the last 10,000 years, to be passed on from generations to generations, each one teach one.

Now with clear vision, look at this picture being painted to visualize, if you knew how to build your spiritual strength, as well as mental skills, all the way up to maximum capacity, do it, & watch the red carpet start getting rolled out for you everywhere you be, rolled out like you a very important person in Hollywood, now recognize every city state you enter, it will test your survival skills, that which has been in betted inside you, & every city will test how expertly you play the game of life, that's mandatory to transpire everywhere you go.

Now check this out, hitting the highway is a route going into the major leagues, when you leave to come back home from hitting the highway, that's what some, not most will consider to be going into the major league, keep this in mind, the boss player association will huddle up when necessary, simply to brake down an important situation worth focusing on in fractions, to deal with it piece by piece.

Now listen to this indigenous individuals, from living life fast recklessly, to living strategically on a pathway towards the good life (also a name of one of too $hort classic song's called, "good life"), we all will reach baller status financially, we all will fall down the ladder, similar to how billy ray did on the movie, "trading places," with a paused play button, so you keep moving until you get where you going, then you get the best of the best every city has to offer, full effort on that journey, see where it lead you, aim to win like Michael Jordan, LeBron James, Magic Johnson, james worthy, wilt chamberlain, tim hardaway, Shawn kemp, Steve francis. Gary payton, terry cummings, Charles Barkley, develop those type of winning mentalities.

Now I see the best global intelligent boss players, identical to the names I name, these type indigenous individuals made it ahead of the world races they found themselves born in, with plenty thoughts on how to read to succeed, live to learn, and learn how to live, we all got a book to write, those that have been touched by the sun, from the beginning of time to now, they shine million dollar diamond bright, they straight Dogon stars in amun ra sunlight to moonlight.

Now if this how you suggest a book is supposed to start, then appreciate the words I provide for the wise to read to succeed, add what this book tell you, to what you already know, it's equipping yourself with game that's called reinforcement skills, to back up your already got skills, the ism you was naturally born with in this game of life, always put game you hear in the air in your pocket, take it with you every city you hit, it will help you recognize how to survive every where you go, how to learn from being in that City's longevity lessons, then add it to what you already know, that's how you get a cross country understanding, about living life with a master mind mentality, which will develop into a global brilliance thinking process on all levels.

This brilliant boss player Association book, is based around the theory of figure out the game of life, the master mind way, to instantaneously know how to read in between the line of everything that demand your attention, life is broke down in fractions inside knowledge, wisdom, good game books like this, take what you need out of everything your ears grab to get your attention, take specifically what you require to use in everyday life, use it to step your game up to the king queen mastermind level, with wisdom as your First Lady, and knowledge as your power, the more knowledge you possess will gradually body build you up to a giant, strategically speaking, on all, or most levels of the game of life.

Always full effort every hour, no half stepping like big daddy Kane said, now it's known if you find your reflection on your pathway, a lifetime player partner is what most boss players title that person, or group of people that Will roll with you for a lifetime, your best partner like Hawaii famous american pimp charm said, or best partners, however you choose to play the game of life, can you feel that wind blow through you, put all your ism in her, or in all your lifetime dedicated to you ladies, however you group up, shine up your diamond, or diamonds, then all y'all will immediately begin to shine brighter, it's all apart of the game of life step by step process, rules laws mandatory successful behavior, I thank the Most

9

High truthfully I reply, I'm thankful I seen every state except one up to this point, it's somebody that been waiting to see you, and finally meet you, it's places to see, to enjoy the energy there, sight see, possibly come up nice, I mean somewhere you get fat at, just for being there, the new home, the home away from home, a place you get the royal treatment day one.

Now when this book finally hit the internet, plus stores such as Barnes & noble, amazon, overseas in places like china, also global stores near you, I probably would have finally seen Oregon, I noticed it's always somebody cool in every state, now stay on point regardless of that, but it's nice to meet & greet in every state, a somebody, or people from each state, that will put you up on how their city state operate, so if you need to have a beneficial stay while you dwell in that city state, boy it's serious on the high levels in life you walk up on, this is a pinch of how you play the game of life, or how it will play you, living in this world is turning into a business, nothing personal, ain't that something to think about, everyday is based around your all around consistent performance, strictly business for some, personal for others, a rule law to live by, is never mix business with pleasure, it's a bad outcome, when you combine those two together.

In the life I live, in some cases when it's time to get back on your feet, with vehicles keys, house keys, businesses generating income money routes, all eyes will be watching to see how you make it happen, I mean how you consistently play to win in everyday life, day to night, even when you traveling just to analyze, just to get game from everywhere, so you can learn how to stay a giant, all while leading who follow your lead like 50 cent said, consistently defining the word king, by staying consistently on your throne, righteously ruling for years, simply by figuring out, exactly how to master the game of life everywhere you touch your feet down at, like uncle juny said.

I tell you what, thank you for your undivided attention, you can be anywhere in the world, but like they always be saying, you here with me pouring my words in your eye contact, therefore now to forever i appreciate you, simply for making it to this level you on in your lifestyle, simply made possible from dedication to surviving, just perfecting the ways of living life to the fullest, or you bout to do just that, while, or after reading this book, I got author names in this Mackology 2nd edition, an their book titles, it's slightly hidden in plain sight, see if you can see what the third supposed to see.

It's difficult for some, not most, just to understand when an indigenous individual is truly blessed, they tend to do things for others, some, not most will consider to be weird, or crazy, because some, not most would never think twice about doing what blessed people do, in fear of losing the root of all evil. Lol

Money is a tool, a trading tool, All royalty do is get money to make everything happen, that's the game of life, baby drew said, "because a little ain't enough," I'm speaking on opportunities every blink of the eye see, royalty like the best, so royalty aim high, shoot for the bullseye, if need be, royalty will re aim royalty aim, sharpen royalty skills, so Royalty can have, get, keep, hold the best in the city, i mean if you playing to win, ain't that what's it's about, having the best for the best.

So this where it's at right now in the game of life, chaos, craziness, out of order, but it's the way of the world, get up get out the trap, figure out how to get paid in full like Eric b and rakim, I mean that's how you play it, I mean the giants gone send limos, to air plain tickets to invite you to meet them, because they respect your game.

This how it go inside the boss player game of life, if I like you, I'm gone airplane you to me if it's space in between us, that's boss player friendly behavior, I mean if my living is luxury, then I got to get busy b busy, to help you get everything big in your pocket, on your money route, it's called community service, give to live, live to give.

This what you call chopping up game with you respectfully, truthfully, honestly, This is straight shots of Cleveland Midwest good game with no chaser, no game spitting with cruel intentions in royalty conversation, I mean Royalty on a journey to get wealthy, tracing the footsteps Of soul survivors to marry longevity.

Turn on willie hutch song, "sunshine lady," its what Memphis juicy j mean when he say, "play me some pimpin," literally, now that's game if you can do that, I say in the words of California King pimps, peace and pimpin, peace to the pimpin, one or the other, I'm John blaze right now, but i'm hip to the game of life scriptures.

You know what Um tum bout, willie hutch talking about a dedication cooperation lady, how she got to be in life to qualify herself to shine, and get the royal treatment.

The last Mack standing scriptures is the last part of this brilliant book, it's the story line of all story lines to enjoy, and it allows you to have the opportunity to explore inside the mind of a king, located on the Mack moon, where game rain, and laims complain, royalty do royalty best to not complain, and just spit more game, & play to win, win, win, win all live long day.

Any person place, or things named inside the creme pages of this brilliantly written book, is only to help promote the best, that life has to offer one to all.

As I edit this beginning part of my book Mackology 2nd edition, I lean back in the comfort inn hotel in Davenport Iowa, not to far from downtown Davenport, by the Mississippi River, I'm watching the historical game of life movie, it's called, "the Mack."

The burning bush in the ten commandments movie, it symbolizes the sun, Moses turned dark to say, that all original indigenous brown skin soul people know the Creator from birth, they been touched by the sun, spell it with o or u, it still will reflect the same way, the sun is the Most High.

Every hour after every hour game is supposed to recognize game, that is, if you focused to hard to be distracted, some individuals will lie about the truth, & simultaneously hide it in plain sight, some individuals put the right words together for personal gain, it's known as word play, real weak but effective sneaky game, stay on point all day every day, power overcomes weakness, polish your knowledge, & turn weakness to strength with your powerful polished knowledge.

In order to get some real money, you got to hit the highway, or the internet, or the airwaves on your phone, straight connecting game on a Money route guiding it to your pockets.

I'm in beaver dam wisconsin right now, I'm sipping Hennessy xo mixed with alkaline water, with a black, its dipped in labrusco wine I'm assuming, snow everywhere out here, & I'm watching richard pryor movie, its called, "bustin loose."

Now close your eyes and see yourself where you at in another world, inside this world I lived my whole life in, a world of game is the world I was born in, it's the opposite of how life transpire at this present moment, it has different results, then it normally has in the fantasy world, some call reality now a days, now think to yourself, do you want to be in my world, or this world opposite of my world, a world of sadness, hate, jealousy, envy, traps, struggling, and in my world, it's solutions to problems, answers to questions, prayers getting answered, unbelievable days to nights, it look like a dream turned into reality if you know royalty.

I used to be solid smooth like waves on the lakefront's in Milwaukee Wisconsin, & Detroit Michigan, then I started sipping liquor, and became sleep, waiting for the special day, that would wake up the sleeping giant, the past gave capital game to the present moment, now I can't be like Ron Jeremy, more like Hugh Hefner when the bread get low, I got to make it rise like yeast.

Most know that, that was part of the game of life success stories, it's time to make everything happen like it's supposed to be done, I mean the king done got the official stamp of approval from mother father Most High, to graduate to greater heights on such short notice, I know you heard that before, but sit back relax and enjoy the show.

My south Carolina cousin just called me, had to tell him why I haven't seen him, he talk to much about what I said don't talk about to me, about to me, game supposed to recognize game right.

I'm in Fargo North Dakota, it's twice nice & good to go, cold in fall, it's a place to be relaxing, also business adding up, now let's not forget about West Virginia the mountain state, now investing in that state is genius, it's a gold mine waiting to be invested in, that's right, I said West Virginia, it's a treasure hidden in plain sight.

Everything gone get better, falling into place every minute of the day to night, it's just mandatory to consistently transpire things to transpire, it's called securing the time to come, securing your position, comfortably living ahead of schedule, and when you see yourself staying ahead of your situations, that's called recognizing how advanced you knowing & growing, this the way boss players speak things into existence, dreams to reality, it's all good game with no cruel intentions, so let it be written, you know the rest, that's right game recognize game.

Now that's what rick james, & snoop dogg call, "the players way," now it's a weird genius that can sell you what you don't need to buy, and it's a whole lifestyle based around that, so stay on your toes, watching everything moving like a surveillance camera, or like a couple Rottweiler dogs guarding nino brown house, while he drunk hiding out.

Respectfully I know, "facts of life," like bobby womack, because I get the game from words out mouths, from every state, now that's a student of the game, it's all apart of prime time hustling, & just survival hustling, I mean if the main door open up to you, to give you what's coming to you in a major way, that's the moves to be made, explore through the traveling door.

Now it's people in the world fresh out of prison, that is figuring out strategically, how to get back what has been took from them in this lifetime, & that's their main objective, simply Because they got that want, & need to win, so they master mind think on how to stay in control, or their second option will be to live in fear.

Always watch for the conversation starring right at you, how it get set up to subdue you, & what it leads up to spiting in your face, not your ear, it's a big difference, so now you prepare your self for a battle of the minds, do that soon as it start coming your way, reconstruct the conversation, so the main idea of somebody speaking to you reveals itself, without that person knowing how you did that, it's all brilliant strategic moves being made, on your thinking process part, happening quickly like fast.

If game recognize game, money, & power is serious from your perspective, the whole existence of those two teaming up in your world, understand everybody got somebody that can play the game exactly how you play it, but more devious then you, so that mean you got to be on your toes at all time.

When you in the right place to hear boss players tell you, or show you how they play their game, take notes, and figure something out from that point on, keep some eyes, & ears around you to see, hear, & make things happen where you ain't at, it's moving as one unit, that's the game the globe is playing to win, now with that on display, it's obvious, it's a tremendous amount of ways this life can be operated on, to figure out what you gone Scooby doo next, that's what is, or will be most anticipated, that which is what will happen next, the outcome, this life lived is meant to be mastered, with global brilliance, to conquer the game of life, globally everybody got a way they play their game, run their game, supreme confidence will strike you, only when you hit the top of the Kilimanjaro mountain, that you climbing.

Some people play on the memories you was taught, so they run their game on those childhood memories, now if you ever in life get the chance to see a round table conversation, it will be extremely educational if your game recognize game, now if you got life long ism, not only will most people be impressed, shocked, & amazed by what you progressively say, to separate yourself from what others say, with the main objective to make your self a beneficially speaking indigenous individual.

Now, to think about hearing boss players brilliant conversations, & peep their verbal patterns, meaning you recognize the script they sticking to, I mean the game is played brilliantly by world geniuses, so it's in you to knowledge your power, wisdom your queen, & watch what happens next, enjoy the show, now that's how the game of life is successfully played with that perspective, now watch all boss players, male, to females be observant, analyzing, then develop longevity moves to make.

Now picture your ancestors, alive in the flesh, in their time they had breath in their lungs, think what would they say to you, study their every moves, pickup where they left off, because it's necessary to know that this world will split people up, so everything got to be hooked up in an unbreakable way, that's what will consistently lead up to longevity.

I been where the king pimps, & boss players was on the prowl at, so I watched their all around performance start to finish literally, not to imitate them (it's called, "imitation of life"), I did it to peep game, so in California, it's said by the elders, "that gang members, gangsters period, some, not all have got into the skin game, but to me, you got to adapt, when it's time to get off a sinking ship, you move fast thinking quickly, ain't no right way to do wrong, so I understand the moves made, now that's why it's important to stay updated, upgraded, globally intelligent to brilliant, mentally developing with that step by step process.

This how game trace back, now a good time for me to have got a team, is when I was in 6th, or 7th, or 8th grade, I should have loved some girl, or girls, which is the same as saying superglue them to what they hear me say, then grow with them girls, United as one, I mean guidance straight to the big money, then by the time we all turned 18, we would have lived all around the country with that togetherness building each other mentality, we all would have been deep in love with each other, so it's less resistance to have a need, to leave a small town, and more so important to see the world on a come up mission, with a see each other live life to the fullest thinking processes, house on the Washington state beach, working to buy own house type currency, it's all game that this relate to, now it should have been played out like that up to now.

When in new land, it only takes one day to see how it go, then you decide decisions, & choose choices, simplE math, slow, & steady win the race, home gone be home when we get back home, explore through the traveling door, put fear in the rear, I'm listening to Curtis mayfield song, it's called, "the makings of you," the live version.

Always Tell all negative thoughts, you got stuff to do, & you ain't got time for no setbacks, not even a minute, all you do is just stay on a pathway paved with blessings, so travel it with prayers in your hands, & more prayers in all your pockets, remember the right combination of indigenous individuals equals the right results, I mean we can chop up game for days, braking everything down in fractions, just figuring everything out to know what to do next, it's all the game of life rules to laws, & always move when that door open, it's like being in school, the teacher call your name, that's the game of life, the door open, & you stand still, watch it close, & keep on living inside the merry go round, recognize it's a trap before it trap you, now to get gone on the highway is the best way, I mean just living correctly for successful, progressing to bless your circle of these, & those people, everybody a phone call away, or in person we connected, royalty play to win on the strength of all that which has been spoken, when crewed up, the motivation to get wealthy is gone stay on the mind of the royal family, now remember you got to know how to speak more than four languages, & know what everybody know, & stay clear away from hate, & jealousy, stick, & move in that order, time limit on arrival, & a designated departure time, it's all part of the game of life mandatory behavior.

Spiritual healing is feeling goodness greatness, that's what it's made for, that's what it's all about, free spirit, not a slave to this world, nor a slave to money, not a slave to being a crowd pleaser, that's what we are, free spirits, just live to serve your purpose, so Money will come to you in this world automatically, that's the game of life professionalism way to play, love is life, life is love, who soul glows, who got personality, who got lovable characteristic traits, you at home when something is yours, indigenous is not an option, it's a birth right, apply that to who you are, it's all the game of life, just play it to perfection, the animal kingdom appreciate their position in this world, they full effort their part in this world.

Always look forward to goodness greatness, worrying is wasting your time, use time wisely.

I'm all in Montana right now, I just went through Wyoming, now tell me this, ain't it a blessing being able to live in this lifetime, ask yourself, "how can I beat you if walking, while you running, now that's a question to figure out, how did I make that happen, complicated is the game of life, that's only if you not wisely educated.

Fools will put dirt on your name if you end up on their mind, so others won't recognize the greatness in your existence.

I'm on the 5th floor, with the city wide view, asking myself how Royalty get to this point, which led up to me thinking about when I was at the ritz Carlton hotel, in Orlando Florida, $500 for one night, just thinking how I got here, seeing what I can see, what I got the chance to say I saw, knowing the thoughts that can't be bought that I know, dressing up in fur coats sense 2008 in winter times, I'm on a mission to do something big is what preacher the gentleman of leisure told me, I still member playing James brown on the lake front in Milwaukee, preacher was doing the James brown foot work, a lady was exercising pass us, I can tell she wanted to stop jogging, just to do some 1970s dances, the dances she used to do, whenever she heard James brown music.

Moments like this happened, during what you call going hard lifestyle, with no breaks, moving fast, everyday working on finding all the laid back longevity retirement plans.

During royalty North America adventures, royalty found out that Cross country living is the only way to travel I found out.

If You ever get the chance to see Indigenous people at the top of their game, they squeezed through that trap door, and came up nice, indigenous individuals got to find the right door to go in.

Life in the fast thinking quick lane, It's all about how tight you can get everything to work together, it's mandatory to have that bread fat like full grown granddaddy hippopotamus necks.

What you gone do if your bread just up, & be gone when you wake up, you got to keep it moving, & get it back fat again, it's the game of life, don't be living to die, always full effortfully be looking to catch up with longevity, live everyday making everything in arms reach happen correctly consistently, moving prosperously progressively straight ahead, then pop up in the spotlight, straight back like You never left, Ed lee said, "shining looking like new money," on tip top for all the right reasons in life again.

If you know how to make money pile up like that, if it's available, mingle with the correct chosen few crowds, no half stepping big daddy Kane would have said, make every step count like Eddie Murphy in the golden child, & don't spill one drop of water, til it's time to water the front lawn grass.

Recycle indigenous money for the indigenous people, within the walls of the indigenous inside circle.

Attach yourself to bread that stretch Armstrong, with no strings attached to it.

Queen khalifa California Mountain indigenous peoples be on some giant type living, Seem like majority of them on the top levels like snoop Dogg, & dr. Dre, welcome home to freeway rick ross, & harry o, little Darryl, meds audio, they playing to win, study how their game developed, analyze how it guided them to the top of the upper classes, it's the game of life, simultaneously recognize the days to night they had to read to figure out how to succeed, and the countless writing to figure out how to build their characteristics traits that made them extremely beneficial, It's good when you can play everything on the highest scale, getting the most for all you worked hard to become, do or die, sypaz, & Danny boy said, "nothing happens over night," Chicago produce truth beyond belief.

Got to be at the top of your game on a fat mission, to setup retirement, believe it or not It's boss players that survive the game of life traps, & they stepped things up to the highest level they could reach,

You will always get to the top of the world, when you reach up to the top of your game.

Everybody out here aiming to get fat with finance, I'm talking big bread, I'm tum bout straight on top living properly, straight grinding for that fat outcome, Gangsta brown mansions in Hollywood type living.

Because around the earth, hard work pay off, straight figuring out how to get crowned with a new throne every year, the pinky ring street king crown, it has been around sense the first day of the first born, in human indigenous peoples history, & it ain't never gone leave, now the throne

18

might get pulled out of your reach, but now memorize, if it can be done once by you, it can be done again by you, if you can make it all happen again, dreams will once again turn into reality, just stay on top of your game qualifying to live on a throne, now game got to recognize that game, I'm speaking specifically on straight moving strategically.

Ancestry indigenous individually speaking, I prefer to be like those who came before myself, I recognized who took their game everywhere they went to play to win, & show nuff it made them powerful, just living like a king supposed to, with unlimited assistance, & financially satisfied on a yearly basis, I mean just here there everywhere, they make it happen, to go building their own pathway to where they want to be, see, & get better acquainted with, I mean you slip you fall, you get back up better then when you left, like 50 cent did, like ray virgil fairly did, get back up harder, smarter, stronger, when the top ones bounce back, they do it to stay on top from that point on, no more hard times, or stomach growling nights, just learning the game on all levels, to master it, straight study it every second they can, see int defeated, down, or out, I'm on pause til everything get put in order again, without any signs of people practicing hesitation, showcasing hatred, or taking a day off in life itself around me.

It take great game, I mean straight polished knowledge, game every brain need to contain, just a boss player stepping in the name of game, in the direction towards the next level, everything a king named Mack has done thus far is cool, but this route gone make gigantic foot prints to walk in, I mean doing the unpredictable when it's convenient, for the king strategic moves to be made, like the chessboard, I mean that's the game of life, knowing which piece you is in life, which piece you want others in your circle to be, again I mean stepping up to the solid gold diamond plate, like baseball royalty Barry bonds, straight aiming to send the ball screaming off your first swing, sending the scared ball on fire screaming going towards the outside streets, outside the stadium, I mean figuring out how to make Michael v Roberts major moves in a billionaire way.

Aiming towards the deluxe apartment in the sky, George Jefferson type moves, with a professional cross country Benjamin Lloyd crump paid lawyer, having a house specifically for sleeping, & cooking a feast for the royal family, it's coming soon for you, if you don't have it already, just be preparing now.

I had teams previously when I was coaching in my lifestyle, each year one, or two new faces, some would leave, & some would stay, rotation rolled through the years like that for the king named Mack, previously I mean, that's the game back then to now, not looking for it to happen the major mackin way right now at this moment, it's just not meant to be right now, I mean it's the business of living to retire right now as the center of attention.

The game of life is custom made for each individual king participant, in an unique individual way for them, life will also customize the king thinking process as well, The King lifeline from ancient ancestors to now is the chosen role models,, "it's just the way it is," like Tupac said.

Kings of this continent also known as indigenous copper complicated complexion groups of divine suns, they was obligated to pass the historical ancestors game down generations to generations, each one reach one, some say I was given that Oakland goldy golden rules book with the great ism in it, as time went on throughout my macknificent life, I begin to quickly fast learn how to read the book of life, all from practice to progress, empowering the mind to interpret what was complicated, to the point it encouraged misunderstandings to happen, so before reading this golden rule book, it's best that you sharpen up the thinking process, pitch black ancient indigenous sumurai katana sword sharp, I mean build your mind up to Superman style, strong beyond belief, with vision to see clear land in muddy waters, I mean straight "surviving the times," like nas said.

THE ORIGINAL LANGUAGE OF THE LAND MACKOLOGY 2ND EDITION 2021

I'm listening to dj screw song, it's called, "new friends new foes," what's up to Texas, them players hustlers gangster business indigenous men is on point down there, believe me, if don't believe me, go visit, see for yourself.

A godfather to a pimp, gangsta, player, hustler, a pinky ring street King, a godfather is supposed to supervise his pinky ring street King son, school him like a college professor will do for a million dollars, with a full effort for a student, studying a subject in their private college class, each game of life participant, requires ancient wisdom, from a polished knowledge life long pinky ring street King professor, to qualify yourself to get a degree in that particular lifestyle.

I'm watching Aaliyah official Virginia video, it's called, "hot like fire," a timbaland Virginia mix, this thought just popped up on mind, therefore it's mandatory to learn how to spot the best woman possible, every city, town, village, state you will stop, & go into, so that means all indigenous men to women got to stay getting better at being who they is, it's the way to play it, in the game of life we was born in.

Now watch this, this some insight to out-sight, when somebody ask you for spare change, ask them to tell you the most important lesson they learned in life, then pay them what you owe, the game is sold not told, this ain't your average book, no miracle whip on this, straight hot sauce is what midwest prefer, now east west south might prefer different hot sauce, but this what midwest be on, this that ketchup syrup sugar sandwich upbringing game.

I said, "Ye are gods, and all of you are children of the Most High." Psalms 82:6

I'm watching Lil Pimpin DPG video, it's called, "Square Biz."

"Thank you Most High for anything to everything, all or nothing, love Is life, life is love."

King Mack millon

Enjoying self accomplishments, picking buds off trees In Pomona pimpin young suga free California, respect to all, past, present, & future, may the Most High bless every pinch of existence, past, present, & future, may royalty truth plus prayers be upon.

I'm listening to marvin gaye song, it's called, "don't mess with mister t," from the trouble man movie soundtrack, to me, trouble man movie was based on Harlem king mr. pee wee kirkland, and black Cesar movie was based on frank mathews.

Game recognizes game right?

THE GAME OF LIFE SCRIPTURES

Playing the game of life is knowing how to roll it, live to give, give to live, the game of life has always been about unity, team work works, it's a proven fact teams have won championships, everybody need everybody, cross country living will explain precisely, what the game of life scriptures is all about.

At the present moment, I'm in oak grove missouri, somewhere near kansas city, sipping watered down patron tequila with a shot of cranberry apple raspberry juice, editing this part of mackology second edition right now, looking forward to spending the week in california. I did love los Angeles, & north Las Vegas, let's be specific to what side was visited, & Hollywood was real peacefully laid back.

The wise man on the corner in the shadows said, "Bring your Game to every city state you touch down in," people gone recognize you from out of town off top, that's indigenous brown folk type stuff, real tribal thinking, & they gone enjoy showing you their land that you visiting, & every city is usually patterned after the original people of that land great grand indigenous children, that is one of the game of life facts, game always gone recognize game, all game of life indigenous participants cross country living is playing to win at all time, game recognize game don't it, I'm listening to pomona california suga free song, it's called, "like what."

MACKOLOGY 2ND EDITION

This Is the game of life scriptures, Mackology the second edition, street life philosophy was Mackology first edition, Mackology second edition Is not raw, or uncut, it is edited, it is strategically written chapter to titles, it is influenced by tax paying cross country living, it is for game that recognize game.

Mackology first edition was notes turned into book form, It was a practice book to get to this book, it was raw, uncut, unedited, it was a test run to see what happens next, it was a book written from traveling through less then ten states, thank you to the unique individuals that bought personal copies of street life philosophy, it was good for the game of life on all levels, words in book form was used to make the reader seek higher learning, It was written under the influence of alcohol, & champagne, this book is under influences of mother earth made herbs, buddha bless like bone nem said, influences to new old influences, which mean jolly green giant, jazz black bands, & unfortunately some cigarettes moments.

Mackology second edition was professionally written with great intentions.

THE LAST MACK STANDING SCRIPTURES

Step in smooth to lay It down thick, straight grinding like they do in Little Rock Arkansas, got to learn how to live, then learn how to earn, then learn how to make money work for you, then learn how to pull up shining brand new, like they say In Memphis, "this what game plus money do for you," if you learn how to direct traffic, Memphis know the business, on some project pat type stuff, It's all about getting life right, wealthy comfortable with longevity, and spirituality.

JOURNEY WEALTHY LONGEVITY SCRIPTURES

Everywhere you go, be on the prowl to see if that city got benefits for you on the business tip, vehicles, homes, a new crew, or new members bringing something to the table, showing a down for life mentality, simply to be in the royal family, to help the royal family get wealthy on the journey to longevity.

Thekingbusiness@aol.com

Thekingbusiness@aol.com is To contact author for movie scriptures, tv shows, song writing, lectures, counseling, spiritual advice, Intros for songs, intros for movies, Intros for concerts, etc.

In the air it was once said, "don't lean on another boss player game, because your game will imitate his," but just like everybody taught you how to talk, everybody got pieces of information for you, to complete the puzzle that will complete your life, and those who aim to know everything on their own, will lack information from directions they don't go in, & will not learn from lessons other people lifestyles taught them, that's what elders Is for, what's up to Chicago, past to present Chicago Indigenous people in old to new projects, or those in Fargo North Dakota, which is how you learn how to master life with everybody help, because everybody, past, present, and future makes the world what it is."

King Mack

JOURNEY WEALTHY LONGEVITY SCRIPTURES

2.

Everywhere you go, be on the prowl to see if that city got benefits for you on the business tip, vehicles, homes, a new crew, or new members bringing something to the table, showing a down for life mentality, simply to be in the royal family, to help the royal family get wealthy on the journey to longevity.

If you stay the same, everybody gone think they know your game, every lifestyle is played on levels, with order, with position, memorize everyday is meant to be how it was, is, & will become, you Just got to stay in motion, follow your right mind, adjust, adapt, update, upgrade, it's all game recognize game business, stay ahead, or get lost, left behind, the truth is trapped in a world of lies, s0 don't miss the big picture, because you looking at the small screen, if you don't distribute the game correctly, & know who it is originally sold to, the way the ancestors did it, because it can come back to hunt you when you start living comfortable, because United we stand, do that early, not when you reach the last days, just like you walk, it ain't backwards, so living backwards is blind leading blind, so don't be surprised when you realize it's more to life then what meets the eyes, which is why game naturally recognize game, & it's sold to who don't deserve it, & told to those touched by the sun, because it's best to take care of home instead of where the buffalo roam, if somebody put you up on game, they concerned about your well being, the closer you get to the truth, the deeper Life becomes.

I'm In Sturbridge Massachusetts right boss player now, I'm In Sturbridge Massachusetts right boss player now, ordered food from Southbridge Massachusetts, got way more then I paid for, people made me feel like I was at home here In Sturbridge, nice weather, a bunch of trees everywhere, I just missed a tornado that came before I did, it's clean all around here, smell good to out here, like a fresh plate of collard greens In a can, I'm editing the final parts of this brilliantly wrote book, I'm watching an espn special, on the 1998 bulls with Jordan narrating, jordan been doing stuff for indigenous people, but he don't get credit for it.

POLISHED KNOWLEDGE MOST HIGH APPROVED ORCHESTRATED CREATED

ALL CAPITOL GAME ENTERTAINMENT

WELCOME TO THE MACK MOON MACKWAUKEE

THE BOSS PLAYER ASSOCIATION

Peace & blessings to the elements above & beyond below & beyond inside & beyond outside & beyond amen ra mut nature ancient ancestors great spirits mother father most high & every pinch of existence from past present to the future may royalty truth & prayers be upon & keep evil away

JOURNEY WEALTHY LONGEVITY SCRIPTURES

3.

Everywhere you go, be on the prowl to see if that city got benefits for you on the business tip, vehicles, homes, a new crew, or new members bringing something to the table, showing a down for life mentality, simply to be in the royal family, to help the royal family get wealthy on the journey to longevity.

When somebody left alone, they grow like that to the point, that's the only life they know, ask nas, he said it in his song, "life we chose," which is now sounding like it should be the title of this book.

I'm back In Milwaukee Wisconsin revitalizing, polishing my knowledge, getting tools I need to go cross country with, sipping you already know Moët, puffing east coast gorilla glue, and smoking black jazz bands, almost finish editing this brilliant book, close to publishing it to, with the Most High allowance.

I want to stand by queens Bridge like cormega, with people from every state, bbqin, bumping nas, cormega, fat Joe, punch from smack DVD, az, lil Kim, notorious big, big pun, tru life & Saigon from smack dvd, jay-z, mobb deep, m o p, Lloyd banks, Tony yayo, & then smoke gorilla glue, drinking ace of Spade, Hennessey xo, & watch the indigenous ladies Of harlem like harlem azealia banks sip rose moet puffing on some snoop dogg, Ez roll Gin & juice blunts, full of white widow, I'm watching project pat video, It's called, "raised in the projects," crunch black professionally doing the memphis tribal dance, he snapping, I can't be taught that dance style, because int indigenous to memphis.

The hotel tv showing little women of atlanta georgia, peace & blessings to ms. Minnie, I'm watching mobile alabama rich boy, his video called, "boy looka here," he did his video in mobile mardi gras parade, now, I was in nashville & alabama told louisiana maradi gras started in alabama first, you tell me who right, where you from, where you been, do you know?, setup a meeting of the minds on YouTube, to discuss the origins of mardi gras, & where it originated first, some call all that black history.

PURE AS A RAIN DROP

I got the hotel window wide open right now, I like to feel the energy in the air in every city I'm in, I'm listening to cross country pimp music past to the present moment, thank you for your undivided attention, I met cool indigenous people, all over the country, from all States, & the news speak on them in a way that is the opposite of how they really is, what is known as the worst places to live, those be the best indigenous people to meet in that state.

I'm watching Baton Rouge boss players from Louisiana: young bleed featuring max minelli, the video is called, "better than the last time."

When you go through the motions in this lifetime ocean, you qualify yourself to be satisfied, I'm all in Massachusetts reflecting on my Mack lifestyle, how I got here, reflections like mjg no more glory album song, I been cross country like a Chicago greyhound bus, more than once in 2020, capital game, Mackology, pimpology, lifeology, g code, flip through the pages in my brilliantly written book, it's all game entertainment, boss player status on all levels, love it, or hate it, no concern to me, yo best bet is beware of those with tricks up their sleeve, usually the rocket burn out before it hit the sun, simply because It don't belong there, stay from out of bounds I recommend, be where you belong, yet I see my throne on the sun, If you don't have a problem looking at the sun, you can see me sitting on my throne, like Don Juan said, "many is called, but only a few is chosen, ain't that a cold statement, let game recognize game is what the original boss players, & original gangsters say, if the tree cut off Its own branch, what you expect that branch to do, that's right, the branch gone plant itself in new soil, that soil that's been there all the time waiting for It to happen, self got to find where your environment Is, then grow into a tree, then grow new branches, that's the game of life, it's way to many more people

In the world, to be devastated by a group you knew in your early years, that's right, don't quit, give up, or stop, or slow down, keep it moving full speed ahead, regroup, recruit, rebuild, it's Indigenous people you can meet all over the country, that live your way, play to win now to forever, two people might hate on you, then ten people will give you your props all In them hating faces, I don't have one thing negative to say about anybody.

Respect to one to all, it's the game of life, customize it, strategize, and improvise in It.

JOURNEY WEALTHY LONGEVITY SCRIPTURES

4.

Everywhere you go, be on the prowl to see if that city got benefits for you on the business tip, vehicles, homes, a new crew, or new members bringing something to the table, showing a down for life mentality, simply to be in the royal family, to help the royal family get wealthy on the journey to longevity.

Now real pimps pimped, I call it wise men living, they studied pimpology, the g code, mackology, lifeology, now these colleges they attended was only, & to this day, only accepting those touched by the sun, with an exception to Chicago international pimpin white folks, now as you read this chapter, the song, "forever mine," by the o'jays, is playing in your mind, as you read this now, within seconds you just heard it, now I'm saying that to say, if you know how to unite words strategically, you will become powerful, it's mandatory to master the art of doing that, because knowledge is power, & as always, & forever like Luther Vandross said years ago, from the beginning to forever, game recognize game, and if you lack game, you ain't been touched by the sun yet, it's mandatory to memorize that words is powerful, if you know how to control them, it will be more powerful then what's printed on paper, in books created to road block indigenous people, but that's why it's mandatory for all Game under four decades in the game of life, or over four decades worth of game, should always recognize game, because everybody touched by the sun, will have an intelligent to brilliant changing point, when they start living life with purpose, plus meaning, that's what the man playing the guitar in Niagara falls park said to royalty.

FROM THE ROOT TO THE FRUIT

Let me start this off by saying this respectfully, with no negativity included, If we all was playing to win in the game of life, what do I do If Individuals in my circle stopped playing to win?, or got put on pause.

Now keep in mind, I got put on pause several times before today, & everybody kept ballin without me, what part of the game is that, if we In the army, & you get wounded, do I leave you stuck, or do I pick you up, to pull you with me til we both straight? John from Waco Texas know what um tum bout, I'm in Oklahoma City & à Group of three employees working at hotel, directly across from the hotel I'm at, they decided to play talk, first own know neither one of the three, one smelt snoop dogg, & Jamaica in the wind blowing, own have time to play, cut that encounter short, got to know how to encourage people to excuse themselves out your environment, master the art of communication conversation expertise talking.

Now If you was the one to keep going, knowing a person reached out for a helping hand, what do you expect to happen if you did that to a person.

That person has to develop a mentality like that from that point on, it's a natural survival instinct.

I mean, I looked left to right, with nobody in sight, not one person that was there with me, which was around me, when I was riding high like the classic song, "riding high," said, before I got put on pause.

how do you look at everybody now?

now while you alone on an island feeling like you standing in quick sand, straight stranded stuck, you gone be thinking a hundred miles an hour, Its like being In prison, you put everybody behavior in your lifetime, on your mind everyday, not every second, but everyday, especially when you hear their voice, or see them calling you, or in your face, or now a days via emails, Facebook, Instagram, etc.

Let's pause to chop up Milwaukee game, one of the top paid rappers in Milwaukee, boss player coo coo cal made a song called, "how does it feel," the song cold, but the video on some MTV type stuff, it's cool, but coo coo cal put his people in the video, & everybody kept it Milwaukee dress code, hairstyles, this song the business, my fault back to the book, I was just watching it back to back.

Now while I'm back up in motion, that's not gone be forgot about, people got to stick with who they start with, now I was told while incarcerated, that if you on a sinking ship, you got to get off, so I respect the thought of that, but if you still got the will to keep everything moving, your Kingdom has no business disappearing, or allowing infiltrators to infiltrate your kingdom (your castle), especially when they know how you taught everything to go, now if you got a partner that don't know how the game of life is played, that mean they possibly just along for the ride, not to help build the king's kingdom, boss player Association call them infiltrators, sent to pull you back down the food chain.

From start to present moment, you learn that you can't be cold hearted all your lifestyle, because what you put in is what you get out.

If your pimp brother, hustle brother, or your gangster brother fall, or slip, don't act like you not aware of what he, or she going through, you do everything to keep your people up, like king bean Chicago said, "let him, or her sleep in the basement," do something to help, he, or she might be down but they not out, so when they get back up, & you see them looking like ed lee nathanal Jones said, "new money," don't act like you see a ghost, respect the game, & remember what they gone remember, because now they trained to spot a fake, hate, & those who will abandon them when it's time to struggle.

So now they will be nice to you from a distance, but you know they not letting you get close to them ever again, this the game of life, ain't no fools wearing crowns, so respect the game of life in every way possible, even if a king, or queen was up, but now they down, treat them the same way, weather they up, or down, only the strong survive, every giant on earth Is thinking like that, because anybody up, is saying who will be there for me, If I fall off the Kilimanjaro mountain top, that plan is coming with

41

all that, stay working on going up higher everyday, millionaire billionaire mentality, simply because that's the destination every live long day, for all indigenous people world wide.

in my lifetime it's all part of the step by step process to the next level, like Chicago king boo said, "it's not how you fall, it's about how fast you get back up, Chuucch."

In Milwaukee you got to be on top of some type of game, to set yourself up comfortable with bread, a house, a vehicle, that's what you call living comfortable, consistently aiming to buy, or start a business, that's how it go in Milwaukee, I mean everybody in Milwaukee make Milwaukee Milwaukee, it's a nice place all year round from winter snow to summer heat, visit Milwaukee, check it out, see what it's about, make it beneficial going state to state, make show the world tell you, long live the king to you, for you, showing respect to you, I'm listening to james brown, the godfather of soul, the man that put on a performance to member, in kinshasa zaire africa in 1974, the song is called, "down & out in New York City."

All over the country everybody is beneficial living this lifetime, if you know how to generate financial Income where ever you go, straight adapting to survive quite, you can move in silence, or stay loud quite, I mean it's Chicago to Milwaukee ways to stay paid in full like Eric b and rakim, In Every city you touch down In, you can see life in different ways, for all the beneficial purposes, inside the corporate buildings negotiating money deals, that's what you call, mr. ken ivy style, stepping up to the highest level eventually, also Referred to as transition living.

It's a movie where somebody built a maze In a basement, and trapped a man in the basement inside a wooden maze, he had to crawl in the maze, then the whoever was doing it started a fire in that same house, and when he got who did it to him, he put them in the position they put him in.

Snoop Dogg's song called, "Stacey Adams," it just slid out the speakers to my environment, I wonder did he have to get an ok from founder of Stacey Adams, (founders), to use the name Stacey Adams as his song title, due to copyright purposes, this a cold song, or did Stacey Adams pay him to make that song, either way it's just business as usual.

I'm all in Georgia at the present moment, of this editing my book moment, I heard somebody in my atmosphere just say, "if you knew better you would do better," that's a cold statement, at this exact moment, game should be recognizing game right now, this my second book of capital game, enjoy life, & don't roll dice with your life, gambling with the time you can be focusing on getting wealthy, on your journey through life, to get better acquainted with longevity.

Look at what I'm saying with your third eye indigenous ones, I'm aiming to retire in a little over a year before I turn 40, or when I turn 40, I'm planning on doing what Mack did In the last Mack standing chapter, it's called, "history in capital letters," my first book was unedited, & used it as bait to see how this book business go.

lets get on the same page with this next statement, this life is about being tight with the Most High, see, age & experience gone teach everybody that, some hear it at teenage years, or 20s, or 30s, or 40s, this how the game of life will get broke down in fractions, inside this brilliantly wrote book, chapter to chapter strategically placed in proper positions, this is not your traditional book format, like other books written before this book came out, what's up to all the first ones to do something new, first in the most intelligent to brilliant way possible, figuring out how to do new moves to progress beneficially for all the right reasons, james brown song called, "payback," it just came on.

I'm on my way to Florida top east side right now, I'm listening to snoop dogg song called, "big pimpin'," I'm sipping figi water with gorilla glue, a real solid player is all about the Benjamin's, this player gorilla glue straight want you to pay to be around him, he charge more If you aim to share him, his time is money on all levels, when money first met him, It never stop running to him, straight dedicated to him on all levels, for all the reasons to make him king, keep him king, and make it possible for him to travel the globe, to meet all the best of the best people at the top of their game, with access to a beneficial lifestyle, that which bring enough bread to keep you around this player, everything is game related like e-40 & the click told you years ago, I just finished reading e-40 novel call the dictionary of slang, what's up mr. Earl Stevens, I heard they sell slurricane liquor on the west coast in Las Vegas, I saw the bottle in colorado, in my little people hotel room, in Colorado.

At this moment in our lifetime, all y'all should already know, game recognize game, if your game recognize my game, you with the in crowd, you helping make the in crowd the in crowd, this crowd is on their toes, acknowledging it's a difference between friends, & foes like e-40 said years ago, I'm on point like a fresh rolled Chicago eddie crum joint.

Now if the wind blowing pass you on south beach, Jamaica, the Bronx, queens New York, Chicago, Milwaukee, Dover Delaware, Phoenix, Ontario California, Southern California, these the places I enjoyed the most, this brilliantly wrote book is for the ones who don't let nothing go to their head, like crucial conflict intro said years ago, the ones that started living on the top levels, simply to never give up, or settle for less, & stay in to the finish.

Crucial conflict intro song called, "don't let it go to your head," just Came in the airwaves, how can you not turn this up three times in a row, all game entertainment is hidden in plain sight, repeat it again, start this song over, at this moment game should be recognizing game, don't let this go to your head, "no no no," is what the background singers is saying, while the boss players take turns to bless this beat, with their words of capital game, every brain need to contain.

This brilliant wrote book Is for those individuals who live to learn, while they simultaneously learn how to live, good game can be said backwards, & forward, making sense twice in one phrase.

Now I'm gone tell you this, intelligent to brilliant reader, It's about to get cold in this world, I mean that in the nicest way possible, I been at my get wealthy goal consistently with no breaks, or day offs sense 1996, when everybody in my age bracket was learning new dance moves, getting their first kiss, & going to house parties, I was In a basement counting currency, breaking down collard greens, reading the basic instructions before leaving earth type books, writing up notebooks, with green eyes watching classic gangster, to pimp movies, hustler movies, even though these was movies, I was still studying how the writer of these movie scripts, wrote these movies, so I peeped game, hidden, & I studied how each character was successful wise, & foolishly slipped up, this what I mean by game recognizing game, I was early in my game, by how I was studying old movies like baby face, & mr. Lucky cary grant, just to name a couple 1900's movies.

Most boss players pop their p's, & q's differently, your game is all based on your upbringing, that's how your game gone develop, your game Is your computer, it work for you, It was custom made for you, then once

44

game start recognizing game, you customize it for you to use as your tool, to go through life with.

I'm listening to Mack 10 song, it's called, "wanted dead," this some highway music, you play this on thanksgiving in my house the west coast king pimp said, on Christmas to, you play this when you walk around with $2000 in your pockets in rubber bands of, $1, $5, $10, $20, & $100 bills, I'm tum bout state to state doing that.

This book is for king hustlers, before the year 2000 came on the scene, this for those who made a way on dead end streets, straight created a new route, through the dead end going the other way, big tymers song called, "how u love that," is what I hear right now.

I be really chilling, I haven't had Moët sense I left New Jersey, which was almost two weeks ago, roll with a king, sometimes you think a king be down, & out the race, then he find away to put his crown back on, then he shine brighter then the Cadillac North harriet tubman Star in 98, I mean he get back on his throne In plain sight on the low, out of sight out of mind, you probably thought he was getting free money from the government, I member I pulled up in the 2014 Kia truck, in 2014, with sunroof open, straight money to burn, green white black diamond faith ann pinky ring, with paks gun powder bracelet, with a little over an inch long row of horizontal diamonds In a line on it, about five pair of different hustler havana joe shoes to coordinate with, Monday to Friday, custom made cds to blast out the sunroof, pitch black rabbit fur for the winter to, I still got that same fur from 2009 right now, I mean it's absolutely mandatory to be at the top of your game, if I do say so myself, is what the original gangster said.

I was having a conversation to discuss who was speaking down on me, then I studied that boss player hater to know why they was hating, so I can fix my movements to stay clear of individuals like this, with these type characteristics traits, recognizing how to avoid haters, debaters, & time wasters, I got to get where I'm going In this lifetime, & get what is coming to me, like the Indigenous lady said on the news, "ain't nobody got time for that."

Boss player hating women will end up in your boss player face, they usually stand out by not bringing something to the table, trying to get what's on the table, if a woman is not in the royal family, she can run to who she see everyday, because I call that a thief, stealing game, and looking to infiltrate for whoever sent her, like that lady said, "ain't nobody got time for that," getting information about you, to pass to somebody, we ain't on none of that right there,

handling business for the kingdom, helping the royal family build an unbreakable lifetime, an everlasting successful lifestyle, I'm talking about retiring In a year, or so, around 2022, I'm talking about figuring life out sooner then later, play time is over, it's time for the dream team to get handpicked, to bring important game, huge face money, & contribution from ten different money routes, to build this kingdom properly.

I'nt never been no hater, I respect it all from everybody, but if i'nt on what you on, I'm gone keep my boss player social distance, straight focusing on longevity moves to be made, with the royal family in the quietest loudest way possible.

Teenage years reading dictionaries to become more sophisticated, picking words to write in sentences, straight studying lifeology to become highly educated, all this is from home schooling, to build up a custom made lifestyle, now here it come again, game should recognize game, take notes on boss players who your style share similarities with, this brilliant wrote book is certified important In more ways then one, which is why it's satisfying to the mind, food for thought y'all.

Tonight I got to get ready for Jacksonville Florida in the morning, out of nowhere kingpin skinny pimp song called, "skinny pimp," straight Memphis Business, he chopping game up about memphis ism on this song, it jumped up, & popped out in my speakers, project pat song called, "you know the business," Chicago is memphis twin brother, gary, detroit, oakland, dallas, houston, jackson, baltimore, d.c., st. Louis, if you'nt know that, you know that now, preacher the gentleman of leisure said, "if it's a secret, it ain't nan one now."

This is a 2020 exclusive confidential classified magnificent global intelligence to brilliance book, it is said by pinky ring street King scholars, that it will change your perspective on life, also everybody around you, due to your changes, that will be influenced by this intelligent to brilliant book, I'm listening to a young cat out of memphis tennessee, kingpin skinny pimp, the song is called, king of da playas ball," smoke one with a poe one."

The 1st line up of chapters Is the game of life scriptures, which will speak on every level of updated life situations, 2nd line up of chapters is the last Mack standing scriptures, that which is a storyline about love, longevity, betrayal, sadness, mystery, unity, leadership, youth living, triumph, dedication, you will not be disappointed at all, respect to how nas song called, "project windows," spoke to the soul, genius move nas, peace Respectfully king, that's a down south play me some pimpin type of song.

It was once said by a cross country game spitter, that, "this is the book of the century for one to all to read, & reread every month, it can be considered a modern day version of Chicago Milwaukee Iceberg slim, donald goines detroit type of writings, midwest best writings for the world to fall in love with," luther vandross, always & forever, enjoy royalty pimp prospective.

Never close your ears, or mind to what will set you free, truthfully speaking, referring to the phrase that prolongs comfortable lifestyles, which is read to succeed.

when you first start walking, consider that as your first steps in the direction of your lifestyle, that which you will start living in your lifetime.

Wise words spoken: don't just be living to repeat every year, doing the robot, doing the same routine, on the same level, everything always gone fall into place, just like a homeless man playing the lottery winning millions, even if he worked a job, that winning lottery ticket of him buying, winning millions, would still have transpired, it's no stopping what is meant to happen.

Wise words spoken: Mother father Most High, praying like that has been known to bring balance, while delivering answers to prayers made for a boss player, each lifestyle has it's set of prayers, look around the country at the styles of indigenous heavy populated cities.

Ancestor boss players had a secret lifestyle, that which was rarely known about to outside races, I mean they was like myths straight legends, they know who they are, see I'm a student, not an original, not when that race started formulating, so I just study the game of life, past to present.

I'm known for rolling well off in my lifestyle situations, it's like taking an amateur player behavior to the king boss player lifestyle, to a level of ray virgil fairley, or don magic Juan, or sir captain, versatile with the lifestyle, provoking your game to advance you to greater heights.

I stayed living comfortable, just young with my knowledge, which king boss players would call unpolished back then, it wasn't polished til I hit this age I'm at now, I was told you don't start living, until you 40 years old, I also learned in order to master something in the game of life, you have to study It for 40 years, like a doctor with good intentions.

See it's all game to me on all levels in every direction, you just got to set everything up right, to set your outcome up long term speaking.

But when you fresh In the lifestyle you living, you got to have a mentor with good intentions, it's mandatory to find longevity In the lifestyle you living, or was living.

But unfortunately a lot of us do not get that in the lifestyle we live, unfortunately a lot of us will not get that in our early years, of living a beneficial lifestyle.

When you fresh In your lifestyle, you will have needs to look for footsteps to walk in, so you can see how your lifestyle is supposed to be done properly, so you can climb the ladder to get on your throne, Like a baby climbing in his, or her crib, as soon as you learn to get paid in full, it's gone be time to start living it up, so stay prepared, so you won't have to focus on what to do next.

The wonder years, a mother once said, "she should have let her daughter stay with a player," sometimes we have different pathways in life, I'm listening to Gerald levert song, it's called, "baby u are," they was midwest stepping in the video, the pimps was stepping Chicago style in the video.

So if your game is in it's amateur stage, you got to fix it up fast, to stay alive in this world, because all game tight living, has traps set for you to fall Into, due to your advanced lifestyle you living.

So the only way to build game up, is to seek capital experienced soul survival game, its naturally mandatory to learn how to recognize game, it's very important to have that skill in this direction, I say that because outsiders will learn to imitate real skillful indigenous boss players in this lifestyle, then they will trick themselves into thinking they know what that boss player knows, then find out acting is dangerous, because when they realize they was only an infiltrator living a life not meant for them, sad to say they find themselves on drugs, in prison, poe, broke, & lonely, like Don Juan said, "it's a very dangerous game if you don't play It right."

I mean it's due time for a level up, with necessary financial satisfaction, to live like a king making things happen, in order to live like a king supposed to live, precisely like that all the way to the extravagant elevators, that will escort you up to the million dollar condo, located in downtown Milwaukee on Wisconsin avenue, you bought it, looking at the city close to the clouds floating pass, and that's the same game played in every city.

It's the highly intelligent to brilliant group that move around the world, strategically to make everything happen, that will enhance their lifestyle to the king levels.

This country cool with me, if I knew I can hit theses states, & leave with money made wisely, I would have been made them type of cross country moves in my early years, see due to lack of mentor to tutor in the early stages of this lifestyle, I had to catch all this valuable information in my later years, but it's straight, because it caused me to be self made, which is rewarding, due to me surviving the times I spent, living my lifestyle, guess what just came on, it's master p classic song, it's called, "true to the game," see life is based on timing, everything always falls into place, due to how It is meant to transpire.

I mean it's to many spots open for a king to sit on a throne, now that was said to make a point of hating is not necessary, it's enough for all us to achieve, receive, retrieve, If full effort is put forth to make things happen, if you play the game right, ogs said, "either you make things happen, you watch things happen, or you wondering what happened," which one is you, slim diamond brought that to my attention, he from Alabama, him & gucci mane.

Once you get crowned king early In your life, that's it, you in for life really though, you got to have a mentor from that point on, some footsteps to walk in, to see what your lifestyle will bring to you, from income to outcome.

See the elder players job I say, was to school not fool, teach the youth & preach the truth, see it's all game of life titles, from amateur players to king boss players, the game had to be distributed correctly to you, from birth to earth to adulthood.

But it has to be distributed according to step one to step two, to every step after that, it's not wise to get retirement game in you're amateur stages, you must be taught to walk after you learn how to crawl first, game must be distributed orderly from A to Z as you graduate to greater heights consistently, like kindergarten to college, addition to subtraction, then algebra to calculus, game must be distributed orderly.

So if you had the footsteps custom made for you to walk in by a mentor, you possibly somewhere riding high like faze-o, if you didn't get kilt due to hatred, jealousy, to envy, but if you lacked the mentor in your early stages of this lifestyle, you did like me, you just got on foot patrol to see what this lifestyle had to offer, you learned from trial to error, mistakes create brilliance on this pathway.

I mean I was learning how to read facial expressions, body language, all the way to analyzing the tone of voice being spoken in, from the words being spoken, sentence being spoken, I watched everything moving like a squirrel hiding in a Texas tree, you got to stay alive, prey or predator, I saw a tremendous amount of what is hidden In plain sight, that's why game recognizing game, is a mandatory skill to be able to do, all that was just said, I learned to do, all this came about because I patrolled the night life, I called it the midnight league, you got your day crowd, evening crew, all the way to the all night flight stalkers, lurking in the midnight league.

Like others in this lifestyle, I ran into plenty lessons learned, from incarceration to Ironing currency, I got the game my brain protects, like a mother holding a new born baby crying, that which king boss player elders considered to be raw to uncut ism, the rated r version in more ways then one, not the pg-13 Disney channel boy scout version of game, I got half my game straight out the belly of the beast from those in it, those stuck in it, those out to get out of it, and those enjoy being in it, rapping 4 tay said, "win or lose," cold song right there.

I learned early that it's plenty to have out of life, Its more to what meets the eyes In one town, it's more land to ground to cover, water to float across to new lands, which also have plenty to offer once you touch dry land, before the boat dock, or airplane land, you gone have, or be hearing your thoughts explain to you, the plan to perfect in new territory, you about to meet greet, just in it to the finish, play to win every hour, on top of the hour, I got one of the people in mind, he had the fangs in his mouth, he told me he from cali, you can see somebody with good game, my godfather said, "you tell when you see somebody, if they at the top of their game.

If you figure out how to make everyday beneficial, progressively satisfying your kingdom consistently, week after week, you gone be considered royalty status to boss players that are you throughout the country, believe the real is moving over the world, some state to state, others country to country, everybody living everywhere, meet greet, I mean here I am with about fifteen hundred in arm reach, sleep with hundred dollar bills & other type of green presidents next to self, sleep with it, keep hands to self, don't touch It, respectfully wake up with it, it's part of the wardrobe, no matter what happens in your day to night, keep going towards the final longevity destination, until it is reached, then kick them feet up, throw your self in retirement, but still conducting money routes to self, so you can stay busy routinely.

Never speak of quitting, speak on get to it, & do it, learn not to want, just keep what self have, it's simple math, it works beneficially better this way, this the serious side of the game of life, see, I stayed from having teenager fun in my teenage years, I stayed studying the game of life, on the streets to off the streets, inside the concrete jungle like New York say, I just participated in activities in this lifestyle, & I learned to just stay busy being occupied with your undivided attention on longevity, retirement before forty years old, buying a rolls Royce with a 18 color viewing choice, this was my youthful thinking process believe it or not.

I stay gentleman with my lifestyle in the coldest way possible, I peep game & see it hiding in plain sight, so I grab it with sticky fingers like onyx, adding it to my own mental repertoire, I saw original indigenous men stacking fat banks in the game of life, & I also saw paycheck original indigenous people along, with other people all on a mission to maintain lavishly, eating five star restaurants good, dressing movie night stylish, luxury vehicle driving good, it's the game they play, but the gentleman look at life as a business, I'm about building a kingdom, plus an empire, it's about king living with me, setting retirement up, simply by figuring out how to make major moves, like easy Eric Wright, respect to his son lil Easy, just to make things happen every live long day, no breaks, no day off just aiming for the big party off days to nights.

See, I been on the up down roller coaster ride, throughout my lifetime, but I got to buy something beneficial for my retirement, a soul food grocery store, a five star soul food restaurant, an indigenous soul people mall, a rhythmic blues supper club, turn low Income poverty houses, to luxury expensive soul people condos, to rent out for low prices, so we can live it up for a small price, tables is supposed to turn, inexpensive luxury apartment buildings for Indigenous soul people to live In, I mean that's the game right there, masterminding the art of living in this lifetime, it's time to get things back on track, to setup the antique fireplace lifestyle.

See, that's just it, if you on that next level thinking process, & somebody else around the way talking about buying a car to stunt in, I'm gone put myself in their shoes, & figure out how to master their situations, plus doing that with my situations, so I studied everybody, & figured out how I would master their situations, & mine, that's how you game tight your game, learn from who got skills.

So I was starting to open my eyes to all that's happening in this country, if you want major results, you got to hit some states, to connect your self to your people, then you get huge face money routes, that's the game of life, that's living intelligent to brilliant.

Then you start watching everything moving everywhere, on the strength to see where you meant to benefit long term at, In each city, or internationally making moves, like indigenous billionaires, like Michael v. Roberts & his brother, moves like that will have you connected to countries, & cities in the states.

That's the game of life way, just putting all the pieces to the puzzle together, on the strength to show you what Is really going on, like payroll the pimp Radio station said.

To start living in castles over seas, & mansions in the United States, buying property to benefit from, businesses all over the world, to set your kingdom up long term, like Anthony moving from Milwaukee to the Dominican republic, that's the game of life, just living It all the way up In this lifetime.

If individuals ain't up on relevant capital game, being updated to upgraded, straight skilled with the motion in the ocean, recognizing what you visualize, seeing the whole picture, not just a small perspective on life, that which is keeping you grounded on the lower level, it's time to get on up to the upper class living, by eliminating habits & setbacks, noun, people places or things.

George Floyd last words was, "I can't breath," them people sat on him, while one put knee to his neck, strategically cutting his air off, All indigenous people over the world saw this, now this Is felt by all us, tears in all eyes listening to him, as we watched him live his last moments, before this, Kobe died in a helicopter, we put in prisons, they burned up black Wall Streets in Oklahoma, they hung Indigenous soul people on trees, I haven't seen my little cousin in over a decade, for his home invasion incarceration, nobody was killed but he got 27 years, plus he have to register as sex offender, because kids was in the house, I got stopped by a female officer In Minneapolis for walking In the airport, in January 2020, same year George Floyd got assassinated, female officer called three men to surround me, all this after I showed her my plane ticket, plus license with four endorsements, she consistently asked did I have weapons, or drugs, or warrants, at an airport, now back to this brilliant book,

Who, or What stopped these boss players from being Kings?

If they didn't get stopped from being hired at jobs, so they would not have to take the back roads to success, if I could have worked a half way decent job, to buy a car, I would have been working all my life to, It's a system of competition going on in this world, if I can't compete with you, I will cheat you out of money, all the way up to jobs, is the mentality of those setting the system up, against indigenous people, all over the world, play fair to see who really qualified.

See, it used to be known, grow your hair, & when you got to disappear, cut your hair, new identity, innocent kind indigenous people have to think like this, it's a sad way to know you born in a position like this, knowing you set up to loose from birth to earth.

Now you tell me in your loudest quietest whispering voice tone, can game recognize game, I need you to really dig down deep, to tell me about what you telling me about, I need to get a job, but how, when I was told, a person girlfriend working In Human Resources, throw away applications, if the name sound like It belongs to an indigenous person, now how you get a job with that being done, can't smoke weed but liquor store is everywhere you look, some say business not personal, yet personal preference Is eliminate who is seen as competition.

It's like now, I keep pimpin in the air I breath, I mean I breath it in hourly, pimpology is wisdom, is it because game recognize game, is it because it was the water I swimmed in at the lakefront, in Milwaukee, let me explain, I lean back to listen to wise words spoken, water plus wisdom, plus good green growed for kings, equals peaceful, calm person balancing thoughts out.

See, you got to watch everything moving, body language, facial expressions, I mean everything moving, a Minnesota squirrel, a Florida lizard, everything moving, because game recognize game, wisdom teaches to study all that is, plus why It is the way it Is, how it exists, so all facial expressions can tell you what's going on where you at, without somebody verbally telling you what's really going on.

Um tum bout this the game of life, it's about wealth and health on all levels, for both them words, I mean to be honest, I keep it pimpin with my mother, my auntie, godfather, pimpin is respect combined with wisdom, I mean game recognize game, in the most gentlemen way possible.

It's around 2am in tifton Georgia, I'm just chopping up game, braking it down in fractions, I mean this how you got to play it, i'nt in retirement yet, so every live long hour, is about putting me in retirement before I'm 41, I made it through the 80s, 90s, 2000s, 2010s on up to now, them four decades, now tell me I can't teach a regular, how to be fantastic, fabulous, exuberayting, how to be a success story, due to the assassination of indigenous men character, most people look at us like we lower then dirt, saying we don't work, we sell drugs, pimp women, we don't grow drugs, we don't set up system where women is looked at as just porn stars, we cornered in those lifestyles, if we could work decent jobs, It wouldn't be money made in prisons.

I'm in Las Vegas at the moment, sipping ace of Spade, hypnotic, jazz black bands, I'm in the lucky casino hotel, Vegas is the place to be, north Vegas got energy that make indigenous people never leave, dude from North India at liquor store, he asked me what am I celebrating because I bought Jay-z champagne, I told him this normal drinking, he said $400 bottle is celebrating something special in his world where he from, indigenous people enjoy being alive everyday, everyday we wake up, we thank the Most High, and go from there, straight like that like New York say.

Now, just like California, I put work in for my royal family, I mean this the king business right here, so game got to recognize game, I mean you don't know how I chill in my leisure time, I mean chilling with royalty is complicated, consistently reading to be wise to help royal family stay wise, it's always been this way from birth to earth, I give the game fairly in balanced doses, I mean, I play well with others at all times, despite what you taught others about indigenous men, respect my game, & the fact my name spit game, this the game of life, the game of life is bigger then me, so game got one option, a mandatory option, and that's recognizing game, make it work for you, train, & tame it, that's all game got to do every chance it get, see own live to be proving something to somebody, I'm boss player status, I got my raise from paying my dues, the more you know, the more you get paid, the more you know the more you grow, also promoted to greater heights from qualifying to escalate, a meaningful way to put it is, I paid my dues seven fold.

I was always taught don't look like you got bread, if you got bread, from indigenous people golden years from kings up to now, it's always been about being updated to adapt properly, it's all good game for those into being highly educated.

I mean how you run pass this polished knowledge, a person who woke not sleep, gone stick like super glue to good game spitters, I mean this truth beyond belief, you got to know it's about staying above average, with hard work, & dedication to elevating to greater heights, I mean talking is like walking, you develop your style to master communication, to become a conversation expert, everyday will lead you up to something better.

If the crowd see a king walking talking dressing all that, then respectfully they will part the sea like Moses, it's the game of life, if you thinking I'm lying, then I'm gone have to get on the solid gold microphone, and say all game entertainment, meaning only assigned seats is for game that recognize game, no outside help distracting the major king mackin, that mean if you don't know what Is really going on, you gone have to pay a coverage charge to come where I'm at, I mean, you got to respect those on top of their game in this lifetime.

See, this right here is showcasing living proof of a sun, of a Chicago mother who once was a gangster, and a son of a godfather, he who which pimped in his lifetime from high school to present moment, so I'm Mack, that combination of game given to me, creating the Mackology, I mean

I been studying the lifestyle I live from birth to earth, I mean what you expect from me, like jay z said, "what more can I say."

See, I been leaning back to stay out of sight, but I wanted to ball to, buying luxury vehicles like big meech, dub them up like the rappers, bass it out like Miami, but I stayed quite, out of sight, out of mind, but why my people got to always look like we not supposed to have the finer things In life, our ancestors had the best life, with the best life had to offer, but we not supposed to, so we supposed to live beneath other races of men, so they can feel important, or look important, because they can't compete with indigenous people in a fair race, I drove through New Mexico to Arizona, it's billboards with Billy the kid picture on it, but people say big meech was wrong for having billboards, I disagree, I'm glad he did it, they doing it, but see it's game involved in why they say big meech should not have done it, but I'm with him for his reasons for doing it, respect his gangster, & the reasons it should have not been done.

I member an older original indigenous soul person gentleman, came to the store where I get my mind right at, he respectfully told me game recognize game, he said, "they can't hit a moving target," I respected that like nobody business, see i'nt a fool to use confuse, I'm In the so called rat race to get paid in full like Eric b & rakim, I just want to see a great life being lived by Indigenous people, without us being stopped from doing so, be the best you was created to be, that's how I play it, don't misunderstand, that statement hitting a moving target, is saying, if you out of sight you out of mind, you got some people who plot at night, & wake up to hate, and time waste, a moving breeze is out of sight out of mind, you ain't on nobody list if self invisible, if you in the spotlight you on people mind, with their thoughts included, it can be good, or bad.

Everybody need everybody, we all living simultaneously, so let's do everyday properly, I mean boss player status, I mean I'm living it my way, the rick James snoop dogg players way, and you got to do it, like Don Juan said.

Now this to every man woman elder & child, respect my game, and my name, I paid my dues like you wouldn't believe, & those I should cut loose, I be keeping it solid with them, cause I'm a righteous man, but now it's later for all that, but it's still relevant to do what is right, words spoken to us through us from the right mind, live & let live, let live to live.

From amateur beginning to years later, its time to boss live, ancient wisdom learn to polish knowledge, I mean hourly shooting straight at luxury living, learning how to be a master of the game of life, like gangster brown from Oakland California, and ain't nobody said it like that, like this, I'm expecting all game to recognize game, like Bushwick bill said, on do or die song, called, "tails," he said, "is it time," I say yes it's been time.

Like Michael mc carter the boss player of boss players said, "we the gentleman gentleman's," we just great indigenous people put In position to look bad, from birth to earth, like others, we have to feed our families, we been stomped on to long, we just like to work, listen to good music, make people laugh, we help people we don't know with no cruel intentions, we spread love not hate, we help the helpless, in order to be a baller, you got to know you gone get fat money to help others more then yourself, a baller biggest fun is the cars, the houses, & that's not saying the money Is not good, but that money Goes to everybody who need help, so a baller enjoyment is his cars to his houses, that's all he get left over after helping everybody to stay living properly.

Breaking news: protest rally all over country, seems like this police killing has woken up the sleeping giants.

Now you ask yourself, has somebody stepped in this smooth, & laid it down thick strategically, in the most quiet way possible.

Keep everybody out your business, I mean straight progressing while being hidden in plain sight, & not to mention, a hand picked Jamaican stepfather, I mean the outcome is obviously understood how I live this lifestyle, I mean I took the game voluntarily that was hand picked, & gave to me, & put it to use.

I understand everybody in my lifetime always say, "it's not where you from, it's about how you do it where you at, but Chicago set the bars highly for me in my innocent childhood years, it's so real in Chicago, if you survived the 80s, & still alive, you a star, a gangster, a pimp, or a Mack.

I know I'm appreciative in more ways then one for my upbringing, Its like a movie how everything been going for royalty thus far, but you know what, I make the most out of the less, &turn nothing to something, you might be somebody who do the same, or you know a professional paid boss player that do That to.

like g Gove the governor, you know Chicago president twin brother, he said, "like trick daddy said, "when a man has done something great, how can you act like you have not seen it."

these words with action, I keep around me dancing in the air Royalty breath: spiritual, pimpology, macklogy, even the g code, lifeology, I mean game got to recognize game, I master the places I'm in, especially if it's a crowd near me, I either run the show, or blend in, or be gone.

In my perspective, Los Angeles, Chicago, & Milwaukee move identical, so if you live in California, & want to leave, pick those three first, then hit Miami, Houston, Dover Delaware, Denver, Seattle, New York City, um tum bout survival skills do this, not the untrained survivalist individuals, I don't recommend these major cities, you got to be prepared not scared facing everything head on, see my bread come first, my father said, "don't let nothing stop me from getting paid in full, like Eric b and rakim.

See, like the bishop don magic Juan said, "I don't get no free living money, that's right I got to get out here to get what is coming to me," now let's give an indigenous man his props, he survived the game of life, then full circle got back spiritual, now that's how a master mind live this life.

Johnny guitar Texas Watson song called, "Cop and blow," pertains to those individuals that's coming to leave, they got a lifeline that keep them bouncing from you to the next player holiday everyday boss player, because that's their purpose in life, they know it, that's why they do it, they here for everybody, they need to run until they reach the stopping point in their life, & then they stay with who they born to be with, they gone run till they come across who they can feel at home with, that's the game of life.

If you don't know what is going on in the world, stay at home til you find out what the game of life is, stay in your city, it's safer that way, but if you ready to explore through the traveling door, & let the game roll on, like afro man said, stay out the way Interfering, like godfather Oasis said, "you in the way of real players," because you gone be known as an infiltrator.

See what you can see from what you hear from real soul survivors, then make a plan to do what can make major things happen, & make it count for the large amount, even if you start with a small amount, don't go to college til you pass the twelve grades first, you can't be a black belt, until you learn why your life is leading you up to the point to be a black belt.

If you gone go into a specific lifestyle mysterious world, you got to play it how it go, & believe you me, I'm here to do everything on the next levels, big daddy kane said, "ain't no half stepping," ain't no stopping, or pushing pause when you in the face of the lion, or time to put a bandage on, the only option Is keep moving, it's serious, & dangerous in the game of life obstacle courses.

Each woman has to know how to pick a mate, choose a king, how to recognize a person they born to be with, Its mandatory to learn how to know how to do that, you got to be learning how to do so, from your first kiss, from the day they got penetrated from choice, force, or being naïve, after losing their innocence, so they will know from that point on how to pick, choose, & you got to know who at you, who choosing, who picking you, it's all part of organized living brilliant with good intentions.

Because if you not into what they into, they gone go pass you to who suit them, it's like eating food, they know what they prefer to put in their body, in their life, it's called the game of life.

Stay true to the game of life correctly, not incorrectly, keep straight ism in the air you breathe, that's how you empower your ism, because diamonds shine brighter around diamonds, and don't give priceless to who don't know it's priceless, because guess what, it's gone be worthless to them, everybody is priceless until they start living worthless.

Keep it real in the field, if a dime piece block you out her mind, not telling you what she thinking, she belongs to somebody else, so let it be known, let it be written, those who share their thoughts with you is free to get at, because the ones in somebody circle will not let you take them, or control their mind, or tell you what they think, or thought, & then you know to keep a social distance from them.

Know when A woman Is out your reach, not your type to deal with, some require thugs, addicts, pimps, it's somebody for everybody, so you got to know yours when you see yours, that's the game right there, know who is who, because game got to recognize game, know who is born to be with the king, allow no one to be lost in character, in the king business.

Everybody got go take care of everybody, pick up where the last one left off, let your lifeline redesign the world you introduce your presents to, one city at a time, our power comes from the sun in the south, distractions come when it's time to do something major in your live long day.

Sometimes you can play yourself out by playing yourself, you make sense out of life by writing about it, study it, take notes, memorize main ideas out of everything you hear, explaining to yourself everything you hear, your interpretation of what you broke down in fractions, specifically to tell you something new, so it speaks clearly to you, in a step by step process, go to sleep with everything right, and wake up with everything right, what you put in is what you get out, if everybody wasn't everywhere, we wouldn't get to see each other, every one from any place in the world, leave that place, then that person introduces the world to everybody where they from, wherever they go, if anybody want money, they have to sell you some of what they know, and the currency adds up to how powerful the information was, that which they gave you to know, for all the need to know basis.

Riddle me this, have you had a thousand, a thou pile in your pockets, or customary jewelry, I mean customize your transportation as you develop into a king on earth, see this the thing to memorize, if you down with the uprise, then you save save save fundraise precisely, that way no matter what happens next, keep moving, everything going on will fix itself, I mean straight like that, so just keep everything moving, I mean do it like it ain't never been done before, stomp hard like dinosaurs, &giants that made footprints that last forever, you will shake up the wrong, when you step in smooth to lay it down thick, I mean take two steps back to visualize a king named Mack, own even trip on people sizing me up, checking out my crocodile shoes, then my wardrobe just to see if I fit the descriptions of characteristic traits they programmed to recognize, but own be presenting myself in no predictable fashion, I mean straight camouflaged from day to night, light in day, dark at night, it's king living in every way possible, I mean playing with billionaire ways to win, not aiming to live plain, & simple in my lifeline, I'm gone lay it out fat on my history, in every way possible.

look at what I'm saying, it's midnight right now.

A king named Mack birth to earth, in a family that had a grandma leave the flesh before I was born, so my mother kept it gangster with me, she survived highly intelligent in Chicago west sides south sides, I mean then we hit the Midwest con son mackwaukee, I mean walk and talk to me, hear my game, watch what drip off my lips, it's game, it's given to those chosen to create an explosion in history making major things transpire, I mean the king crowns the chosen indigenous people person individuals, I mean my mother once kept it gangster, Mother Earth decided to retire from that, then took us to Mack town Milwaukee, just like Todd Shaw, I went from a pimp city to another pimp city that kept it gangster, so I adapted Chicago with Milwaukee and became a king named Mack, & i survived after mistakes was made, got smarter to smarter intelligent to brilliant, I mean I had hate fakes, those who bark behind your back like poodles, but I kept it together, I didn't really get into gangster living, it just seemed like to many sleepless nights living on the edge, I assumed the position I was born to be in.

life was setup nice to create a king named Mack, my moTher was a gangster, and my godfather a retired gangsta pimp, now you ask yourself what do that combination of lifestyles create, that's right a king named Mack, so I'm effortlessly being me, it's been plenty fun under the sun, but respect to my elders, I paid my dues & adapted, upgraded, updated, a king named Mack all through the lifeline up to the present moment, I mean it's real in the field, I be on the front line, but I be out of sight, out of mine, I mean really on a come up mission, as flawless as possible, with not one weak link in my chain, I mean not one in my chain, that's when game recognize game, i mean it was known, then up to now, 96 to now, my style started.

Just out here to get wealthy, & retire like a truck driver, I was born in the 80s, I'nt into nothing but the best for the best, a king, & queen born in the 80's, will do everything bigger then big, in silence.

Unseen unheard, just hanging with success, sleeping with bankrolls next to the king crown.

I can't go to sleep until it's time to close my eyes, I mean I got stuff to do, that which should have been did properly right my first time around, now I got to do it right, this second time around the best time around, now I hit the top of my game, & like san Diego said, "i had a good run," mine ran for over a decade recently, & this time it's to stay up forever, all in retirement before I'm 41, that's the 80s babies, late 70s babies game plan, goal to accomplish, see that's top ism to mix regular with extraordinary game, to speak clean to both sides of the game of life track.

See, in Milwaukee, own know about where you from in Milwaukee, statements in conversation in my surroundings, was speaking on the elders, how they rumoredly slipped, or fell, it's lame to me, your Business ain't my business, like pimpin' snooky said, over a couple decades ago, "I respect it all," but I'm in the race to the top to, I'm with that crowd, so I respect who paid their dues with hard work, dedication to build with bricks not wood, I mean straight aiming for gigantic living, not small things to a giant, now royalty game has a job to mandatorily recognize game, precisely everything that is hidden in plain sight.

I was in indiana, land of the Indians, close to Indianapolis, I'm in the store, and they had dom pérignon on sale for under $150, so I got two, right, I said all man, because I was thinking I should get three, save money from budgeting money, the clerk said, you gone spend your whole pay check, I said nawl this regular money, but I was showing my player card by having a conversation with her, gentlemen first at all times, I learned when doing business of any type, stay focused on getting everything done, never mix business with pleasure, keep personal out the business at all time, don't mix that up, it's a bad combination, eightball wrote a song called, "down and out."

You can tell a king by how he sit in any seat, as if it is his throne, he the king, you can recognize that when you see him, I mean he on business straight to the point, not cracking under pressure, you can watch his performance, take notes, he the king, look how he get treated, I mean he customize the world that surrounds him, wherever he at, that's what King's do, it's a skill that been under construction, like tiara said, for years to have it ready for longevity, the final destination like star trek said, the obstacle course, some call Milwaukee Wisconsin, I mean to be the king, it take game on the brain, skills to pay bills, make mills, I mean fast learning due to fast living, keep up with yourself, is what the king says, because he know it's from studying a life worth living, not remaining stuck on stupid, that's behind schedule behavior, straight unacceptable, but we all know it go on around us, but later for that, it's time to big tymers, big time my lifestyle, my custom made way, according to how growth develop, putting on a show, living a lifestyle identical to their behavioral characteristics traits, that which will become the reason for a movie, to be made about a king.

"Ain't nobody here except us Mack's, musical mackin on the microphone for money," like king jb stomp down said, it's from the baileys album, its called, "san Fransisco giants."

I mean, look at this what I say, I mean literally, now if I can be invisible in plain sight, huge face stacking, major mackin, when I talk how I walk, I speak to game that recognize game, so it's all us who see the invisible in plain sight, those letting their game speak for them, it's boss players status living, I mean interacting simultaneously adapting, updated, upgraded, in it to the finish being stupendous, fantastic, and fabulous, living to learn, learning how to live simultaneously, I mean all that at once, I mean with a dream team turning dreams to reality, bout to press play soon, I'm on pause at the moment, under construction, like tiara said, I mean making room for improvement, like p said, spring cleaning, process of elimination, with intentions to rise, and surprise those sleep walking, then they wake up, the grind don't stop, or take breaks, even when I'm sleeping, the brain building game with wisdom knowledge, creating more power, you see me walking built up, like a gorilla glue strong, confident ahead handling business, read to succeed, routine in leisure time, straight watching the history from start to present moment, see it's a movie called, "long kiss goodnight, a lady was a gangster to me, then she had to change her identity, because a move she made went wrong, she was camouflaging her self, respect to Savannah Georgia camaflauge, back to Gina davis, she was thinking intelligent to brilliant to last a lifetime.

It take great game, I mean straight polished knowledge, game every brain need to contain, just a boss player stepping in the name of game, in the direction towards the next level, everything done thus far, perfecting the game of life is cool, but this route gone make gigantic foot prints to walk in, I mean doing the unpredictable, when it's convenient for the king, strategic moves, like the chessboard directly in front of hillside biggie, I mean that's the game of life, which piece is you, which piece you want to be, again I mean stepping up to the solid gold diamond plate, like barry bonds, baseball royalty, straight aiming to send the ball screaming off the first swing, to outside streets near the stadium, making major moves, like kanye west type billionaires, on my way to the deluxe apartment in the sky, for recreational purposes, and a Benjamin Lloyd crump laywer, & on a mission to buy a lifetime mansion, property paid in full, just for sleeping, and cooking, a feast for the royal family, it's coming soon, I had teams previously I was coaching, each year, some will leave, & some stay, it rolled through the years like that for the king previously, I mean that's the game back then to now, not looking for it to happen the major mackin way, it's just meant to be, I mean it's the business, it's the lifetime, it's the lifestyle, custom made for each individual king, in an unique individual way to customize the king, I mean King lifeline from ancient ancestors that stomped this country called America now, I mean indigenous copper complected complexion groups of divine suns, that passed the historical game, passed down from the beginning to now, from the first Indigenous ancestors journey in this lifetime, I was given that golden book with the great ism in it, now I know how to read the book of life from practice to progress, empowering the mind, to interpret what was complicated to the point, it encouraged misunderstandings to happen, so it's best to sharpen the thinking process, with a pitch black ancient japan indigenous sumari sword sharp game, I mean built up to Superman style strong beyond belief, with vision to see clear land in muddy water, I mean surviving the times, like nas said, surviving the game, like too $hort said.

It ain't close to over, it's just getting started, I mean sound the alarm right now, you know that bell in Pennsylvania, bang it hard, Because it's time to get down with the get down, to get up and stay up, I seen top individuals at their best, and it's time for imitation of life to transpire, with all their skills in one person, that's qualified to inherit that type of ism.

I see this game of life from one to all perspective, I just prefer to be like those who came before now, I recognized who took their game everywhere they went to play to win, and show nuff, it made them powerful, if while, & they survived that lifestyle, just living like a king supposed to, with unlimited assistance, and financially satisfied on a yearly basis, I mean just here there everywhere, they make it happen to go building their own pathway, to where they want to be, see, and get better acquainted with, I mean you slip you fall, you get back up like everybody told you to do, come better then when you left, like Curtis 50 cent Jackson, get back up harder smarter stronger, when the top ones bounce back, they do it to stay up from that point on, no more hard times, or trouble, just learning the game to master it, straight study it, see i'nt defeated, down, or out, I'm on pause til everything get put in order, without hesitation, hatred, or down time lurking.

My game 90s all the way down to the early 1900s, straight solid individual, with respect for all I meet next.

See this game of life is nice if you play it right, just keep a grip so you wont slip, if you can't take your money in rubber bands with you, you going to the wrong place, I mean be around the next levels individuals, see, i'nt get the game from those who aim to keep me down, or standing still, see, it's more realer then jack & Jill going down the hill, we going up the hill to see how it feel to live correctly, like it was meant to be, miami rick ross said something about, somebody, "can't hold y'all back."

Everybody out here aiming to get fat with finance, I'm talking big bread, I'm tum bout straight on top living properly, straight grinding for that fat outcome, Because around the earth, I heard hard work pay off, straight figuring out how to get crowned, with a new type of throne to, these crowns been around sense the first day, & it ain't never left, now the throne might get pulled out of arm reach temporary, but now if it can be done once, it can be done again, and if you can make it all happen, dreams to reality type stuff, on top of your game, sitting on a throne, now game got to recognize game, straight moving strategically.

The wise players get jobs with less work as possible, with more pay, with intentions to make more money, demanding money work for them, all from how their business is lined up to be handled.

Cross country living is the only way to travel.

You see people at top of their game, they squeezed through that door, & came up nice, got to find the right door for all that.

It's all about, how tight you can get everything, it's mandatory to have that bread fat.

What you gone do if the bread gone, Its mandatory to keep everything moving, & get it again, it's the game of life, not living, looking to catch up with longevity, live everyday correctly, mandatory to stay ahead, the king found his way back, like he never left, on tip top for all the right reasons.

Its mandatory, to know how to make money pile up like that, if it's available in arm reach to practice with, mingle with the crowd all over the country, no half stepping, make every step count precisely.

Recycle indigenous money for the indigenous, within the walls of the indigenous, all inside their inside circle.

Mandatory to be Attached to bread, that stretch Armstrong.

Them indigenous soul people from the Mountains, be on some giant type living all live long day.

Everybody at the top of the food chain, it's mandatory, for them to forever be playing to win, exactly how their game develop, as it guided them to the top, it's the game of life successful way.

It's mandatory to play everything on the highest scale, getting the most for all you worked to become, why stop when you know it's mandatory to make everything happen, especially when you can't stop that from happening, everything lined up to go up, or down, sometimes the game of life need wise words of game, to encourage encouragement, to convince the game of life consistently, to keep building your pathway towards longevity.

Got to be at the top of your game, on a fat mission to setup retirement, before you turn 40 years living.

It's boss players that survived the game of fast living, sitting on a throne, & get things stepped up to the highest level they could reach, levels they never saw themselves on, so early in their lifestyle, within the realm of The game of life.

You will get to the top of the lane you in, when you reach up to the top of your game, it's mandatory to step your game up every chance you get, every hour you woke.

Chicago said if you got to count your bread, you don't have no money, it's mandatory to get fat, the wise rise to surprise all eyes watching, and all ears listening, scarface got a classic song, it's called, "dollar," & mc breed got a classic movie called, "dollar."

Keep up with your people, is like watching black exploitation movies, it's the motion in the ocean, each one is a piece to the puzzle of history, it's all the game of life, respect to all that opened doors,,& kicked down doors, so the next ones can step in smooth, & lay it down thick, like Waukegan tay said.

Don't be here to entertain, like a dog running around in circles, do the matrix, make everything work for you, be here to maintain, it's mandatory action to stay on top, or get back on top.

Those who survived the lifestyle, can live to talk about it, it's walking libraries everywhere you walk, & talk.

If you know the trap game, why stay in it to play it how it go, especially if you know it's a losing game.

Crucial conflict said, "don't let it go to your head man."

Pimpin is survival, different spellings, but same meaning.

You told me what to do, but I got to deal with what I did, or do, not the one who told me what to do, now I'm in prison, it's all weak game made cool, see most people gone cover their end, saying I didn't make you do it, so then props get dropped, and respect leaves the spotlight you in, for weak game used for financial gain.

The wise man said to the household, "if you mad, go sit by an antique fireplace, & if you sad, go to the pacific ocean to relax, it's mandatory to have life setup to a point, to be able to say that to your circle.

Everything gone come back around full circle.

Crucial conflict group member by the name of never said, "here's a little something that I think y'all should know."

Milwaukee cool, but it's a prison town, because it's in a prison state, so be prepared for that type of Atmosphere, when you cross that state line indigenous people.

I got to put the fat meat in this book, you know everybody like to eat to be full, so that's how it get served up, It got to be served right, you know I'm also a survivor of the Chicago 80s, & Milwaukee 90s, that's that gangster schooling in childhood, Int saying I'm gangster but game recognizes game, & I learned how to mingle with everybody, survive with anybody, get wealthy with a royal family, & maintain that way, longevity is a lifetime goal mandatory to accomplish, with a solid circle around me, put yourself in my crocodile shoes I got from Philadelphia, I pulled up to the front door of that exotic shoe store,, see game got to recognize game, because it's mandatory in this lifetime, I mean to be on point, it mean you on that John trovota type stuff, you staying alive strong, built to last, building yourself to last long strong, unbreakable, um tum bout staying afloat in the ocean with a life protector on, figuring out what to do about the sharks swimming circles around your feet, living your lifestyle everyday, no breaks, I mean it's a full time job staying alive, aiming for mansions, 24 hour procedure watching everything moving, like Bill gates surveillance cameras, it's real in the world from the front, to the present moment, appreciate what transpired, every pinch of everything happening, all in the globe, do that with a complete understanding about it.

It's mandatory to learn consistently, fools moves can stop you from living a major lifestyle, california mack breed, he said, "minor setback in exchange for a major comeback," like shooter said, in the classic gambler movie called, "Cincinnati kid," shooter said, "I only play for percentage," nothing major far as eyes can see, I been where I'm going, it's mandatory to be into global learning, the kingdom way, I'm turn bout, having a boss player counsel, an x female gangster, & an international uncle all the way from hawaii with it, a boss retired pimp born again boss player godfather, a boss player counsel, Chicago step father in my first 2 years old to 7, 8 years old, some where in that time frame, I got my gangster step father gangster lifestyle ways upbringing, Chicago was top of the line home schooling, if you got game from soul survivors With game, you got to know the business, I'm just a modest fella, a great motivational speaker, good game story teller, I can inspire the youth to focus on retirement before 30, I call that community service, I mean the golden child's, they shine in the day, & night, past present to the future, I mean it looks, & looked like heaven spotlight, beaming out the clouds, on the pyramid golden brown, indigenous people in the universe.

I'm in Oklahoma, twenty miles from texas, breathing the thought, & smell of california to colorado scent, just keeping the peace, staying, remaining humble in the jungle known as the world we live in, still around forty to fifty degrees out here in middle December, and texas born erykah badu is singing saying, "she understands the game," now that's a real woman with age, & experience, & the best upbringing with excellent home schooling, in texas, I say that in the highest form of respect, cold statement, so strong, if it hit the ground, it would cause an earthquake, she said, she understands the game," she singing live, I think her good spirit started singing, that's a cold woman, young women should attend her college she teach, I mean sing to you at, it's absolutely mandatory for all good game to recognize game, when you in the race for first place, ain't no turning back, you only going up, like driving in the rocky mountains, you climbing the ladder, to get back on your throne, if you on your thrown now, respect to you, I know it didn't come easy, It takes time to build, & seconds to destroy, got to move strategically hand picking everything strategically, like slim diamond alabama said, "get rid of them vices player, now one more time, third eye watch me, erykah badu said, "she understands the game," now if a woman said that because she mean that, like don juan said, "say what you mean & mean what you say," respect to Chicago past present to future, now you get what I'm saying, if you got a third eye watching, that means game recognize game, it's all elementary if you polish your knowledge, & got schooled properly, with a boss player status counsel, a one time female gangster turn retired lpn nurse, international from hawaii to Chicago cross country uncle, a boss pimp retired still active checking money godfather, original gangster Chicago step father, he the start of what I saw, that said we supposed to stay paid in full, take care of air body, & figure out what to do to retire early, & not be a slave to currency, green backs, miami call hundreds, yards, enjoy what you read, & read what you enjoy, you could have been anywhere in the world, but you choose, & decided to read my book, I very much so appreciate this.

JOURNEY WEALTHY LONGEVITY SCRIPTURES

5.

Everywhere you go, be on the prowl, to see if that city got benefits for you, on the business tip, vehicles, homes, a new crew, or new members bringing something to the table, showing a down for life mentality, simply to be in the royal family, to help the royal family get wealthy, on the journey to longevity.

No good deed goes unnoticed, and what you do shall pile up to be done for you, just keep self in motion, consistently making things happen, I'm watching, "she done him wrong," respect to louise beavers, she was the center character, she had the game, knew what was happening, she played the background, peeping everything, waiting for the right time to run her own business, her opinion was most important to main character in movie,

GRANDMA'S HAND FULL OF TRUTH

As I sit in the Ritz Carlton hotel in orlando, I sit on the balcony looking at palm trees, I notice from my smart tv Bill weather's song, it's called, "grandma's hand," it just came on my playlist, as Bill starts to sing, as the beat starts to perform, I hear my grandma voice say, "ma'cus…"

My ancestors, the indigenous peoples, pass the truth through the bloodline, till it touched my grandma, then one day, Grandma hands me a hand full of truth, she says, "yesterday will teach you what to do today, to setup a comfortable beneficial longevity tomorrow, learn all languages available to learn in this world, past to present…."

I sit on my throne in the present moment, I continue to sip my Armand de Brignac, puffing my jazz band black mild, a bottle of Hennessy xo, another bottle of Remy xo, none of this would ever transpire in her presence, I would not be doing this sipping & smoking, respect is very seriously important.

So as her voice speaks to me, I relax in the most comfortable way possible, I whisper in the wind, thank you to the Most High for her, and all she about to hand to me, through words to my ears, from her life after death to me, in this present moment…

She continues to speak in the most grandma way possible, saying, "understand what is required to be understood, luck is for those who lack knowledge, spirituality is for the Most High chosen, when you put pimpin in something, that' which will make it formulate, into what the wise title, a powerful thinking process, ism is wisdom, capital game is knowledge, is what she keeps telling me, live learn look listen, sit back enjoy the show, everything is lined up to happen exactly how it was written to transpire…"

The more things stay the same, the more it will progress to change, everything is lined up to move to the next level, think positive before the negative, don't get ahead of yourself, or scoot nobody ahead of themselves, synchronized people enjoy life more, I know you, I comprehend you, we one on all levels, if something is real, you will not have to fight it to be right, you got to get up, then stay up, new waves splashing in the ocean, same game of life, new participants...."

Grandma just running It all down from A to Z, I took a sip of my Moët, then i proceeded to listen, she continued saying, "lifetime partnership is mandatory, a lot of questions can make people become nervous, represent the truth at all times, some people gone stay the way they programmed to be, stay clean away from all people who do not respect a person hard work efforts, a lot is to much, a little is not enough, you will not be exposed to what you can not handle at any given moment in your lifetime, the best for the best at any given moment, never allow self to be knocked off your square, everything must happen so everything else can transpire....

As her voice continued to speak to me, I was inhaling my jazz band black, I exhaled then continued to listen to her voice speak to me, saying, "infiltrators come to take over, to destroy what you spent years building, don't give up ever, no matter what happens, keep rolling, it's a specific way to play on each level, with a specific way to play on each level, and a specific way to make every situation pay, & teach you how to master what comes next on your wealthy pathway, to longevity.

A leader has to be at the top of their game, mentally physically financially spiritually, straight blessed all the way in the truth, shining with love, that southern california san Diego sun bright sun shine, good vibrations, all signs point to yes, words grouped up releasing power, dress code releasing power, that which attracts those lifetime partners that respect your game, alot of times, it's best to just connect for networking purposes, to uplift your net work.

Hills to the top of life, time builds, the man the myth the legend, stay humble, it's always been a strategy to reading, stay humble, what some do, will change the way others live their lifestyle, time traveling gives people a chance to make things happen, sad mad create jealousy...

If the head is not strong, the body becomes weak, people have expectations on what you gone speak on with them, respect is very important, first impression is last impression, let truth be spoken, let the truth be heard, when temporary people try to get to close, create some space, educate to motivate, use brilliance consistently, master your muscle, strategize, always keep space around you, huddle up with correct counsel, pick championship winning players, like hall of famer quarterbacks did, do, like Warren moon houston oilers, bernie custis, marlin briscoe, james harris, George preston, geno smith, Doug williams, lamar jackson, andre ware, charlie ward, troy smith, tyros taylor.

Business is business everywhere none stop, anybody under the influence should not be spoken to about importance, keep eyes on everybody that will, is, or did transpire, people is just like books, read their facial expressions, body language, voice tones, no more drink to think, master life twice as nice, do thorough background checks, check resumes, distractions mandatory purpose is to put you back where you started...

I noticed the orlando summer breeze blow through the palm tree's leaves, I heard somebody yell hole in one by the golf course, then I sipped my Moët again, then inhaled my jazz band black, exhaled to the sky, I teary eyedly sat on my throne, listening to the voice of grandma, as she continue to hand me her hands full of truth, I heard aunt Shirley from south Carolina saying, "stay soulfully full, when people smell currency, they get real nice real quick, real ballers share what they get, look pass muddy water to see dry land, with every negativity, a positivity must be put with it, if something is out your reach, it's in the hands of the Most High..."

I'm listening to suga free song, it's called, "you can't lie to yourself," this some real california music, sipping on some fruit punch infused 100, while editing this chapter, with fiji water, and jazz band blacks playing smoke in the hotel room, now 8ball song, it's called, "down and out," it got me thinking about my first time in miami, 2003 with low money, looking for new land to get wealthy, on a journey to find longevity in.

Recognize what great ism can bring you, produce for you, create accumulate, & accommodate for you, life is meant to be studied, & learned, instead of the ocean, surf on blessings with prayers in your hands, keep them people out your mix, practice brings progress, years of continuous studying, will bring rewarded knowledge, & wisdom, keep everything to self to understand it better, meaning, analyze new found information first, before you distribute it in your own words, it's a privilege to enjoy being blessed, with the opportunity to be at the top of your game.

Get what is coming to you, by way of moving with the motion in the ocean, more ground covered is new land explored, when the right door open, walk in, travel to unravel what is waiting to be seen, also meet greet who waiting to see self, mackology is the study of mastering your own mind, it is studied by Macks, stick to what you know, grow with it, develop with it, progress with it, manifest with it, master it, get a master degree with it, elevate to greater heights with it, wisdom will speak reach teach preach school educate, and motivate...

Watch everybody from start to finish, keep out everybody business, timing is everything, when the time is right, the time is right, time builds, & creates, a partner listens, & learns from your words of guidance, you never know who is who, what they know, or who they know, don't make all of the sudden moves, because it's not planned out, everybody gone be how they taught, and learn to be....

Knowledge get passed down to the keepers of the sacred ism, your spirit must be fed through all senses, through vision, what you can touch feel hear & taste, what you take out, you got to put back, what you put in is what you get out, no deed goes unnoticed, certain people are limited, to spend time with certain people, verbally& physically...

Life teaches us lessons for us to learn, how to survive with longevity, give people a chance to see if they down with you, everything that happens is getting you ready for what is coming up next, avoid hear say, know for show, cause effect, income outcome, got to be able to live without substance, to really feel alive, and live enjoyably.

Business is business, everybody will be who they aim to be, second time around, you will learn to be more appreciative, the more time you stay busy, the more what is needed is received, everybody has to be coachable, money making is just a hobby, meaning, money has not made a slave out of you, meaning you not willing to lose your life for currency, a piece of cloth, a lifeless piece of nothing...

Everybody play a part in everybody life, allow no interference on your pathway to your destination, always stay out everybody business, you got to disappear off the radar, stay low key, moving at your own strategic pace, speak with precise communication, recognize everything bad is temporary, never get caught up in any moment becoming lost in character, it's two sides to every pinch of all that exists, look good without looking for attention, everything seen also heard will guide you….

The king is always in the background overseeing, being rarely seen, rarely heard, everything in life is lined up to happen, everything you do, will be based on strategic timing, if you see someone doing something successfully, that mean you can study them to improve self, that mean you can do it successfully to…

Let your busy behavior have a great impact on the world everyday, focus on doing real estate business, preserve yourself for tomorrow everyday, stay true to the game of life, with knowledge always polished fresh updated upgraded, always put first things first, needs not wants, need don't want, want don't need, it absolutely is about what you need, not what you want, necessities is primarily most important every live long day…

Keep in mind, being righteous is a natural instinct for some not all, no good deed goes unnoticed, your main purpose of waking up is to make progress, rise to shine, a good day is a great day to be thankful for, a powerful man can change the weather when he walk in the room, depending on who you know will increase what you know, forever to always analyze the game of life, play the game of life on a master mind level, top to bottom, side to side it will cost a fee, to everything that goes into a life worth living…

Make it a habit to build important beneficial bridges, read to succeed, if you in the minor league, leave them giants alone, day to night will take your life to the next level, master the art of creating naturally powerful statements, sentences, plus paragraphs, study the life you live, then master the life you live, understand weakness can be heard, and seen by the strong minded…

When people down play your intelligence, keep distance from them, recognize when you reach another boss player level(4/27/19), write the date down so you can monitor your progress, life is a chessboard, figure out which piece you is, or if you need to be a different piece, live to learn, stay in it to the finish, progress without stress, you, and everybody in your business, got to contribute to you going up the ladder, so you can live on your throne…

Understand how to naturally have a professional attitude, control your expensive thinking, never get ahead of yourself, always stay in your world, know the titles of the land you end up in everyday, recognize descriptions that dwell the land you end up in, absorbing data is called thinking, memorized data is called intelligence, hidden history waiting to give complete understanding to those who been given false information, stay in control of your mind, because your brain will attempt periodically to create conflict in your mind of thoughts, no fairytale type thinking process, will be allowed around the master minds…

If you got to work overtime to get a woman on your level, she don't need to be up on your level, because it's not meant to happen, get rid of downfalls, embrace what contributes to prosperity in your lifestyle, always respect individuals at the top of their game, help the world, not in your power to save the world, if you not ready to make moves, moves do not get made, the king has to be well protected, equipped with skills, plus updated upgraded rules, and laws every year….

Stash your ism for your royal family, the game is sold not told, for your royal family it's in you for them only, they guaranteed to do something with your words of wisdom, the safest place to be is inside your enemy house, the enemy will not destroy their home, it's protection from the enemy in the enemy home, the rejected stone has always been the corner stone…

I don't recall who said It best, but I heard, "Its crowded at the bottom," with that being said, I just chose to not indulge In that war zone, I rather be comfortable enjoying life on the level a born king supposed to live on, I'm back in Wisconsin, randomly ran into a gentleman from England, my second person I met from England, we had a deep conversation that probably confirmed what he was recognizing here in the states, it's a money game here, this country is a business district, if you want to live happy go overseas, because here, Its strictly business not personal, sad for some, & a playground for the indigenous soul people, why you ask, because ain't no place like home, & those here from the beginning, they know to stay updated upgraded to maintain a nice life, in it to the finish, live to learn, learn to live, this the game of life, this country the center of attention, ask any foreigner that came here past to present, ask them if they gone leave, air body here got one thing on their mind, that's live it up to the fullest, welcome to calusa.

The fact of life is, if you play your cards to win, you win, but you got to have the hand book to do it correctly, it's plenty books to show the way to go, I used to say, ain't no book to say how to do your day to night, but it is if you know how to read to succeed, like indigenous peoples said for years, "If you didn't know, now you know."

I'm watching, "billionaires mindframe," 1st episode with Mac lucci, if I do say so my boss player self, I'm enjoying this event of upper class learn how to livers, it's like I'm there with them, without being there, soon come, like Jamaican Richard said from Milwaukee Wisconsin, I mean it's nice when everybody all share a memory together, the energy is life changing, also I saw The Godfather Fillmore slim 85th birthday clip, which also was nice twice, I like to name individuals I saw clips of to, such as Roosevelt Taylor from the movie the Mack, pimp dragon, pimp t, stripper amber, meiko a fast liver, all from the show, "soft white under belly," Its real nice to see the bishop don magic Juan from west side Chicago, he get to be seen by the world, to show truth beyond belief, United we stand divided somebody gone fall, or sink in quick sand.

I'm just seeing, & hearing cross the country how Chicago get respected for being organized, & highly advanced, I mean Chicago reputation is major, I been all over the country, I seem to run into Chicago, or somebody who loved what Chicago did to them, or for them, it's just a blessing that I spent my first, almost ten years, a decade growing up In Chicago, like Mack 10 said, "I wouldn't change it for nothing in the world," it's the game of life that keep some comfortable, others uncomfortable, I'm in texas on cloud 1981 right now, just leaning back editing this chapter in the king business Mackology 2nd edition book of the century.

THE GAME OF LIFE SCRIPTURES

3.

Playing the game of life is knowing how to roll it, live to give, give to live, it's about unity, team work works, it's a proven fact teams have won championships, everybody need everybody, cross country living, will explain what the game of life scriptures is all about.

A teacher should never tell indigenous peoples in their youth," they can die before turning the age of 21," the message in all that being said, was somebody was setting our lives up to end early.

Now this informational, those who take drugs is informational, ask a question after You voluntarily respond to their financial request.

I'm leaning back with time to finish editing this brilliant book, I'm in ardmore oklahoma, it's 50 degrees in January, I'm watching, "room service," staring the marx brothers, I'm ready to method man some tical strains, but it's to early in the day, royalty still got business to handle.

BOSS PLAYER ASSOCIATION

INTRODUCTION

"Meek is a humble person, they have a certain peace, so what I get is a spiritual aspect, The meek and humble God will take care of, in the end, they would inherit the earth, and live in peace."

C. Hardy

I'm watching lovely sade, her official video, "nothing can come between us," seem like the classic songs made, the musicians had dance moves to explain the song they performing, to know the game of life, is the same as saying you working on mastering it, in the most indigenous way possible, same as saying in a real player (word) way.

I'm in Edwardsville Illinois, sipping kernel brut champagne.

It took 38 years, & counting, to write this book Properly, I'm back in Wisconsin, Lacrosse to be precise.

I'm leaning back, looking at the city from my 4th floor room, in the historic lacrosse Wisconsin charmant hotel, it's the end of February, I got green green on my mind, with intentions, to put it on my menu soon.

I put everybody I came across musically, historically, appliances, places, to vehicles, in this brilliantly wrote book.

Respect to the game of life, I edited this book me self, my way, my style of talking, me, regular Hennessy, h20, green tea, & a jazz band is hanging together right now.

It's snow outside right now, it came to see me before it had to melt, with more snow coming from the northern West coast,

It's blowing towards the east coast, my Indiana people just left Denver saying, "he just went through the snow storm, coming my way," unfortunately I'm gone be gone before it visit Wisconsin.

I enjoyed reading this intriguing book, as I was editing it, I tell you what, life is nice if you play it right, people gone argue just to forgive each other, without even knowing, that's exactly, what is waiting to transpire..

I made a list of music I put inside this unbelievable book, on the strength so you can see what I was listening to, as I was editing this historical book, the days, to places I did exactly that, I made a list of appliances I used in this special book also, I made a list of names I slid in this book to, I also made a list of United States cities I was in, through out this unbelievable book, I made a list of vehicles I wrote in this fabulous fantastic book, along with vehicle parts, also a clothing list I wrote in this brilliant book, including shoes, I made a list of animal kingdom individuals I wrote in this intellectual book, I made a list of hotel motels I wrote inside this global book, I made a list of words I wrote in this simply remarkable book, words I compensated from the Mack Moon.

I put a full effort in this book described as stupendously spectacular, I appreciate you for reading my ism, knowing knowledge is what really creates power.

THE GAME OF LIFE SCRIPTURES

4.

Playing the game of life is knowing how to roll it, live to give, give to live, it's about unity, team work works, it's a proven fact teams have won championships, everybody need everybody, cross country living, will explain what the game of life scriptures is all about.

A teacher should never tell indigenous peoples in their youth," they can die before turning the age of 21," the message in all that being said, was somebody was setting our lives up to end early, Sade said, "oooh what a lifeee, give you the world if it was mine, I'm yours, your mine, like paradise, give you the world if it was mine."

Feed who around you, and they not gone think about eating off your plate.

Got to know where you at, the face of the hungry, and the face of the thirsty, big difference, and they come in all shapes, sizes, plus shades of complexions, You only can do what you can do, when it's time to do it, it's natural adaption instincts, I'm watching, "the cotton club," with gregory hines.

Million mackin for millions of green backs, that's the game I play, The money will not make you, and the money will not break you, some call it mind over matter.

UNDERSTAND WHAT IS REQUIRED
TO BE UNDERSTOOD

APPRECIATION FOR YOU
IS IN FULL EFFECT

I'm in clean, 7000 feet in the air, inside a mountain made city, called flagstaff Arizona, real real nice looking city, I can't believe a city is so well put together, this high up in the mountains, a little cold, but it's nice in a way, you can't believe right now, go see what I saw if you ever in Arizona.

I'm listening to Sir Charles, & Suga Ray song, it's called, "Running Game," I'm in North Carolina, I'm sipping Biltmore Zinfandel Blanc De Noir, puffing on Jazz blacks, while I proudly edit this section of this highly anticipated, Alaska cold book.

You finally made it family, is what the ancient ancestors would say too, you know who, congratulations on surviving in North America to dive moony pool, ten feet deep, inside this specific boss player status classroom, that which is in the form of a brilliantly written book.

The author has an unlimited wealth of knowledge, that which was passed down, hand picked from the ancient indigenous ancestors, which certifies him to speak on several specific unique topics, living in this longevity book, I mean these titles is walking with you, talking to you, and enjoying you reading this book with you.

Appreciation is in full effect, is what I'm saying in simplest terms, like slapping cigarettes out of random peoples hand, tyrone said, "no disrespect."

The oba author, also will include a childhood to adulthood storyline, to memorize, it is based around expensive living, life in the fast lane, unique rare life situations, that can only be told from a survivor of the Game of Life perspective, so naturally dig deep, read deeply between the lines, it's all ism releasing the energy, in this unbelievable book.

Inside this 2021 unavoidable book, your new favorite intelligent to brilliant author, will share unbelievable Capital Game, that's really meant to be sold, not told, which means all you shall read, in this brilliant book, is beyond priceless, similar to an Eric b. & Rakim versus scarface concert in the mgm Las Vegas Nevada.

To more explain the point of this book, being priceless is to say, that no dollar amount, can be enough to purchase the power of this book, and the knowledge in this brilliant book, this magnificent book holds sentimental value, only you have been given the opportunity to be blessed with.

I say to you humbly, proud with a feeling, often described as heavenly privileged, With honor, I welcomingly say this with diamond gold teeth, straight from a Fort Leonard Wood Missouri born smile, I welcome you into a well known unknown world, I call the Mack Moon, it's a place only chosen handpicked individuals is allowed to dwell, a place where only the strong survive, year after powerful year.

A classified confidential world inside your once in a lifetime world, I will discretely invite you inside the King's castle, only through this marvelous book, universally known as the Mack Moon, in the solar system amongst the stars, indigenous peoples is stars, daytime to moonlight, past present future.

While diving neck deep inside my 38 year old book, you will need the following accessories, access to EarthLink internet service, and a rare first edition Encyclopedia Britannica, then watch lectures by Dr. John henrik clarke, some ministry by louis farrakhan, and teachings from Dr. Ishhakamusa barashango, malcom x, bobby hemmit, pastor tony smith, dr. Sebi, dr. Ray higgins, dr. Umar johnson, dr. Laila afrika.

Don't get nervous, that's some philosophical playing I do periodically throughout this brilliantly written book, wipe the sweat off your Russell Simmons solid gold toilet bowl round forehead, relax, it's not that serious, supposedly.

If you haven't been living your life to the fullest comfortably, after reading this book, it will be time for you to start traveling state to state, continent to continent to see what you been missing out on all your life, to see if you been missing out on something.

Get a passport to vacation visit other countries, its time to step your game all the Empire State Building way up, just to see what's going on, inside this gigantic Mother Earth.

The earth is your turf indigenous copper brown soul people, like Master P said, "ain't no limit," explore and enjoy your journey, to become wealthy, while you seek to marry longevity, for a lifetime.

Sincerely I Thank you for your purchase, memorize this one time, put this in your long term memory bank, if you see it, you can obtain it with good game, only because knowledge is power, use your brain game, not your back being a slave to currency, play the reverse game, make currency work for you.

If your heart desires it, hard work mastering your Most High given gift, will make it greet you, when you ready to meet it, and keep it.

Last thing to memorize, never quit, give up, stop, hate, debate, or time waste.

You important to this world, in a way you will not understand, til you turn 40 years old, without you in this world, & all those that saw you, know you, need you, this lifetime would be missing an important piece to the puzzle, that completes this lifetime.

Enjoy what you read, read what you enjoy, real game can be said backwards, and forwards, appreciate yourself for being good to yourself, I mean that truthfully in this lifetime.

I started writing in a halfway house, a couple people I was cool with, we was having pushup contest everyday, this older European man had dice hid in the ceiling, so my room held dice games before count time, the look out, got paid by whoever won the most that night, so after a while, I played once, or twice, but I got more into writing a book, I used to get gone from there everyday, because I checked in to community college, to avoid going to the house of correction, I was in ccc half way house, that's what it was called, so during my classes at matc college, I used to let this pretty round brown attractive gal, she was in school to be a lawyer, I let her voluntarily read what I wrote, and everyday she wanted to read the next pages I wrote, so it motivated me to keep writing, to finish the book, I was stunned that she was really anxious to read what I wrote, and here we are now with my second book, plus those who bought copies of my original printed up books I put in folders, I thank that hand full, without support,?a person place or thing cannot develop.

JOURNEY WEALTHY LONGEVITY SCRIPTURES

6.

Everywhere you go, be on the prowl to see if that city got benefits for you on the business tip, vehicles, homes, a new crew, or new members bringing something to the table, showing a down for life mentality, simply to be in the royal family, to help the royal family get wealthy on the journey to longevity.

You want to pimp, ok push play, baby drew song, it's called, "you my weakness," playing in the background, now let's discuss the bullseye, then let's calculate time to strike, while the iron hot, while we discuss what get the bullseye, hot under the collar, then the move is made, I mean approach a roach with a plan, same thing with anything, when it's a queen bee, you got to approach with caution, a plàn to set the scene up right, a bird dance, flapping wings, foot work, and colorful feathers, now that's the game of life, broke down in fractions, so if it's anything more important, and directly strategically spoken today, prove it now, or forever hold your piece, no hating, just respect for what's polished, shining, earning, turn, and time to shine.

Las Vegas is just a playground, a stop, and go, respectfully I say that with all game entertainment, every city is made a way to be dealt with it, knowing that, is the only way to travel.

Life is like going through the atmosphere, that go into outer space, you gone see some stuff, when you climb the later, going to the top, you gone see in windows, you gone see from a birds eye view, what is really going on, that's all this about, and spontaneously stay super glued to the Most High.

I'm watching droop-e video, "I'm loaded," sounds like a truck driver theme song, this the business, california got the game, ism, energy, don't believe me go visit then, northern, & southern california indigenous people, a life worth living is a life worth learning, e-40 got to get his selection in stores in all the chocolate cities all over the country, know what um tum bout, we want some to, in the Midwest maine.

THE SECOND ROUND

THE PHILOSOPHICAL PHILOSOPHER PRESENTS

PURE AS A RAIN DROP

THOUGHTS THAT CAN'T BE BOUGHT MACKOLOGY 1981: 2ND EDITION

I'm In Ontario California, near Rancho Cucamonga, with the mountains in the background, Right boss player now.

THE GAME OF LIFE SCRIPTURES

5.

Playing the game of life is knowing how to roll it, live to give, give to live, it's about unity, team work works, it's a proven fact, teams have won championships, everybody need everybody, cross country living, will explain what the game of life scriptures is all about.

Let's chop it up, if I can sharpen my game with your game, seeing how it's mandatory to keep your game tight, steel sharpen steel, same thing, it's mandatory to happen, it's absolutely mandatory for steel to sharpen steel, now let's chop up game, and brake it down in fractions.

I'm watching og cj mac, indigenous movie star, community activist, his video, it's called, "come and take a ride," sex c kilt the chorus, now I'm watching e-40 &the click video, it's called, "slurricane," now tell me we ain't make this country important, popular, and powerful, indigenous people, suga t doing motivational speaking, she get plenty points for that right there.

RESPECT TO ALL WILLING PARTICIPANTS

Now check this out one time, a woman that understands the game of life like Erykah Badu, is extremely unique, on some rare type stuff, now how do she understand the game, listen to me now, like the pastor In grandma nem church say, how do she understand the game is what I'm asking, she knows the indigenous man goes through life with traps, every step he take, waiting on him to not pay attention, improvise, is how he defines living life, it's the game of life, a woman that plays her part, is crowned the queen, ain't no time to play, no need for excitement, that will come with setbacks from a woman In the royal family, a queen gone get down with the get down, she know we got to build an empire, the king ain't got time for half steeper's, stop playing, kids is kids, they waste time without knowing they wasting time, the king queen thinking, it's make it happen time, every hour on top of the hour, even when we sleeping, y'all don't hear me, I said, "even when we sleeping, when we in motion, it's Chicago do or die," big daddy kane, said, "no half stepping," it's real out here, that's my word, we pushing it to the limit like Rick Ross the rapper, and on some brilliant freeway Ricky Ross the giant type stuff, read to succeed type living.

You got to know me, I got to know that you understand the game of life is played on a boat load of levels, we know what level we discussed to play it on, to satisfy the royal family, the royal family is dedicated to accumulating accommodations for the royal family, after we first spiritually heal the royal family, each member receives the king royal treatment, we all a family brought together, hand picked to combine properly, no hate, no jealousy, just unity to happify each member, together we create progress, prosperity, success, blessings, love, respect, we all here to better each other on all levels to live this life, for all the Most High purposes.

Respect to my lifestyle, lifetime ladies, one way, or anotherr, who fed me, housed me, let me in their house to be me, or kept bread in my pockets, or just loved me, it is others who name I can't remember, in my early years after 1996, oh, to the ones who left the flesh, I say Rest peacefully, a good woman is a life long friend, To the ladies that gave me house keys, when I was homeless, or the ones that housed me when a lady kick me out her house, I was green limousining in Milwaukee, to those that kept my hair braided, Miami godfather I met on greyhound leaving Chicago, he came to get me from ft. Lauderdale when I got stranded there, with a suitcase, & fox fur coat on, I didn't want to leave it in Milwaukee, he came to get me the next day, to bring me to Miami, I painted a house with him, it was his buddy house, to pay for my ticket to get back to Wisconsin, all this happened right before hurricane Katrina hit in 2003, to the ladies from Madison Wisconsin that was gone hit me with bread, to jolly green giant get me up on my feet, & to all my cross country people that welcomed me to their city, or house, from Lebron James home town, to all over the country, Oh, and green eyes, she hit me with qp money from her rent money, oh, mc breed, he saw me in an airport, when I was knee high, he called me lil dog, to tell me the airport personnel was talking to me, when I was minor not major, oh yeah, baby drew, I met the boss player by a pool table in st. Francis, & coo coo cal, I met the boss player at Melvin bass runnerz video shoot, and that's a hand full of people who played a part in my lifetime, they played major roles in me life, weather they know it, or not, oh, preacher the gentleman of leisure from Milwaukee, & Stan Stack Jefferson, Chicago Eddie crum, plus his twin brother John crumb, to geno, to the chocolate young lady that depended on me for a whole year, she was showing me how to take care of my ladies, she wanted to get loose leaf money on the streets, but I told her no, that's it, that I remember, that played a part in my Macklifestyle, also I appreciate the women that turned on me, one way, or another, teaching me how to read those closet to me, no hate for them at all, it's just survival.

A Waukegan Illinois Gangster, by the name of tae, crunchy black business partner uncle beats brother, he told me to, "step in smooth, and lay it down thick."

Look up the names I use in this book, to see who is who, & what is what, look listen learn every live long day, that's how you earn your turn, & time to shine.

On behalf of the (BPA) Boss Player Association, Once again, I want to take this time out, to anxiously say, "welcome to The Mack Moon everybody, thank you very much for your undivided attention, and time."

You gone enjoy this magnificent book in a way you never knew was possible, I got Ism for you, rare capitol game that will live with you for a lifetime, sometimes I say random stuff that has purpose to meaning, where I'm from, game get chopped up, so I write how boss players conversate communicate, so no worries about that, game recognizes game when it presents itself is what the ancestors will whisper in the wind.

I'm listening to 8ball & MJG song, it's called, "Pimps," and it says, "I can't seem to get my feet on the grounddddd."

I'm watching the Mack, the movie made in oakland, I'm in Southern California right now, watching it right now, in Southern California, that's major for all boss players to do.

I want to say this, I went to miami, I met a lady working at some gas station, well a few, each one intelligence level was impressively above average, their sun colored complexion was like no other state, Miami just impressed me in every way possible, my first day in Miami gardens, most known to indigenous in that land as liberty city, I saw a parade of four wheelers, motor bikes doing wheelies down the street, Miami was, and is my favorite place to this day, all the water colors everywhere you look, I call Florida the water world, wet and wild lifestyles, perfect people, perfect weather, perfect scenary, perfect location, water world miami florida, 2003 my first time going there, lizards to iguanas laying in the grass, water world, alligator in water areas, it's a lot of living going on in miami.

JOURNEY WEALTHY LONGEVITY SCRIPTURES

7.

Everywhere you go, be on the prowl to see if that city got benefits for you on the business tip, vehicles, homes, a new crew, or new members bringing something to the table, showing a down for life mentality, simply to be in the royal family, to help the royal family get wealthy on the journey to longevity.

The original indigenous peoples language of the land, We talk our talk, from past to present, just listen to us: two birds in a bush is worth one in the hand " stay on your square " see no evil speak no evil hear no evil " we speak powerful inside the English language, that only us can interpret, to the point they can't respond, or comprehend it, so you hear indigenous peoples say, "you know what I'm saying," it's incase you don't know what they saying, say you don't respectfully, respectfully they will break it down in fractions for those who don't speak the indigenous language of the land.

if the soul people, some call black people, is truly infact the original indigenous to the land they dwell in, then all, not some, should say that then, if it's a game being played, it's mandatory to know how to play it to win in it.

If you speak what some call, ghetto, or Ebonics, you speak the original language of your land, in modern day interpretation, modern day terminology, in the most indigenous way possible, not to be confused with the geechi people, respect to those unique bloodline, original language of their land, in modern day English, similar but not identical, and indigenous peoples speak with their hands, & body, it's a past down style, when ancestors had to describe something, to those foreigners, who didn't speak the original language of the land.

If you speak of mother father Most High blessings, and reap what you sow, good game put in you from mama from grandma, father from grandfather, good game from my elders, in the areas I rotated in, I got game from men, good game from they grand daddy, cover all angels, connect the dots, put all the pieces to the puzzle together, look at the big picture, and it stay in the past, present, future, straight like that, like new York say, if you don't know that right there, you don't know as much as you thought you knew.

All indigenous peoples teach what they taught, which is the original indigenous peoples way of life, it's been updating upgrading sense the beginning of Life, from when it first started being lived.

Don't sell game to indigenous, give it freely, and get your blessings.

All indigenous peoples got songs, and tribal dances, to represent what land they indigenous to, look on the rap videos, the truth is hidden in plain sight, third Eye got to be open watching, to feel what I let drip off my lip, on paper in forms of words, in spectacular simply remarkable intellectual intelligent to brilliant sentences.

Ask the indigenous people to speak indigenous to you, the original language spoken in modern day terminology, straight updated from the original ancestors, past present, to future generations.

Word of mouth travel faster, than the speed of life, faster than a starving cheetah chasing an impala, I mean faster then a flight leaving los Angeles, to miami, I mean fast, it's drums beating across the land, with huddled up smoke symbols, in the air, sending symbols of the 2021 blueprint.

PLANT A SEED WATCH IT GROW

Missouri Born inside the well known Fort Leonard wood Army Base in 1981, Army folks call it fort lost in the woods.

This book right here, Its Gone be better then food, drugs, & alcohol, this can be considered, to be unforgettable memorable fascinating intriguing exuberating revidalizing empowering Words to the wise.

To beat mike Tyson, you got to be a giant, Hercules strong, and bishop Don magic Juan smart.

Stay on the money route til it's time to get comfortable.

Your auntie April just reminded me of something you used to always say, she said, "Boo used to say its money all over the world, and now he going all over the world getting it."

JOURNEY WEALTHY LONGEVITY SCRIPTURES

8.

Everywhere you go, be on the prowl, to see if that city got benefits for you, on the business tip, vehicles, homes, a new crew, or new members bringing something to the table, showing a down for life mentality, simply to be in the royal family, to help the royal family get wealthy, on the journey to longevity.

Erykah badu, let me say it again, queen soul indigenous texas erykah badu, respectfully I speak this name, kollen Mari hopsin daughter, erykah badu, her spirit will sing for her a lot, you hear it, you feel it, erykah badu airbody, when I get a chance, I'm gone have a show on an island, handpick everybody that come to mind, from all over the country, past to present, I'm gone squeeze everybody together, how I see it in my mind, I'm gone paint a picture of it, in the round table meeting chapter, when you play your part, knowing you serving your boss player purpose in life, everything fall into place, trust me on that, like Kenny red said, to his ears listening, in his first mansion, I worked hard for this, soul survivors rewards be appreciated.

WORKING ON RETIREMENT

I'm somewhere at the bottom of New Mexico, just editing this magnificent book, it's slightly Southern California raining, thank you to the Most High, for anything, everything, all, or nothing, like snoop, & don juan said, "you got to do it."

I'm in Blue Island Illinois, sipping Rose Moet discreetly, puffing on A jazz band black slowly, sight seeing like a Disney World tourists, and my bread low at the moment, at the same time I got another loaf of wheat bread, in the oven baking, what really started me up, hillside finches, I might be pronouncing that right, somebody told him I got license, he found me walking, ask me, " did I want to drive to Madison," I said yeah, plus I verbal contract a percentage of the money for driving to Madison Wisconsin, he was jumping up when we got back, excited we made it back, & he got his bread on the journey to the badgers stadium, boss player was impressed I got us in, & us out, peace to blessings to the boss player, may amen ra hands be holding you big bra.

I'm listening to J Diggs song, it's called, "Santa Claus," its the month of colorful leaf trees November, I got it blasting loud for all ears near to hear, ain't nothing like that, it's solid talking music, in a major earl Stevens major way.

I was privileged to be Raised up cold, on the West Side Of Chicago, appreciation to the Most High, the great spirits, and ancient ancestors, I said that in the most respectful boss player way possible, I'm very thankful to have the privilege to exist, because the 80s, 90s was serious.

I'm Still here, like 2pac said, not to mention I wrote two books, I didn't full effort the first book properly, so this book is my first book rewrote with precise strategic word selection, intelligent sentence creating, and I did it with a brilliant lower class upbringing thinking process, ain't that something, all game recognize game, erykah badu said, "she understands the game," live show, so you know she, & her spirit put it down legendary.

This is the city, a man from New York City, he told me was based on influences, that helped create the scene in New Jack City, the scene that which they took over the Carter.

New York City LB said, "New York City didn't roll like that, on the strength everybody was strapped in the projects in New York City," and Chicago he said, "had worst projects then New York City had," I just heard that from somebody else in Orlando Florida yesterday, I never knew that.

I was fortunate to grow up Inside the organized Henry Horner Projects in the early 1980's, al capone Chicago, don magic jian west side Chicago, it made me who I am today, and taught me major facts of life, on some bobby womack type stuff, cleveland ohio bobby womack, in more ways then one, in Chicago you grow up quicker then time allows, about five years is childhood, then you get adulthood raised, five years own up.

I Lived in Chicago 1982 till 1988, that's all I needed to get ready for everything in this world, I mean everything, come on now, Westside hornets projects, we playing baseball in the hallway by the, "don't get on me elevators," I was back catcher, got hit in the lip by the batter, blood everywhere, own know how he got a real wooden baseball bat, I member in the same halls one night, somebody had plenty frogs loose on the hallway floor, & a boy hit each one with a hammer, I mean you grow up fast, learning life faster than a Bugatti go zero to sixty, big city fast living fast learning..

Respect to Crucial Conflict, Do or Die, Psychodrama, Don Magic Juan, King June Bug, 4J, etc.

I'm listening to Oakland Legend, Philthy Rich's song, it's called, "East Oakland legend," as I edit this brilliantly written section, once again I say this is Spanish, muchas gracias (Spanish), for your undivided attention, and for purchasing my thoughts.

I want to say, respect to Alabama born, Atlanta king, sir Gucci mane, I respect how he bounce back after doing time in prison, he bounced back so cold, rumor started up saying he was a clone, respect a mane when he at the top of his game, they didn't want to give him his props, for bouncing back, so they said he a clone, boss player Association approved this message, y'all don't hear me, erykah badu said, "she understands the game."

It was once said in Ontario California, "if los angles recognize what you promoting, it's gone be known nationwide, los Angeles got big time media going on there, it stretch all over the world, los Angeles a top city in the world, very important far as money is concerned, it was created strategically molded to pay, like Las Vegas casinos to the owner of the casino, you at the top of your game all across the country, for some money making reason, los angles got top access to the best media, that's why so many people travel to California, I call California fun in the sun, In the most beneficial way possible.

THE LAST MACK STANDING SCRIPTURES

2.

Step in smooth to lay It down thick, straight grinding like they said, on hood to hood part 1, the people was in Little Rock Arkansas, got to learn how to live, then learn how to earn, then learn how to make money work for you, then learn how to pull up where ever you go, straight shining brand new, like they say In Memphis, "this what game plus money do for you," if you learn how to direct traffic, Memphis know the business, on some project pat type stuff, It's all about getting life right, wealthy, comfortable with longevity, and spirituality.

The real be doing things their elder nem style, red said, "you hear me," I love being places Where people be minding to their own business, I'm out here in new Orleans, feel like I'm at home, went to utp skip spot, "chicken and watermelon," got something to eat, food the business, chopped it up with chef outside when I pulled up, ask could I park how I parked, talking to him for a minute, then asked do og skip come here, he said he right there, he was just chilling, it was some cool ladies inside working behind the counter taking orders, they was real cool, super 8 on east side of New Orleans, (Soulja slim) from what I was told, I was by the 9th ward, super 8 look like a hilton hotel, feel like I'm at home, weather 60 in February, watching cable tv, I turned to mardi gras history on tv, new orleans look way different then it be looking on tv, everybody was cool, 100 percent chocolate city, puffed my last california here, that was the business seeing og skip at his restaurant, I think I'm gone work on getting me a restaurant to, new orleans I think is the birthplace of rhythm & blues.

Respect to lapham park maine, this boss player was good for sharing game with indigenous people, classic solid boss player, biggie said, "yeah he had some words of knowledge."

CHILDHOOD MEMORABLE MOMENT

Humbly, I ask you to allow me to share an unforgettable, childhood memory: the place was Buddy bears grocery store, the location is In the land of snow, the land of the father of modern Chicago blues, Muddy Waters, not to mention Jeff Ford, a born and raised Chicago brilliant man, I'm watching mjg video, "it's called that girl," it got Stacey dash, damon dash sister in it, mjg got some stepping going on at the end of this video, with some Indigenous ladies, I would have paid vip price to be on that video shoot, this a king pimp video fa show, I like the women that be dancing in rap videos, they be full effort dancing, them be big money moves for them, if you know how to shoot for the money, if you on point as a woman, it mean learn the business, then qualify to be the boss, own it, be a billionaire like oprah winfrey, isabel dos santos, folorusho alakija, or strive masiyiwa, respect to cloverland c note, og red, li flip nem, for having the slab parade for the video, "ride'n slabs video version 2," bra nem kilt it, bloc boyz, houston be chilling, linked up though, safety in numbers, United all stand, "gripping grain, everybody do it but it's a houston thang," og red snap though, gangsters keep it gangster in all indigenous cities, "rollin In the slab, ride slow tip left, beat on knock, botany block, hit the park and turn heads, when I touch down in h-town," this a straight gangster song, respect it, or check it type gangster song video, texas indigenous nem be on the next level, come with your game tight, and your mannerism when you touch down in the land of giants, provincia de texas, caddoan caddo raudha mean friend, jumano,

Near Buddy Bears was the grocery store, a friend of me (mut maut mout) Mother Earth family, he saw me pimp stick walking in a pamper, I was a brave heart, like queensbridge Jungle and Wyz, I was a three foot

120

tall pyramid golden brown toddler, by myself, in Chicago streets, strolling in my childhood.

I thank the Most High daily, this man I never seen again, he not only saw a toddler, he recognized it was little bitty ms. Cornbread son, and without thinking twice, he decided to bring me back to me mother, that day became a boss player holiday day, it's celebrated every August, possibly in a city, or state near you.

Who knows, he might have told this same story a million times from then to now, and believe him, or not, he ain't lying, it's a true 1980's Chicago story that transpired.

That was my first time on my own, in this world, I pimpishly presume I was born ready to explore every pinch of this world, with a purpose, and meaning.

During my time in unforgettable Westside Chicago, my crime family years later, we stayed right by the Bulls stadium, where Don Juan got picked by the Pimp God, to pimp for over 30 years, and Michael Jordan brought millions, millions of dollars to the area of the so called ghetto, Too Short made a song around this time, it's called, "money in the ghetto."

This was near the time frame, Mr. Brooklyn born Michael Jordan, he was hand picked to win six National Basketball Association championships, in the pay detectives off, crack cocaine, gang bang capitol, pimp capital, mississippi migrating people loves it, it's called billionaire Chicago Illinois, that's a serious combination of statements referring to one city.

A place where race means, let's see who can get the most currency first, believe that, Memphis said it best, making money easy is serious, those who know the Memphis abbreviation understand me. (Memphis means making easy money pimpin hoes in style, black indigenous magic).

I member seeing a window with chipped paint around it, on the side of a burgundy brick brown building, it was across the street from the Henry Horner project building, it was a building where they gave free food to us, project Soul indigenous people that is, the so called less fortunate.

Once again, a New York City LB told me that, "free food was food waiting to be throwed in the garbage, but instead, churches, and non profit organizations gave it to the less fortunate," right or wrong, it fed people.

For hungry poor purposes, a soul brother had his black brown hands in the window to long, asking for more food for those who didn't get anything.

Simultaneously, a regretful person from inside the building, own know if it was unintentionally, but that window was slammed down with force on them fingers, hard plus fast, and blood was everywhere.

I mean everywhere was blood, straight from that soul brother hands, from getting his hands slammed in the window, on the side of that building.

Memories like these let me know, years later in more ways then one, Chicago got me prepared to maintain, and survive anywhere in the world, and not be surprised, or shocked by anything I see.

I'm listening to the last mack standing soundtrack, hosted by international red, c-murder featuring monica song called, "streets keep calling me."

THE LAST MACK
STANDING SCRIPTURES

3.

Step in smooth to lay It down thick, straight grinding like they do in Little Rock Arkansas, got to learn how to live, then learn how to earn, then learn how to make money work for you, then learn how to pull up shining brand new, like they say In Memphis, "this what game plus money do for you," if you learn how to direct traffic, Memphis know the business, on some project pat type stuff, It's all about getting life right, wealthy comfortable with longevity, and spirituality.

MILWAUKEE INFLUENCED FROM 1988 TILL 2018

Now let's speak on money making just a hobby, chocolate brown Milwaukee Wisconsin, rest easy to CJ Nickolas, forgive me if his last name spelt differently, hillside marshal, nunu Antoine Ahmad, Chris John brother, Pooter, Jj Havin Bread, Mr. Finches from hillside, several more names I will say this to, may truth, and my prayers, be put on y'all, by mother father the Most High.

I'm in Jacksonville Florida, it rain like it's a timer out here, signs in the grass saying danger, alligators, snakes, also frogs be jumping on the road when it rain hard, everybody I encounter here just be relaxed like they in heaven, Jacksonville is real nice, and one of the original indigenous people most important indigenous places to be.

I'm sipping Moet mix with hypnotic, bra in the store, he was talking about making kush cologne to sell, I think he can get big bread for that, Jacksonville all year around like Hawaii weather, it seem like you in heaven, brown black faces everywhere, instantly made me feel at home, just by seeing everybody in motion to get paid.

I'm listening to Nippsey Hussle song, it's called, "Blue Laces 2," I never listened to new geniuses before, I been traveling consistently, coming up on two years straight, finding myself introducing myself, to what I'm not a custom to, it updates, upgrades me properly, to hear what original indigenous people have to say, from their right mind, about where they from, let me know what's going on in your land you indigenous to, especially when I'm there, school me, so I can know what to be aware of, when I'm in your city, b legit got a song, it's called, "city to city."

Rest easy Nippsey, and may the Most High, place my truth to prayers around you, forever to always, it's good to make big moves, especially when you can produce jobs for other indigenous people.

I tell you what, it ain't nothing like sipping champagne, writing a book, I'm listening to Milwaukee finest, Chicago born, Mr. Baby Gold Fangers Drew.

I member this like it happened five minutes ago, I was in the University of Pimpology Mackology (UPM), I was with my professor, Pimp Stanley Stack Jefferson, as Professor Ken Ivy would say, Mr. Stanley Jefferson got a pimpin hoes degree (PHD), a true lifeologist.

It was me, professor Stanley Stack Jefferson, his Pimp brother Tommy Dixon, plus Big pimpin Tommy Dixon Pimp friend was in the moment to, us four shared this magnificent memory together, I can feel the energy from them, a tremendous amount of wisdom, history, love, respect, a powerful combination.

We took a pimpin ride through Mackwaukee, in TD pink old school Cadillac, I think it was after Tommy Dixon got out of prison, he had randomly came to visit Stan, and I also was randomly visiting the Milwaukee Legend, Stan the man at that time.

Um tum bout this Cadillac was antique, he started it up with the key sideways on the dashboard, from north to south is how new cars is started up, this key turned left to right on the dashboard area.

After the classic pimp movie scene ride, we ended up back in professor Stanley Stack Jefferson pink house, this house was on 28th state street, where I first met Stan, I felt some strong energy from them three, it was so strong my eyes got watery.

When I first met professor Stanley Stack Jefferson, I was on my way to Ricky's strip club, on 26th state street, to see if I could talk the strippers, or a stripper into choosing to be with me, young man pimpin, straight practicing on perfecting my king mackin'.

I used to post up on the side of this strip club, it is across the street where the liquor store at, I did this, before they went into the strip club, to get their hustle on, and from there on, he started putting me up on OG pimp game, this was around 1999.

He told me, after a while of chopping up game with me, he told me he was gone write a book, but I ended up writing me a book first, which is now my second brilliantly wrote book, so I guess Its true what the ancient language says, "if you walk with giants, you become a giant."

I'm gone put his life chapter in this book later on, after a few chapters.

I don't remember everybody name all the time, because I seen a tremendous amount of solid players in my lifetime, but I met a true hustler on 35th Wells, with two California gang bang dokey braids, in his head.

I knew from the moment this happened, I was certified, destined to be boss player status in my teenage wonder years, the true hustler, had one of his people, come in the store, to snatch me up a hand size bottle of J. Roget, straight on chill out the wine cooler.

Anybody who knows me, knows I started off living the champagne sparkling wine lifestyle, so J. Roget was my partner, until Og Aj introduce me to Moet, during this time, he was Alabama kiyahotpeppa ballin hard, I mean all year round.

This was the time when Snoop Dogg album, " Da Game is Sold not Told," came out, Og Aj had a purple bat mobile looking Camaro, he had gold ds on it, all four rims was a $1000 a piece, um tum bout big tymer ballin, his theme song was, "Hustle and Ball," by Snoop dogg, when Snoop was living in New Orleans with Soulja slim nem.

Back to the story, the 35th wells Og, his people did it like a thief in the night, without anybody seeing him grab it, then stuffed it out of sight, like it was rightfully his, then he gave it to me, when I came out the liquor store front door.

To my knowledge, I think it was some big brother stuff he was showing me, he was watching me develop, and I was safe as long as he was around, he taught me how to do the boss player association hand shake, with two hands, max julien did this with his brother on the mack, when he got out of prison, "this my brother man."

I was moving quietly, every time I came that way to that store, at least I thought I was invisible, til that day happened, I always left right away out that area, when I left out a store, I was always being seen by myself consistently.

I think he respected how young I was, dressing in snakeskin Stacey Adams, you know it, and coordinately wearing five different types of Godfather Dobb hats, and driving throughout the weeks, days to nights by myself.

I used to buy swishers so much, from Sams corner store, it was located directly across the street, from the 35th Wells liquor store.

So much so to the point, I was titled mr swisher, other than that in Milwaukee, I stayed basket balling in the king center, on 17th Vilet street, I was known for killing people on the court with Bob, Enis, Jamale, Popi, D block, Terrel, Sam, Willie, Ricky, Jabar, li billy, Chris & Rico, Cedric, big 10, and plenty moe, they know who they is.

All the true basket ballers in Milwaukee know what um tum bout, respect to Marcus Greer, and Joe, they two of Milwaukee basketball kings.

Respect to All four corners in Milwaukee: Northside, Eastside, Westside, and Southside.

I'm listening to Fabulous & Troy Ave, song, called, "only life I know," it's from Fabulous album Soul Tape 2, these two if they haven't already, they should make a album, or short film together.

JOURNEY WEALTHY LONGEVITY SCRIPTURES

9.

Everywhere you go, be on the prowl, to see if that city got benefits for you, on the business tip, vehicles, homes, a new crew, or new members bringing something to the table, showing a down for life mentality, simply to be in the royal family, to help the royal family get wealthy, on the journey to longevity.

Psalms is prayers, proverbs is wisdom, it's best, from what I was told, to read three chapters a day, wake up to read, read before you go to sleep, to cover yourself from day, to night with truth, and effort to keep the Most High in your day, to night.

AUTHOR APPRECIATION DAY

Respect to authors such as Iceberg Slim, Don Magic Juan, Mickey Royal, Mr. Ken Ivy, Ron Newt, Chicago Red, Rosebud, Jack Coleman Jr., Noble Dee, Eric Culpepper, Dr. Muata Ashby, James Robinson, just to name a few authors, those of which who books I read, the following authors get top of the line respect, world wide, I haven't bought their book yet, by the time this book come out, I will already have bought their book, j.a. rogers, o.g. Fillmore slim, Stanley tookie Williams, king bert, Gucci mane, James prince, big meech, freeway Ricky ross, Daniel r. Day, king flex nasheed, wainsworth m. Hall, just to name a few right now, I'm listening to Troy ave song, it's called, "New York city."

Oh I like to say congratulations to birdman, also Chicago native Kanye West, for reaching billionaire status, if I do another book, I'm going to see if he can do an acceptance speech chapter, about him becoming a billionaire from hard work, and dedication to paying his dues.

I Am King Mack Millon Dollars, I'm a polite philosophical philosopher, possibly the game spitting smartest, & a well-known cool breeze floating around the United States, it's my pleasure meeting you all honestly.

Pimpology, Mackology, The G Code, con game, spirituality, drugs, alcohol, hate, love, betrayal, trickery, hooking to hoeing, (hoe abbreviated is hands on everything), racism, 1981 to 2020 has made me into the intellectual intelligent to brilliant individual I am today, & still I'm motion.

Last thing I feel the need to display, I never hated, debated, I been grinding all my life like Nipsey Hussle, simply to get up to stay up, people always told me to stay up, out of all I went through, I sit here reflecting on cross country living, I never seen none of this coming, that which I wrote about in this book, transpiring, I was just maintaining soulfully surviving.

It's time to get this book started properly, I'm listening to Troy Ave song, called, "More Money More Problems," I want to say to you reading this, I respect you for reading this brilliantly full effort wrote book, if I could, I would thank you a thousand times for your purchase, and your undivided attention.

Front cover to last page of this boss player status book, I will Show respect to powerful people, while I politely escort you narratively through some of my breath taking thoughts, that couldn't be bought by you, until now.

These is Supreme thoughts I present to you, that which me lovely mother told me, that which will continue to exist deep inside of me, specifically created, to introduce to a specific special person, that which is you, I'm listening to droop e song, it's called, 'n the traffic'.

I shall give you delightful unbelievable details, I shall walk you through my simply remarkable birthday events, events that introduced me to growth, development, great decision making, so I could know incomes to outcomes, simultaneously while living my Macklifestyle.

All of this I present to you in this brilliantly wrote book, it happened, all the while I was one of the innocent boys, raised up inside the prejudice systematic trap in North America, created to keep Indigenous people from their powerful position in life, indigenous people was setup to lose, and all the Soul people in the world, know the business of living.

I'm listening to Trinidad James, song, it's called, "All Gold everything," he said, "own frank with no snitches, so don't tell me who telling."

I'm listening to erykah badu song, it's called, "orange moon," one of them summer night songs, that you supposed to listen to in Miami, floating on water, in a 2020 Dilbar yacht, with cecil's a. Iftikhar on deck, taking instagram selfies in front of the sun setting, & the moon slowly rising reflection on top of the ocean.

Simultaneously while I write his story(history), I will introduce you to amazing soul people, great supreme individuals, unique powerful people you wish you met, brilliant people who you never knew existed, wonderful wealth of knowledge, heaven sent soul people you see in everyday life, like Og Don, who left prison in a limo, In Wisconsin, just like Dolomite did, respect to Milwaukee og j ro.

These the soul people you see shaking hands fancifully, drinking Hennessy Xo, Ace of Spades, Don Perigion, Rose Moet, smoking dispensary strains, such as Leafs by Snoop, Berner Cherry Kush, Dizzy OG, Freddie Kane OG, Khalifa Kush, Dr. Greenthumbs, Tangie, Kurupt Moon Rocks, and OG Skizs, also known as medical healing herbs, also los Angeles method man tical, I'm listening to snoop dogg song called, "a dogg named snoop."

Once again I need to say this, ain't nothing better for me, than enjoying Jacksonville Florida, sipping Moet mixed with Hypnotic, writing this historic book.

Just for you my highly intelligent reader, I will demonstrate how longevity game is passed around, mind to mind, ear to ear, who it is given to, why they receive it, where it came from, & why it is passed around state to state, county to county, continent to continent, and prison to gladiator school prison.

I'm going to highlight, unbelievable events in my pinky ring street king Macklifestyle, that which stand out to me, through out this Missouri born, wise written book.

Simultaneously, I will add historical pyramid golden brown colors to these events, & some special Indigenous decorations, around these specific dates, and times of my privileged indigenous lifetime.

I'm listening to Ron Browz song, it's called, "pop Champagne," he said, "how we ball in clubs, we need more bottles, tell ma hurry up," respect to Harlem World, once known as, one of the chocolate cities in North America, think about it.

Respectfully I'm going to use my life events, to entertain hidden messages that will highly educate you, to get all your undivided attention, also to shock, and amaze you, with a millennium book, that which all soul people can relate to.

I'm listening to Baltimore Tupac Amaru Shakur song, it's called, "my block," now g-unit song called, "g-unit soldiers," featuring bang em smurf, that's my Favorite Trinidad gangster right there, ll cool j said, "it's a queens thing."

Just like any other knowledge created powerful book, that has ever been written, or will be written, there is a unique purpose for my book to be read, and studied, it's up to you to figure that out kings, and queens.

The reason why you ask, its Dover Delaware Milwaukee elementary school, simple math, common sense, I full effortly will explain what is unexplained, recognize people fear what they do not understand, so I will Chicago Milwaukee educate you with my black magic.

This book is created, to Specifically teach you about all that has been created, specifically that which was created strategically to confuse you, and about why certain people live the way they live.

Good game recognizes good game, bad game recognizes bad game, my main aim is to get people from different walks of life, to meet, & greet each other, to connect on all necessary levels.

I'm not doing not one book signing, guest appearances, lectures, so if you see me, believe royalty, it will be because it was written in the book of life, to transpire.

Translation, meaning I want everybody all over the world, to get to know each other, for all the righteous spiritual reasons, that's it, that's all.

I'm listening to Mr. Curtis Jackson, that's what I'm assuming business partners of his, address him, this 50cent song is called, " hold on," sometimes it's hard as hell not to touch stuff, we came from nothing now they saying we straight, boy you better be easy, i woke up this morning, supply and demand, my man got knowledge of self, New York type stuff, we came from nothing, now they saying we straight, let yayo hold the straps, to my beliefs, that money coming in like we run the streets, hold up hold on," got to respect 50 word play, true lyricist, strategically hand picking words to group up to create black magic power.

Now his song called, "when it rains it pours," it just came on, "usually goes down over money and 304s, people be in the hood doing the same ol smith, yet they think they game so slick."

For example, sense I wear a pitch black JJ Havin' Bread waist line rabbit fur coat, some people would like to think I did illegal transactions to get it, I been mackin all my life from prince to king, with no breaks, you can ask me mother.

Foolishly they will keep their distance from me, yet if those people who tend to look at me fearfully, sideways, took the time out of their day, to get better aquatinted with me, they would really really regret not wanting to get to know me, I'm cooler than snoop dogg number one fan.

This brilliantly wrote book, is guaranteed to politely, humbly, give you a rare look at what you hear rookies speak often about, or see classic black exploitation movies talk about, or hear black haven Tela lyrical rap songs rap about, and throwback soul people speak on naturally.

Respectfully I say this, this boss player status book excitedly will give you a Dom Perignon champagne, crystal glass clear perspective from the inside, not the outside looking in.

I want you to relax like you living in an east side lake drive mansion, in Milwaukee, Chicago, Detroit, or Cleveland while sitting inside your back yard waterfall infinity pool Jacuzzi, get 5 star Paris Hilton Hotel, Orlando Florida Ritz Carlton comfortable.

Then put your Xiaomi Redmi 6A expensive phone on airplane mode, let the Big Boi Bully Kennel barking family dog go play outside in your backyard.

Next I King Mack Millon Dollar want you to put the Penny candy loving kids to sleep, & turn the Vizio M Series Quantum TV off.

Then finally, I want you to find an anechoic chamber at Orfield, that type of quiet peaceful area, to be at peace with yourself, & direct all your yoga meditating undivided attention to this fascinating childhood to adulthood book.

Now, don't get saint Claire lazy bones, I'm bout to sling shot big words to you, look these words up that you don't know, you got internet to look up words, & names, watch how cold I introduce you to the next level, that millions of people be on right now, this Royalty book ain't for lazy thinking, simple minds, or slow boats, it's for those who game recognize game, good to bad game.

What you will voluntarily read with your Remy XO crystal glass clear vision, in this brilliantly wrote book, shall change the way you look at life, unless you listening to audio books being read, this most definitely is a universal brilliant book, Texas to Arkansas be saying, already bra, we gone buy the king business Mackology 2nd edition book.

I think it will change the way books get wrote, & it also will give people who don't read books, a perfectly good reason, to read reality based books, believe that, believe, or let it alone, like Minister Farrakhan be saying.

I'm listening to Chris brown sing on 50 cent song, it's called, "I'm the man," "I came in the world crying, and fussing, every ghetto the same,

138

once I'm on, in't never gone stop, i came in the game getting money, I'm on the grind right now, you know I'm the man," Chris brown, "i came in the game getting money, come for free," 50, "I'm on the grind right now."

This is my own global intellectual historical personal perspective, through my eyes in my lifetime of life itself, I laid all this out, on the strength of all that, with infinity respect for the Most High, already, finally a book from us for us, already, on some fubu type stuff.

Humbly I say this respectfully, my life experiences has given me certified understanding to speak on a numerous amount of topics, that's in this powerful brilliantly wrote book, seasoned veterans know what um tum bout, I got it from them to know that, and all this you bout to read.

Therefore throughout this Missouri born book, respect to Saint Louis, I will enlighten you in a way you never knew was possible, reading this book will have you feeling right at home from this point on, all over your world indigenous people, like nas said, "the world is yours, who's world is it."

I met a white Mink coat wearing boss player in St. Louis Missouri, at the fabulous Sheraton Hotel in downtown Saint Louis, he told me hit him up, and he would show me how it go in Saint Louis.

I'm listening to Snoop song, it's called, "A Dogg named snoop," I mean this brilliantly poet lyrics says, "mother loving dog named snoop, what's up homie, where you from, moms put a bottle to my grill, I can't walk yet, I can't talk yet, doing it up, given it up," California Soul people be on point with how they play the game of life.

"Roll with me, this is the dopiest g that you ever will see, by the grace of God, you loving me," also I heard this scholarly man speak during the Blood Crip truce, respect to the man the myth the legend, Mr.T Rogers, a brilliantly created man.

Allow me to speak humbly about me self, I am a Missouri born king named Mack, I studied in the land of giants, also known as Mackwaukee Wisconsin, from Chicagoland, then globally to be really updated, upgraded is a privilege to be still progressing.

The cold hearted baby New York, Chicago Illinois raised me up for almost a decade, much respect to all from Chicago, we everywhere in the country, all over like a 2020 Range Rover.

I deliver to you my conclusion, I was influenced by Indigenous soul survivors in North America, those who survived the 1950's, 1960's, 1970's, 1980's, and 1990's.

I'm listening to 8ball & MJG song, called, "Take a Picture," they part of the underground kings, this video is brilliantly made, it says, "we taking everybody with us."

My polished knowledge is my power, ancient wisdom is my longevity queen, I am her longevity king, she qualified me to be worthy of being crowned lifetime king, by the Most High.

Recognize this which then is how I became King Mack, God son, and possibly one of the last Mack's standing in the universe.

Respect to Og Fillmore Slim, the Pope of the game of life, he made a song called, "Mackin," he start the song off by schooling not fooling, then he speak on what he did, that which made him the strongest, wise man he is today, pimpishyly speaking, with a lifetime of respect I wrote this book for indigenous people cross country first, to indigenous people worldwide, everybody got a book except indigenous soul people in this country, that's why I said first, it's all love from above, don't be offended, not even a pinch of a little bit, of offended.

THE GAME OF LIFE SCRIPTURES

6.

Playing the game of life is knowing how to roll it, live to give, give to live, it's about unity, team work works, it's a proven fact teams have won championships, everybody need everybody, cross country living will explain what the game of life scriptures is all about.

I'm in Las Vegas, big city, bright lights, you can smell money in the air, and everything that comes with it, with good game floating in the air to anybody listening, Vallejo O.G. J. Diggs once said, "don't come to Las Vegas trying to get up, you got to come here already up."

Waking up in this Good north Las Vegas heat, don't know what to expect today, when I got here, an indigenous player to this land, he put me up on some retirement game, in a way you wouldn't believe, so today I'm gone sight see like a tourist, and take pictures, to see what to decide to do for long-term purposes, I'm watching miss universe 2013 preliminary competition, the o'jays song, "forever mine," just came on, I'm in the air with california smoke signals, editing this all game sharpen game chapter, I member a player named Lawrence, from Hamilton, I never seen him off his square, I think I got that in me, from seeing him like that, game recognize game, so I copied that style he had, never crack under pressure, built in air conditioner, stay cool at all times, the humble rules the jungle.

Did my sight seeing on the Fabulous strip in Las Vegas, weather nicer then nice, people everywhere from everywhere, it's all types of stuff to do, eat, buy, try, explore in one day, all the way to the night, it look like somebody turned the now desert mountains into something beneficial, in a way a billionaire will appreciate everyday he, or she live there, beneficially speaking, my grandma said money talk, she gave me the game on what to make work for royalty, that's right the currency.

I'm listening to Florida Maybach Music group song, its called, "Magnificent," respect to the tennis expert, slash true millionaire businessman from the ground on up(E-40), Mr. Dispensary Freeway Rick Ross from California, a round of applause everybody, a standing ovation, he represented himself, taught his self how to read write while in the belly of the beast, he found out how to get out the whale mouth, both of these indigenous pinky ring street kings, is true definitions of soul people, they made it out traps they was born in, one day they will sit down to speak on what they need to speak on, big time stuff I presume, that's how indigenous masterminds figure situations out.

Respect to street life philosophers, such as Ray Virgil Fairley, Ice-T, White Folks from Georgia, Pimpin whitefolks from you guessed it, Chicago, Too $hort from Oakland, just to name a few, I heard these soul people break capitol game down in the English language, in fractions, in a way the average man can't do, in a way I never seen done before, I came across them, it's good game at home, but it's more game from each state, cover all angles to connect game.

I'm listening to Staten Island Capadonna, the ultimate lyricist, this song Is called, "Cuban links kings," he a Staten Island master of word play, king on the chessboard, Wu, Tang, wu, tang is what the 10,000 concert full of fans is chanting together.

I'm listening to the soulful beautiful Goapele, her song, it's called, "closer to my dreams," if you need soul music right now, she sing this song with indigenous angels cheering her on, and I mean those resting in peace will feel her voice vibrations, each, & everytime you play this song.

INTRODUCTION TO STREET LIFE PHILOSOPHY

I'm in New Jersey the garden state, I'm bout to edit my brilliant book, while I'm watching Kane & able video, with master p, it's called, "gangstafied," what year did it come out?

Every city is made for a certain lifestyle, it's known its boss player cities, king pimp cities, gangster cities, hustler cities, gangsta paradise like Coolio said, I'm saying this to say, each city is setup for a specific lifestyle to reign supreme in comfortably, now titles is known where money fall out the sky, college students do the same, they go where the money at, that which they specialize in making money, see, if you game tight, you know how the grass grow, I think rapping 4 tay made the most consistent boss player songs, about being a boss player.

The game of life, lifeology, mackology, pimpology, the philosophical philosopher presents street life philosophy, written by King Mack Millon Dollar.

You need to enjoy knowing what other peoples know, at all times, including different languages (native tongues), at any given moment anywhere in the world you end up in next, this is mandatory to have in your possession, it's all part of what you call soul survivors lifestyle, all information is good information.

Some times a lot of times in life, it's well known by the wise soul people, you do not need a whole lot, to do a whole lot, because everything is based on your wisdom to make situations progress consistently, not what tools you use to get the job done, because it's natural instinct for some soul people, to turn nothing into to something.

Yesterday, will teach you what to do today, and tomorrow will explain how great your performance was yesterday, time will tell you everything you need to know, or waiting to figure out, from this perspective, time is on your side.

Learn the language of the land you find your self in, also the language inside that language, and the ancient languages of that land you dwell in, understand what is required to be understood every live long day.

DJ Quik said, "Balance & options," self explanatory, learn to say a lot by saying as less as possible, learn how to be a communication conversationist, master word play on all levels.

It will always be truth in lies, and it is always lies chasing the tail of the truth.

If you don't know, Game came from whence rain came from, and now you know, it's pure clean and powerfully unpolluted, with good intentions like most people in federal prison, prison, jail, dead gone, all their intentions is best described as good, speak for those who speak on the microphone to the crowds gathering up, or having round table meetings.

Paid royalties, meaning getting paid by those that respect you, in exchange for what you got to offer that which they want, or need, it's the proper way a kingdom operate, otherwise if the wrong kind, is present, yet not playing their part, aiming to get all they can get their hands on, they turn into infiltrators, on a mission to destroy, what you built up, that which is in your lifetime.

8ball song, called, "lost," just went off, if it's raining Game, like mac dre vallejo said, why complain, get more game, then spit more game, that's how you fight, let your game speak for you.

Strategically place everything in the proper position, for long term effects, and beneficial reasons, that's how a situation last forever, when everything is in its correct position, & working properly.

Always for a lifetime, keep enough to do enough, at any given moment, some might say, "always stay ready for war," I say, "stay prepared not scared," in so many words, it just means, stay ahead of what is going on every hour, on top of the next hour, that's what the news channels is for, peep game from every angle.

The weak is in a trance sleep living, the quiet is hidden in plain sight starting specific types of riots, in more ways than one, the strong will always last long, the wise will rise unexpectedly surprisingly, fools do not know {rules, laws}, or how to use their Most High, hand picked given tools, because they go left instead of stay right here.

Royalty definition: king perspective is, seeing life as a giant sees it, king mentality, is learn everything about history, from every angle possible, ancient knowledge, and all natives to every land, in boss player terminology, it means have a global brilliance, that's the king perspective.

Earth is land of the star child, North America is the land of the Soul people, my native lands is Missouri, Illinois, and Wisconsin, which is my tribal lands, confused ain't you, miseducated was you, trickery teach kids lies, so they live with a lie, and don't even know, until they crash into the deadend wall.

Never ever, in a million years, school a fool, or give game to a lame, if this individual, has potential to have a lifetime of hidden hate towards you, trust me, don't do it wise one, leave the anchor in the boat, keep moving, til you find dry land, that's welcoming with money falling out the sky.

This is why, simply because, it's to much powerful knowledge for the unqualified, therefore it will mess their life up, and backfire on you, they subject to misuse it, hence the ancient expression, "the game is sold not told."

Because power in the hands of those untrained, it will get miss used, or it will be used hatefully on who gave it to them, then you like why did I give the game away foolishly, if they can't pay for what they seek, they not ready to have it, simple mathematics.

Being in the wrong group, is the same as being isolated, because each person mind must be on the same page in a group, so no one in the group has a hidden issue, that which will create friction amongst the whole group.

So with that being said, incorrect grouping up is the same as self destruction isolation, because a group structure must be unbreakable, simply because they all in the same boat, on the same pathway, same lifestyle, with the same lifetime goals, now friction amongst that group, gone go good, or end bad.

You can not change what is, into what you want it to be, unless it is the Will of the Most High.

It is a source to all that is, what is being said is only important, if the person saying it, is important to the person, it is being said to.

Groom self to suit the journey self on, which is spiritually being wealthy, finding soulful longevity, in conclusion, stay ahead of what is going on, updated, and upgraded, now to forever, because it's a most definitely mandatory requirement in this lifetime.

Learn how to stay equipped with new {ism} everyday, seek lip service, catch what drip off lips, everybody got something to say, but can you catch what is helpful to you, out of everything each person speaks their mind saying what you allowed to hear.

If the Most High put you in a privileged position, the Most High can take you out of that privileged position, appreciation is mandatory in everyday life.

Life lessons come from all directions, in all types of ways, in more ways than one, for one to reach out to all, all over the world, we all teach preach to each other directly, or indirectly, think about it.

Everything will work itself out, because that is how life is setup to go, no worries, or need for you to allow fear to hold you hostage, it's to much to do in this lifetime, find them formulas of success on correct pathways, stay on them.

Make lifetime plans to invest in spiritually delivered literature, buy tools necessarily needed for your life journey, for business, and during leisure time situations.

Make your currency get three jobs, to create more options for you, it's called turning nothing into something, by way of making your money work for you.

With the cards you was dealt from birth to earth, play to win, introduce what you got going on to what produce progress, continue to maintain while monitoring what transpire next, at any given moment.

Suns of the Most High, should not sleep with foolish, rebellious, jealousy women, only women who dedicated to being the greatest woman, they was created to be.

Darkness is what created me, so I embrace it, and all it represents.

Life will teach you what you need to know about life itself, I am learning what is required to be understood, and memorizing while simultaneously recognizing everything is based around timing.

Be where you belong at all times, find those who live your lifestyle, get in where you fit in, earn your turn to time to shine, learn to live, live to learn, put all this in your long term memory bank, a life worth living is a life worth learning indigenous peoples.

Today is in competition with tomorrow, today is in competition with yesterday, this year is in competition with last year, the present moment is in competition with the future, the present moment is in competition with the past, the present moment is in competition with the past, and future.

Never let currency make you need it, currency need you, make the currency work for you, and stay down to earth for you, and yours.

Some specific people in your lifetime, will stand tall through it all, with you no matter what, others will fall victim to anything, they will be showcasing weakness for curiosity, some will slip into traps, and still stand tall through it all for you.

What the streets got to offer, is for those living the street life, one option goes down a dead end street, which is midnight love.

I'm more of a house mack, less of a cross country professional paid rich street pimp, that is to everybody reading this, and wondering what I specialize in.

A piece on the chessboard that will stand up for a king, while a king stand down on her, will bring progress for their kingdom guaranteed.

A king should motivate his kingdom at all times, inspiring his kingdom, encouraging all women to be at their best at all times, two times a day is minimum, three times at the most, every live long day.

If a king is not positive, it is well known, that he do not have longevity to offer, all those in his kingdom.

Everything you hear in life, will play a part in what you think about, or influence what pop up in your head, that's at any given moment.

A wicked individual will twist you up in a world of trouble, also confusion, this only can happen if you get lost in their eyes, or participate in their conversations, which is the door to your downfall.

Have something brilliant to say to every person you communicate with, male, female, all ethic backgrounds, individually, one on one, in any place in the world, you dwell in.

The words you speak will reach out to comprehenders, to let them know how sharp your thinking process is.

So for those who can catch what you throw verbally to ears listening, those individuals is most likely on the level you on, or on their way to the level, you been working hard to get on.

Those who aim to master all levels of life everyday, is who you need to communicate conversate with, every chance you get, ain't no time to waste at all, not a second, minute, hour, day, week, month, or year, I'm editing this chapter watching e-40 & too $hort vs. concert.

Take time, to properly enjoy every moment you serve your purpose in life, everyday you wake up is a new beginning, blessings to the Most High.

Beware of those who use what you say, or do against you, to big up themselves, to look down on you, or to gain power over you.

Iron Mike Tyson bob weave, Muhammad Ali move with style, Don King dictionary talk, Memphis Gangsta walk with confidence, never stay longer then the time planned to leave, like Jay-Z, precisely pick what you say like Condoleezza Rice, and speak like you in a court of law.

Let your Cleveland Good Game speak for you, like the greatest of all time, like brooklyn born Micheal Jordan do, just keep scoring, winning, focus on first things first, self preservation, with money routes all year round, a fat mansion to kick your feet up in.

Keep something on the table, so you can stay paid in full like Eric B. & Rakim, keep everything in motion like Mac Dre, keep the ocean clean to, ready for you to swim in it comfortably, and don't burn no bridges, get the jacuzzi built in the bedroom.

Grow into your higher self, master the art of being self, the wise man said, "I did not want to accept the truth on meat, because I did not want to stop eating it," if you can interpret that, you on your way to your destination.

When it is time to deal with real reality, all forms of nonsense will cancel itself out.

When players find out what the coaches know, it cause all types of friction, argumentative confusion, which will then disrupts the natural way of things existing in order.

Meaning everyone from top title, to lowest rank, should daily, nightly aim to advance themselves in their line of business of mastering life.

I'm listening to the great Ja Rule's song, it's called, "One of Us," and this song speaks deeply spiritually, I'm sipping my second bottle of Moët mixed with Hypnotic.

The gate keepers of the universal black magic Good Game, should know what to share, how to discipline, meaning, know who gone put to use what is important, that which they have to place in others minds.

Its well known by intellectual individuals, that, if the mind is not strong, the body will be weak, falling victim to infiltrators.

Study ancient fools, to present moment fools, a safety commercial, once said, "you can learn a lot from dummies."

All over the country, how you treat people is how they treat you, do things that highlight your life, look, listen, learn.

Some of the same faces, be in different places, these be the people who travel through the world, to make things happen, and they know, all action gone present itself looking for them, in different places, all over the country, & then the world.

Go to sleep in the right state of mind, to wake up in the right state of mind, to conquer all obstacles on your pathway, Kemet pyramid golden rule for a lifetime of success, simple math, stick to the script.

Simple minded schools, teach kids to think as groups, & not independently, not putting them on the last long retirement game.

Your reflection is those who is the closest to you, it's called imitation of life.

You never know how the grass may grow around the world, or where the invisible wind gone blow you to, seeing is believing, here say is what they say, seeing is believing, travel to unravel.

Royalty Power can be seen, in a person existence, their personality, and their characteristics traits.

Trust or bust, sink or swim, plain, and simple math.

Royalty requires everything to be automatic in their lifetime, which helps them make things happen instantaneously, because it is mandatory to bring the kingdom to longevity.

The land of giants, is where only the strong indigenous survive on major levels, Miami, Chicago, New York City, Harlem, Milwaukee, Fargo North Dakota, Los Angels, San Francisco, Oakland, Memphis, Houston, Dallas, Newark, Youngstown, Montgomery, Tucson, Denver, Montana, Bronx, Queens, Atlanta, Gary, Detroit, Minniapolis, New Orleans, Africa, Brazil, London, Germany, Russia, India, Asia, Tasmania, Mexico, just to name a few.

Saint Louis got my foot in the door, and Memphis started my journey.

Everybody got a pathway they on, or getting on, either you in, or you out.

Four, or five, what you call power points, is strength, power, knowledge, wisdom, leadership.

Always Have a reason for starting a conversation, with whom you start a conversation with, which is those you will meet on your journey, to get wealthy.

Keep everything all the way classified, and strictly confidential, at all times.

If the head person in charge is not strong, the body becomes weak, and vulnerable.

Do not speak to a magnificent king, if you do not know what to say to him, people always have high expectations on what you gone speak on, with them.

Worldwide Respect is very important, and first impression is your last impression.

Business is business everywhere none stop, no matter where you go.

Life is meant to be studied consistently, everyday of your life, learn from every lesson presented to you directly, and indirectly.

Learn how others surfed on, above to beyond blessings, with necessary prayers.

Work your way up to God body status, Soul people is closer to the sun, everything is setup to know, and not know.

Who is naturally, or programmed to be, or not be, on a spiritual journey?, is the question amongst questions.

Sit back like you in the Maybach, relax like you just cashed a 7 million dollar check, then enjoy the show, Jay-Z called, " In my lifetime."

Keep everything confidentially classified to your self, so you can be free to understand it better, meaning that's how you analyze new found information.

Rumor has it, down south moves slow, they relaxed, with no pressure, because everything around them is plentiful, so if you don't know, they always think fast, visit the southern, see how they play to win there, and it will stand out as soon as you get there.

Move silent like the Great Grey Owl, think with caution, trust or bust, sink or swim, it is a treasure at the end of the rainbow in Dover Delaware, ask Harriet Tubman.

City to every North America city, state to every North America state, life is being lived, learned, so it's mandatory to stay updated, upgraded.

Get what is coming to you out of life, simply by moving with the crowd that accumulates beneficial accommodations.

Surfing on the motion in the ocean, always aim to cover more ground in the world, seek out to discover land that's new to your family.

When the opportunity door open, humbly walk in with intentions to see what is waiting to be seen, this includes pretty places, also you will meet greet who waiting to see you.

Cleveland Good Game add years to peers, study what teaches you how to become built to last, pay attention to thoughts explaining how to use time wisely, every person alive will never have time to waste, hate, negotiate, now benefit is great, then negotiate, compromise.

Gigantic living transpires every live long day, here to everywhere, ask the powerful highly intelligent people with those longevity mentalities, respect to Olive Branch Mississippi, love that city.

Mackology schooled me properly, lifeology paid my Dickie pockets, button up shirt, to creased up pants, days to nights in the Midwest, cross country luxury lifestyle is most appreciated, learn how to stay blessed, surfing on the ups to downs of life, the waves, simultaneously praying.

Some take specific routes in life others will not think twice about taking, some people just scared to take a chance to advance.

Dudley do right all your live long life, if you just so happen to possess Cleveland Good Game, keep it Excalibur sharp, simultaneously learning as much as possible, earning power points for hard work dedication, also respect, showing respect, focusing on being in it to the finish.

Spitting your {ism} in a way considered stupendous, releasing goodness verbally, dressing spectacular, putting vision in a blur, always let your Cleveland Good Game speak for you, never brag, never boast, and your God given name will speak for itself, never glorify negativity.

Dreams to reality, is the goal to accomplish, forever will the truth be spoken, on the strength, to make happiness get rid of sadness.

Complete understanding about what is required to be understood, to eliminate madness off your pathway, on your journey to get wealthy, while finding longevity.

Reality based conversations with longevity conversationalist, which always will be leading up to progressive prosperity, all because you learned the brilliant ways to create self improvement communication.

Stay out of sight, out of mind, no time to sell lemons to limes, be bout your business, with long term decisions, to get old mentally, before you get old physically, and retire three decades, before you supposed to retire.

Wisdom will naturally speak genuinely, reaching to those aiming to uprise, teaching the youth, preaching the unlimited truth, schooling the students in UPM, educating the Soul People, and motivating those Kings to queens, aiming to get back on their throne.

Practice will forever bring progress, focus on eliminating stress, this will transpire when you know what need to be known, and start recognizing all life lessons being presented to you, hidden in plain sight.

Big dogs see big dogs, and good game recognize good game.

Be righteous as much as possible, righteousness creates a magnetism that draws good to bad, also bad to good, so be prepared to avoid distractions from every direction, truth be spoken, because the truth must be heard, to set you free from that which caught you in traps.

Talking is identical to walking, it is all on how you aim to progress with it, when either is done correctly, it will prosper it self.

First thing first, Most High, the beginning forever, and always.

Mind your business, occupy self, none stop, no breaks, full time job staying alive.

Think intelligent while reacting brilliant.

Blessed be one, blessed be all, love is life, life is love, truth be spoken, because the truth must be heard floating in the oxygen you breath from trees.

Prayer is made for all types of players, on all levels, find yourself before you, find yourself by yourself.

Timing is everything, when the time is right, the time is right on time, patience builds empires, and creates generations of wealth.

A partner always listens, and learns.

You never know who is who, what they know, or who they know, or when you will need that person, so be nice, or pay the price for not being nice, in more ways than one.

Do not make all of the sudden moves, because it is not planned out, straight fools moves, think intelligent, react brilliant.

Everything automatic, is good to go, if you know what to do when situations transpire, everybody to everything, that's on automatic, will protect you with no hesitation.

Every person requires solid ground to walk on, to understand who they is precisely, so every one else will understand who you is, how you live, your perspective, your {izm}, your truth, your lifestyle, what ropes you went through, the rings you had to enter, the matches you had, and the fights you had to win.

Strength around strength, creates power, unity, balance, answering questions, bringing solutions to problems, all you got to do, is build with longevity, build in an unbreakable way, show me state, Missouri, says it all.

Business is business as usual, pleasure is pleasure as usual, rise above your human nature, master the mind, body, the life you live is the life you given to conquer, not let it conquer, and destroy you.

Not just words, but action speaks loud with a message, meaning to a definition, allow a smile to smile at you, if it is connected to your well being, meaning only trust a heart warming smile, because, like the o'jays said, "smiling faces tell lies."

Pick your battles, know who to battle, how to battle, who to avoid, who to seek, meet, greet, approach, choose your choices, bring comfortability to you, and like who like you.

Choose choices that demand necessary attention, that which suit your necessity needs, to accommodate your lifestyle, accumulate greatness, cheese eggs steak breakfast, Pimp C Texas driveway, 2020 Rolls Royce type stuff.

Yours is yours all yours, it can not be took, broke, bit, hit, stole, bought, used, abused, confused, those who must be reprogrammed, is not born to be in your kingdom, that is a battle, a George Foreman verse Deontay Wilder fight, waiting to happen.

Time consuming situations often appear at night, which teaches you how to have permanent dedication, to make everything progress prosperously, meaning stay focused on what is permanent, distractions got to leave a message, or make an appointment.

Being in a comfortable position in this world, meaning, relax when you established in a permanent position, enjoy what you deserve to have, explore the things life puts on your solid gold brick road, keep the peace in full effect, respect is needed, it's about choice not force, never no hostage situations.

Stop, look left, right, proceed with caution, know which way to go long term, maybe it will go right, know for show what's happening, no time to guess, hope, or wish on a star that everything go right, instead of that, just conduct traffic, figure out how to make all your business go right, E-40 said, "play chess not checkers."

Know that the Most High, hand picked every situation to transpire, hand pick all that you set your focus on, like Shawty Lo, full effortfully, strictly dedicated to being the greatest you was created to be.

No hitch hiking, only driver seat living, pick up who automatically down with you, love at first sight type stuff, lifetime respect on first sight, that is the sun shining through clouds, a show nuff sign, that spotlight glowing type stuff, pick permanent players.

Do not spit where you live, or break plates in your house, or let food mold, or let your electric get cut off, or allow yourself to get evicted, keep home peaceful, and setup to bring you enjoyment, keep everything in motion consistently.

Know that your home is home, kick your feet up, relax, cry with tears of joy, meditate at home by a fireplace, and love home with no restrictions.

Just love everything about home, good, bad, from horrible to wonderful, no discrimination, everything is everything like Baby Drew said.

Change for the better like Gucci Mane Alabama style, ain't no right way to do wrong, if you think it is, Ice-T said, "you gone play yourself," never get better at being at your worst, I assume that's exactly what they say in federal prisons, & around the world.

Do not entertain the wrong route, with any type of eye contact, stay your self away from it, that's deeper then the Atlantic Ocean, so with that being said, always be on your Academy Award winning best performance.

Everybody tend to say things, then do other things, it is about those who will be able to stick to the script, which will be the individuals to grow with, learn with, be happy with, stay true with, and be dedicated to being the greatest with.

I'm listening to the great Dj Warren G, song, called, "Midnight Hour," with the greatest vocalist, Mr. Nate Dogg, another classic song from these geniuses.

D-Shot made a classic song called, "true world wide players," with global intelligence, aim everyday to live a brilliant lifestyle.

Reroute your route if it is a dead end, leave space for goodness to present itself to your environment, give it the Kemet pyramid golden opportunity, to be righteous for you.

Know when to be close to individuals, or distant from individuals, and always to forever, what works best is always best.

Learn in every way possible, how the grass grow, what it displays is truth, honesty, guidance, companionship, dedication to the Most High, natural laws is what is being specifically referred to, I'm listening to Mack 10 song called, "hoo banging".

Stay true to the ancient ancestors, believe or not, they created the present moment, truth be told, life is for the living, let everything be on automatic, in your circle of associates, recognizing obedience creates excellence.

All it takes is the secret password, to get people to reveal their true colors, showing who they truly are, and how they gone be in your longevity game plans.

Live and let live, understand who you is, has brought you to this point in your life, to the position you in, accept all life lessons for you to learn from, next, keep your thought process updated every day to night, to all living inside the mack lifestyle, you must stay in it to the finish.

It's obvious who live their life, to be true to the game of life prospering progressively, study thy lifestyle, everybody born to be perfect, master, conquer, over coming all obstacles, and side stepping pass all traps.

Think like a global ancient historically taught king pharaoh, react like a million dollar mack, build like ancient imhotep, you can not teach a peach how to be a peach, it got to come natural, automatic, sometimes your wants, is not your needs.

Stay low key under the radar like preach mack, meet lifetime friends, make heaven sent goals to accomplish.

Play offense like Kobe Bryant, keep ball in your court, play to win like James Harden, so you don't have to play defense, see without being seen, like Eddie Murphy mansion surveillance cameras.

Your birth to earth childhood to adulthood upbringing, will build you up for success, or set you up for self destruction, yet a natural will figure it all out with no hesitation, without being given a flashlight, to see what is going on in this world.

These individuals will figure out which way to go in the dark, meeting requirements, showing worthiness to qualify to be put in great positions, because they was dedicated to being qualified to be satisfied.

Hard work pay off, James Brown paid the cost to be the boss, 8ball & MJG paid their dues to be living legends today, ask P. Diddy, seek your long term journey pathway, to find longevity, then earn your turn, and time to shine.

Consistently royalty grind for the royal family, like the Clipse, king Mack Millon Dollar think consistently, perfecting my mack lifestyle, remaining in it to the finish, good times to bad times, live to learn, learn to live, surviving the times, with good intentions.

Vision to see who apart of your need to know basis, be approachable when necessary, or unapproachable when you need to be unapproachable.

Move with the days wisely, like a desert lion, hunting at night, precise step by strategic step, watch a chameleon every slow movement, like you a fly flying, remember the feeling is great, to be free from the same old same, hit the main cities in the country, watch everything moving, see what everywhere got to offer you, I'm listening to fiend international Jones's song, it's called, "corner store."

Words is extremely powerful, how you group up words, which words you aim to use according to what you aim to say, how you want to lead up to saying something, setup every next point you aiming to make, to win the battle of the minds, like Johnny Cochran played his game.

The cause to effect perspective, is an important skill to learn, and every moment you wake up, look around to see where your life at.

Everything mean something, who you is, what you know, your skills, your lifetime resume, your wisdom, your knowledge, weather, or not it is polished, how you adapt, your patience, if you don't believe me, ask the Most High.

Everything is always based on your best foot being put forward, your overall performance, your team, your partner, your dedication, your communication, your conversation, your deeds, your rights, wrongs, your focus, your comprehension skills, all of which leads up to your God Body perspectives on this Mother Earth, ancient times to the present moment.

Every live long day read to succeed, explain the game of life to your self, define your name, maintain throughout your life time, sink or swim, or keep your head above water.

Everything is lined up, meant to happen, silence is a form of intelligence.

You got to know when to make great moves, and when not to make bad moves.

Get better acquainted with the north American soul indigenous ancient ancestors, know what is required to be known, according to thy bloodline roots, it's mandatory to have self understanding.

We all live in our own world, inside this world, balance the thoughts living in your mind, seek only long term options.

Wake up with head in clouds, meaning stay connected with the Most High, by whispering in the wind to your Creator, having continuous conversations with the Most High.

To really get better aquatinted with someone, you have to go deep inside their world.

Leave the truth, with everyone you have the pleasure to meet, & greet.

The Most High speak through us to us, always remember, some people, not all, but some might not want to hear about your good times, or happiness, I'm listening to g. Dep song called, "let's get it."

Put in work, so you can be to busy for all nonsense, which will always bring forth the realness, directly to you.

Pushing it to the limit, cross country grinding, with longevity as your final destination.

Sometimes you can not move the crowd, only those who moving in your direction you going into, because some will remain stuck until they decide to move.

One of a kind, unique like today, right now this year, ain't no duplicating the present moment, no come back, take advantage of time you have, rare opportunities do not come, but every sixteen years.

I was here in Florida 2002, now I am back better then ever, more ready, more prepared, more skilled, with income coming in, mental strength more powerful, incredible like the hulk personality, no strings attached, and free to be the king, self was created to be, I'm listening to westside connection song called, "bow down."

You made it this far, you being rewarded because you deserve it, you have to be thankful every second of your life, good days to bad days.

Your mind knows what your body needs, it is called central intelligence, also game came from whence rain came, memorize that, I'm listening to 21 savage song called, "a lot."

It is best to ask the Most High Spirit, to teach you what need to be known about everything you need to know about, in your lifetime.

A lot of time, self need to be isolated from the world, to put thoughts in order, simply to know what is the best decisions to make, to determine if self moving to fast, because decisions made without thinking clearly, can, and will cause accidents, I'm listening to swizz beats song called, "bigger business."

It is always something to do, even when you do not have something to do, believe that.

The key is, always know it is a better way to play to win, you do not have to settle for being a pawn on the chessboard, that position is optional, it is an inheritance for you undoubtedly, search your historic history, to learn what is your birth right.

It's two sides to all that is, and a source to all that is.

Never set yourself up for disappointment, all I do is read everything I get my hands on, I do pushups for physical fitness, and drink Armand de Brignac when my day is complete, that's cold, don juan said, " ain't it man."

Men of power, soul people, not color folks, the color black symbolizes power, men of great power, be your own person, true to your ancestry bra, it's mother loving mandatory.

Blackness is power, it is what light reveals, stay away from fantasy living, or make believe, living a lie, never deal with, what is a setup to make you slaves in your mysterious mind, recognize your mind is been being studied buddy boy.

Everything is based on time, time is key to figuring everything out, if you don't believe me, ask benjamin Big Ben banneker in London, my good man.

Follow your right mind, and you will be just fine, which is your spirit.

Any person not on drugs, is destine to turn dreams to reality.

Stay in your own world, invite qualified participants in your circle only, stay away from those with competitors spirit, it brings hate, jealousy, envy, confusion, and also lies.

Some places want, need, should have you there, even if it's for a split second, just to make your presence felt, more than other places that aim to have you in one state, for years, as a slave, slash prisoner wasting life away, hit the highway indigenous soul peoples.

It is definitely something wrong, when the suns of the Most High, is being used, confused, abused and looked down on.

When the feeling of something is missing, something is coming, you felt it before it arrived, the saying is, I been feeling something bout to change, and that's exactly what it is, that's what it's gone transpire to be.

Move in silence like humming birds, age plus experience will create intelligence, and brilliance.

You got to deal with what comes next, let the past past, let everything fall in to place, do that without applying pressure, let every situation be automatic, naturally waiting to happen, as it's meant to be.

Mature your lifestyle, know what you getting into, before you get into it, see if it's water in the pool, before you dive in.

Everyday is the piece to the puzzle, that complete your whole reason for existing in this lifetime, day, and age you is.

Everyday class is in session, where you from is your training course, to prepare you for the world you live every long day in.

You either in, or you out, be without or without it, what you like can be used against you, everything is setup to go a certain way, so get in where you fit in.

What is yours, to have in your life, will be just like you, a reflection, everything always falls into place, from ancient times to the present moment.

I Am therefore I exist, is so deep, only students of ancient history will be able to translate that small, yet gigantic statement.

You got to be prepared, before you get where you going, on your pathway to your final destination, stay fresh, clean, whisper in the wind, stay ready to look, listen, and learn.

Make money work for you, {ism} is a hidden treasure spreaded all over the world, see how one to all prosper progressively, globally intelligently maintaining surviving brilliantly.

It is all about your introduction presentation, every psychic knows if something did not happen it is not meant to happen, what is meant to be will be exactly that.

Get acquainted with the source that empowers you, the tree, the root, the seed, the one who planted your seed, should be your center of attention.

Study the ancient knowledge, past to present moment, the ancient wisdom of people, who started what led up to everything transpiring today, courtesy of the Most High allowance.

Avoid being trapped in unnecessary obligations, and never crack under pressure.

Whatever you present to the world, will be exactly what type of reaction you get back, pertaining to that which you hand out, will be what you receive in return.

Always remember to read between the lines, simply to discover the hidden truth, It's mandatory to be in sink with reality, to be balanced in the life you live, keep over a few options, practice weekly, how to master your mind, body, and lifestyle.

The Game of life quietly says, "read consistently to succeed successfully, learn why it's important to enjoy when the sun rise, figure out why the sun decides to set, start counting your blessings, when you see the moon rising, and relax comfortably when the moon has ten minutes to set."

The hidden messages in Arizona's Indian Country, explains humbly that, its always gone be a right direction to go into, which will lead you to that which will equal the right results for you.

It's very mandatory to Keep head above water, at all times, and your feet out of quick sand.

Separating mind wants from body wants is mandatory, strictly focus on mind necessities, and what the body mandatorily requires consistently.

Self preservation is also first priority, recognize when your train could possibly be being rerouted, right before your eyes, mastering the mind is also a priority, and mastering the body, helps create a lifetime of balance.

A person can seek to be in some one else home, for security safety purposes, simply for stay alive purposes, for comfort purposes, for rehabilitation purposes, to avoid old habits, in trouble making environments, think about it, queen t is next to me, awfully close, it's John legend song called, "best you ever had."

Know what world a person preferably prefer to be in, is it a drug type environment scenery, or the Big Meech entrepreneur baller type scene, etc, respect to Big Meech, now to forever.

Self preservation is the mandatory center of attention, seek longevity in good Hawaii type climates, self discipline is very important, learn Godly practices, and seek books teaching ancient king queen behavior, queen t is listening to jodeci song called, "you & I," I like k-cj & jojo on players club soundtrack, I think it's called, "all about the Benjamin's baby."

162

Keep your head held high in the clouds, with your chest strongly built poking out, consistently associate with great decision making individuals, those who be looking up to say thank you mother Father Creator, and never ever ever set self up for disappointment.

Respect a woman enough to look her in the eyes, analyze what she say, what her focus is on, and how she respond to everything she responds to, that which you say.

Never do wrong on purpose, just to foolishly see what will happen next, let everything fall into place naturally.

Forever to always, Stick to the script, memorize the right combination will equal the right results, what you put in, is what you get out, meaning, you will get, exactly what is coming to you.

Purpose, meaning lifestyle, the more you learn, the more powerful your conversation becomes.

Your life, most important prized possession, is thy self, you will forever be priceless until you start living worthless.

Rewards for righteousness, is gone be unbelievable, when each reward presents itself, to the chosen ones.

Control the mind every live long day to night, learn more about self control every day, always anticipate income outcome, every hour, every situation you find yourself in.

Do not foolishly dominate someone, use time above ground wisely, it is always ears listening, eyes watching, let the past teach you the lessons, in all that has transpired.

Consistently turn your weakness to strength, you can not have a weakness in your lifestyle, because your weakness, can be used, as a life threatening weapon, against you.

Wait till your turn roll around, until then, keep quiet, observe, while preparing for the top positions in your lifestyle, simply to stay on the top level, all this is done before you get on the top level, hard work pays off, in more ways then one.

Weak minds fall for anything manipulation say to that person, precise movement is strategically made for every move made, handpicked cautiously is how choices get chosen, every person in your life, is getting you ready, for the person you will meet next.

A woman can be a man worst enemy, if she not raised up properly, in her wonder years, or if her best friend is overwhelmed with hatred, and she unfortunately was raised up incorrectly.

Every title of a specific person, gets a chance to shine bright, above all titles, only with the correct amount of full effort, also when going the extra mile, to make competition wish they was qualified, to be that individual title, competition.

During beneficial hours, it's always business as usual, no breaks, strictly dedicated to the come up missions.

Permission to graduate to greater heights, will come from what your mind progress to understand, know your birth right, seek to know what type of people your soul people ancestors truly was, so you know who you are, so you can reclaim your throne, that which someone else, falsely sits on, fraudulently.

Knowledge is the source to your true power, study father & Mother Earth bloodline ancient past, all the way up to this present moment, earth, water, fire, air, weather, animal kingdom, human life cycle, outer space, the whole galaxy, every pinch of existence, every year, must be thoroughly investigated past, to present.

Be above, beyond, recognizing all that is, consistently associate with the source responsible for every pinch of existence.

Those individuals who willing to disregard ancient knowledge, will avoid serving their purpose, foolishly, in exchange for the thrill of seeking fun.

Exchange valuable information with those who have valuable information, respectfully, do it for the righteous soulful reasons, not for foolish gain, that will eventually fade away.

R I appreciate you Mother Father Creator, for the game my brain contain, to help me maintain, that's right you guessed it, I'm in to the finish, and straight down for my crown, you know it.

I'm listening to Shyne song, it's called, "Quasi Og," straight classic, I think he in the votes for mayor of Belize.

P funk star child said, "swing down sweet, do y'all want to ride on the mothership, put your hands together y'all, it's gone take energy," snap your fingers, clap your hands, ladies and gentlemen, a live performance, from Parliament mothership, do you want to ride.

THE GAME OF LIFE SCRIPTURES

7.

Playing the game of life is knowing how to roll it, live to give, give to live, it's about unity, team work works, it's a proven fact, teams have won championships, everybody need everybody, cross country living, will explain what the game of life scriptures is all about.

I'm watching christìòn, the twin brothers videos, with dame dash, & orange juice jones in the video, it's called, "full of smoke," you might have heard them on the beginning of the classic movie called, "the streets Iz watching," now I'm watching red café video called, " bad chick alert," I'm listening to red café song called, "paper touching'.

UNCLE JUNY JB BUNS

Max julien once said, "you ever had a hands on everything business woman, from Hawaii?, I'm listening to Rick Ross song called, "magnificent."

uncle Juny said, "yeah," with a straight face, in fact, he took her from Hawaii to America, I think some call that straight international professional paid pimpin, you know the rest If game recognize game, if game recognize game, you will know the rest.

For that's his past, but uncle Juny jb still remembers it, like It happened five seconds ago, as you will read, his thoughts in this random chapter.

I'm an international professional paid person, into making progress nephew, everywhere he sat his feet at, he was ready, beneficially live, uncle Juny pulled two comfortable garage seats, out, for us to sit in, one night I was in town, we was sitting in in the garage to enjoy the sun setting, he playing his 70s soul music, in his bronze badge colored Camry, with the windows down, with the sunroof open, It sat parked in front of us, with the headlights spotlighting us, creating a memorable moment scenery, he bout to sip Moët with me, the sun still up at the moment, he listening to the floaters, he said what's up cc, to my mother on speaker phone, he said make a long story short, it's the thought that count, I popped the rose Moët, he ask for the cork screw, he said, it bring back memories of his crew, In his early 20s, he always tell me, that champagne you drinking now nephew, it was more expensive when he was drinking it in the clubs in his early years, when you survive the game, then that mean you not a perpetrator, or fraud, the game look out for you, he cutting his son hair in the garage, straight multi tasking, he said, "he make show everybody alright in his circle," he said, "anybody got to be right, & ready with him," he said, "he had a special crew, that did his hair," we listening to a group of ladies, called the terrels, he said when we lived in the gardens, all gal gardens In Chicago, we had more around there, If the season funny, the people be funny, you got to stay international, he said, he really known for his singing, like the stylistics, hitting them high notes, queen t is listening to Brooklyn fabulous song, it's called, "it's gone be a cold summer.

The queen bee is listening to rini x earthgang song called, "out of the blue," & I'm watching unique Mecca audio "dc for the people cookout" with dc"s finest Larry mo, the queen bee is listening to lucky day song called, "love you to much."

THE LAST MACK STANDING SCRIPTURES

4.

Step in smooth to lay It down thick, straight grinding like they do in Little Rock Arkansas, got to learn how to live, then learn how to earn, then learn how to make money work for you, then learn how to pull up shining brand new, like they say In Memphis, "this what game plus money do for you," if you learn how to direct traffic, Memphis know the business, on some project pat type stuff, It's all about getting life right, wealthy comfortable with longevity, and spirituality.

I'm in the mountains inside Virginia, dwelling in a city called max meadows, watching all game entertainment, known as the podcast network, just saw Lamar Odom with nore, it's real cool hearing Lamar speak, chill, and be himself, boss player television in full effect.

It's a formula to learn in your lifestyle, to help you master living in this reality.

FROM BIRTH TO EARTH

On a hot seventy-five degrees August 3rd,1981 summer time day, in the show me state of Missouri, an Akenu-Lan pyramid golden brown baby boy was born, precisely inside the world famous Fort Leonard Wood, Missouri, inside a loyalty before betrayal, well known army base, cross country it is known as, fort lost in the woods.

Meanwhile, inside the heavily guarded infant facility I wou enter this world in, the proper procedure occurred, with me leaving the womb of my growth & development,(respect to Chicago), the first home I ever knew was me beautiful mother, that deep dark place which kept me hostage, also safe for nine months, safe because animals have to be born, then run to save their life, at that something, now, after I was discovered by Chicago Dr. Leon, I was politely escorted to a handpicked, top of the line incubator, soulfully escorted by a Hattie McDaniel Wichita Kansas born looking nurse, & it was inside a grass green, Serpent Mound, Ohio sky royal blue, peaceful painted room.

The peaceful royal Repoblikan'i Madagasikara water blue room, was full of freshly innocent born, birth to earth, Vanessa Williams 34c, breast milk wanting infants.

This mysterious room had different categories of innocent infants, not one fruit fly, or any type of fly was was allowed in this room of infants, I think it's called protecting the future, some will live a Barack Obama blessed incredible life in a wealthy family, & some will live a ruff, tuff, horrible, unbelievable Henry "Box" Brown, trapped in a crime family lifestyle.

For some Most High only knows, Roman kind of a man, unexplainable reason, a Thutmosis III, Martin Luther King Jr. anciently looking tribe of georgia Cherokee, Mdewakanton specific hand picked guardian angels, out of nowhere began to gather around me while I was laying down alone, deep blue sea great white shark hunting quietly this was happening, one Nile valley mosquito flying pass you quietly this was happening, this unbelievable scene had began to transpire without a sound alerting anybody.

The August 3rd, 1981 heaven-sent black brown turtle island indigenous angels, synchronized together simultaneously all of a sudden, they started formulating a shikaakwa Bears 1985, we about to win the super bowl type of huddle around me, without making any sound to alert anybody of what was transpiring.

I received an Moquelumnan Orange County tanning bed, Himalayan summer warmth from those August 3rd, 1981, Most high hand picked guardian spirits..

For some soul people spiritual reason, the warmth from these specific Chaloklowa Chickasaw angles made me spiritually glow, it looked like I just read the basic instructions before leaving earth three times in a row, back to back, cover to cover, while sitting inside a riverboat, on the world famous Mahn-ah-wauk River, it runs directly underneath Ouisconsin Avenue bridge, directly inside downtown Millioke Wishkonsing.

Thank you for reading my 2nd book, I'm editing it in South Boston Virginia, while drinking a pitch black bottle of Hennessy, mixed with Roc a Fella jay-Z Memphis Bleek Beanie Sigel hypnotic, and Body Armor sports water, now back to this brilliantly wrote boss player status book.

Simultaneously, it seemed like time was standing still for me at that exact moment this was transpiring, or time was watching this happen in slow motion, when these 1981 handpicked Amen ra sent, black golden brown spirits guarded me, I was looking like I was the Honorable Minister Louis Farrakhan, and Malcom X sitting in a meeting together, now that's serious protection.

Maybe these Oglala Lakota Sioux soulful indigenous spirits was sent to protect me, so evil spirits couldn't possess me, & ruin my chances of serving my purpose in life, for the Most High, by telling me what I'm required to know, before I can all the way comprehend it.

Maybe something disturbing wanted to get to me before I could start living my royal life, specifically, so I couldn't be granted the King Tutankhamun solid gold opportunity, to walk on the onyx paved pathway, that which leads up to the priceless white gold gate, in front of Heaven drive way, three thousand feet, from the front door of Ptah Hotep mansion, right next door to Osiris Honolulu, dry lava, black white diamond, Johnny Dang custom made gold castle.

A James Earl Jones, Lou Ross older man, deep voice tone, & Freda Josephine Baker, sexy, seductive voice tone, was creeping up towards my room door, these voices, was coming faster then Usain Bolt won his Olympic gold medals.

When this Athabascan woman appeared, she was a Chickmaka accent speaking nurse, mixed with a beautiful Rosie Perez accent; & she was attractive like New School for Community Service Theresa Magma.

She was walking like Buffie Carruth right pass my Abraham Lincoln copper brown room door, directly on the left side of a, "Guess who's coming to Dinner," Sidney Poitier Bahamian island dark skin looking Caribbean doctor.

Then two heartwarming, eye pleasing, one appeared closer looking like Della Reese from Black Bottom Detroit, nice welcoming facial expression like James Boggs, with a Nina Somone looking soulful spirit, directly above my left shoulder, & the other directly above my right shoulder, synchronized together simultaneously both started speaking to me federal prison whisperering quietly, in Kriol accents, it felt like they were my great great great grandma, & great great great granddaddy.

Then, in a love me long time Bangkok phone sex unaggressive voice tone, they spoke with a Tsalagi accent, synchronized together simultaneously they both started saying, "To have eyes to see, to see mean to have vision, to have vision, mean to recognize what you visualize, to recognize what you visualize, mean to understand what is to be required, to be understood."

Out of nowhere, a XF-84H airplane, loud as an earthquake in Valdivia, it roared louder than a Cecil lion, directly over the well-built army base hospital, as that sound got quite, I could hear a northern long eared bat whistling flying pass the window, then it sounded like a cottonmouth snake was fighting a wild turkey, then it just got silent again, then the wonderful mysterious wind began blowing all around the army base.

While that was transpiring, then out of nowhere two Lemhi-Shoshone soulful indigenous golden brown spirits was covering my ears, then when the second XF-84H African king lion roaring airplane flew pass this army

176

base, the Choctaw soulful indigenous golden brown spirits starred deeply in my third eye, synchronized together simultaneously they both started back schooling me, speaking with an soulful golden brown indigenous Onondaga accent, saying, "Teach the youth, preach the truth, plant a seed, watch it grow, don't hesitate to motivate, procrastinate, when it comes to showcasing hate, & creating reasons to hate," these ancient wisdom parables these soulful spirits is planting in my mind, is so rare to get from soulful spirits during birth to earth, a lot of indigenous golden brown people of modern times say that's why game is sold not told, simply because of the origins of it, it's unique rareness makes it valuable to those who posses, the game keepers that pass it down generations to generations, some people pass money down to generations, others pass most valuable understanding about is required to be understood game generations to generations.

The sound of these copper brown skin Polynesians soulful golden brown indigenous spirits voices was soothing to the point, I became NyQuil sleepy, when I peacefully woke up, I felt like a tremendous amount of love was kissing me all over my body, inside to outside.

Just for me, My dark & lovely, bold & beautiful chicagoua Illiniwek born mother, out of nowhere she was walking happily into my room of future stars, & crooks.

She came with a Milwaukee born, West Division, slim tall, High School graduated, pimp till his last breath, indigenous doctor, by the name of Mr. Stanley Stack Jefferson, if you know this man this myth this legend, congratulate him on being placed in Milwaukee Wisconsin historic hall of game permanently.

A Linda Jefferson, Kim Jefferson, Gloria bell, Leomie Anderson looking nurse, she came towards me pakalolo Maui Hawaii weed smoking happily, Anna faris smiley facing, with one intention, which was to pick me up gently, up out the incubator, to give me to my beauty contest, Chicago Carver High School, cheerleader mother.

She proudly picked me up, thinking to herself, how much she loved holding me close to her giant heart, she was staring proudly at me, saying, "you my first-born child, and I truly love you."

Then she felt the urgent need to escort me to her heartwarming private first rank room, it seemed like a Choctaw ancient soulful spirit was telling her to take me to her first born, child room.

All of this happened, exactly after she got permission from the Ostrich skin, knee high boot wearing, street wise, Dr. Stanley Stack Jefferson, just to see if she could keep me for the night.

The whole time this was transpiring, I had a Baby Evangeline, toothless, helpless, gummy bear, no teeth, Melyssa Savannah Ford, breast milk craving, with a cute like a million dollars falling out the sky, type of look on my Chickamauga looking baby face.

I think at an early age from birth to earth, I was learning how to play my part, to keep myself looking innocent, & keep people thinking I'm unaware of exactly of what's specifically transpiring around me.

I sadly with two tears in both my eyes, I began looking heart brokenly at my beauty contest, 1957 born September 14th, 24-year-young mother, & with seven tears in both her eyes, she said, "God blessed me with a Shinnecock looking, Tsuu T"ina baby boy."

At the same time, she was looking deep in my 803 Hillside project, 8th & walnut, 1988, robert Barisford, Bobby Brown eyes.

Which would in time to come, mesmerize Wisconsin to Illinois, lovely ladies, who got a fetish for 1974 Barry White deep voice, game spitter like American Pimp, Andre Taylor, who live to give, & give to live, like Dr. Sebi lived.

A pretty, melting Bomb POP banana yellow round brown, Keshia Cole Oakland California sexy attractive, lena horne elegant looking nurse named Kenyette Culberson, she Peggy Bundy bounced, switching a Buffy the body booty side to side turtle walking in my room.

All she came to do was pick me up out the incubator, Ritz Carlton pillow fluffing professionally, then my private in the U.S. army, hard nosed attitude, stone cold, strong Khalifian descendant mother, she reached to grab me from her, like I was a one-way ticket to the lifestyle of the rich, & famous.

As soon as my in time to come, soon to be a gangster in Chicago mother, was holding me, inside her Orlando Florida Ritz Carlton pillow soft skin, Yellie Olive Oil skinny arms, I felt more welcomed then copper skin people, in Australia.

She gently genuinely sincerely said to me, "Booby, you Jacuzzi in Russel Simmons $11 million New York penthouse warm," & with a Davey Crockett squatter suspicious crooked smile, on her Pokanoket forever young looking face, she said, "You already Arsenio Rogers ready to live a dream to reality, neil degrasse tyson lifestyle."

As she tightly held me, she first love, main squeezed, & polar bear hugged me, she hugged me like I was her best friend mavis.

She did that while she turtle walked quietly holding me, still somewhat hurting from my arrival; we were 88 Stacey Dash feet size away from her Trugernanner Tasmania warm tropical colored, earth tone decorated comfortable room.

When she entered her room with innocent little me, for some, "watch lifetime channel for four hours straight," strange reason, she aimed for the fuzzy Dorothy ruby red slippers colored wooden chair.

The chair was by the 50-inch flat screen size window, with the canary, st. Augustine Florida sunshine egg yolk yellow curtains, hanging exactly two feet from the old, loud, rusty, rattling heater.

As she sat in the ruby falls red chair, she was slowly bouncing her left leg up, down, & somewhat gently, simply to rock me to sleep, & she held me tightly in her fifty pushups, in twenty-five minutes' arms.

Outside the 50 inch flat screen window, I noticed the happy, semi truck 2020 peterbilt high beam light bright, off white, Barbados July looking full moon, it was shining brighter then head lights on a pickup truck on a dirt road in Olive Branch Mississippi, directly after midnight, around 12:01a.m.

At the same time, all the Dogon ancestor's stars, twankled twankled, each important star in the midnight hour, was attempting to get their 15 minutes of fame, in the first few hours of my life.

It seems like, the entire galaxy solar system constellations wanted to introduce itself to my curious eyesight, then three specific stars, was coming from Fargo North Dakota, shining brighter then November 10th, 1775 Philadelphia Pennysvania marine search lights, flying south west through the sky, towards 27 hour raining Jacksonville Florida.

These specific stars, intentionally was throwing light in me moma room window, causing her 24 bugs bunny karat, 58 diamond pinky ring, to shine bright like convertible Burt, diamond bright, in a picture with mike Tyson, it almost blinded my weak baby vision, of her.

For some Sponge Bob got square pants strange reason, she turned the black & white 18-inch TV off, it was showing George Jefferson Sherman

Hemsley doing the funky chicken dance, ask Nelly batters up video what um tum bout.

She Tyra Banks yarned, prettily looking at her black power fist afro pick, which fell on the floor, straight out her Barney purple, Shell Cordovan leather purse, she was listening to Anita baker song called, "angel," it was playing on her clock radio staticing a little.

Next, she put me in her just right for a new born infant, such as myself, Puffy Mattress princess Christina Cindrch, private island sized bed.

Then she closed, the Tucson Arizona desert baby mouse, squeaky downtown Julie Brown colored, comfortable, Gioconda Shineroom door.

Then swiftly like a Malaysia leopard sneaking up on a Southern Sudan Ethiopia Gazelle in Alkbulan, she walked up to me & said, "I will never stop loving you son," then two crystal benson clear tears dripped down her face, from her left eye to the bottom of her small jaw bone, then it screamed silently as it speeded down to the floor, this scene looked so sad, it would make six flesh walking demons start crying.

Then she Colin Rand Kaepernick, kneeled down, to kiss my International guion bluford Bernard Anthony Harris jr. Mae c. Jemison Space Station, Toilet bowl round forehead.

She then bent over, to pick up her Brazilian bull frog, deep Everglades rain forest green afro pick, then she started to pick out her Huey P. Newton, Bobby seale, elbert Howard black panther party afro.

Next, she pondered through her thoughts, fixed her Tennessee Kaskinampo mother inherited given lips, to say to me, "how a person carries themselves, either demands respect, or loose respect," on the tv was an unbelievable commercial, it was a picture of a golden brown indigenous man from Tennessee, by the name of Nathan nearest green, it was showing an exhibit acknowledging him for creating jack daniels whisky.

She paused to wipe away an Whoopi Goldberg Academy award winning tear, then she said, "People just like books, read their body language, facial expressions, analyze what they let drip off their lip, & figure them out, before they know that you studying them."

She prayerfully closed her eyes, only for a minute, took a simone manuel Olympic gold medal winning deep breath, exhaled like Angela Bassett, then she opened her pretty almond brown eyes, & said, "What you say can be used against you; therefore it's mandatory to pick what you spit out your mouth, and let drip off your lip."

She stopped talking to grab some Puffs Facial tissues, then she said, "Be careful what questions you answer, it's called good decision making skills, knowing about the weather before it's about to change," like Mr. Earl Stevens said, on the tv the next commercial came on about unknown inventions of soulful brown indigenous peoples, first it showed Sarah Boone in 1892 standing by her iron board invention, she smiling happily next to proudly, then it showed a man pointing at the 1923 traffic light smiling proudly, it was garret Morgan the soulful golden brown indigenous man who invented the stoplight, then me mother caught my undivided attention.

Once again, she paused like she was taking a deep breath like sabir muhammad, to wipe away two Murano Glassware Crystal clear tears this time, then she said, "Listen to food for thought, good, longevity, progressive, positive, powerful, inspiring, motivational, encouraging game, every brain needs to contain."

She took a deep breath again, like 4 time Olympic winning Simone Manuel, & said, "Also be around helpful, kind hearted, giving, strong minded people, let soul survivor's behavior rub off on you, learn from everybody mistakes, count your blessings, thrive to stay alive, & build a team that will be with you all your life, also known as lifetime partners," then I noticed a man talking on the clock radio, he sounded like wilt chamberlain voice tone talking, he said, "4 time grand slam tournament winner Naomi Osaka has quit the French open after news conference disputes.

Forgive any editing mistakes I make, I'm editing my book myself, I'm in wonderful Paleo West Virginia, by the bottom of the Appalachia's mountain, they call it the foot hills, I'm at the pleasant Travel Lodge, ducked off in the outskirts, playing laid back soul music, sipping Don Pérignon, & regular Hennessy, enjoy what you read, and enjoy life, two important things to stay true to, ok back to the book, forgive my interruption.

The next morning, magnificently I woke up quietly, my vicuna soft skin eyelids, opened slowly, one at a time, innocently, specifically to see who was around me, so I could determine how to behaviorally present myself properly, when I opened both my eyes, I noticed I was in a Philips

181

Atom infant incubator, and once again me mother was nowhere to be found.

When I finally decided to open my baby big Bobby Brown eyes wider, two pretty delicate Monica Philly Calhoun, UTE looking female angels kissed me, directly on my left, & right cheek bones, Hugh hefner style, that means simultaneously.

The kisses they gave me, was so appreciated by me, I mean these kisses was like sitting in a J 470 warm jacuzzi, with Susan Rosen, with Steinmetz Diamonds bikini wearing Patrice Fisher, lovely, pure, & heavenly, these kisses brought two tears to my eyes instantaneously.

I tell you what, if I could post a picture of that on instagram, It would get a million views in less than an hour.

Simultaneously, these Iva La'Shawn chauvon higgins looking angles, they looked deep in my eyes, directly at my Algonquian eternal spirit, starring at my Clyde Jones soul glow, at the same time, Amun Ra sun rays Butterbean punched through the window, & shined on all three of us, like we were underneath a spotlight, in a Tyler Perry play called the, "have's & the have nots."

They started smiling like they was posing on the red carpet, then they both started saying, "in life its best to stay updated, upgraded, thinking quick, live to learn, learn to live, train yourself to interpret what everybody aim to insinuate, & never forget what you being told Royalty, this all parts of the king business, which is now presented to you In Mackology 2nd edition."

They glanced at their unbelievable reflection inside the window behind me, then slowly licked their Veronica Webb type lips, flapped their Quetzalcoatlus sized wings, like a magnificent silver bird, blinked their eyes twice like something flew in their eyes, then georgia Cherokee grandma style kissed me again, & they slowly like smoke from a Miami Beach suga knight Fidel Castro Cuban cigar faded away, while Black-chinned hummingbird flying away from me, towards that same 50 inch window, into their reflection.

Then out of nowhere, two Jordan Carver German, pleasantly plumped females, Virgin Island Carib, Arawak and Ciboney peacefully, quiet like wind blowing off the waves above Lake Michigan, began to walk in my room, literally out of somewhere, a place where simple minded fools is not allowed to visit, that's where I assume they came from with round trip tickets with no intentions staying long.

They beautifully stood over me, soulfully, spiritually glowing, both of these Great Lakhóta soulful indigenous Spirits, was on my picture-perfect Hollywood right side, staring in my Whitney Houston Bobby Christina teary eyes, that never cry, all the while, with their Montalvo's Queen Califia evanGaline rose jewell praying eyes.

Then one of the Great indigenous ancestor soulful indigenous women said, "Baby boy, when you get to your spending currency stage in life, leave if somebody try to trick, con, manipulate, persuade, or provoke, or convince you to do what's wrong for you to do, just to entertain them."

Then the other ancient indigenous soulful pyramid golden brown ancestor woman, she locked her Chicago black hawk eyes on me, like I was proposing to her, then she touched my hands gently with her elise neal, cullen Leslie Jones Memphis Tennessee warm, small, Hilton hotel, pillow soft pretty golden brown finger tips.

She took an cullen Andrew jones Olympic swimming class, deep breath, blinked twice faster than Mack 10 Eddie griffin, then two tears dropped on my pillow from her Raven Symone type hazel eyes, & my legs started moving, then my arms Harlem shakenly began to move, then two more tears fell on my wrist, & my body felt like I was sitting inside Halle Berry master bedroom Neorest Air Bathtub.

She started spiritually glowing, then she said, "baby boy, the life we live, good or bad, will lead us right where we want to be, exactly where we belong, it takes time to build, it takes seconds to destroy, have patience, do not rush to turn to dust, what's anticipated, will be retrieved, when you qualified to be satisfied, as soon as you meet the requirements."

Oh yeah, if you didn't know where the end of the rainbow is, it's in Dover Delaware, that's been waiting to be said for years, forgive my facts of life, informational interruptions.

I'm listening to Red Café song, with Cardi B, while editing this chapter right now.

Then the Bavarian Cuckoo Clock, in between the windows behind me, with no hesitation leaving 11:59am, it struck 12 on the dot, and then the bird started jaw jacking, in a bird singing sort of way, simply to symbolize lunch time.

183

Then simultaneously, the two-lovely netherlands enith brigitha soft, gentle Osage accent, grandma spoken, healthy looking soulful indigenous golden brown sprits, started glowing together, & together started saying, "Heaven, mind, body, soul," while touching my head, heart, then the right side of my chest, & then my stomach symbolizing an Anhk.

My baby eyes began to fall asleep, when my baby eyes got heavy like the 17th Vilite King Center hundred pound barbells, they just closed; then the miraculous, marvelous, extraordinary ancient soulful ancestors walked towards the door, & disappeared before they touched the doorknob.

Ten New York, Los Angeles, Miami rush hour minutes later, my busy body mother, walked in my hand-picked room, unaware of all that's been happening, she paused with an overwhelming feeling, on her facial expression, with a faraway look in her eyes, you can tell she felt the different energy in the room, & then she reached her olive oil skinny arms out, like christopher reeve, then eventually she began to pick me up.

After she picked me up, she walked towards the antique designed window, switching like Nia Long on Friday, and then the sunlight, sugar Ray Leonard, Joe louis, jack johnson punched through the window, kissing us all over, head to toe, you hear me, I had to put that in the book.

For some stunned & amazed reason, she stood stolen benin bronzes, Nigerian statue stiff, & silent, like the Martin Luther King statue, on historic 3rd street, in Milwaukee Wisconsin, home of Harambee (pulling together) neighborhoods, you like that.

Breaking news: dj screw said, "he want to be known for putting south on the map, the way he did his music."

She stood there strong, right by the window, in the spot light, with a thousand years' worth of blessings, type of look on her face, simultaneously while she looked at me, out of nowhere, she smiled with sixty-six tears in her eyes, crying like she was looking at a Detroit pit bull, fight a Beverly Hills fluffy puppy poodle.

At the same time, she was happy, like a poor boy in Michael Jordan house, on Christmas, with two million dollars' worth of gifts for him, under a seven-foot-tall, Emirates Palace Christmas tree.

She then lifted her right hand up, directly above my face, tapped my nose with her ring finger, leaned closer to me, & kissed my Russell Simmons, solid gold, toilet bowl round forehead.

She then lifted her head up off my face, at the same time, she glanced at her, delightful first time giving birth reflection, in the window, admiring her Julius Erving David Thompson George Ice man Gervin ABA afro, & sadly smiled like, she was never gone see me again.

Ten tears fell down her face, in less than sixty-six seconds, with a facial expression so heart broken, Mr. T would feel her pain, & get teary eyed, & put his hand over his mouth, right before he start crying, like a four month infant, laying in the dumpster, in Seattle.

She blinked once; & then her heart started pounding, faster than twenty-two piranhas will attack a drowning, two-day old baby duck.

She took a deep breath, like she was going through a sandstorm in Kuwait, or deep sea diving, inside Nnalubaale, in Luganda, to swim with shark bate in her hands, without scuba diving gear.

Then she looked in the sky to the Amun Ra, & said, "I love you Booby, you priceless until you start living worthless, never discriminate, yet don't settle for less, if one person is not with your program, find somebody who is, it will be well worth it, it's about choice not force, it's about love at first sight, find your kind, & like who like you, like District of Columbia gentlemen juju said.

One tear fell down her pretty round brown cheek, running faster than Jacky Joyner, to the bottom of her face, & then she said, "some people gone try to put chains on your neck, arms, or legs, to keep you close to them, also they might feed you bread, to keep you coming back to the hand that feed you, that's why you play it how it go, don't be no pawn on the chessboard, education is mental strength, stay ahead of everybody who will intentionally attempt to run over you, & everybody who lives to search for your weakness."

Waking up mean, it's time to rise, & shine, it's an old meaning, spoken in english second language that way, most indigenous people speak English in the original way, it was spoken when it first started.

So let it be written as it shall be done, you can't chill if you got business to handle, respect to the harlem globetrotters from the beginning to the present moment, learn how to drive behind your people with no plates on car, until they get where they going safely.

Starting to count currency in digits, then times digits by the bill amount, just progressing towards longevity, I'm leaning back in indianapolis, the land of Indians, indigenous, love being in Gary Indiana, I'm sipping Don pérignon, it was on sale, guess ain't nobody drinking it out here, in whitestown indiana, I'm making soundtrack to this brilliant book, something to iron wrinkle currency to, & I'm finishing up Mackology 2nd edition book, If I could I would thank you a thousand times, for rereading Mackology 2nd edition, it should be out right now, soft copy, hard copy, kindle books, google books, in china, also street life philosophy Mackology 1st edition written by royalty, is available on Amazon, barnes and noble, etc, I'm listening to 8ball & mjg song, it's called, "reason for rhyme," and father dom song just went off, it's called, "same old song."

JOURNEY WEALTHY LONGEVITY SCRIPTURES

10.

Everywhere you go, be on the prowl, to see if that city got benefits for you, on the business tip, vehicles, homes, a new crew, or new members bringing something to the table, showing a down for life mentality, simply to be in the royal family, to help the royal family get wealthy, on the journey to longevity.

I'm in New Hampshire right now, I was in Maine earlier, this my first time coming to the farthest north east corner of the United States, it's looking good with lakes of clean water, to rivers running around different parts of the state, blueberries to lobsters is Americas most wanted from this specific part of the country, plus it got islands all around these areas in the north east of the country to.

THIRD EYE WATCHING

This book, is about a cold piece named Hazel, named by me, her respect for her king, her staying true to her king, her staying down with her king with a master plan, their unity amongst each other, how these two took a chance, to advance, being consciously woke, with global intelligence, and growing historically intelligent.

Thank you to my elders, who gave me capital game, appreciation

all those who invested in me, specifically those who rolled with me, through traps I didn't see on my pathway, & unexpectedly fell in.

I wrote this book years ago, around the time when the Iphone 4, was brand new, I got more literature I left out of this book, but all that is in this book, available to be read, completes the book in every way possible.

The Game of Life, Lifeology, Mackology, Pimpology, The Philosophical Philosopher presents, Street Life Philosophy, written by the game spitting smartest, the mayor of everywhere, and the king of everything in the world he develops in.

Its well known, you will need to know what other people know, sometimes you don't need a whole lot, to do a whole lot, yesterday will teach you what to do today, & tomorrow, learn all the languages of all the lands, mandatorily conceal balance, and options.

Its truth in lies, its lies in truth, game came from whence rain came, royalties means getting paid respect.

Strategically place everything in its proper position, keep enough to do enough, at any given moment, the weak will remain sleep, and the quiet will forever start riots.

The strong last long, the wise will rise, & surprise, fools don't know the rules, or how to use their Most High given tools.

Never school a fool, or give game to a lame, it's gone mess their life up, then backfire on you, being in a group is identical, to being isolated, because all huddled up minds, must be on the same page.

So that one person will not have an issue, that will create conflicted confusion amongst the whole group, a groups is isolated because they all in the same boat, same cage, same trap.

You can't change what is, into what you want it to be unless the Most High will it to be done, its a source to all that is, what's being said, is only important, if the person saying it, is important to the person its being said to.

Daily groom self, to suit the journey to longevity, stay ahead of what is going on at all times.

Seek interpreters, those who can explain what you do not know, how to brake down in fractions, this book is the business, a group of geniuses, all contributed, to me figuring out how to write this book, I'm watching New Orleans dancing Toni with his stepping in the name of love horse, all I can hear is fiend saying is, "welcome to New Orleans.

People who aim to be wiser, will huddle up with honest knowledgeable people, on the strength, to figure out the hidden truth, hidden in plain sight, this book is the.

Silent nights, silent days is necessary, read write, instead of giving the game {ism} away for free.

Fools is tools for other fools to use, abuse, confuse, everybody got to respect the game of life wise ones, the watchers, the keepers of the longevity game, the youth, and elders at all times, respect to Mac minister minister of defense.

A person that has a plan worth a hundred grand, support that, put your bid in stock markets, all celebrity, stand out In spot light situations, is target central, always be low key, under the radar, that's what you call modified lifestyle being lived.

Boss player status, is learning, earning, qualifying to be satisfied, and progressing hourly.

If your lifestyle similar to mine, we got something in common, we can chop up capital game, then brake it down in fractions.

Its all about surviving on all levels, in any climate, all locations in the country, under all circumstances.

Celebrity entertainment talking, is for some, not for most skillful thinkers, that aim to keep people out their business.

I'm Speaking the number one language right now, which is silence, which is another way, of saying the game is sold, not told, press play, & let the games begin, spend correct currency, to get exactly what you pay for.

No guarantees, that sacred talk, will not be spit on, or drug through the mud, that's mainly why, the keepers of the game, say, "the game is sold not we told."

Always be thankfully appreciative, let nothing inside of you that will take control of you, or puppet master you, never look for rewards, just be at your at all times, & qualify to get what is coming to you.

Every pinch of life, is hand picked, & placed specifically where it's at, which will be true, now to forever.

Got to tighten up, tell nobody about your business, because if they get what is yours, you will be upset, with only yourself to be the blame, I'm watching an officer of the law with his dancing horse in New Orleans, black golden brown officer with his dancing horse, unbelievable to some, but this horse getting down with the get down, people of all races is watching the show, let indigenous brown people entertain you, educate you on life how it supposed to go.

No mack in motion, wants to hear, not even a little bit, about no pimp problems, consistently weekly, these two only supposed to speak on lifestyle solutions, amongst each other, & solve their own problems.

By trusting the Most High to lead self through trials, to tribulations is a fearless characteristic trait, also no mack, wants to hear a man bragging on himself, to impress a crowd.

Real beneficial living, obligated to consistently be stepping up to new levels, doing what ain't being done, full effort living, going extra miles, when the average person-will not, and being focused, like a Atlana hawk eye in the sky.

No outside interference, can't carry dead weight, or baby sit grown folks, special requirements is road runners, intentionally staying with polished knowledge, so you don't have to rely on somebody else, to think for self.

A new team bring new progress, it's best to hand pick winners, that's born to win, solid individuals, determined to take their life to the next level, I'm watching dirty boys song called, "hit da floe."

Never wake up to down play yourself, stay doing what keeps you feeling uplifted, either keep up, or get left behind, turn weakness to strength, strengthen your mind, like Dezarie said, if you sense you losing, learn how to win, learn from winners how to stay up, like four corner hustlers told you.

You can tell who been sharpening up, their communication conversation survival skills, consistently step up to higher levels, let your game speak for itself, like Steve Francis did.

Keep slick mouths out your business, watch those who specialize in word play, no need to rush, just wait to escape poverty, with patience, everything always fall into place, if you don't block your blessings that is.

Everything connected, has a special way to communicate in conversations, together, it's mandatory to follow the hand picked leaders, share ism with those all in, if you gone live, live with a full effort, because every move made counts.

Focus on what self got going on, like an Alaskan Polar Bear, pass up on what you want, to be good for what is great, eliminate the middle man, a team is always in sink, dedicated to playing to win together, for each other to succeed successfully.

Norfolk Virginia bootney said, "It was some of the best of times, it was some of the worst times."

THE GAME OF LIFE SCRIPTURES

8.

Playing the game of life is knowing how to roll it, live to give, give to live, it's about unity, team work works, it's a proven fact teams have won championships, everybody need everybody, cross country living will explain what the game of life scriptures is all about.

I'm In Milford Connecticut, with jazz band, with pink face Moet, with California love in the air, I'm watching drink champs, episode 13, legendary guest such as dpg, Tony yayo, Capone, dru hill, lil pimpin, and Jack thriller.

MACKOLOGY

Mackology is the art of major mackin for a lifetime, the Mack lifestyle is very serious, it deals with life on all levels, it's a global intelligent to brilliant thinking process.

If you live this very serious lifestyle, daily nightly you learn from it, recognizing every day is one step closer to longevity, it's a very informational step by step process, with no brakes included, until the Kilimanjaro Mountain top is reached.

A magnificent great Mack, is most definitely a mastermind, the aim is to figure every pinch of life out, the key is to know all that will be allowed to be known, to make life a plain, simple, and an easy process.

Women gone bust moves like New York City alley cats, without leaving trails, or evidence, or reveal the moves they make, or made, if you ever with a woman in public, then she points at something to look at, with a man in that direction, she scanning him with out you recognizing she wreckless eyeballing.

Mackology is directly aimed to qualify a male to be crowned king, also to be given a throne to sit on, and a kingdom to rule wisely righteously brilliantly.

Mackology is a direct life course to being an intellectual, intelligent to fascinatingly brilliant wise king, it is a course of supreme advanced higher learning.

Mackology is the action of living to learn, simultaneously learning how to live, it is advanced intelligence, and brilliance.

Mackology teaches the youth, preaches the truth, it schools the uneducated, it also opens the third eye, to see what is written between the lines, and hidden in plain sight, like you a radiologic technologists.

Mackology prevents one from losing identity, it will always bring truth to lies, and automatically brightens up the darkest saddest days.

Mackology is studied by all pinky ring street kings, all the way up to those who sit on the top floors, in the Royal Penthouse Suites, it is also studied by those born to Mack, and it is well known, Macks will spit capitol game consistently with good intentions.

A Mack will study mackology, so he can know, how to conquer life on all levels, it is well known, by all pinky ring street kings, that mackology is truth beyond belief.

Mackology teaches excellent conscious awareness, it also teaches born participants, how to master the mind, body, mentally, physically, and financially also spiritually.

To a Mack, spirituality is seeking to be the greatest one was created to be, now, and forever.

Mackology is about studying the truth in plain sight, it also enhances mental skills, to recognize what is being visualized, with allowance to do so by the Most High.

A Mack mind his business, he doesn't hate, debate, or time waste, he sticks to the script, and don't change like the weather.

A Mack knows the game of life, the game of life knows him, a Mack is known for staying strong, and lasting long.

A Mack will automatically analyze, strategize, and improvise when necessary to overcome obstacles.

I think Lil flip from Houston, & mr. Fab from Oakland should do a freestyle album with freestyle kings all around the country, from every state.

THE LAST MACK STANDING SCRIPTURES

5.

Step in smooth to lay It down thick, straight grinding like they do in Little Rock Arkansa, got to learn how to live, then learn how to earn, then learn how to make money work for you, then learn how to pull up shining brand new, like they say In Memphis, "this what game plus money do for you," if you learn how to direct traffic, Memphis know the business, on some project pat type stuff, It's all about, getting life right wealthy, comfortable with longevity, & spirituality.

Indigenous soul peoples got unique characteristics, and unique behavior that can be seen by all eyes that got game that recognize game, respect to Lapham park projects hillside projects Milwaukee Wisconsin mr. Boss player Maine.

MACKOLOGY

The way she Métisly style cradled me, in her arms, was Muhheconnuck heartwarming, it was a feeling I will never receive again until I lay inside the clouds in comfortable enjoyable pimp paradise (hawaii island), & for some original soul people indigenous spiritual reason, I don't think I wanted to feel it again, to understand what this paragraph is saying, your third eye has to be active, so it can project a visual of what you reading, to explain the meaning of what the unique author is insinuating.

With a Tiara Rogers mother loving facial expression on her pretty copper brown face, she looked out the antique designed windows, at the long summer fresh Schoenoplectus prairie grassy field, simultaneously, while she new born mother held me, Jake the anaconda tight, in her pyramid golden brown arms, an April Rogers Barbara Hardy Simmons looking nurse walked passed my mother room door smiling, the nurse had one of them Jean Rogers Tennessee Mississippi type of walks on her.

She gently, motherly, respectfully kissed me on my copper brown baby Blake looking jaw, she had a Cicely Harlem New York Tyson serious thinking facial expression on her face, while she looked out the antique designed window, & she said, "Your father belongs to a group of smooth operators, & that world famous Ibadan Nigeria soul singer Sade made a song specifically about them, called, "smooth operator."

At this present moment, I'm Listening to the Bankhead Georgia king, sir Shawty lo, his 1st classic album song, it's called, "cut the check," he relaxing in gangsta paradise right now, but his name spit game, plus his legacy, will reign supreme for time to come.

My nice height, pretty copper brown mother earth, said, "they called themselves Mack's, or boss players," & I member he looked directly at me, to say, "You gone be just like him in more ways than one, luxry living, flossing tossing currency in the air, straight professional king mackin."

My mother earth said, "the last day I saw your smooth operator father alive, in living color, he told me to tell you, he wanted you to know, "that it seems like every person that is in a rush to get rich, either lose their life, or accumulate a numerous amount of bad memories, or end up finding the Most High."

Your Big Boi, idlewild, foghorn legion, silver fox fur coat wearing father also said, "Tell my million dollar son, his father was born on the Mack Moon, south of Saint Louis Missouri, where Stagger Lee song was created.."

Then she smiled happily, like three time Olympian Dominique dawes, then me mother started saying, "Your father schooled me, when other people attempted to fool me, he laced me with good capitol longevity game, & it most definitely prepared me for life, simply so I wouldn't be scared to expect the unexpected, never in this lifetime."

"One thing about your hard knock life father, is the elders was saying he grew up on the wrong side of the track, where king pimps lived in mansions, with Namibia lioness simba cubs as pets," then my mother earth whispered to me, supposedly my mama said, "your boss player, Memphis pimpin lucky, abcp game spitting father, was learning directly from what dripped off the pimp God mouth, faithfully studying pimpology with his pimp brothers."

My mother earth, teary eyedly said, boo I grew up under your simply remarkable Choctaw copper brown indigenous, great righteous wisdom talking grandma, she loved cooking fried okra, fried green tomatoes, Turkey wings, daily to nightly, we saw her studying the Soul People Spirituality, basic instructions before leaving earth hand written book, this book was hand written by grandma's, when they turned 74 years old, to pass down to the next generation, your simply remarkable South Carolina Choctaw indigenous grandma taught me that the Soul People Spirituality, Holy bible is abbreviated, & it historically means, basic instruction before leaving earth."

Then with two Krystal Benson clear tears in her right eye, she proudly said, "Son I always wondered why an indigenous soul person, dislikes learning new ways to live life information, information that will put them back on their birth right throne in this world."

The two Krystal Benson stripper tears crawled down her copper brown face, then my mother earth said, "Some people got a fear of flying;" she paused, turned her black exploitation Pam Grier afro head, & pretty lady Michelle Williams, Latvia Roberson, LeToya Luckett, Farrah Franklin quietly sneezed.

I'm listening to Sam clarksdale Mississippi Cooke song, it's called, "change is gonna come," my loving mother earth, laid me down gently, so she could grab a Golden Crisp Sugar Bear, brown napkin, to clean up the respiratory system mucous mess, her snotty nose made, the pyramid brown hermle tellurium II mechanical table clock was playing snoop dogg song, it's called, "just a baby boy," featuring tyreese, he singing from his California soul.

Then she politely respectfully kissed my jigsaw jaw, next she looked Lake Tanganyika deep in my eyes, & finally she said, "what you put in is what you get out, you got to put back in what you take out, it's a fair exchange no robbery in the game of life, how you play the game of life, will be exactly how you get played with, what you give, shall be exactly what you receive, speak no evil hear no evil, doubt the wrong route, & persue the righteous direction."

She happily sad faced Divine Brown smiled at me, with glossy Laura London teary eyes, she was gently saying, "love is life, life is love, never think you know it all, everybody following in somebody footsteps, when handling important business, pay attention to what's in front of you, business first, pleasure last, give your life your undivided attention, & do what need to be done, to make other accommodations come directly to you."

It seemed like, me wonderful Black River Chippewa bloodline mother earth, was teaching me 18 years worth of mother son knowledge, in my first two days on this big water infested bubble called mother earth, also known as Mut nature.

My eyes closed shut, like a New York JPMorgan Chase gold bank vault.

I didn't know, that this was gone be the last time I saw her.

When I unexpectedly woke up, from feeling the breath of the Most High, also known as a cool breeze off the waves running above The Pacific Ocean .

The Mack Moon was T.C. sniper infrared scoping me, the light from it was blushing, blowing kisses at me nonstop, & the 1998 Cadillac north starlight, was winking at me periodically consistently, I stood their bold as little bryan in Texas.

I saw six Ramapough copper brown looking soulful spirits with glowing thousand dollar smiles, & they was Pelican Bay, prison guard, secret service guarding my bed, with ancient knowledge, and ancient wisdom that's hidden presently in books, that you choose not to read, that which would be wise to read, with undivided attention, day to night.

Then a Bernie Mac Chicago born king of comedy talking looking angel was tickling my feet, with a pyramid golden brown feather, off one of his big Bird sesame street angel wings.

Simultaneously, a saint ann's bay, richard Jamaica born, Marcus Garvey strong, onxy copper brown looking soulful spirit started to stand out, like a Texas yellow rose in an Oklahoma City red rose garden.

He was Dallas Texas, George Bush, Barack Obama presidential inauguration smiling, with bright ivory white colored Mr. Lucky Cary Grant teeth, & starred at me with Kavango broccoli antonia thomas green eyes.

Then he looked at the soulful spirit on his right side, pointing at me with his pyramid golden brown thumb, smiling sideways, with a Milwaukee look at dude facial expression.

Then he said, "young cool breeze, follow the rules to last long, it's always somebody more clever then you in more ways than one, you might be fast, but it's always gone be somebody faster, have the truth with you every day, all day, to fight liars, duck nonsense, dodge pointless situations, & trouble makers," then the hermle tellurium II mechanical table clock started playing sade song, its called, "cherish the day."

His voice was Mozambique lion growling deep, & it released a Saint Paul Minnesota spring time Lake Michigan Sun Setting cool breeze, on copper brown baby me, I felt it when he spoke to me.

For some soulful reason, he rubbed my somewhat bald head, when my eyes blinked twice, he walked to the window, praying quieter than a 1983 L.A. Mayer Museum thief, walking in the neighbor multi million dollar palace, talking on the 1938 reproduction royal Victoria house phone.

My eyes blinked again humbly, when my Amazon tree frog size eyes opened, he was gone, & once that Genízaros copper brown soulful spirit left, the other Montauk copper brown looking soulful spirit disappeared.

After feasting my eyes on all that, I started falling asleep again peacefully, like a Chicora-Siouan New born infant, & the night walked pass me, like it was a 1977 $1000 a night Los Angeles Figueroa prostitute, while I slept like it wasn't no tomorrow, a radio in the room started playing Luther Vandross song, it's called, "Having a Party."

A few capuchin monkey face months swung pass me, I was getting bigger, my boss player long hair was growing, & my vision was getting stronger then an adult great grey owl eyesight.

Then one morning in August, I woke up to a colorful Desmond Merrion Supreme Bespoke suit wearing, Russian sable fur coat wearing, with a Godfather Dobb hat to match, Don Magic Juan coordinated man, who I never seen before, yet he looked like I was supposed to know him.

He stood about six foot one, with an Excel Barber shop, on 6th center street bald fade, chin strap, sky blue bumpy face Full Quill Smooth Ostrich skin boots on, and a custom made Versace suit.

A full-length pitch black Russian sable fur coat, with droop-e, E-40 eyes, two gold white diamond fronts, a 58-diamond pinky ring on each pinky finger, like Peewee Kirkland, & a look in his eyes that had to be worth more than a 2019 rolls Royce, with a 28-color viewing choice.

He looked at me, like a six-figure gentleman of leisure, who just woke up going to cash a $45,000 check; his deep dark dangerous eyes, Mike Tyson punched me in the face, I mean harder then a young George Edward foreman, January 10, 1976 Marshall Texas rib punch.

It seems like everything in the world paused except us, & he said, "look at my mini me, the million dollar Mack, the chosen explosion, the game spitting smartest, and universe hardest, mack dulo, the pimp professional, the h taker, the b braker."

He reached for me with his diamonds studio 54 discoball shining, twinkling brighter then mister twankle, from North division summer school, he was picking me up, like I was a Michael clarke's Louis Vuitton luxury trunk, full of tens, & twenties in sets of five hundred stacks.

He lifted me up over his head, like he was the Undertaker, or rafiki, lifting limbs up in the air, then he said, "Everybody got to listen to somebody, it's a source to all that is, its two sides to all that is, good vs. bad, evil vs. righteous, truth vs. lies, strength vs. weakness, love vs. hate, happy vs. sad, young vs. old, & whoever answer a question with a question, is attempting to take over the conversation, its chess not checkers," that's what California solid gold diamond teeth hustlers be popping, when they be counting money like J. Diggs.

He held me close to his heart proudly, I felt like I was safe from any harm in the world, then he said, "I will be back in a New York County jail month," next he said, "your mother went overseas to fight in the Arab Israel war, so it's just me, & you until she come back home DJ quick safe & sound.

"I'm going to put you up on game, my only seed I planted, it's all about incredible discipline, accurate correct choices, handpicked decisions, & that's just a pinch of different ways to keep your head above flooding Pacific Ocean water, with your feet on the solid ground," then the hermle tellurium II mechanical table clock starting playing jay-z song, it's called, "family feud," all I heard was Beyonce singing amen, with the spiritual singing voice of 1965 Aretha franklin, when she was singing with million dollar vocals.

He laid me back down, like I was a baby bird, going back into the horned coot nest, made of pennanitia baylisiana tree branches, he shook my little miniature sized hand, & said, "I love you solid gold, priceless, unique, strong, incredible, highly intelligent, John Henrik Clarke intellectual God body son of mine, you gone be cashing hansom checks, like Shawn Brooklyn Marcy projects carter."

He reached inside his expensive suit coat, he dug playerrifically inside his expensive suit pocket to grab his money Martell Phoenix Rogers currency clip, of twenties, fifties, & hundreds.

He pulled two fifties out his bank roll; his bank roll was so fat, it would make Lebron James think about robbing him.

Then he put the two small face fifties in my infant pamper, & then he said, "Tell everybody you had money before you knew what to do with it."

He turned his head slightly, coughed with a fist balled up covering his mouth, & turned back to me saying, "I want you to stay around positive, polite, powerful, pleasant, respectful, helpful, food for thought capitol longevity good game giving people."

"Simply because they will make your life so much more enjoyable, & it will become a breath-taking experience, awesome, fantastic, stupendous, unbelievable dream to reality life worth living."

For some odd reason, I suddenly became sad, he looked at me with a $200 an hour jack bobo smile, then he pimp stick walked out the door, it looked like a million dollar grossing movie of the 2022 summer.

At that time of my early millon mackin life, I didn't know that this was going to be, the last time I saw my father in this life time, I was more sadder then a 1929 most racist man, seeing an Asian, European, Mexican, & indigenous golden brown group of kids playing together in 2020, or the day sad like the day snoop dogg knew Shreveport Louisiana Stanley tookie Williams, was in San Quentin State prison facing the death penalty on December 13th 2005.

I'm listening to Roger and Zapp song, it's called, "computer love," I'm still sipping Don pérignon and Hennessy, I hope you enjoying the book so far, because I'm putting my foot knee deep in this, its like a death row inmate last request was for me to write this book with all I got, before he got electrocuted in Huntsville on February 8th 1924.

Thank you for your interest in my second book, I'm putting my full effort into this, the same way fat Joe & Remy ma, put in making lean back, or big pun, put in his song, it's called John blaze, or how fat Joe hand picked everybody to be on that song, simply so you can get what you looking for in a money worthy type way, this book is an investment in yourself, put to use what you get from this book, and make it beneficial long termly.

I'm also thinking about going to a strip club, it could be interesting, I can lean back to analyze, and study everybody.

Respect to Lapham park bra mr. Maine, the pimp player gangster hustler business man.

JOURNEY WEALTHY LONGEVITY SCRIPTURES

11.

Everywhere you go, be on the prowl to see if that city got benefits for you on the business tip, vehicles, homes, a new crew, or new members bringing something to the table, showing a down for life mentality, simply to be in the royal family, to help the royal family get wealthy on the journey to longevity.

I'm in Pennysvania listening to master p song, it's called, "best hustler, it's hot out here in June, next Sunday is the Fourth of July, I'm aiming to finalize this macknificent book before august 3rdthe boss player holiday all over the world, I heard a song called, "the bigger picture, " it's made by an artist by the name of Lil baby, very interesting, I also heard a song called, "bad," made by an artist named xxxtentaction, it's cool to me how it's made, now I'm listening to classic song by tela, it's called, "ride."

THE PINKY RING STREET KINGS

What you reading is considered sacred thoughts that can't be bought, I take it that you intrigued by what you reading in this simply remarkable book of the century, I strategically painted this genius book with handpicked dictionary words while being in my right mind, allowance from the Most High to know what is known how to do what can be done by royalty, names I use that you will read is to highlight important people in my perspective, this book is historical & musical.

It has been my ultimate pleasure to entertain you with encyclopedia words, not only that, but educate you about what is knee deep in the fast lane, forbidden unknown topics people decided not to speak on.

I aimed to make this brilliant book complicated for the globally historically uneducated, it was my intention to put uncommon sentences, statements, paragraphs, exactly where I handpicked to put them in this macknificent book, only a soulful person with extraordinary game can translate this book to somebody with little, or no game at all.

I'm listening to afroman song, it's called, "roll on," "they said we used to be local, now we world wide."

This spectacular book is reality based, it has certain situations that did not occur exactly how I wrote them, & I think I wrote this how I think my life should have transpired, I rewrote my lifetime the way it could have transpired, this is not his story, or their story, this is my story.

The next book will be complete with more details, also a much more intriguing storyline, which is this book, so thank you, one, & all, live long, love your Creator, and prosper, Respect to mr. Bushwick bill.

Rick ross said, "The devil is a lie," the truth is with the Father of the Universe is what indigenous elders always been saying, welcome to a world were friends become enemies, enemies becomes friends, myths gets replaced by truth hidden in the past, a place indigenous men have been strategically kept down only to eventually, or instantaneously rise up to become kings, once again sitting on their solid gold throne hand made in pimp paradise, or gangster heaven, or the supreme every day is a piece to the puzzle that will complete your life, so understand you cannot be weak if you want to be strong living life to the fullest, remember prayers was made for a boss player, whisper in the wind every chance you have to do so.

Truthfully I reply to you, who would I be without you, if it was no you, it would be no me, think about it, when you roll legit sitting on your throne at home in y'all castle.

Oba mean King, King mean God, Mack mean son, I am who I was created to be now, I am my mother father, my Creator's sun, I am King Mack.

Women ask men do they know how to treat a woman, yet they themselves should ask their self, do they know how to treat a man, then they can get treated like a woman, which is a fair exchange in the game of life.

Dive deeper into your teachings, to achieve, receive, retrieve higher learning, because the deeper you get in life, the closer you get to the truth.

I'm listening to James Brown song, it's called, "like it is like it was, he said, "just messing around with the blues, with the blues, with the blues," biggie Brooklyn smalls song called, "me & my bt$h," it just came on.

To know, you must be equipped with proper enlightenment, in order to step by step process, graduate to greater heights mentally, physically, and spiritually.

Truth beyond belief, to say a person is not educated, you must have proof of that, if that person was not taught what you were taught, the way you was taught, that which makes you feel enlightened, and feel like that person is not educated.

I was lost until I found myself, I'm listening to Lil flip song, it's called, "It's a fact," he said I had to bag back, it's a fact, you reap what you sow."

Realize what is going on, then understand what to do, pursue the truth, pursue solutions to problems, pursue answers to questions, pursue not death, nor danger.

The key to life is see, not be seen, like motion detectors, or let's say, wearing a hoodie, be were to be, far as your well being is concerned, every pinch of life will be how it is setup to be, and created to be.

The Most High is Almighty, simply because The most is, & always will be, it's a fact like Lil Flip said.

Keep an eye on what grabs your attention, analyze it till you know why it grabbed your attention, understand your race (unfortunately race stands for competition), and all your history you allowed to be introduced to.

When you save a life, that person will save your life, so if it is a woman, you two will be soul mates, ask the China wise Buddha man, life goes on until The Most High says no more, never be in the face of danger, accept not love that will one day hate you.

Everything is lined up with precise moves, the more you know, the more you grow, the past has to transpire, so the present moment can exist.

I'm listening to legendary Long Island Rakim song, it's called, "stay a while."

Levels stepped on, means you graduating to greater heights, enabling progress to transpire with prosperity leading the way towards the pathway to longevity.

If the wind is not ready to blow, the leaves on the trees will not move, the sun will shine when it is time, and the moon was made to shed light on all the ancestor Pharaohs Tombs.

It is impossible to find a right way to do wrong right, a fool is known by what he, or she say, said, saying, did, done did, or doing.

Different moods produce different modes, only what is written to be kept is what will be for the keeping.

Understand what is required to be memorized, recognize what you visualize, read to succeed, live learn how to live, and stay in it to the finish.

Lies exist as well as the truth, it takes a penny to get wealthy, if you make chess moves, you will not have to make checker decisions.

All will go through life to become who they is, simply because, that is the way all will learn to be, who they created to become.

Anybody will tell somebody anything, if that person willing to listen, if you not paying attention, this world will use you, confuse you, abuse you, and destroy you.

Add new found information to self-repertoire, some people want to be informed, some do not want to be informed, because it is easier to do what the world is doing.

To fool a person you must trick them, tricks is for kids, a thief is not above the person being stolen from, some brains can interpret what is being insinuated.

In this lifetime, it's absolutely mandatory to have everything, I mean everything in order, straight prepared not scared, fearless powerful wise knowledgeable day to night.

I'm listening to 8ball & MJG song, it's called, "just like candy," they said, "it's just like candy, it takes over me, yeahhh yeahhh yeaah."

It is more to life then what meets the eyes, like transformers said in September 17, 1984, gi joe said, "knowing is half the battle," every experience is a learning experience, leave what do not put you ahead, know what you getting into before you get into it, know the value of every pinch of life The Most High created, knowing the value of every pinch of creations, is mandatory.

The deeper you get in life, the closer you get to the truth, the more self pass the blessings around, the more the blessings stack up for self, ask Dudley do right.

This book is dedicated to people who is playing to win on royal levels, paying dues, surviving to be enlightened by King Imhotep, King Mansa Musa, Tehuti Maat, Ptah Hotep, Osiris, Horus, Netjer Maat, Alkebulan, Turtle island, Black Madona, Aset, Seti, Atum, Amon-Ra & others who names is being uncovered as time reveals their contributions to indigenous soul peoples existence today.

The truth is forever imbedded inside indigenous soul peoples all over the world, past present, future, forever, and always.

I'm listening to, Dallas Texas Choctaw Erykah Badu song, it's called, "orange moon."

The philosophical philosopher street life philosophy author is available for: lectures, and individual, or group counseling, life coach, for further information, go to thekingbusinss@aol.com to contact Royalty.

When air body get together, everything will get better, unity, United States, cover all angles, & connect game, to bring back balance, and options. (Dj quik album is called, balance and options.

217

THE GAME OF LIFE SCRIPTURES

9.

Playing the game of life, is knowing how to roll it, live to give, give to live, it's about unity, team work works, it's a proven fact that teams have won championships, everybody need everybody, cross country living, will explain what the game of life scriptures is all about, I'm listening to a song called, "premium game," by the tightest p spitter, the first man to make a song about being on my way, the street life genius, king suga free from Pomona pimpin' young, respect to the giants, Alabama dirty boys just came on, "wood grain," this real down south classic street life philosophy, you can read cleaner then ray virgil fairley favorite fur coat, um tum bout riding through side streets in the neighborhood just turning heads, playing this song gone talk loud gangster pimpish for you to everybody who attention you caught.

CURRENCY LIFESTYLE

If you get any amount of currency, evil will lurk around you, historical top money rules always says, "keep your business uninfiltrated, & keep laims out your game, in every way possible."

Money making is just a hobby for prime time hustlers hitting the highway, simply because, they mastered the game of life on every level possible, that they got access to that which they graduated to play on.

The money game is specifically for trading purposes, fair exchange no robbery, my price in exchange for what you got, that which I need, being a service, like world known Amazon, it can be food that can get your bank up, like Dallas resident, Mr. Pickles with a twist, etc.

It Is unknown to most, that every lifestyle, is a slave to who it cater to, simply to stay paid in full, if you a slave to currency, you got to start demanding money work for you, it's a formula to be figured out.

The big time Money game, it's played by those who aim for luxury living, yacht parties in Tswalu Kalahari South Africa, vacations in tropical Ecuador places, also buying evening Rolls Royces to push when the day half way over, rolls Royce with eight-teen color viewing choices, you know, let the soul people see how to top this game is played, they they say, one gone say, it's time to get what's mine now, & forever, state to state steak to steak, when out here to get paid, & laid under palm tree shade, with some burgundy alligator pimpin ken ivy sandals, comfortable like the male safari lion, I'm listening to busta busta rhymes, round of applause everybody, this bout to be the most unbelievable unforgettable performance, this song is called, "where we about take this."

The money game is for individuals, that which who collect new hundred dollar bills, also those who anticipate saving thousands of dollars a week, more than they like spending currency, that's saved for specific longevity reasons, and personal investments.

Brilliant individuals that participate in the money game, living a lifestyle that play to win, every hour of the day to night to morning, money makers will eventually master the formula of eliminating hate, debates, weak links in their chain, also those who can destroy the empire from the inside, empires that which took them a lifetime to build.

The millionaire money game, its for globe traveling high rollers, also for cross country clever wise people, who can make the unbelievable things in life happen, become believable, with no problem, assistance, or help needed to proceed, consistently making that happen.

Paper chasing is about having lightning quick thinking, um tum bout, Shakopee Mdewakanton Tribe intelligent to brilliant money moves, Imhotep advanced intelligence, studying ancient global higher learning, with specific intentions, to master the game of life.

Paper chasing is not about half stepping, its all about investing in your self, and putting self in long term powerful positions.

The Rolls Royce perspective, you either going to buy the expensive cars that can be purchased privately, or publicly, or you wishing on a star, for it to magically appear.

Bad business is anything, or anybody in your circle, your business, a destination, a situation, a place to be, an investment, all of which that is not beneficial to you, or your empire, all of which is simply creating bad business outcomes, that will put you back down the ladder, distractions can be people interfering with how the king play to win with the royal family.

The true career money game participants, all address themselves as beneficial people, twenty four hours a day, & longevity is their final, & only destination, welcome to the game of life, if you don't know, you better ask the correct somebody, I'm listening to the green eyed bandit, legendary epmd Eric sermon, round of applause for the performance gone put some pep in your step, it's called, "come thru," all game entertainment, like Burt said in Milwaukee players ball, "I love all y'all."

The money game says know what you getting into, before you get into it, stay building yourself up to last, always prepared to expect the unexpected, and equipped with soul survivor skills to make life comfortable.

In the expert master mind professional money game, its all about having city to city, state to state, country to country, continent to continent currency routes, along with a thinking process that makes all that possible, with a natural hands on relationship, with the Most High.

it's well known around the whole wide world, that you will stay broke around the consistent broke, & when you around the wealthy, look broke around the wealthy, look less but at your best, no flash, no standout, never speak cash money, unless it's a business orientated situations conversation, I'm listening to Scarface, we out here," performed by utp boss player gangsters.

The money game is strictly about a come up mission, getting wealthy, becoming wealthy for a lifetime, is strictly about luxury living in the most righteous way possible, respecting the Most High every live long day.

The millionaire money game is about upgrading, staying updated, picking beneficial decisions, & longevity choices.

The millionaire money game, is played in your home town, on all levels, meaning, you deal with everybody one way, or another, for specific beneficial reasons, & purposes.

Money will almost, aways bring money, driving a Rolls Royce, will bring money makers if you work the wheel right, it also brings money takers, even if you don't show weakness, everybody got to get rich now, So all Indigenous can live in peace.

A mansion also will bring money makers, if you charge to get in your mansion, also infiltrators that which look to get inside, & not leave empty handed, they will attempt to infiltrate through your front door to.

When you in the money game, recognize who in your line of business, visualize who would invest in your line of business, cover all angles, of possible business options.

Always know its snakes in the grass, weather it's high or cut low grass, watch for traps, always have a bank vault, & stay hidden in plain sight.

Avoid bad investments, & appreciate what is coming to you, and never be greedy.

Learn from other money moves you made that failed, plus the consequential outcomes, keep living legends on your dream team to help keep everything progressing in your empire.

If you running weak game, & it's being noticeable, just be yourself, stop making yourself look like you up to something, it's local brilliant Indigenous peoples with their game Virgin Islands tight, what you do in their presence will stand all the way out to them, it was once said to royalty, "You need to tighten up," jack from Virginia told royalty that exact statement in missouri, tell the copper wise complected main, or woman, you need to be schooled not fooled, it's time somebody sharpened up my game, fair exchange no robbery, make money work for you, if they prefer bread for giving game, sharing is caring, or get what they personal preference is, that which can be bought, gifts will encourage the brain to tell the mouth what to say, it's that simple, tighten up, everybody had to get schooled, it's the indigenous route to get your game tight, it's plenty elders that be saying, "keep your game getting tighter," that is being spoken all around the country from words out of soulful mouths, peace & blessings to the whole south soulful indigenous pyramid golden brown peoples around the country.

Money that is being used properly, it can be a defense, also it can be used as an offense technique, to defeat opponents presently, also future opponents, & attract more money to the bank vault, only if the millionaire technique is learned how to be used beneficially, now check this, California original gangster c-bo song called, "die broke," it just came on gangster walking stomping dinosaur, bass banging his voice krystal benson clear, specifically for all up the downtown area near you can hear the whole song, respect where you live to give, & give to live.

In the complicated forever changing currency lifestyle, the hand picked starting players that which you coach, who you teaching leadership skills to, they mandatorily have to study every lesson of yours thoroughly.

Also, how you coach them about how to learn is important, how to separate good information from bad information, which includes how, & why to be loyal to what is mandatory in the lifestyle being lived, I'm listening to too short song, it's called, "call me daddy," got me some chrystale wilson champagne in arkansas, first bottle of it, it taste great, jazz black bands, california smoke signals, while editing this brilliant book, if you in a new city, if you park, wait a while, if you don't see Indigenous soul people anywhere in sight, that's not where you gone feel good energy.

For the rest of their life, they must be schooled by you daily, nightly, consistently, on how to dedicate themselves to building your empire, that which they belong to, lifetime partnership, not a hostage situation, why be near if you temporary, but I guess, even the fly by night, need to run off on you to figure out how to last long, so just play to win with them, even if they got a 30 second shot clock, enjoy, let them enjoy their time under your wing, bless them, get your blessings, don't do it, & you might be blocking your blessings, I don't make the rules, I just know the business.

Sometimes you will slip, but don't allow self to fall down, off top it's mandatory to recognize problems, then mandatorily solve those problems, next retrace your steps, all the way back to childhood, to see what all went wrong, & then professionally participate full effortlessly in the currency lifestyle, and rewrite your history, exactly how mistakes could have been prevented, I'm just listening to dj screwed up click, he gave Lil flip a trophy plaque on a stage, simply specifically mainly for being the freestyle king, for paying his dues, being dedicated to being the greatest early, that's the ultimate, I'm still sipping chrystale wilson right now, watching 2013 miss universe preliminary competition, all that's going on is royalty creating the king boss player proofreading environment, I just like to get paid in full, and lean back in different states, it's winter time, it's 60 down here, no snow on Christmas, this playerrifical.

If you ever hear about a king cheating to win in the game of life, instead of flying straight, its gone be in the front page of the Journal Sentinel newspaper.

In order to stack up fat currency to increase big riches, or have something wealthily pile up, currency must be left alone, not picked up, just touched with moderation intentions, not greedily, or unplanned out intentions.

When it come to living this life, its best to hold what you got, because what you want might not be what you need.

Its always several ways to do everything, the styles, a time limit, specific certain places with specific certain people, to do the do with, sometimes what you think, will not apply to everybody you know, or meet.

The objective with currency is simple math, keep it flowing your way hourly, by making it work for you, at all time, its your tool towards getting on your lifetime throne.

226

I'm watching retired International Red show, the fashion experience, title of show is, "Keep it Boss Player," and he speaks Pacific Ocean deep on the game of life, from a seasoned veteran perspective.

Know what you doing, before doing it, income outcome, long term effect, short term effect, its all about mastering the game of life.

In order to know how to make currency work for you, you got to have experience with it, to know what to do with it, beware of those who will take credit, for what somebody else did, stay out of sight, out of mind.

In these times, money make the man work for it, instead of the man making currency get a lot of jobs, investmently speaking, men now a days, don't know, that they supposed to make money work for him.

A currency maker, aims to steer away from checking somebody else traps, its better, to stay paid specifically from self own blessed money routes.

Reality is if its meant for you to be wealthy, well off sort of speak, it will happen, that's no matter what happens, to prevent it from happening.

Show & tell purposes is, I show you how to be advanced mentally to progress physically, & financially for a life time, for a fee, so if you super glue yourself to the coach who schooled you, a lifetime of turning dreams to reality, will be in full effect, in fractions, that mean game is sold not told for free to those who don't respect game.

When it come to being financially satisfied, self discipline is mandatory, control your nature, master your mind, body, & soul.

Self Discipline, is what creates a wealthy person, in more ways then one.

Build longevity on solid ground, a man is, he who plays by the rules, & laws, he fly straight ahead with out taking no short cuts.

Its all about learning the language of every land you touch down on, also being where people is respected, and not being in love with currency.

Its a solution to every problem, an answer to every question, eliminate hazardous situations, walk light, think priceless, & sacrifice wants for needs.

Business is not a back & forward war, its negotiating, making verbal, paper contracts, its priceless suggestions, to generate long term consistent income.

Keep everybody out your business, if you ain't gone be doing no business with them you like that.

Having more then one currency route is comfortable living, financial satisfaction, save, & fund raise.

Business partners must be helpful, beneficial, not distractions, also they must serve a purpose, & have good intentions.

A fool is bad for business, deal with everybody on the level they on, be with progress, or without progress.

A boss player day to night, is based around stocks, bonds, shares, owning businesses, properties with intentions to master real estate on all levels, straight monopoly living Sean puffy combs style, Percy Miller Master P, j. Prince, jermaine dupri entrepreneur style

I'm in half moon New York watching the New York Yankees verse Los angles angels, Yankees is up 11 in bottom of 8th, & angels has 5, gas station is selling jolly green giants, New York upstate is aggressive unnecessarily, but it's probably the way to be in the mountains.

Leigh s. Truth beyond belief: You ever feel like God is telling you something? Maybe you're worried to try something new but you don't realize you been surviving out there for awhile. Maybe he's leading you right now to where you are meant to be,You always said you wanted to be somewhere else he lead you hundreds of places and meet so many people for a reason, He's literally been doing what you asked. Maybe he's slowing you down to try to make you see it.

THE LAST MACK STANDING SCRIPTURES

6.

Step in smooth to lay It down thick, straight grinding like they do in Little Rock Arkansas, got to learn how to live, then learn how to earn, then learn how to make money work for you, then learn how to pull up shining brand new, like they say In Memphis, "this what game plus money do for you," if you learn how to direct traffic, Memphis know the business, on some project pat type stuff, It's all about getting life right, wealthy comfortable with longevity, and spirituality.

THE GAME OF LIFE

A person never knows, or knew what type of cards they was gone be dealt, from birth to earth, & who they will be surrounded by, so it's best to study lifeology, in order to stay ahead of the game of life, in style.

Neither does a person know what state, or city they will start their life in, or what type of situation they will be put in the middle of, or what type of family they will grow up with, so therefore it's mandatorily important to analyze everyday, all day to night, everything that which will transpire.

My tenth magnificent birthday, it was on Sturgeon Moon August 3rd, 1991, the 215th day of the year, on this well known boss player holiday, I found myself eating a Heinz ketchup sandwich, feeling poe, broke, & lonely inside my Auntie Barbara Diane's one bedroom single family house, with all that being said, I wasn't sad mad, or glad, I call it surviving, and in my childhood, I recognized that off top, it could have been my natural ability to adapt to everyday life in this lifetime, from that point on.

When I finished my creative hood meal, for some unexpected reason I looked at the Black, old town wall clock on the wall, I saw two German born roaches, both German born roaches was together crawling inside the black wall clock, & the arrows inside the black wall clock was pointing at the number ten, & six, symbolizing ten-thirty in the morning, inside the 100 square foot, one of a kind, was an unionville New York mansions looking carpet, laid out nice in the living room, the tv was on, it was showing a tv show called, "the players' tribune," with Quinton richardson, and darius miles, they was interviewing Kobe Bryant.

Then something in my thoughts inspired me to leave the 29th wells street studio apartment sized kitchen immediately, so I decided to aim myself towards my auntie nice sized master bathroom, it was two doors inside the bathroom, I went through the door by the hunter Douglas, silhouettes looking blinds that covered the window, it would lead me straight up towards the pigeon squirrel headquarters, also known as my auntie attic, I slid the door open quietly, I did it right before I aimed myself up the stairs, minutes later I found myself sitting in the dusty attic, directly in front of the wooden window ceil, with a Bald Eagle's eye type of view directly in front of the house.

While sitting like Chicago pimp king baby bell on his solid gold diamond infested throne, I was being entertained by the sounds of three African olive baby pigeons, they was hidden in the ceiling somewhere, one baby pigeon was crying for food, I think they was living inside a nest, it was inside somewhere in the roof of my auntie attic.

Sounds of 1991 Nike air max squeaking tennis shoes started creeping up behind me, I started hearing soft, yet strong feet, that which was walking up the dusty attic squeaking steps, I played like I didn't hear it, at the same time, like a Chicago muzzle mouth Hebert Horner project pit bull, I was looking out the corner of my eyes.

But for some reason, I couldn't resist turning my head to look, it was wise, witty, slick, kind hearted, comedian uncle Geno, the unsigned soul singer with my other uncle, John twin brother Mr. Eddie Crum, the nickel tall man, with the six-foot spouse.

Simultaneously, synchronized together like they planned it out, they said, "happy birthday little boss player nephew with a gangster mother."

I somewhat smiled sadly siamotainously full effortlessly attempting to look excited with a crooked smile, then I said, "pimp pimp," & right after I spoke those two words, they both replied, "hurray."

Respect to the McBride sisters collection.

Something in my round brown wavy hair bald fade, with an Larry Johnson Stephen Marbury part in the middle of my head, with a demonic evil voice in my mind, it was telling me to say it again, then I said, "Pimp pimp," & once again with a devilish grin on both their faces, they replied hurray, followed by some sneaky Mike Myers, Dr. Evil type laughing, it can be pictured wrong, but I know they was being right, with good elder intentions to a close youth to them.

My uncle Geno ladies love cool j licked his lips, then within a night owl blink of an eye, he took a R.J. Reynolds pull off his Newport 100 cigarette, identical to a Chinese pitch black samurai dragon, smoke viciously fought its way out his nose.

For some reason he just paused for the cause to think brilliant, he memorable momently Was thinking specifically exactly about what my father would say to me right now, for some reason, I already, like Jesse say, knew what he was thinking, as I looked deep in his eyes directly at his eternal soulful spirit, it was like I was admiring my reflection in the glare of his eyes.

Stuttering, then he buster douglas punched his words out his voicebox, he did it with house party full force strength, & then he said, "b b bbefore taking that next step, concentrate on looking in the direction you going into, from more than one angle, such as the income, outcome, the benefits, & the consequences before you get into the situation, you aim to get yourself into."

Before my uncle Geno finished passing capitol good longevity game to me, rudely yet respectfully with Old English on his breath, my humble uncle Eddie Crum said, "nephew, here go a hand size bottle of Moet, strictly for your 1st decade on earth, because, I know you going in the major leagues professionally as a minor, so get prepared not scared."

Uncle lightskin Eddie Chicago born Crum, he was looking directly at me with Cheech & Chong looking eyes, his Brandon Roy, comedian reeno light skin eyelids was slowly dropping lower than Redman Brick City eyelids, & with capital game coming out his mouth, he was drunk with ism ready to be passed to the next generation, like 1998 Tywon, he was smiling from ear to ear, like he was taking a Chicago picture, sitting in a hay straw made chair gangstsfied, like New York bronx born kane & able.

My uncle Eddie Crum stood on his square the boss player way, respect to Harlem world Mase, uncle Eddie crum wiped his mouth with some Acanthus Napkins, on the low, he stole the napkins swiftly out his work pants pocket, then he said, "The earth is your turf nephew," he was saying that with a Shine's 24-karat gold rolling paper joint In between his lipes(pleural) you like that, at the same time he had one of them gas station thumb burner lighters in his hand, he was ready to make yoga flame up his John Wayne.

My fast Harlem world hustler, slick talking uncle Geno said, "memorize that capitol game recognize capitol game little pimp," I opened the dusty chipped paint led poison window, it was a 2020 Lexus RX hybrid riding

234

pass, with a 6th street hustler named bud, he was driving, sub woofing twista song, it was called, "game recognize game."

To my knowledge, my hustle hard(resrespect to mr. Ace hood), 9 to 5 working uncles, truthfully they was tow down that morning, but they meant well, and they only had good game to hit me with, that which would last a lifetime for me, and I'm still using that throwback longevity good game til this day, right now, at this present moment.

So I paid close direct undivided very serious attention, specifically to what dripped off both their lips, even though they weren't sober at that moment, they had Cleveland Good Game on their mind, in them, with good intentions to put me up on, um tum bout, straight capitol game, strictly to succeed successfully in my lifetime, identical, similar like billionaire Shawn Carter.

Then my uncle John twin brother Eddie Crum said, "before you go where you gone be at today nephew, take this good game with you," then he said, "dedication, determined to accomplish goals, hard work payoff, live to learn, learn to live, give to receive, receive to give, look, listen, learn, pay attention to details, stick close to who stick close to you, they have to have good long-term intentions to uplift you, & do that all y'all life, it's absolutely mandatory to master the art of separating real from fake."

I looked all the way down at me feet mon (respect to Jamaicans wherever you at in the world), I began noticing my right foot Belvedere crocodile sneaker shoe strings with the plastic tip, it was untied & tearing off, so I kneeled down boss player wearing a mink style, to tie up my 1991 Belvedere crocodile sneakers, being sold today in moshoes store in downtown, skinny crowded streets, Bill Cosby, Leon muhammed noi, absalom Jones, James forten, mrs. Frances e. W. Harper, John t. Gibson, crystal bird fauset, jill Scott, freeway, Cassidy, gillie the king Philadelphia, that's boss talk, brought to you by the boss player Association.

Then my uncle Geno, he struck an el clasico match, he did it to flame up my Uncle Eddie Crum leaves, these was some leaves that got cut off Cecropia rain forest trees, these Cabrini greens was rolled up in a Juicy Jay's rolling paper joint.

Keep in mind, some of us skipped boss players classes, game is mandatory in this lifetime, miss one day of all game classes, is identical to missing years worth of game, once again, find who got their game tight, ask not want not, I tell myself to do as the king does, it's mandatory king thinking.

Then uncle Eddie Crum inhaled deeply, like Teddy Lenox Bruckshot, next he just let the smoke escape out his nose, it was like it was being held hostage, like private ryan, it looked like he was in a Native American peace treaty(indigenous), then the money green smoke crawled out his mouth, before I knew it, he was surrounded by "weed is from the earth, it was put here for me & you, take advantage man," Chris Tucker Smokey smoke.

Then uncle eddie said, "let me lace you up with this Westside Chicago ism," when he said that, smoke was Robert Taylor, beat street, break dancing out his mouth, he said, "the game of life exists because we all participants in this lifetime for a reason, simply to serve our purpose, receive what's coming to us, for us doing what's required to transpire, to qualify us to be satisfied by the source to all that is."

From All I saw, it was when the smoke clear, like three 6 mafia, then every time the smoke tried to clear, uncle Chicago born Eddie twin brother Crum, he took a fat Mavado Popcaan, snoop Lion, up in smoke tour pull from his Raw pre rolled Compton style rolled joint, it was creating more smoke then a 1970's building burning in the Bronx, no disrespect.

It was like a horror movie mist of smoke rain mountain top fog, it was dancing around us, it was Smokey like a Los Angeles California wild fire in Northern California, similar to when motion picture film ghost appear in mysterious scenes.

Then uncle hard working Eddie Crum said, "your shoes have been officially laced up, now put some pep in your step, & get where you going young pimpin', go start your king of the royal family lifestyle, you been blessed with ism to master the game of life, & build your future comfortable for you, and your future kingdom, peace & blessings."

Then he smoke choked, then he turned his head coughing, barking like a beans & honesty, rocky & caine pitbull, he was trying to cough talk as smoke escaped out his bbq grill, he said, "this some Harry Anslinger banned killer weed, do this for your uncle little pimpin, don't be like me, learn from me."

While sitting his old English 40 oz down on the dusty wooden floor, my uncle Geno said, "put yourself in park, put your hazard lights on before you burn rubber, like too $hort, I got a Jay-Z Too Short real boss player,

236

two new York Knicks to give you, "golden opportunities come when they supposed to, just like blessings, or an eclipse, meaning stay ahead of what's occurring, simply because you can walk right into your soul mate, wife, or guardian angel, without even knowing, or seeing that day coming around the corner."

Then uncle Eddie Crum parachuted from off cloud 9, then he said, "You getting this good game for free, always remember the game is sold not told, so appreciate what's handed picked, & given to you nephew, that's from now to forever in our country, and outside of our country, to where ever you end up next royalty."

I'm watching roy jones fight percy Harris, what a fight this is, I would pay to see this fight, thousand dollars, or better, only cause I know it's gone be entertaining, own agree with indigenous soul people fighting one another, or killing Indigenous soul people, respect to all, just found out j prince from the land of houston, king j was setting up boxing matches worth armor trucks of currency, for mike & roy to fight years ago.

Next he said, "Open your eyes, find out why you got the solid gold chance to be handpicked to exist."

After that, I grab my small nine-inch bottle of Moet, pimp stick walked hood rich style sideways down the dusty attic steps, you know how the real ones did just that, I made my way down the steps to the first floor, grabbed some Daishowa tissue for my pocket, & shot like a dart out Nate Wingo hand, straight out the front door, down the porch steps, fearlessly into the concrete jungle.

As I walked flat footed on the side walk, right pass Melvin grandma yellow white house, straight up the street towards Mr. Dicks grocery store, all I could think about was what both my parents told me in the hospital, & what my uncles just told me today.

I saw Sam with the curvy mustache, he was riding his horse twenty feet north of excel barber shop, on 6th and center street, what's up mr. Terry, & lapham park projects butch, he drove pass on a pitch black north star Cadillac, he was playing Curtis Mayfield song, it's called, "little child running wild."

Curvy mustache boss player status Sam, he was going north up six street, while the boys of the struggle was grouped up, all was wearing suave tan {Clarks} hustlers, they was standing gangster style, right on 6th Hadley, directly across the street from Hispanic Sam's corner store.

Funny was still alive around this time, I saw Tim dog, Snoop Steven, Cory, & Shawn dog on 7th Hadley, they was throwing rocks over the fence onto oncoming traffic on Interstate 43 high way, this what kids do when they not supervised.

Without thinking, a kid being a kid, with no adult supervision in sight, I joined in the rock throwing, we threw rocks until we heard tires screeching, then we ran like we was being chased by Los Angeles police helicopter, straight scattering like German roaches when somebody turns the lights on in our home, back then.

We then would find ourselves picking sour plums off some older lady back yard tree; she had a garden of fruit trees, & vegetable garden, this was right by 6th Hadley, she had the only house in a 5 mile radius, with some real fruit trees, and a vegetable gardens, far as I knew.

Mean while, my bow legged little cousin named Deon D Block, he was flipping on the hood mattresses, on the side of his mother house, in the open field by that present moment tree stump, it's still there today surprisingly.

After I left my once in a lifetime childhood friends, I aimed for D Block doing backwards hand springs on the dirty alley hood mattresses; I was walking to him eating the sour plums, with intentions to do the most backwards handsprings any of us ever done, in that Indian summer grassy field I did around 21 backwards hand springs, ain't gone catch me going upside down now a days, we was flipping for real back then on some olympic gymnastics type stuff, what's funny is how good we was why didn't get chance to compete in gymnastics Olympic tournaments.

When I was walking pass the corner store, a man stood on a gray house porch, he was pimpishyly wearing a beaver brown borsalino fur felt hat, with a matching al capone three piece suit, with a black brown silver silk tie, with a Patek Philippe watch, with a pink gold bracelet, it had to have over 50 pink diamonds, & two chopard blue diamond pinky rings, he was the definition of a pinky ring street king, and he was wearing pitch black jungle predator hornback lizard dress shoes, he was at a house going towards 6th & locust, right near the alley, three, or four houses down from Ms. Linda Jefferson house.

At the same time, I noticed across the street, I saw preach mack, & his brother Shawn, they was headed to the corner store to buy old English, & swisher sweet blunts, og aj I think was locked up, then I noticed they was wearing suave tan hustlers, hugging tight on their feet, also known across the country as Clarke wallabees, Milwaukee called these shoes hustlers.

Something told me to stop walking to watch the brown copper skin man in the suit, I started watching him telling a young lady, a pretty like Janelle commissiong, & sexy like 2011 Miss Wisconsin Shaletta Porterfield, he told her to, "kick rocks, pet your feet on the concrete, zip your lips, stop back talking, & get a pimp currency stacking."

Her face looked Cynthia Brown sad, she licked her Rachel Acenas lips, fixed her Linda Li number one prostitution clevage, then she magan the stallion donkey walked away, she was shay shaunda sister wiggling her hips, it was similar to Amber Rose walk, & she said, "yes big money sunny."

She wore an Aubrey O'Day mahagony see through short skirt, with an eye grabbing appearance, she was looking tight, & right for all night, she was wearing Christian louboutin, alley cat black, constella ankle boots.

I stood twenty feet from him, it was like I was a Fox 6 cameraman, my eyes turned into Binoculars, I started looking at all this with amazement, I was standing by the corner, on the block, then I began to start tossing the plum at the sewer, I did it with my 187 ml hand size bottle of Moet in my hand, I peeped somebody california looking, he was coming west from 5th Hadley, it was double trouble, he was driving his lowrider, driving on three wheels, he was bumping kid frost song called, "la Rasa."

I stood froze motionless, I was watching that Kim Murphy, she was a nice height lady, she disappeared out his sight, he saw me watching her; he started smiling like he saw a chicken eating an orange, he had his eyes on his money, and his money on his mind.

Then he fixed his Flawless Fancy Vivid pink diamond index ring, then he straightened his herringbone chain out right, & he said, "hey little pimp, let me buy that Moet from you, what you doing with that anyway?"

I peeled my eyes off her; I looked at him silently simultaneously scrunching my eyes, because the sun was triple beaming that day, brighter than a 2017 Ford F-150 pickup truck head lights, in the middle of Bradford Beach, after midnight in January.

Then I timidly with a shy scared voice tone, I said, "my birthday today."

He smiled happily, so hard his teeth almost cracked, then he said, "how bout that, happy birthday, guess what, my birthday today, not only that, my uncle Iceberg Slim's birthday is tomorrow."

With an awkward moment confused look on my baby face, I just stood there speechless.

Then he looked at the 1991 grey Honda Civic going pass us, then he turned back looking at me, & he said, "Here's twenty dollars for that Moet."

I looked at the twenty, then I said, "Just for this little bottle, you gone give me twenty dollars?"

He looked up at the red Chevrolet Corvette ZR1 zooming pass us, it was behind me, then he said, "that's why you in front of me, you getting setup to lose early in your life little pimping, that's why it take a village to raise a child."

He pet his pants pocket to search for his box of R. J. Reynolds Newport 100s, I guess he changed his mind, or didn't have the cigs on him, so he looked at his porch table, directly at an silver jadeite ashtray, it had a half smoked sugar knight Fred Williamson Fidel castro favorite cohiba cigar in it, next he picked it up, just to put it in between his lips, finally he covered it like the wind was blowing, & with a Vic lighter flame, he lit it up Gangsta Player Con Man Pimpishly.

The giant Inhaled cool as he knew how to do, roaring twenties style, out of nowhere, he pointed his lips towards the sky, straight blowing 65 cent worth of smoke out his mouth, then he said, "you saw who I was talking to?"

I said, "Yes sir," he took another pull off his cigar, just to blow a fat ball of smoke out his mouth, directly in circles, then dragon style out his nostrils, the rest of the smoke came out aggressively.

He elderly Humbly looked at me fearlessly, with the eye of the tiger, then he said, "That's a lady of leisure, she a member of my spectacular blessed royal family, due to me being unable to get a real job with benefits because of my police record, we working for the devil disappointingly."

Then his face started looking frowned up after what he said, looking directly up to the sky, it was if he hated what he was doing, giving a hint

240

to above to beyond, simply to say he was living a lifestyle he didn't want to live no more, or later, but he was good at living this lifestyle, one way, or another.

Then He said, "before she walked off, I told her there is no time for nonsense, life is too serious to be playing games, let certain people, meaning your royal family know what you thinking, not everybody plays fair, although its fair game in my lifestyle, running game on people that recognize what they visualize, makes them loose respect for you."

He told me to, "Come close to hear what royalty got to say."

To me, it seemed like everybody felt like they had to pour out their heart for some reason, when they stood in front of me, & make all types of confessions so I can pray for them, I found that out years later.

He then began saying, "sometimes in life, people end up next to people who will say something to redirect them towards their destination, because certain people is trying to send them off course, Directly, or indirectly towards a dead end, literally."

When he paused to puff on his cigar, he did it big shot in a yacht style again, I said, "You talk like my father, this the same way he spoke to me, & that lady you were talking to, she looked sad, but happy, like my mother looked the last time I saw her."

He blew out grams of smoke, then he said, "Were they at now little pimp?"

With my face falling down low to the floor, my eyes looked down at my Belvedere crocodile sneakers, then I said, "All I know is what my auntie Barbara Diane told me," he interrupted me, & said, "hold on I know your auntie.

I'm watching knuckleheads s6: e4 the players' tribune with Jamal mashburn.

JOURNEY WEALTHY LONGEVITY SCRIPTURES

12.

Everywhere you go, be on the prowl to see if that city got benefits for you on the business tip, vehicles, homes, a new crew, or new members bringing something to the table, showing a down for life mentality, simply to be in the royal family, to help the royal family get wealthy on the journey to longevity.

I'm In Forsyth Georgia chilling with a gangster lady from Ohio, Im editing this part of this brilliant book, sad to say, in Texas It was an 100 plus vehicle pile up, something about an ice storm.

CROSS COUNTRY LIFEOLOGY

Go through these days to nights, go through none stop til self get to self final longevity destination, Michael Jackson said, "don't stop til you get enough," sometimes specific people have to leave your jurisdiction, simply so you can grow, & develop into your full potential.

Competition be wishing to be competition, two different directions will not have the same map, being yourself brings growth, & development.

I'm watching California classics hood movies, a street life philosophy movie called, "the art of thug pimpin,"& it's well known about royalty, royalty will study the game from all angles, by analyzing all the genius ways the world play the game of life, straight boss player global classrooms be in session every day, everywhere, student of the game of life be working on a lifeology master degree, never forget in a million mackin years that game came from whence the rain came.

We all must learn how to be strong consistently in the lifestyle we assigned to live, do what you can when you can immediately, so you will not have to do it when it's time to do something else.

You got to go through something to know something about something, spiritual enlightenment will present itself to you politely properly in the most gentle way possible, which will transpire when you get down with the truth, In the most responsible way possible, all in the air you breathe.

In order to comprehend higher learning, you will have to study advanced intelligence, it's usually hidden in dusty books all over the world, straight hidden in darkness, books like this.

Adjust to what is going on where you stomp your crocodile sneakers at, then it will reveal more then what meets your eyes, specifically about this land of giants, also known as Mother Earth.

{Chicago raised indigenous individuals will be all over the world soul surviving, staying alive} Move swiftly smooth, quietly, unknown in an undetected way, like the rain when it politely falls out the sky in the land of Unconquered People, known as Florida.

Life naturally revolves around choice not force, simply because pressure bust pipes, pick who you let give respect to you, no force persuasion manipulation, it's known that reckless people will create chaos.

Because they sad mad reacting without thinking, with no regards to what the outcome will be, in what they make happen, similar to hurricane Katrina, or an inconsiderate tornado did on March 23, 1913 in Nebraska.

The eyes is the door to the soul, like ancient proverbs said, look in the eyes to the soul, of who you talking to, and who you looking at.

It's mandatory to have your kingdom tuned into your perspective, at all times, each member of the royal family, has to learn fast how to peep signs, signals, warnings, and patterns to protect themselves, as well as their royal family.

Depending on where you at, it reflects on what is important to you in your world, you need not more than what you have, the queen wisdom has once, or twice strongly spoke quiet to your long term memory bank.

All your present moment tools is exactly what you require specifically to do what need to be done, in your unique lifetime.

Woke up all in sweet home Alabama, sun just beaming proudly, I can smell in the air the presents of the past people with old old money, upholding wicked ways around me.

The long gone past behavior here has dug a hole to fall in, those who wasted their life showcasing hate, hunts this land in the shadows, simultaneously, truth lives with a chosen few here, for all the righteous reasons, simply to rewrite history, the way how it should have been.

The Most High sees all, knows all, truth be spoken, truth be heard, two eyes in the sky, the sun, and the moon see all, past present future, peace and blessings.

When somebody try to feed you crumbs off the dinner table, but you require a full meal, find a new way to feed your hungry desires, without leading self down dead end streets to eternal traps.

Associate with major lifetime come up moves, moves with no short cuts, distance yourself from set backs, it's mandatory for everybody to respect great longevity game.

Survival of the fittest is the life long truth, dedicate time to strengthen your mind, like Dezarie said, it's a mandatory survival method, it's most definitely necessary to practice perfecting life every time you wake up, day, or night.

I'm still in sunny little rock Arkansas listening to lil flip, "recline and shine," song, at the same time watching bikini destination, all that while editing me giant book, puffing jazz band black smoke, reflecting on the word family true meaning, and purpose, it's usually to bring the best out of you, in more ways then one.

Absorb no one negative energy, allow them to release it another way, stay out of sight, and out of mind.

Allow only specific individuals in your business, specific individuals who ready to surf on blessings, with prayers in their hands, all the way into your Kingdom.

Don't speak less expecting to get the best results, what you put in is what you get out, and continuously listen to mother father Most High.

First things first, which is the Most High, recognizing those last will be first, do on to others as you want others to do to you.

Change will organize things in your lifestyle, liquor opens doors to the mind for spirits to possess the body, stay distance from the evil spirits playgrounds.

Keep a distance from holes in the wall, places of illusions, a place wicked spirits gather to dwell, occupy time with what helps you, not what destroys the goodness in your existence.

When the wrong people in control, it stops people light from shining, if somebody road trip with you, in advance hit them with greyhound money, just in case it's time for them to get back where they came from.

Somebody can bring the best out of you with words, and somebody can bring the worst out of you with words, it's a fact of life that words is powerful, words grouped together properly creates power for the communication conversationist.

Successful people become who they lined up to be, because others believe in them, following their lead, learning fast how to help themselves, and their leader.

Enjoy knowing what to say, when to say it, how to say it, why to say it, where to say it, what to do, when to do it, how to do it, why to do it, and where to do it.

When why how why where, sentence, and paragraph these w's til you master communication conversation.

Know what details you issuing out, who you issuing it out to, why you issuing it out, where you issuing it out, and how you issuing it out.

Who you are, and what you see ain't always the same.

When drifting off from the truth, distractions will full effortly attempt to distract you, while temptations sneaks up on you to tempt you, all this happens after drifting off away from the forever beautiful truth.

It's always strictly business, recognize decorations symbolize graduating to greater heights, every part of your lifestyle, it has a spiritual personal, & business side to it, believe that.

It's mandatory to know if anyone ignores you, you, or what you saying is unimportant to them, possibly that person is a distraction, setting up to tempt you, to drift you away from what is important.

One situation always leads to another situation, it's rewards for actions provoking progress to escalate to higher levels, with that being said, steer clear of uncomfortable currency.

Beware of infiltrators hiding in plain sight, when hidden doors slowly open, step in smooth to lay your game down thick.

Be well aware of those who entertain people, while others aiming to educate people, practice keeping everything above sea level progressively, stay in your own realm.

Never assume the roll of somebody spokesperson, it's obvious we all influenced by what transpired in our lifetime, mainly during our childhood.

Super glue yourself to the ancient wisdom seeking speakers, get your higher learning from what drip off their lips, grow with their daily lessons, and be their student with a full effort.

Advance your intelligence, find your kind, game recognize game, if they lacking in that department, share game with them to help them step their game up, lend a hand to your brother man.

Looking directly in eyes is reading a person inner thoughts, so you either get studied, or you study others, the Indigenous soul people is the true most high thinkers of the lands.

Cleverly discreetly teach them, train them without them knowing, because they might get offended pridefully, or scared to go outside the box they stuck in unknowingly.

The mysterious advanced mind with good intentions is consistently feared in a horrible way unfortunately, also hated in a misunderstood way, very rarely is this type of thinker loved, and appreciated.

I'm listening to Suga Free song, its called, "I need my doe."

Respectfully recognize those ahead of their time, keep enough distance to study them in an unrehearsed way, let their unrehearsed life be your study guide of what not to say, do, or think, or be fooled how theY prevent themselves from being fooled, by anyone.

People everywhere is books, read them, study them, master self mind, body, also the world you live in, that's what capital game helps make happen, don't be mastered, or figured out.

Boss Player haters gone make excuses why a solid player outshining them, an Iowa encounter was showcasing hateful upbringing behavior characteristics traits, from only one person, everybody else was straight like Tim Hardaway, and Shawn Kemp mansions gates.

Memorize that it's mandatory to keep those who lack capital game out the business you handle, strictly deal with the solid real ones that strictly deals with reality.

Journey Wealthy Longevity, the sun gone shine, Game gone rain supreme, it's all about accumulating accommodations in this lifetime.

All up in Oklahoma reflecting on this lifestyle journey thus far, simultaneously on top of my game getting ready for next year, taking December January off from currency route.

Thinking about Daytona beach, sipping on a Corona, making my royal family millionaires, like Antonino Fernandez, just by working hard preserving self, analyzing visualizing, earning turn time to shine.

Gone had let the heavenly rain fall on you, when it chose to, prepare for tomorrow today, no distractions while king mackin majorly, you know the business.

This the year to get down with the get down, longevity approved approves this brilliantly written book, and the insightful messages issued to you in unforgettable sentences.

Now the game you play, step it up to the highest level on some Mountain Kilimanjaro type stuff, step by step process, no time for nonsense if it doesn't add up, or create progress.

Live this life up in this world not down, if you join a team, bring something to the table that will help more then you will.

Know what needs to be known, to get to the next level in your journey to get wealthy, simultaneously finding longevity, you can't guide those sleep while their woke, we don't live for mankind, mankind lives for us.

Watch for the Roy Jones left hook sneaking up on you, it comes from those telling us they against us progressing, recognize when you ask the slick talker for something, you only giving out permission to the slick talking word play individual to ask you for something.

Master minds naturally master minds, not get their minds mastered, meaning never try to trick wisdom, unless you want to be tricked into a trap.

THE GAME OF LIFE SCRIPTURES

10.

Playing the game of life, is knowing how to roll it, live to give, give to live, it's about unity, team work works, it's a proven fact, teams have won championships, everybody need everybody, cross country living, will explain what the game of life scriptures is all about.

Respect to Kobe Bryant, respect to nba supreme legends, Ricky Davis, jr rider, Darwin ham, Tim hardaway, Richard dumas, Lindsey hunter, rafer Alston, Stacey augmon, god shamgod.

MASTERS OF THE GAME OF LIFE

Eliminating self-destruction, self-pollution, no smoking, no drinking alcohol, learn to live, while living to learn.

Rewards, gifts, trophies, enjoyment is for mastering the mind, and the body.

Saving currency, beneficial investments, stacking huge face colorful green backs, making it possible to buy property on all levels.

Age brackets, friendship memories, decades shared, brotherhood from birth will often lead up to identical perspectives.

A leader, a role model, a trend setter, a king to be, or not to be, sacrifice wants for needs, and keep doing what is mandatory to do.

Two eyes in the sky know all, see all, the sun, the moon, today analyze yesterday, so tomorrow you will know what to do from that point on, simple math, yesterday said do this tomorrow.

Focused eyes on the prize, standing on solid ground, keep a grip in more ways than one, so you won't slip, dedicated to being the greatest self-created to be.

Recognize what you visualize, know what need to be learned, look, listen, learn, earn your turn, time to shine, qualify to be satisfied, analyze, and strategizing.

Experience experiences, studying each specific detail, mistakes make prosperous progress, intelligence forms into brilliance, by way of seeking higher intelligence, aiming to memorize, and master the unwritten knowledge wisdom higher learning.

First sign of do not enter, dead end, one way street, don't hesitate to find an escape route, or hidden exit, follow your right mind, third eye guidance.

I'm listening to Fabulous song, its called, "throw it in the bag."

Aim high, shoot for the stars, have mandatory permanent standards, organize the lifestyle, stay in sync with reality, keep heads in clouds, super glue self to the Most High, and create a permanent relationship.

I'm listening to Wyclef song, its called, "low income."

In order to master the game of life, one must know what the game of life is, the game is an obstacle course, it is a purpose, and meaning to the game of life, dig deep to figure out what it's all about, also why you been chosen to exist, many are called to exist, but only a few is chosen.

Business beneficial decisions, at least ten bank vaults, at least ten business beneficial investments, stay gone in the wind, and make it your mandatory business to explore through the traveling door.

Small things to a giant, play with full effort, no weak links in the chain, those who keep you from drowning when you swim to deep, they deserve the royal treatment, & the highest form of respect, all kings have respect for the game of life.

Certain individuals will derail your train putting it on the wrong track, then you will consistently keep getting the wrong results, because you letting them stay attached to you.

Let time formulate what will transpire, recognize in society it's traps awaiting your arrival, its all about what you want to remain the same, & who you want to elevate with, united we stand, divided we fall, connect game, & cover all angels.

Its all about timing, a weak mind will be made a slave to the wicked clever, everyone must have an open mind to change, & respect the life everybody lives, life is setup by the Most High, make your best moves at all times, follow nonsense, & something that makes no sense will happen.

I'm listening to E-40 song, its called, "earl that's your life," the grandson said, "grandma I got a job like you told me," it's always cause & effect, words spoken, & moves get made.

Weak moves gone come when the mind being strong, never lose your identity biggie said, the humble always rule the jungle, & the quiet always starts the riots, if you want more in your possession, self got to qualify to get more.

The king show will go the royal way, either get ready to go, or stay here when its time to leave, when you know what is required of you, devise a plan to achieve it, receive it, & retrieve it.

I'm listening to, "Santa Clause Goes Straight to the Ghetto," it's a song by Snoop Dogg, Nate Dogg, Daz, and Bad Azz, straight classic death row suge knight california Christmas song, texas big pokey song, "hardest pit in the liter," it's playing now.

JOURNEY WEALTHY LONGEVITY SCRIPTURES

13.

Everywhere you go, be on the prowl to see if that city got benefits for you on the business tip, vehicles, homes, a new crew, or new members bringing something to the table, showing a down for life mentality, simply to be in the royal family, to help the royal family get wealthy on the journey to longevity.

Just left Columbus Ohio, stop & go visit, headed to New Mexico to do some sight seeing like a tourist, & escape the hate In the winter weather, the cold up here Is disrespectful, south for the winter is the way the game of life get played to win, rotate to regulate.

WHISPER IN THE WIND

Blessings, & love to the Most High, peace to the elements, peace to Amun Ra, peace to Mut nature, peace to above and beyond, peace to below and beyond, peace to inside and beyond, peace to outside and beyond, peace to all existence, may unity be amongst every pinch of Life, for all life that past present to future, may all Rest In Peace, peace to the soulful indigenous ancestors on earth doing the Will of the Most High, as we do the Will of the Most High, may they be born again to correct their mistakes, help others correct their mistakes, not making the mistakes they made, may they be blessed with the opportunity to make peace with the ancient ancestors, from the beginning to present moment, to time to come.

Whisper in the wind, cover all angels, connect game, John Amos said, "one to grow on."

THE LAST MACK STANDING SCRIPTURES

7.

Step in smooth to lay It down thick, straight grinding like they do in Little Rock Arkansas, got to learn how to live, then learn how to earn, then learn how to make money work for you, then learn how to pull up shining brand new, like they say In Memphis, "this what game plus money do for you," if you learn how to direct traffic, Memphis know the business, on some project pat type stuff, It's all about getting life right, wealthy comfortable with longevity, and spirituality.

I'm listening to Paul Pizzel, a cool breeze from Memphis, seem like he dedicated a song to his pimp brother named Pk, as well as others that played a part in his boss player lifestyle, the song is called, "Cadillac pimpin."

I'm in Famous Olive Branch Mississippi, I love this city with no hesitation, down south all in your mouth, indigenous soul people ask you your last name, just to see if they know your family, or is your family, ain't nothing like it.

I'm In Niagara Falls New York, I'm almost less than a thousand feet from Niagara Falls reservation state park, it's March with 32 degrees, a lot of businesses here is closed down, I'm in the heart of their downtown, right by the helicopter ride, it's closed for the season.

At this moment, thank you infinity to the Most High, specifically for the opportunity to have this journey through this lifetime, if I didn't get put on pause, I would be pimpin a hundred miles an hour, & not serving my purpose in life.

LIVING WITH A LIE

My eyes opened wider then tarsiers eyes, then I said, "My auntie said, my father was a worldwide gentleman of leisure, & me mother was a fearless lady in the United States army."

He took his last pull off his h. Upmann cigar, then he smashed the butt in a Versace home ashtray, simultaneously while blowing smoke out his nose looking like a Chinese Lou kang dragon, then he said, "look here young pimpin, let me run it down to you like this, appreciate what's handpicked to be given to you, always expect the unexpected, E-40 said, "know about the weather before it's about to change," & don't burn no bridges."

"Simply because you know not where you bound to end up next, believe not all you see, or hear, some people got preschool game underneath their belt, which will lead them to people above the level they on, which can be bad ending up good, or start off good ending up bad."

"Also be considerate, thoughtfully sensitive towards other people needs, when you meet your match, don't try to overrule them, or run over them, two brains work better than one, a good combination will equal accommodations, plus accumulation, see, people be so slick they become fools to wise people."

"Simply because slick people tend to overdo things, making themselves look suspicious."

What big money sunny was saying to royalty, it sounded like I needed to memorize it, so I said, "I hear you talking," then he said, "I know your daddy, I know your mother, & how I live young blood, this is exactly how your mother & father was living."

I was looking at him like I saw a haunted oak alley slave plantation West African ghost, then I said, "how you living?"

He looked directly at me without blinking once, it was like he was in judge thurdgood marshall courtroom, simultaneously he dug in his stomach for the best answer to answer my most important question, full effortly..

When he found the best statement to g. Dep, special deliver to me, with a life lasting message, he said, "to be Frank Sinatra with you, I pimpishly investigate Milwaukee professionally!"

A 1990 tree bark brown Buick Riviera, It road pass us very Bradypus pygmaeus slowly, creeping like an Angola cheetah, the kleinn automotive air horn started honking at him, he looked at the classic car, & threw up two fingers showing the player sign, then pimpishly started saying, "what up though," Midwest style, then he copped a seat in his eileen Gray designed dragons chair.

A clueless computer getting reprogrammed type of look, it snuck up on my baby brown Vaseline shining face, I stood their possum stiff, like I just heard somebody say, "a Japanese giant hornet is behind you."

He hiked up his hundred dollar Kiton K-50 looking slacks, simultaneously putting his hand on my shoulder, saying, "it's not about changing people, it's about working well with others, together we can make life better, never speak down on nobody, or broadcast somebody mistakes."

Once again like a respectful Louisville Kentucky young man, I looked up at him, & I said, "I hear you," he said, "as long as you listen, you gone learn."

He took a pause for the cause, & started talking again, he started saying, "don't cheat yourself, treat yourself, running from somebody, or something can sometimes back fire, because you could be running from who, or what was sent to you."

"Everything happens for an explainable reason, look for the main idea in stories, statements, sentences, opinions, & figure out who you dealing with, before you start dealing with them, & if you can't trust somebody, how can you put your life in their hands?"

Stunned, & amazed I said, "Tell me about my moma nem, how they were, what they were about, & how they live like you."

Out of nowhere literally, a Regina lady bug, It landed on his right shoulder, he gently fanned it off his shoulder, & said, "well your father was a true boss player everywhere he went, your loyalty before betrayal

267

mother, she was his number one lady of leisure, & they hustled the land with ancient wisdom."

With a Charlotte North Carolina respectful look on his face, he was admiring what popped up in his head to say to me, he said, "All that brother did was just sit back relaxing, rolling smooth in new luxury Vehicles, year after monkey face year, your father organized crime, somehow he managed to escape local hate, floss expensive Congo diamonds that shine like starlight in sunlight, on the weekends to holidays, he was tossing money in the air, it was like money grew on trees in his backyard, I think he had two African grey Congo birds In his pimp palace to, the California music gangster genius made a song called, "money by the ton."

"Now, your mother was game tight pimpin for him, on some truck turner Nichelle Nichols type stuff, as the main lady in his stable of certified hustling indigenous females, all year around she regrouped when need be, she recruited, she used greedy people like tools to get your father job done, so he could sit on a throne, she crowned him king, & everybody knew what was going on simply because she laid it out like that."

I'm watching Pomona Pimpin Young video, it's called, "I want to go home," featuring Pomona Drey, all Capital game entertainment, if you don't believe me, ask your local homeless man, or woman asking for help, ask them what Is the definition of all game entertainment.

"She harassed encyclopedias, dictionaries, also the soul people ancient wisdom books, with her pretty happy golden brown eyes, all the way until they gave her what she wanted, and she confused anybody trying to infiltrate their empire, your momma wasn't no weak sister, she was stone cold to the bone, her main aim was to be the number one queen in the country, for her Pinky ring street king, which was your daddy."

My heart was pounding like Andre Nickatina song, it's called, "six 15's," it was pounding like it was in Mac Dre's Mercedes-Benz 300 class's trunk, I looked straight up in the sky, & then I looked back directly at him, & I said, "I been living with a lie all my life."

He said, "Excuse my language; forgive me for cussing little man, but f?ck all that sentimental boo hoo sh!t."

He touched his head, his heart, his left side of his chest, his stomach, symbolizing an ankh, then he pimpishly blew a kiss to the sky, & said, "May the Most High bless the past, present, & future," then a black white Lamborghini with 24 inch rims in the back, with 23 inch rims in front, it was some Wayne Gretzky looking person driving the car, he was playing nbc spectrum sports radio station, the number 1nhl announcer Sean McDonough was saying, "welcome to the 2021 Stanley cup finals, the Canadians vs Tampa bay, " then the police came around the corner screeching tires zooming behind the Lamborghini, then the Lamborghini did a hat trick move on the police car, then all you saw was tires burning rubber, & smoke going down the block.

Then he opened the Moet Chandon Brut Imperial, It's the hand sized bottle that he bought from me, then he started pouring it up directly inside a Kohl's Chrystal king goblet glass.

Rest in pimp paradise to Sir C, a cross country pimping documentary dvd giant, he was from Wisconsin the world famous dairy state, It was once said, "he fount a fat money route in Las Vegas."

The glass, It had a couple tea spoons of that which look like famous Rhine wine my auntie used to be drinking during her leisure Time, simultaneously, he had a Sugar Bear brown napkin in his other hand.

I stood up on his top boss players palace porch, I was looking San Quentin state penitentiary angry, my face got Iraqi solider mad at me, because I made it frown, & before I knew it, I said, "my auntie lied to me," he said, "pause your voice box, respect the fact I revealed the hidden truth to you, I just put you ahead of what's going on, don't fall behind again."

"Now look little man, your auntie did what she was told to do, you a minor, not a major yet, meaning, you don't got no clout, or respect, or power yet, you got to put in work, earn your turn, and time to shine, to give orders, in order to move the crowd."

Coming from the direction of 6th Locust, It was the Jackson Mississippi chicken man, far as I know he always had fresh whole chicken, also fresh beef for sale, as he walked pass, he said, "hello brother Sunny," so Big Money Sunny said, "I'm just doing my best to be on my best behavior."

The chicken man said, "ok young brother, I know you is, do your best to teach the youth how to stay away from dead end streets, see you a little later brother Sunny."

Big Money Sunny said, "yes sir Mr. Nathaniel Wingo, I finally went to Olive Branch Mississippi, just like you told me, I miss it already, see you later Mr. Wingo."

He looked at me to say, "that's a hard working independent indigenous man, I respect him to the fullest, and I'm glad you got to see how indigenous men speak, and greet each other respectfully."

I respectfully interrupted him to say, "why you in my ear giving me all this good game, own even know you?"

He shook his glass in a circler motion, the Moet bubbles sizzled to the top, then he looked to the sky, & once again he said, "Most high, bless those that past."

When he swallowed his Moet Chandon that he bought from little, minor not a major yet me.

He said, "look little indigenous soulful original young man, don't make me regret schooling you, you got sent to me so I can pull your coat, and put some longevity game in your pocket."

Then with a terrorist ready to die serious look on his face he said, "from this point on little amateur pimp, whatever you do, or doing, put a full effort into it, be the best at whatever it is you put your life on the line to do, because you can get what's coming to you if you play to win, by playing with the cards you were dealt accurately."

He looked behind him, then turned around swiftly, next he started to get up out the chair he was sitting in, to tell me to sit down, next he sat in the California jalapeño pepper colored chair made out of straw, you know that chair everybody in 1980's Chicago took pictures sitting in, it had a mahogany colored wooden table, with dollar bills underneath the circle glass top, it was sitting next to the chair.

It had a bottle of Remy Martin Louis XIII sitting on the glass top, with a fresh unopened pack of Newport 100s, and a Rare Tiffany & Co Chrysanthemum Sterling Soup Tureen, it was full of cut up apples, kiwi, pomegranate, and blueberries inside of it, he said, "help yourself to these healthy body fruit, if you like nephew."

As he sat down, he took a Waupon prison inmate pull off his cig, exhaled it out his nose, siamotainously he was saying, "Keep up with what people saying, or doing, so you won't get played, or caught up in something, or become an innocent bystander in a cross fire."

He sipped the Moet Chandon again, then he said, "let me go get some Johnny Witherspoon ice cubes, you relax while watching everything moving like a surveillance camera," he got up to go in his boss player palace, he open the odl brisa standard retractable screen door, he walked in smoother than a billionaire will start up a garia edition soleil de minuit golf cart, in his living room the tv was playing the solid gold classic movie, "Harlem night," the volume was turned all the way down, in his dining room there was a 1935 zenith stratosphere 1000z radio, it was playing 8ball song called, "starships & rockets," then he stepped in the kitchen to the meneghini la cambusa refrigerator, just to get some o'shea Jackson ice cubes, then he made his way back to the porch, directly next to the smeg fab 28 dolce & gabbana maiolica collection refrigerator, on the marble counter top was a bottle of dame dash's dusko whiskey, and 50 cent's le chemin du roi rose champagne, & Memphis Bleek's dusse xo.

When he came out the screen door to sit down He said, "check this out lower case p," then out of the house front door, I heard his Sony cordless house phone ringing excitedly loud, and proud.

Quickly he said, "Keep an eye on what's going on out here, until I come back."

I sat in the chair scratching my head, like what am I suppose to be looking for, but I said, "yes sir," then I saw some fancy hood cars rolling about five deep, I heard the expensive car in the front banging a song called, "in Milwaukee," made by tha d.r.e.

Swiftly quickly like ball control Ricky from the king center crossover move, he slid in quick, and slid back out the front door in less than 98 seconds.

When he came back out the house front door, he had his game face on, he was pulling strings from his beard, genius thinking, simultaneously he said, "yeah you got sent to me for a life changing reason little p."

He licked his capitol game spitting' lips, his Benjamin Moor Pacific Ocean blue diamond's on his pinky rings, both started shining brighter than they ever did before, maybe because the burning bush of fire, I mean the Amun Ra sun was setting, at this time the degrees dropped to about 68 degrees.

Then I noticed he turned on some summer of soul music, all I heard was Soul brother James Brown Augusta Georgia say, "I paid the cost to be the boss."

One more time I saw him sip the Moet Chandon out his crystal king clear goblet glass; & once again, the bubbles sizzled to the top, when he sat down in his needle in a hay stack, straw made chair, he sat his glass of bubbly Moet down directly on the round Aisu glass table.

He blinked once, he blinked twice, then He said, "yeah like I was saying little p, some people will say the saddest stuff to get out of a corner, a trapped rat will bite its way out of harm's way, it's called the guilt trip game, that's when somebody get in your head, simply turning you into a bully in your mind, making you think they a victim in your head, were in fact, they actually tricking you mentally, by way of verbal conversation, communication."

I was thinking to myself, this man is not to be played with, he like a four-month-old Gator pit-bull with a muzzle on its face.

The stuff he telling me sounds so serious, I'm respectfully scared to interrupt him.

He took another sip of the Moet Chandon, then out of nowhere his hillbilly goat mustache mouth started smiling sideways, his eyes got wide, it was like he saw Micheal Jackson moonwalking down 6th street, curiously I turned to look at what was lighting up his candle.

It was a Hugh Grant European middle age looking man pulling up slowly, quietly in a black man wish, a BMW, that same pretty face lady I saw him having a conversation with earlier was sitting in the passenger seat smiling from ear to ear, smoking a hydro filled optimo, it was like she won the mega ball lottery, or something.

He said, "Ok lowercase p, make your way home before the street lights come on, you can stop by tomorrow for your second day in my class, I'm your professor, my porch is the University of Pimpology & Mackology."

He said, "What's your name?"

I said, "Mack Millon," he said, "that sound like your daddy gave you that name, but you need to put Mr. in front of that name."

He said, "It was nice talking to a good listener," I said, "it's important to look, listen, and learn," then he said, "I got king pimp business to handle."

He said, "Everybody call me Big Money Sunny, but you can call me uncle sunny nephew."

It was like I got adopted by the game of life, a cool breeze blew pass me whispering in my childish ears saying, "the game of life handpicked you to be the next pinky ring street king."

Now, looking back at all this, I come to the conclusion, I was too young to completely comprehend what all this meant for my future.

I'm in Phoenix Arizona, it's January, it's a warm pleasant 75 degrees, no snow, just cartoon looking cactuses, short height palm trees, traffic, don't even look like winter, I'm listening to New Orleans second line songs, it's close to Mardi Gras time, where did it start first, Louisiana, or Alabama, when you get proof, let everybody know.

THE LAST MACK STANDING SCRIPTURES

8.

Step in smooth to lay It down thick, straight grinding like they do in Little Rock Arkansa, got to learn how to live, then learn how to earn, then learn how to make money work for you, then learn how to pull up shining brand new, like they say In Memphis, "this what game plus money do for you," if you learn how to direct traffic, Memphis know the business on some project pat type stuff, It's all about getting life right wealthy comfortable with longevity, and spirituality.

I'm listening to New Orleans artist group, they called ghetto slaves utp, the song is called, "we out here," a song dedicated to the after effect of hurricane Katrina, after levees was said to have got blown up, it was said that it was a move made to rebuild New Orleans.

Now I'm listening to Chicago rap kings, and r&b king, the song is called, "overnight," do or die, snypaz, And Danny boy.

I'm in Phoenix Arizona, I'm listening to the spiritual greatness of bob marley, the song is called, "natural mystic," he said, "if you listen, there's a naturalistic blowing through the air," & he right, if you don't believe me, just ask the right indigenous soul person, anyone asking you for spare change in your so called ghetto, never liked that word, or used it in a sentence til now, the right Indigenous consciously aware soulful king, or queen, he, or she will give you a rundown, of exactly what is going on, Inside the world that we exist in at this moment.

Respect to Shaquille O'Neal, just drove through Newark New Jersey, happy birthday to mr. O'Neal, Orlando became the center of attention, Orlando became important, after shaq fu got drafted by the Orlando Magic, he brought millions of dollars to that city, maybe billions, leaning back on this March 6th 2021, I'm In Niagara Falls New York, appropriate place to get away from the money game, it's a new home waiting for you, saw the light show on Niagara Falls, saw Canada across the waterfalls other side, always enjoy Niagara Falls every time I park there.

CHURCH

The next day came faster than a Malibu California FedEx delivery; it was soulful Sunday morning, the day ingenious people call the spirituality day, the seventh day of the week, it's specifically for relaxing plus resting, & it was around burning bush Amun Ra sun rise 7am, a lot of the Eurasian wrench birds was singing, & dancing before people started coming outside, and the copper brown squirrels was running up & down trees, playing tag with each other, it was just a good feeling giving Sunday morning.

Every indigenous lady spiritual Sunday morning, a Christopher Columbus settler European man, descendant of a pilgrim European family, he known as Al, "Brown Station wagon," Rebbie, he would pull up listening to, "smile FM Christian radio station," he was coming to take me, and my cousins to East Brook church, also well known as Sunday school, services was being held inside riverside high school, it's purpose was strictly to show us how to become great Christians, it was like he was recruiting us for his pastor.

Al, "Station wagon," Reebie, he arrived at 7:50 something early every indigenous spiritual Sunday morning, wearing a Christian smile, camo hyperlight performance vest, & some blue Levi's with some white thrift store looking sneakers, the same shoes people buying today to wear, like Philadelphia Tyrone said, "no disrespect."

When he arrived to my auntie's four family single family house, I was in the small living room, I was watching: international red fashion experience tv show, the episode was called, "keeping it 100% boss player," then I heard al, "station wagon," rebbie, he would honk his horn three times when he pulled up, my auntie Lisa, she would be up making auntie Reese Eddie bean Chicago style coffee, all while talking to her spiritual adviser, auntie reesie, then my auntie would send us out the front door, one by one, directly after she put Vaseline on all our faces, and lips, she straight had us shining like New money, we all was on our way to church, ask Jim Jones.

He waved at my auntie, simply to confirm we under his supervision, he did that all while sitting in his pyramid golden brown station wagon, my auntie Barbara Diane stood in her door way, she was smoking a Newport 100, all while holding the screen door open, all while waving back at al as she watched us walk to his James Brown station wagon, she began to smile happily at her son, sir D, 13 kids Block, he was walking bowlegged behind me.

this routine took place all around this country, due to how the crooked system was setup to divide families, causing original indigenous soulful men presents to be absent for lack of currency, these indigenous men would be gone consistently, just to figure out how to survive in a world specifically setup to keep them down, when all the indigenous man wanted to do was just have a good job to provide for his family, specifically to afford a good life.

My little cousin Martell, Tells, Telly Toes, Phoenix, he was the last to get to the car; he was eating his food, and whatever we didn't bite off of, that which was left on our plate, you know in most poverty families the baby is usually the first to get the less, and last to get the most, so his survival instincts kicked in, especially when an opportunity presented itself, like indigenous soulful peoples say, "a closed mouth don't get fed," so he learned to get what is coming to him, especially when it's in arm reach.

Al, "Blue Jeans," Rebbie, he didn't watch TV much, all due to him knowing it would eventually control his mind, only if he watched to much of it, but he did have one tv in his house, but on our way to church, like Jim Jones, we would listen to, "talk smile FM Christian radio," & for the player life of me, I never could remember what was being said, it just was never music to my ears, I think my spirit rejected what was being said, the way it was being said.

I'm listening to Shawty (the giant) lo, his song is called, "that's shawty lo."

I'm listening to a world known usher song, it's called, "superstar," I mean he kilt it on this one, this that ocean side, or lake front song, it's that type of song, that song when you with a lady who stayed down with

279

you, a lady who play her part on all levels with no breaks no matter if she mad, sad, or jealous.

While in the passenger seat, I was thinking about my father taking me to church, instead of Al, "blue jeans," Rebbie, I also wanted my auntie to be my mother standing in that door way, and these thoughts would last all the way to the Sunday school, all the way to our chairs we would sit in, inside the Riverside High School church, we was all year around members of this unforgettable chuuuch.

When we walked in the sermon, the preacher was saying, "flattery being flirtatious, trying to hypnotize people with your eyes, it can be the same as digging a hole then falling in it, when you don't realize it's underneath your feet."

Then he wiped the sweat off his chin, & forehead, he did it with that custom made handkerchief, it was customized to match his fresh pin stripe two-piece wardrobe, for some reason, he never wore the custom made same suit, or alligator shoes ever in the same year.

If the preacher is preaching right, let him preach, if this world wasn't revolving around currency, he, or she would preach nonprofitable, but it don't work like that, so let them get paid, because if the congregation taught their self spirituality, what need would the preacher have in life, or purpose to be in a church, so each one helps the next one to be who they are, which is true facts of life, believe it or not, truth be spoken truth be heard, you can deny a lie, but you can't deny the truth, the truth will make love to your conscious until you finally embrace it.

Then he said, "Be well aware, that it's always ears listening, eyes watching, faces smiling, and faces frowning."

She was ocean cornbread fed thick, a very extremely beautiful lady, I never seen before.

My taller than me, Olympic Michael Jordan shoe wearing little cousin, he was eye contacting & smiling at her daughter, her daughter looked like she could be her identical twin sister, just a little taller, and they sat down quietly, they had proper Cheetah Strip Club etiquette.

I noticed all the man on the mother & daughter's left side, these man was sitting behind the mother, & daughter, these men was starring so hard, at these two lovely ladies, their eyes were kissing the mother, and daughter appearance all over.

I had a good life changing feeling, it was that this, Belleville Illinois looking girl's mother, my thoughts was, that she was going to be my reason for breathing, one day.

I never told anybody I love them, but my mind, body, and soul fell in love with her on first sight.

Then I grab my face, turned it towards the preacher, grabbing my ears to give them back to his voice box, and he then said, "turn to Romans 13:4."

He said, "love suffers long, and is kind, love does not envy, love does not parade itself, love does not behave rudely, or is not provoked, love thinks no evil, it rejoices in the truth enduring all things, because love never fails."

Then he said, "When I was a child, i spoke as a child, I understood as a child, I thought as a child, but when I became a man, I put away childish things, and faith, hope, love, these three was important, but the greatest of these is love."

The more he spoke, the more I looked at this lady, she caught me sneaking a peak at her, this was directly after she first sat down, she look like she was 8 years older than me, and that girl next to her, she started looking like her sister, not her daughter.

Then something told me to listen to every memorable words, that the preacher spoke, this spontaneous thought, it told me to pay full attention, full close attention to what dripped off the well dressed, the olive branch Mississippi born, cayman Islands alligator shoes wearing, Sean Diddy combs suit wearing, this John marrant type of powerful preacher, it was mandatory to catch everything that dripped off this Martin Luther king influenced by, preacher's lips.

Then the preacher said, "Now just give me your undivided attention everybody, focus with your mind on what I say, the most High speak through us to us, so as I preach the hidden truth in plain sight, I need everybody to hear me out, understand that my intentions is to stay focused on teaching the powerful youth of the past, present, & future of tomorrow."

It got Kalahari Desert silent, it was like somebody pressed the mute button on a Panasonic 152 inch plasma tv, nobody moved, yarned, coughed, whispered, no Oklahoma crickets made a sound, all babies fell asleep, and all ears was given to him.

The preacher said, "Who forsakes the companion of her youth, and forgets the covenant of her God?"

"Do not be wise in your own eyes, be fearless with righteousness as your protection, depart from evil," nobody blinked, or made any sudden moves, it was like we were all getting robbed by DMX, all the way back then, when dmx was in his twenties.

The preacher continued, he read from the African Heritage study bible, then he felt the spirit take over him, then he started preaching like bishop g.e. Patterson, he started saying, "a beautiful thing is never perfect my indigenous soul people."

I never paid attention to what this David unaipon aboriginal Australian looking man said before now, i never listened to nothing he said before right now, but right now, it's like my brain starving for the hidden truth, the hidden truth that which is living inside Indigenous soul people's wise minds, and he gave me straight food for thought, all game every brain needs to contain.

The preacher said, "For whom the Most High Loves, He corrects, just as a father mothers the sun, daughter in whom he she delights."

"The Most High by wisdom, founded the earth, by understanding, He established the heavens."

He said, "I enjoy what I do, because what I do, it enjoy me, I speak forward, and backwards."

Then the knowledgeable humble approachable preacher got a note from a member of the congregation, somebody was crying in the crowd peacefully, the preacher said, "pardon me everybody, I have to read these very important names, I need all to pray prayers for these soulful indigenous peoples, here's the names to y'all to pray for, peace & blessings to breonna Taylor, Marvelous Marvin hagler, & a young man named Lil d from Milwaukee Wisconsin, dorlett son, peace to blessings to all their families, let's all pray for their very important souls today."

Then he said, "something telling me, oh yeah somebody in here, I said somebody in here right now, they gone be great on their journey to find longevity, yes I said now, yes great, created to be the greatest."

"This person I'm speaking of is one out of a million suns blessed on a pathway that their lifestyle walks on, & royalty is loved by all people universally speaking, now, and forever."

I started feeling warm inside all over, it was like laying on the beach in liberty city Florida, as the s.m lockridge type preacher spoke, he speaking brilliance to the gathering of the indigenous spiritual soulful people, I started thinking about what he was speaking into existence, and about this lovely banana brown complexion lady, the type of tiara ashleigh looking woman, the type of woman every man couldn't stop looking at, it was like her existence was putting all eyes looking in a hypnosis type trance.

I sensed something from this Mississippi born spirit, I felt her baptized spiritual presence, everybody else in the church disappeared at that moment, it was just me, and her starring deep in each other eyes, Tony tone tones top song, it's called, "just me & you," that song was playing in everybody head as they all watched us, as they watched us starring deep in each other eyes at each other soul glow.

I started thinking about that unbelievable feeling, it was the feeling I had, the feeling I had the last time my mother held me, it was the time when she was telling me, "love is life, and life is love, she called me her, "soon to be crowned king."

Then I, "went back down memory lane," like I was Minnie riperton, I was thinking about when I was going to Dover elementary school, one day after a long day at school, I was on the glossy yellow school bus, this unique very attractive fifth grade girl, everyday almost after school every week, she would lay me down on her legs, just so I could go to sleep until my stop came up, she part of the reasons, the main reasons I enjoy laying on a woman so much.

Now this lady in church, this very unique beautiful lady, she got my heart beating fast, faster then Giovanni Hidalgo plays the Congo drums, i just want to rush to her, hug her, kiss her, and tell her I love her right now, I still feel the exact same way years later.

We both smiled like husband and wife, it was like we both was saying I do, and then we focused back on the Indigenous, reverend b. W. Smith looking pastor, he was preaching words, powerful words, renowned words straight from the Most High truth, he spoke from the book of life wisdom chapter, he also said, "the young cannot be born with wisdom and that they need the experience given by advanced age," he then said, "those was words from Ptah hotep."

THE GAME OF LIFE SCRIPTURES

11.

Playing the game of life is knowing how to roll it, live to give give to live, it's about unity, team work works, it's a proven fact teams have won championships, everybody need everybody, cross country living will explain what the game of life scriptures is all about.

I'm 30 minutes from Boston in Marlborough Massachuetes, me sour apple diesel, silver bullet kush, it's alright out here, plenty hills out here, wind blow hard so you can know it's coming, cost money out here, property value is over 3 4 hundred thousand, motel 6 super 8 cost hundred dollars plus for one night, Connecticut & Massachuetes Is big time money states.

SPIRITUALITY RESPECT
TO THE MOST HIGH

I'm in Houston texas, weather nice, looking good from what I see, plenty businesses everywhere, plenty lanes to drive, big city to me, right now Devin the dude banging, you know his song, it's called, "the dude," made me a Texas playlist to hear while I'm in Houston, I can hear Texas saying, "already," got to hit Milwaukee John up, he planted his roots in Waco texas, respect to the Most High for letting this transpire.

Respect to the land of rhythm & blues New Orleans, I'm listening to Rebirth Brass Band song, It's called, "rebirth groove," "if you gone roll with me, let's ride, let's ride," I'm in Phoenix Arizona letting New Orleans talk to the desert, "ain't nothing like a rebirth groove," February is Mardi Gras month, which state, Louisiana, or Alabama, which one you going to, let's ride if you gone roll with me, what's up to G from Georgia, he invited me to the Alabama Mardi Gras, he said we gone show y'all up north Midwest indigenous soul folks a down south tradition.

The Supreme Being is above all, below everything anywhere everywhere, beyond every distance, out of sight out of arms reach, the Most High is truth beyond belief with no competition, with two eyes in the sky, those eyes know all, & see all, so remember the Moon, and Sun is watching everything everywhere.

Guidance to paradise island comes from the Most High with a number one perspective, including knowledge that which is solid, and unbreakable.

The Most High delivers reliable help that is always ready to explain everything about everything, about everything that is required to be understood.

The Most High has ultimate patience, extreme intelligence, a brilliant captain, soul people one, & only Most High.

The Most High is the Master teacher, stupendous excellent preacher, soul people exclusive friend leading the way to longevity.

The Great Grand Father, the unseen, the most heard, the brightest light, and Creator of all that is.

The Most High is the greatest team coach, the true definition of real reality, lasting forever, being forever meaningful, always revealing ancient historic history.

The Most High is priceless, forever righteous, certified truth beyond belief, and automatically purified.

The Most High is Innocent with no guilt, the light in the dark, the dark in the light is the Most High.

I'm listening to Bob Marley song, it's called, "natural mystic," very spiritual for aboriginal folks around the globe.

The Most High is All that is, will be, has been, the pathway to wants, needs, and should haves.

The Most High is Always active with no pause button, intelligence to brilliance, and beyond the wisest ever will know to explain.

The Most High is Beyond powerful, beyond great, beyond exciting, beyond dependable, beyond loving, the Most High is the Almighty as the words was spoken in Chicago echoing to this present moment.

The Most High is Second to none, memorize that it will never get no better than the Most High allows it to be.

The Most High is Unidentified uniqueness, one is all, all is one, I Am therefore I exist.

Purpose, meaning united with no division, what is taught to be feared should be embraced by indigenous soulful people, which is truth beyond belief, welcome it, accept it, get better acquainted with it, build a relationship with it, that which is the Most High.

Stayed down mackin all my years, all I know is the Most High makes me who I am.

Countless hours of full speed ahead mackin with incorrect individuals, which led up to me being distracted away from the Most High, which is what I will use to build me up for the future.

This so deep you might fall asleep traveling this deep, antiques hold hidden messages from your life time time line, when dinosaurs lived in the animal kingdom, their was my ancient indigenous soulful ancestors, and all of them were serious factors in life, despite what you don't know yet.

I'm listening to Rakim song, it's called, "the mystery."

Those who talk the most is not in control, the native tongue of the land speaks loud, & clear.

So if a weak mind can't interpret what you insinuating, don't force them to understand, change subjects.

Then tell yourself to hold that thought like Gucci Mane said, and talk it to those who speak your language.

Memorize a new day is a new beginning, everyday will bring a battle of the minds, because it's a battle of truth verse lies, which will explain why today verse yesterday will be brought to your attention, which then will explain why a new day is a new beginning.

Entertainment is education, because education is your entertainment, that combination equals entertaining higher learning.

It's always eyes watching, ears listening, every life being lived is a life being learned by one, and all.

Think intelligent, react brilliant, memorize you live your life to earn your turn, & time, to shine.

Maturity, growth, development, progress without stress, leads up to true self-improvement.

Memorize that it will always be a solution to every problem, and an answer to every question.

The Most High is Wonderfully mysterious, recognize why people fear, and hate what they don't understand.

A San Diego pimp once said to me in my mind, "street ladies reincarnate into birds flying high exploring the world, as they please," the way they naturally needed to live their life.

A man is a man, a woman is something specialier than a man, with a unique purpose, and meaning, in a way a man will never be able to exist naturally as she does.

Sadness lives with the unhappy rich, while they survive their unbelievable days, and unspoken of nights.

Appreciate what is given to thou from above, and beyond, so use it with good intentions.

Spiritual enlightenment is a very necessary necessity, I was advised to tighten up once in Oklahoma, then in Missouri by my Virginia people, if your screws loose find yourself before your screws end up missing.

The truth will set your mind free, reprogram your computer (brain), get self-education from the Most High inspired inspirations that is hidden in every day life plain sight, and in books, and minds.

Hidden messages from here, there, everywhere, all the way to Texas, memorize, and always forever think positive before the negative.

Ask not want not, tricks lead to traps, and illusions create confusion.

Don't chase the trick, or traps, keep hands clean, don't powder your nose, look at everything from all angles.

Game is blood in the soul that you naturally born with it soul people, it flows powerfully from one generation to the next generation, recognize it drips off specific lips.

Recognize what you visualize while climbing up the food chain to the top of the ladder, it's like being born again, or in so many words escaping the womb all over again.

Truth is deeper than the ocean floor, you need a soul survivor to explore through the traveling door.

Don't test the best, test the rest, if you stand in the spotlight, you will lose all necessary sleep every night.

I Am therefore I exist, business is personal, personally business is always personal.

I'm listening to rapper rick Ross song called, "boss," featuring Miami Dre

THE GAME OF LIFE
SCRIPTURES

12.

Playing the game of life professionally is knowing how to roll it, live to give, give to live, it's about unity, team work works, it's a proven fact, that teams have won championships, everybody need everybody, cross country living will explain exactly what the game of life scriptures is all about.

Respect to the ancient soulful ancestors, and ancient great spirits, past, present, & future..

Respect to California giant freeway Ricky Ross, born in Texas, I'm listening to the rapper rick Ross song, its called, "blow," I believe one day, they will sit down, and chop it up.

Respect to Kobe Bryant, that's messed up he left how he did with his daughter, my auntie told me, "sometimes, it's just time to leave after you lived your timeline, you know."

SPIRITUALITY

Spiritual healing is feeling goodness greatness, that's what it's made for, that's what it's all about, free spirit, New Hampshire welcome sign says, "live free or die," not a slave to this world, that's what we are, free spirits, slaves to money, which is attached to this world, just live to serve your purpose, so Money will come to you in this world, that's the game of life professionalism, love is love new york say, life is love, love is life, who soul glow, who got personality, who got a love-able characteristic trait, you at home when something, somebody, something is yours, that's comfortabilities, it's the game of life, being soulfully indigenous is not an option, it's a privilege, it's a birth right, apply that to who you are, it's all the game of life, just play it to perfection, when you see the states you see it will tell you what life is about, it's like the animal kingdom, you appreciate your position, to have, or to have not, look forward to goodness, worrying is wasting time, I'm all in Montana, just went through Wyoming, now tell me this, ain't a blessing is called living life, if I can beat you walking, while you running, now that's the game of life, you got to respect when you realize that, it's mandatory, the truth will set you free.

Some preferably prefer to steer clear of truth beyond belief, soul music makes you feel sad, or happy because it touches your eternal internal spirit, it will be in a way, in a way the average person cannot begin to know exactly how to touch your eternal internal spirit, but if they know the formula, be impressed.

The strength of words is very powerful, a sentence can strike fear, uplift the depressed, it can motivate the discouraged, the art of communicating can perfect a person life, or create reasons to self-destruct it.

Whisper in the wind, speak to the unseen, guide the sleep walkers, send a message, send it to those who exist in life, after what is called death, because they doing it after they leave the physical self, you once knew.

To kiss the sky, to appreciate the Creator, is to close your eyes meditating escaping reality, just to meet your maker in a spiritual session.

To feel the energy from the sun, to feel the love from above, to bath in what you can't touch, yet only feel, is the truth beyond belief.

I'm listening to New Orleans artist utp song, Its called, "we out here," indigenous soul people out here world wide, take a look around.

What you put in is what you get out, what you say will be said to you, or yours, what you do shall be done to you, or yours, life is what you make it to be, or not to be.

Love is spoken, yet what is felt, is indescribable, no title, no definition, no way to know it unless you feel it, so saying it will be pointless, show, and prove like Missouri the show me state.

Head in the clouds, while feeling the breeze, sitting inside your drop top Chevrolet Camaro ZL1, while on your spiritual journey, wake up a sleeping giant so they can walk on a fallen star, to live on a shooting star, or just be down to earth, living in a lake front Michigan mansion, dealing with the lifestyle, & staying in your right mind.

Dr. Charles Finch said, "Heaven is where the spirit is, mind is where your world exist."

Inside your mind is what you allow inside, you spring clean it, process of elimination what pollutes your mind, body, soul, aim to only listen to feel good spiritual healing music, & associate only with spiritual people with good spiritual healing energy.

seek the Creator, and complete your 24 hours brilliantly, progressively, in a prosperous way, for longevity purposes.

What does biblos mean? What does ta biblia mean? What was the soulful capital of Phoenicia? What does papyrus mean? What in the world Is an ancient history encyclopedia?

THE LAST MACK
STANDING SCRIPTURES

7.

Step in smooth to lay It down thick, straight grinding like they do in Little Rock Arkansa, got to learn how to live, then learn how to earn, then learn how to make money work for you, then learn how to pull up shining brand new, like they say In Memphis, "this what game plus money do for you," if you learn how to direct traffic, Memphis know the business on some project pat type stuff, It's all about getting life right wealthy comfortable with longevity, and spirituality.

I'm listening to Sean Paul unforgettable song, it's called, "I'm still in love with you," he said, "I'm just a hustler and player," ain't nothing better then a woman singing to a man, the video ms. Sasha singing in the most attractive way possible, siamotainously It shows the native to Jamaica lady dancing better than any woman in any strip club in Atlanta, like Tyrone said, "no disrespect."

CHILDHOOD TO ADULTHOOD

A day right before Barrack Obama 36th birthday on August 3rd, 1997, was my sixteenth birthday, I was in a dark lovely bold, beautiful perm head 21-year-old lady named Salena's apartment on 24th Vilet, she had a Puerto Rican accent for some reason, like Raquel Lee accent, I was in her house sitting on cloud nine, like a true Ivory Coast Jamaican born Rastafarians.

Big Money Sunny always told me I was ahead of my time, he also said, "if somebody down with you it shows by actions, some people know what to say to get people to reveal the hidden truth, so to all from intelligent to brilliant never think you know everything."

"But know what you getting into before getting into it, see if the water cold before you get into it, see if its water in the pool before you dive in it, & don't tell nobody how you conquered them, because it will back fire."

While I sat on cloud nine like Tanzanian Jamaican born Rastafarian, I keep my brain working hard by taking notes from movies I watch, and what I learned that day.

I found myself writing true friends, also a lifetime boss lady is hard to find, so that's why you wait for the Most High to send it to you, so listen to every word being spoken to paint a clear picture, any word left out is like a piece missing out a puzzle, demand no word, or detail is be left out what you listening to be spoken, or what you choose to be reading.

I think my childhood was turning me into a game tight person that will pimpishly investigate Milwaukee professionally, all that before I reach adulthood.

An echo from my pitch-black Dickies pants pocket, caught my attention, when I grabbed it, it vibrated in my hand, and the screen said incoming call from Baby Ghetto.

I'm listening to shawty lo song called, "I got it for the l o," "stunt man my spot you can drop it, Int stunting."

I said, "What's going on baby ghetto the number one prettiest, sexiest, smartest Mong lady in Milwaukee County history."

She said, "Where you at Millon mackin?"

I said, "Standing like a Cherry street mob gangster on a balcony, on 24th Vilet Street, feeling a cool breeze coming from the moonlight, siamotainously talking to who every man wish they had access to, & also access to your mind, body, & soul."

She said, "who Mack Millon?"

I said, "You Baby Ghetto," she said, "I got a credit card to spend on us," I said, "where you at Zoo nkauj ooh niam?"

She said, "I'm somewhere in Capitol Court Mall by marshal high school."

I said, "Were you gone be at, because Im already In route towards you, Im your heat seeking missile?"

She said, "I'm just Sitting in them chairs by the jewelry store with a banana yellow chocolate pop sickle," I said, "give me 20 minutes, or less like your local dominos, my uncle dirty south gave me his Delta 88 to move, and shake with throughout the county, on journey to get wealthy with longevity."

I said, "before I step away from this prime co cell phone nice & smooth like Bronx New York City style, listen to me young beauty queen," she said, "ok," I said, "it's always somebody who can interpret what's being insinuated, it's a solution to every problem, it's an answer to every question, taking the long route makes you stronger, short cuts can be like rushing, and cheating yourself stopping you from getting all that's for you to have."

She said, "I know the routine, think about what you say, while you on your way." I said, "Don't say that, then don't do it," she said, "I got you baby."

I hung the bling bling Prime Co cell phone up, then I called nice height, unique, pretty Salena, I said, "I got to dip," she said, "keep the keys, and come get me on your way back Millon mackin."

I said, "What you want from the store I will get for you easy?"

She said, "A pack of Newport, and a six pack of Meister Brau miller lit," I said, "I will not buy you no beer, I might get you the cigs though."

She said, "yeah yeah, but what you gone say before you be on your way?"

I said, "words are powerful, the right group of words can make the earth shake, rain drop, waves splash, wind blow, sun shine, grass grow, faces smile, eyes cry, stars fall, people will hug each other from hearing a word, or words, sex will transpire from words, and people will die after hearing a word, or words."

She said, "You moving too fast Royalty, learning to dj quick, and I know now you got an old soul in a young body."

I said, "Baby be patient I will take care of your wants, needs, and should haves, sooner than later, I had that Barry white look In my eyes, "you first my last my everything," but I smiled it off with a scooby, & shaggy red eyes hunger sensation."

I'm listening to my first game coach, sir goldy album, it's called, "in the land of funk," he straight from Oakland, certified individual.

She said, "how you gone satisfy me Mack Millon?"

I said, "this the last question, the last answer in this brief conversation, because I got a few things transpiring begging for my attention, "if you remain the number one lady in my royal family, you gone get mental, physical, and financial satisfaction in more ways then one, so let it be written, so let it be done," I had that Ten Commandments look in my eyes.

Then I said, "I will call you when I'm in the front boss lady," I poured up me some Mack Juice, I filled my cup up with J Roget Extra Dry Champaign, then mixed it with Bombay Gin in a cool laid pitcher, & I called it mack juice, after I poe my cup up, I left the pitcher In unique very attractive Salena's dacor refrigerator.

I sipped it four times out my goblet glass, then put four west coast ice cubes in it, and then sat it on the metal rack in beautiful delicate Salena's Sub Zero Pro 48 refrigerator.

Then I pushed my pretty tony Lance Feurtado king way out the door, locked the browning security door six panel lock, & pimp stick walked to the $50 bill money green Delta 88, then I went down the steps out the apartment front door.

I unlocked my down south mean green delta 88 car door, snuck inside it like the police was watching me, then I pulled out the ash tray, & grabbed my Crystal Ball Cigar that came in a glass tube.

Then I grab my Fabergé Imperial Table Lighter, then I lit up my crystal ball pimp c smoking hydroponics filled cigar, stuck my key in the kangaroo pouch, twisted it gently until the car growled like a pit-bull name Rocky cocaine.

Then I smashed on the gas, simultaneously turning the last mr bigg up, I skip to the song he made called, "when I'm gone."

Maybe ten minutes, before I pulled up to the famous Marshall high school Capitol Court Mall, Baby Ghetto called my Prime Co cell phone from a pay phone saying, "Mack, this guy keeps trying to talk to me."

I said, "where he at?"

She said, "on the bus stop staring at me," I said, "tell him King Mack want to talk to him," Snoop dog song called, "promise I," it came on as I heard her say that to the local brown soulful brother.

Then she got back on the phone laughing, saying, "he walking away," I said, "meet me by the store that sell godfather dobb hats," she said, "ok Millon mackin," & laughed with her before I pressed end phone call, you like that.

Before I hung up, I heard her singing, "my king's the game spiting smartest, and universe hardest."

I arrived at the mall smooth cool, parked the car like I was in a Bugatti Veyron by Mansory Vivere, put my pimp c smoking hydroponics crystal ball cigar out in the ash tray, while I was doing this, fabolous song called, "cold summer," was punching the speakers extremely hard, then I got out the car king mackishly, & it took five minutes to get to the front door of the mall from the parking lot the way I walk, I move like 200 year Madagascar elder tortoise, you like that.

So ah, well I Chicago Milwaukee pimp stick walked directly in the mall specifically to the store she was in, she was buying Golconda Diamond ear rings, I said, "Baby Ghetto," she said, "hey Millon mackin," hugged me like she got out of the cheetah women prison, hugs like that make me nervous, you like that, she kissed me on my neck like I was in the friend zone, my name ain't screech, I wrapped my Floyd Mayweather skinny strong arm around her little neck, and guided her outside the store with royalty.

I said, "what's the business young one," she said, "i'nt gone lie to you Millon mackin, I got sticky fingers, this plastic bound to melt, its hands on everything hot baby," I said, "ok let's spend where they won't ask for a signature after you buy them pretty diamond ear rings."

We went back in the store, I said, "what can I get boss Hmong young pretty high, & tempting lady?" (Respect to the comedy king Chris Georgia tucker)

She said, "You can have whatever you like," she was sounding like the female version of T.I., "there's no limit mack," is what she said blushing smiling so hard her teeth almost cracked.

I said, "Ok Baby G, music to my ears, wise words spoken, just what I been waiting to hear today baby ghetto you a true player in my perspective, from this point on."

I strategically picked five godfather dobb hats, sky blue, coffee aboriginal indigenous soulful brown, smoke signals gray, pitch Chopi black, cream white, $50 plus for each with socks to match each hat, you got to understand me right, game got to recognize game.

I heard the country boy clique song called, "we dere," playing on the mall intercom to entertain all in the mall, it was j roll, playboy d, baby drew, and d note rapping, Milwaukee Wisconsin a boss player city if you didn't know, now you got to know, welcome to one of the lands of snow, July 3rd 2021 Congratulations to the Milwaukee bucks for making it to the nba finals, last time that happened, Kareem, & Oscar Robertson won the nba championship In 1972 If my memory serve me correctly.

I looked at my picture perfect mong lady smiling proudly, then. I said, "Swipe it Baby G."

We said thank you to the cashier, smiled like we just won the lottery, and quietly like ten thief's in a millionaire 1950's master king pimp Beverly Hills mansion, we left out with the quickness like we knocked his main money maker.

We humbly walked through the hallway full of Marshall High School Students, they were cold warming up while waiting on the city bus, you already know they was escaping the Milwaukee attic cold.

I had five bags in my hands, Asian eye candy on my side, two sets of separate house keys for separate houses, then when we got in the classic antique delta 88, she broke herself, ain't that nice of her, and we dipped off playing tru life song, it's called, "freestyle intro, it was jay-z talking Brooklyn finest literature on It mainly, then tru life song called, "bag for i," it bumped out the speakers for us two sticking together, futuristic living.

Now Baby G was sweet 16, her birthday is on August 15th, or the 17th; she fell in love with royalty when she first saw me at a park near High

Mount neighborhood, hustlers call that uptown, close by Wauwatosa area, I was just finishing up killing everybody on the basketball court.

When I first laid my Narmer golden eyes on her, she was at the same playground park babysitting her phauj kids, I had just finish Marcus Greer killing people on the basketball court, right next to the playground where she was looking out for youthful family members.

A Mercedes-Benz GLA-Class was parked in front on a house across the street from the park, all the windows was down playing Michael Jackson's song called, "butterflies," it was playing loud in the background like we was on a Hollywood movie set.

I spotted her big cleavage, then I saw her wreck less eye balling me, sizing me up, she peep my Italian shining, the Money Madeline Italian sterling silver heroin bone chain, with my money currency sign Madeline straight shining, similar to Houston Simone biles Olympic gold medal.

I stepped to her like Chicago King James would have; I said, "Do you like what you see pretty attractive lady?"

She started blushing prettily smiling so hard her teeth almost cracked, & my dr. Cliff huxtable Philadelphia beeper started beeping, then I noticed an Eldorado Biarritz was at the stop light, it was banging Gucci mane song called, "I get the bag," featuring migos, "take it easy baby," I heard migos say, "moma," peace to blessings to biz markie.

I said, "Do you have an ink pen pretty lady?"

She said, "Here," then I wrote my beeper number down, next her family members kids started calling her name when they slid down the slide.

I said, "Go do what them kids need you to do," she said, "you don't even know my name, & own know your name."

I said, "Me, and you gone be super tight," she said, "give me a hug, and you can go boy."

We South Dakota original brown bear hugged, I said, "I got to get to a phone," she said, "I can help you get a phone if you treat me right Day to night all year around," and we were tighter then the Virgin Islands every sense then.

As I walked away from her out the park, a stankin lancoln on three wheels hitting switches drove pass, it was j rigg ballin through the neighborhood, he was bumping e-40 song called, "bout my money."

THE GAME OF LIFE
SCRIPTURES

13.

Playing the game of life professionally, is knowing how to roll it, live to give, give to live, it's about unity, team work works, it's a proven fact that teams have won championships, everybody need everybody, cross country living, will explain exactly what the game of life scriptures is all about.

I'm in Dallas Texas right now, Respect to advanced intelligent indigenous Soul people, from the land of Texas, such as Ugk, Scarface, Devin the Dude, Typ, Chamillionaire, Paul Wall, Mr. J Prince, I got to buy his book soon, Bessie Coleman native American to first hold pilot license, George Thomas Mickey leland, juanita craft, Etta moten Barnett, I supposed to been bought j prince book, probably gone buy it today, Quint Black, Willie D, Jamaican born Bushwick Bill, Lil Flip, just to name a few, Respect to all the king's business all over the country.

THE KING BUSINESS

I'm listening to the Isley brothers song, its called, "between the sheets," they from the gemstone state, Cincinnati Ohio to be precise, three major cities stacked on top of each other, I found that out in florida, from an indigenous man from Ohio.

Wisdom stays ahead of what is going on in the world, global intellectual brilliance, learn how to be the greatest you were created to be, keep from the pathway of no return, your spirit is free when you master self-control, it will make the vision clearer.

Unity keeps life in order, always make self-improvement, aim to strengthen every part of your lifestyle consistently.

Rise and surprise, become low yet beyond low just to see all that can be seen, and studied.

Learn all that is available to be studied, think not failure, study the uplifting ways of the world, aim to live long as forever is, learn to master life with lessons taught by the Most High.

Learn everything available to know about life, and after life, above, and beyond, including what is out of sight, that which is out of your mind, that is until you put it in your brilliant mind.

Stay far away from fools, keep fools away, keep trouble away, choose truth over lies, live, and let live, consequences is rewards for those volunteering to be fools.

Fools speak of trouble making, the wise plant seeds, and watch them grow.

Infiltrators is always lurking, stay away from those who feed off negative energy, The Most High always speaks through the indigenous soul people to the indigenous soul people, then to all mankind.

It's always best to speak on what you know about, not hear say, simply because you studied it, learned about it, and memorize the wise will rise, and surprise.

Seek to be motivated by the Creator, speak loud silent, always remember what good who did for you.

Let everything pay for itself, you can't rise with the wrong people, you have to distance yourself from them, can't brake yourself, memorize mankind happiness will lead you towards sadness.

If things is hard, make it easy, anything of importance revolves around indigenous, pyramid king tut brown people of North America, turtle island.

In the concrete jungle, I'm a Mack, in my lifetime I reached a king level, in the Mack lifestyle, which is why I'm King Mack, also known as a King named Mack.

Because it's not just a name, it's what I was born to do, so it is me, so it's not Mack joe, or mackin joe, it's King Mack, a Mack crowned King by the Most High, with forever prosperity from the Most High allowance.

Always put elders first, and those of higher rank, stay away from where you not invited, memorize all this once you get your foot in the door, no faults, or you will be put back out the door.

See without saying what you see, master feelings, emotions, mind, body, memories, also existence with permission from the Creator, seek not sadness, anger, or excitement, just stay solid stainless steel.

THE LAST MACK STANDING SCRIPTURES

10.

Step in smooth to lay It down thick, straight grinding like they do in Little Rock Arkansas, got to learn how to live, then learn how to earn, then learn how to make money work for you, then learn how to pull up shining brand new, like they say In Memphis, "this what game plus money do for you," if you learn how to direct traffic, Memphis know the business, on some project pat type stuff, It's all about getting life right, wealthy comfortable with longevity, and spirituality.

I'm listening to Alphonso Mays song, it's called, "Sex, Love, and Romance, I'm in Hendersonville North Carolina, now I'm in saint louis by the arch, me california, & denver is blowing smoke signals, jazz band black, I'm by some race track next to the highway, I'm watching the 2018 miss national costume full show, I'm listening to baby drew song, it's called, "goldfangaz," it's officially Milwaukee business, from start to finish, he chopping up good game about Milwaukee lifestyles, straight facts of life, respect, peace, & blessings to bobby womack.

I'm watching aspen Colorado 2021 fis snowboard, & freeski world championship, I admit this stuff takes true skills, switch right 180, a lady skiing doing twist turns backwards, her name Tess ledeux from France, sponsored by visa, another lady skiing backwards down hill, left cork 720 tail, Kirsten Muir a 16 year old, they earning the money they make for this sport, Kirsten is from France also, very impressive ladies.

THE ROYAL FAMILY

said, "give me a players club 1998 sexy diamond, Lisa Raye kiss, royal lady of leisure," she licked them Barbadian Robyn Rihanna Fenty looking lips of hers, then she lifted her hand up, like it was a royal copenhagen flora danica plate, next she blew me a nichelle nichols lieutenant uhura kiss, at the same time she was prettily laughing, I laughed with her, I started calling her a boss Player hater, see, I knew she had a time limit with me, so automatically it's mandatory to know she always on business, so it's mandatory to stay on business, you know you play but not being sincere, I knew she was here to pay not stay, so my feelings don't be sad mad or glad, appreciation is always in full effect 24 hours every day plus nights, on the strength because without willing participants, my pockets would be low to the flow, the average player would be sad mad confused with a response like that, but I know I taught my ladies to speak their mind, so problems won't be hidden behind lies, because smiling faces do tell lies, ask the O'Jays about back stabbers, so I tell all women, if you find a better king then me, choose him, now check this out, I rather them play this how it go, then be Throwed off throughout the 24 hours, best to just focus on what will stay in motion, if she on her way out the door, live and let live, so instead of making complaints, all because they with me thinking about somebody else, never hold who want, need, should get away from you, so that's why I love my ladies under my wing, because wise kings know if she listening, it most definitely shows, if they born to be with a king, he don't have to ask them to do, what they already been told what need to be done, verbal agreement understanding transpire day one encounter, connection to being on the same page happens automatically, know how to enjoy having fun with your royal family, all that keeping them sad mad will backfire if you get stuck, they gone weigh their options to leave, or stay, if you put good game in them, they will always listen to their right mind to come to assist you, weather it's prison time you do, or get shot in the hospital, it's real in the battlefield, New York call it the concrete jungle.

Silly smiling baby ghetto, she was sneaking peaks at me, studying me, looking to see if my feelings was hurt, then she said, "Crystal Ball cigar breath, own like you like that, but I love your king mackin self though," then she smiled so hard, her teeth almost cracked, see what I'm saying, she on point, because I'm on point, she my reflection, she learn from my ways, she mimic me how I handle life situations, so for those after your business ladies, the best move is, put you in their mind with a full effort consistently, if you on her mind, she can get comfortable doing something, she know you will be in her face, asking her why she doing what she know not to be doing, then anybody looking to put your business lady, on their team, guess what, they better be prepared to battle everything that was put in her mind, by her king.

I said, "I love my royal family Maine," then I started the Andrew Jackson mean green colored Delta 88, I started it up, to me, she gone be contemplating on coming back home, to a king named mack million, I leaned over to the window, to drive leaned all the way back, you already know, boss player style, she reached to skip to TYP's Thowed Young Playas's song, it's the song that say, "I will be everything with a matching pinky ring," she did that, only because she knows, that's my favorite song, she studying me, it's the game of life, and to show me she respectfully love me, in more ways then one, this also showed the world that I'm in her head, on her mind consistently, past to present moment, I got two wins, she got one, she also protecting her feelings, in case she decided to leave, now it's two wins me, two wins her, it won't hurt so much if she not attached to me, in every way possible, now she got three wins, I got two wins, own know how others run their program, I say, "bang good longevity game in the correct brains," every chance possible, create leaders not followers, you know what I'm tum bout, straight king mackin.

I'm editing this all game entertainment chapter, I'm lstening to Jay-Z song, he kicking knowledge, it's called, "the story of o.j.," I'm in ft. Pierce Florida, it's January, it's 80 degrees, 80 degrees, supposedly I'm sipping regular Hennessy, puffing on a Louis Armstrong jazz band black, straight chilling, I was told this the city of no pity, it look nice to me though, Now the next song on is Jay-Z & Beyoncé song, its called, "family feud," it just, just came on, I feel that amen part beyonce scream out her soul, in the most soulful way, like rose royce, minnie ripleton, back to the story, pardon me, Beyoncé killing that higher singing part though, I just see her crunching down dancing in my head, while she singing higher.

Baby ghetto know every time she interacts with me, I know she seeing, and doing it to keep me in a good mood, and on my toes, what you put in is what you get out, steel gone have to sharpen steel, she know if I'm up, she guaranteed to stay up to, if I'm straight, she straight, two peas in a pot, the right combination equals the right results, men done hit her before, can't talk with their words, so they have to talk with their hands, you rate that performance, vs verbal word play, with nothing but hand gestures to highlight what's being said, so she knows I'm cool on all that, but it's in her, to control who around her, to keep herself safe & comfortable, you got to respect she on her toes to, it's the game of life behavior characteristic traits in full effect.

She Looked at me smiling, touching my indigenous downtown Judy brown right hand, she did it with her powerful seductive touching soft Asian mhong hands, women know it's power in the touch of a woman fingers, she either was doing it naturally off experience with the opposite sex, or she was taught that by who, I don't know, women pass game like Indigenous men do to, then she said, "Let me spray your Michael Jordan air freshener Mack," I said, "you already doing it, but I appreciate you asking first, or last, before, or after," my royal family be on some being funny type stuff, play with your players you coach, they funny you funny, enjoy the time spent, we always have fun with each other, happy family, happy money, you know what um tum bout.

We pulled up on 27ᵗʰ & Capitol, at the stop light, it was next to an Amazon tree frog green colored bentley, it was lapham Park project's dalone, he head nodded at me, respectfully to the boss player, I head nodded back at him, you should call that keeping it real, texas call it keeping it treal, We was by the bar hopping, north side hood McDonalds, we didn't know all about soul food restaurants in the city back then, I said, "you hungry baby ghetto," she said, "Not yet, I'm hungry for you," see, always talking that talk, she just be practicing her game, if your hands on everything, don't do that, I know something is bothering her because they have fun figuring out what they can say, that which will excite a man to the point he become hypnotized by them in a trance, but I smiled with my face, it was saying you know in't falling for your trickery, then I said, "here some food for thought baby ghetto."

"Peep game, know who for you, know everybody around you, what they be thinking, where they head at, what they want, what they willing to do to get it, it's all about protecting your neck against who, or what can stop you from breathing, walking, or talking."

She said, "How you know so much, you ain't even that much older than me Mackology?"

One more time I want to say, I'm listening to Jay-Z song, its called, "party life," this lady on the chorus killing it, "headed to the party life, ohh ohh party life, big city and bright lights, welcome to the 70s," ok back to the unforgettable story.

I said, "Just be concerned about putting what I say to you, to mother trucking good use," I started smiling, then she said, "ok I thought you was serious, I was about to say, I'm all in his head," then she started smiling.

She said, "where everybody at Mackology," I said, "it's a cold world In Wisconsin, if anybody wants to come in with me, to kick off their shoes, & relax their feet where it's warm, they got to be consistently chasing bread, getting loaves of bread, setting up bread to come, just handling business as we all be doing baby ghetto."

We pushed through the Mackwaukee Wisconsin spotlight, we was going south bound, straight down 27th towards downtown, I said, "Salena at her sister house, on 24th Juneau, & this Tousha Dominique calling right now," now keep in mind when a king kingdom love Is strong, it shows from him to them, and them to him, let them grow with you, because you growing because of what they doing for you, what you put in is what you get out.

She said, "Let me answer Mackology," she said, "I know what to say first," she said, "hello." Then Tousha Dominique said, "hey girl where y'all at,?" see, this how it go, she knows how to assist me from learning my talks I talk, at the same time, she know my phone greetings, I gave her that look, that look that say, "don't try to be me, just help me, help us."

Baby Ghetto said, "He just picked my ghetto self up, in his mean Green colored delta 88, His clean engine blue nose pitbull growling limousine delta 88."

Tosha Dominique said, "How much you brought to the table tonight baby ghetto?"

They really be thinking they cooler than me how they be talking, but they my reflection in the coolest way possible, in a major way, I'm analyzing how their conversation go, start to finish, also I'm letting them stay close with communication, we the royal family with no tolerance hatred Ins the royal family, jealousy, or envy, just all in the royal family surviving together, unified from start to finish, now, while she was on the prime co cell phone, she was chopping up game out of nowhere, don keke world famous Texas song, its called, "slab holiday," it just came on.

Ms. Baby Ghetto said, "Two, plus a credit card," Tosha Dominique said, "for real, I barely got 6 50s, & I got some Rose Moet for royalty, to celebrate with us with, she laughed some, then baby g was smiling at me, don't ask how my sticky fingers got it, hands on everything girl, you know he said, "don't do that," good thing i got the rose kind of moet, I know he like rose moet, it might help him don't be mad at me about the credit card, he be looking at all that, as doing desperate money making for our royal family."

Ms. Baby ghetto said, "You did good, he in a good mood to, here go Mackology."

I said, "What's going on baby 380?"

She said, "Something better than nothing b Mack," I said, "you know that's right right now, where you at pretty lady?"

She said, "I just got dropped off on 27th & North Avenue, I'm at Golden Chicken, I'm buying your king mackin self some French fries to go with 3 Miami yards, plus a bottle of Rose Moet."

I said, "you show right something better than nothing, we making everything count tonight boss lady, we will be there in ten minutes, order you, Ms. Baby ghetto, & Salena some food, with that Miami yard inside your Heavenly Star bra, that which you left the house wearing this morning, or that Ulysses S. Grant in your gucci gg tulle lingerie panties."

She said, "Mack," I said, "you know the business, don't lie, or defend yourself, just make it happen," she said, "I love you to mack daddy," she mumbled something under her breath, saying, you think you know everything," but I didn't give attention to it, but I should have, major mistake on my part, you know what I'm saying.

We were passing through the street, where Milwaukee runs through the yellow lights, it was on 27th & Locust, then I told Mrs. Baby ghetto, I told her to call Salena, to tell her, that we will be there in 20 minutes, or less, like your local dominos, Diana Fletcher was a Black pyramid golden brown Indian who lived with the Kiowa in the 1800s back to this unforgettable storyline, & we bringing food cooked the way she would have cooked chicken to eat.

I skipped to Big Tymers song, its called, "Pimp On," after I gave her the prime co cell phone, then she dialed the number, it rang twice, next I heard her say, "hey girl, how you been?"

Salena said, "Everything cool, work was cool at New Yorkers on north avenue," baby ghetto was smiling saying, "I got 2 plus a credit card, I can't complain," Salena said, "how was school today?"

Keep in mind, Salena was a fresh few years out of high school, with her own apartment, a job, nice height, dark lovely bold beautiful, she was top prize for an upcoming player such as royalty.

Ms. Baby ghetto said, "I missed classes today," Salena said, "don't fall behind," Mrs. Baby ghetto said, "I won't, but I was told to tell you, that we all gone be there in 20 minutes, i was in the background saying like dominos, then baby g said, "like dominos," she was smiling at me, & we coming with Some pyramid golden chicken," I said, "Diana fletcher cooking style," then she said, "Diana fletcher style."

Salena said, "tell him don't forget my wants, my needs, & my should haves," Mrs. Baby ghetto said, "Mack don't forget Salena Newport's," Salena said, "what he say?"

Mrs. Baby ghetto said, "He nodded his head with his game face on, we on our way to get tousha Dominique, & I won't let him forget big sister."

Salena said, "Thank you little sister," Mrs. Baby ghetto said, "I got you."

I said, "we here, let's go get her, own know why she come to this police chicken spot," Mrs. Baby ghetto said, "we in, & out baby."

I placed my arm around her neck, I leaned my mouth to speak gently in her ear, I said, "Don't miss no more days of school," then we pushed inside the restaurant, to see some player looking indigenous hustler, he look like he was spitting game to Dominique, she said to the indigenous player, "I can't talk no more, my royal family here."

We watched him walking off confused, with a disappointing look on his face, baby ghetto was watching, but she minded her business, she know I want silence, when I need to see what's going on.

I said, "in't concerned with that conversation you was just having, unless I see him again, sticking his hustler player hands inside your royal family, baby phat embroidered fuzzy joggers pants pockets."

I said, "Grab the food Mrs. Baby Ghetto, give me a hug first Dominique," she ran to me like I was her happiest first, & last day of her lifetime, she was smiling so hard her teeth almost cracked, & she kissed my neck, like she was Erykah badu, & she squeezed the warmth off me, until it went inside her, she usually do that to block out who put something in her head, good, or bad thoughts.

After she grabbed the rest of our food off the counter, I wrapped my Manny Pacquiao 39 knockouts skinny arms around her, I was guiding her out Golden Chicken; I told Mrs. Baby Ghetto, baby g lead the way, I said, "I'm show glad you back in my arms reach boss lady."

I said, "let's get in our mean green colored limousine, we gone sit on top of the city tonight ladies," Dominique gave me the Rose Moet, plus the $300, it was wrinkled up, but the faces pointed the same way, she know that's how I like my cash in hand, when paper is being put in my pocket.

I said, "you bet not be planning on leaving, without telling me ahead of time, hugging me like this, it feels like we at a pine bluff little rock Arkansas family reunion, you know when somebody hug because they know they not gone see you no more, now dig in your baby phat clothes, for that currency your hips lips, and fingertips is stashing."

"Because I know you spent little bills first on this food," I said, "you know I love Moet, & I know what my royal family love, when we get Salena, we gone see what I got y'all."

I said, "give me a kiss Dominique," Mrs. Baby ghetto was smiling prettily giggling, she was saying, "he got crystal ball cigar breath," Dominique said, "own like you like that, but I love you though, & own want to leave you Mackology," I smiled at baby g saying, "player hater," then we pulled off with the engine growling, the paint job looking like the color of New money, fresh out of the federal building in the district of columbia, and the music playing, it was scarface song, it's called, "dollar," it reminds me of downtown los Angeles, by the staples center.

I said, "this for both y'all to know, "what people don't like about themselves, somebody else will love, a friend is eternal, an enemy is temporary, a wife, or husband is eternal, a girlfriend, or boyfriend is a stepping stone towards higher ground."

I said, "Dominique call Salena, tell her come out in 5 minutes," Mrs. Baby ghetto said, "her Newport's," I said, "we gone stop at the gas station on 27th & Walnut, the one where that pretty short round brown mother, and her daughters used to own around 1996.

I skip to Too $hort song, its called, "Call me Daddy," & Dominique said, "hey girl, we almost there, he getting your Newport's, come out in ten minutes, we pulling up at the gas station right now, on 27th & Walnut, we pulling up right now."

Salena said, "It's packed in that gas station ain't it?"

Dominique said, "You already know," Salena said, "y'all be careful & stay on point, if y'all see a Mary j blige cd they selling in the cashier window, ask the king to bless his family with her cd, she was laughing, & seriously watch each other back, you know it's always eyes watching talking on cell phones, I'll see y'all when y'all get here."

Dominique said, "Pray for us girl, bye sister."

I said, "Mrs. Baby ghetto take this Andrew Jackson, buy a pack of newports, point to the car if she don't sell them to you, & get all y'all something to drink, & your sister Newport's 100s."

She said, "Ok Mack, I'll be right back," then she kissed my jaw, asked Dominique, "did she want anything out the ordinary?"

Dominique said, "Not today sister, oh some hawaii alkaline water bottles," baby ghetto said, "Ok," & then left out the car, she show nuff was looking tight, and right for all night, Like Aaliyah in her rock the boat video, she wearing a Shawn Kemp jersey dress, with airmax to match, just regular dressed up to catch bread, to meet our monthly requirements is her daily mission, all the way to the end of the month.

I said, "when people realize you don't need them, they start to appreciate you, I said that to say, don't try to get over on me, you hear me Dominique?"

She said, "Yeah baby I see the point you making," I said, "go in there to help her speed up the process baby," & she gave me a Foxxy Brown kiss, It was like I was Kurupt, I turned the music up, it was playing scarface

325

song, the classic song is called, "untouchable," I lit up a jazz black, while I watched everything moving, I saw Clifton from Hamilton high school, I member some women in high school told me, he was hating on me during a phone call they had, I guess my name got brought up in a way, in a way he had to put me down, to big himself up, remember no feelings interfere with everyday life, plus it was hear say they say, so I got out to speak to him, like a man i shook his hand, to let him see my shining diamonds in my teeth, on my wrist, all the way to the ones on my fingers, and when the ladies got to the register, then they started paying for their purchased items, I excused myself from our conversation, I also was watching where my royal ladies was at, at the same time, I was playing It off small talking simply because Milwaukee be out of line sometimes, plus that's mandatory in the midnight league, I'm a gentleman at all times, and on point at all times to, he knew I wasn't happy with him, he knew I was just showing respect, just in case it was true, I got to keep my eye on him, til I talk him into telling me how the conversation really went, then I can compare versions, and determine what really was said.

Respect to king bean from Chicago, a master of the game of life, rest easy royalty.

I'm watching drink champs, thinking about hanging out with sour diesel fluid tonight, I'm still in Massachusetts leaning back, on drink champs is slim thug, amerie stoudamire, I didn't know his first name squeezed out his last name, Jadakiss is on the show to, that's three different perspectives In life, information they share is pieces to the puzzle that complete the game of life scriptures, we all need to know what each other know.

I'm watching Larry "grandma" Johnson joins q and d knuckleheads s6: e3 the players' tribune, just saw Shawn kemp, & Tim hardaway on this same show.

Always bring your truth with you.

THE GAME OF LIFE SCRIPTURES

14.

Playing the game of life is knowing how to roll it, live to give, give to live, it's about unity, team work works, it's a proven fact, teams have won championships, everybody need everybody, cross country living, will explain what the game of life scriptures is all about.

I'm listening to Jay-Z song, its called, "rulers back," the rulers back.

Now I'm in hebron ohio, pure as a rain drop falling out the sky in my hair, let it water the grass in my head, it's raining so peacefully I can hear buju banton, peace to jamaicans workd wide, especially in Hartford Connecticut, his song is called, "trust," it's dancing in the rain for all Indigenous ears to hear it, respect from a king named mack to buju banton, appreciation for this song, I'm sipping waiakea water mixed with pink moscato, california deliciously sweet, with a black jazz band, berner & do or die song, it's called, "highway," it just came on, with hartford connecticut, decatur georgia, jagged edge singing the chorus.

THE KING BUSINESS

[MACKOLOGY - LIFEOLOGY]

It's not natural for the suns of the Most High, to hate without probable cause, that which is what they supposed to love, sometimes silence speaks louder than words, learn how to know when to let the good spirits speak for you.

According to what's going on in the world [the city where you from], it will reflect on the motion in the ocean, it's always a source to all that is, study where you at, far as life go, past, and present, historically speaking.

Just because you with, or standing near someone great [a person who worked hard to become a wise king], or something that exist above sea level [above average], it doesn't make you equal to that person, place, or thing, you got to earn your turn, and time to shine [it's the ways of the giants, past and present, sophisticated mentality].

Intelligence to brilliance [age, and experience] turns boys to men, and girls to full grown ancient wisdom women, born to succeed successfully, on all levels of life, with their knowledgeable kings.

Right your wrongs, understand what is required of a person such as yourself to be understood [know what need to be known], embrace what seeks you, knowing that it will bring you to a new level in your lifetime every time, forever teach the youth, and consistently preach the truth.

Remain in this lifetime, low key under the radar, rarely seen by cameras [internet], never be heard about by snakes in the grass [move silent like leaves growing on trees].

Seek higher learning daily, be around the wise nightly, find your kind in every city you enter, forever learn the ways of the world.

Appreciate love that's shining down on you from above, turn down not the truth beyond belief, keep food for thought in the long-term memory bank, it will forever automatically feed you when you hunger for more.

Avoid all forms of temptation, ignore all wicked distractions, carefully cautiously hand pick who you choose to be around, and those you deal with, on any level of existence.

What you put in, seems to be exactly what you get out, it's been that way sense the beginning of time, the Almighty truth lives in the air you breath in, every second, believe it, or not, everything you need to succeed has always been in your arm reach, tools, plus rules, always have, and forever will be in your face, winking & blowing kisses at you.

Appreciation to the Most High [who, or what you consider your Creator], prosper not in the wrong ways, if you going in the wrong directions, take everything to the next level [elevation is the destination], continuously consistently repeatedly graduate to greater heights, every week all month, all year, every year.

When you dealing with the best of the best, you got to be at your best, sometimes you don't have to say something, until the time is right.

We all seem to be inspired by somebody, past, or present, most indigenous soulful Brown folks of the past 1900s, they migrated north to west to east, to seek jobs, from the segregated south, & see a new change of scenery, Indigenous soul people before the 1900s, 1800s, all the way to beginning of time, they all had different purposes year after year, all the way to indigenous soulful peoples of today.

People fear what they don't understand, and hate change.

Find something new to do every day, only speak deep to the deep, soft talk to the soft, talk baby talk to babies [meaning you can't speak mature to childish adults], and always have a conversation for everybody looking in your eyes.

Always know who you bringing in your royal family, when it comes to activities, only participate with next level behavior, not under graduates, rookies, or half steppers, when you playing to win, do exactly that, brilliantly play to win long term style, with longevity as your final destination.

Never reveal your game plan to those outside your counsel of wise ones, until it's time to shock the show, (respect to San quin song, "shock the show"), [meaning write a book], lead your own way, study greatness to add it to your style, if it's not wicked, and live under the wings of ancient powerful knowledge.

Seeking higher learning will bring you closer to the Most High, let the Most High speak out your mouth, for all those who aim to maintain God body style.

The pathway going towards longevity, it's paved with truth beyond belief, for all those who serve the Almighty purpose, they will be taken care of, from start to finish, believe that.

For who that is, or become, all things in life will reveal their true colors, being seen for who, or what they truly are, or is.

Keep a boss pimp Italy Mauro gator foot distance, from faking hating nonsense, get the lame out your system, that's learned from swimming in shallow waters, it's called a step by step process, when it comes to being at your best.

I'm listening to Jay-Z song, its called, "momma loves me," (d block love this song),"unless you was me, how can you judge me, I was brought up in pain, In't trying to change you, just give you some game."

You can't pull people to the top, because they might not belong on top, before they qualify to be on top, that's deep, it's like stopping a lioness from catching an impala, all, individually will switch from minor league to the major league, after meeting all requirements.

Quiet, unseen, unheard shall always be special weapons of survival, also praying to be taught ancient knowledge, also ancient wisdom, which will highlight distraction, and temptations so you can avoid it.

Avoid all that is consequences, that which is creating evil on earth, also all that which loves trouble making evil, duck, dodge all women sent to destroy goodness in a king, or king to be.

Life is for the living, build your life on solid ground forever to always.

No weak link in the stainless steel chain, only stainless steel links built to last, will be in it to the finish.

Titles is just another way to categorize self, give the ism to those who buy it, one way, or another, some is taught to buy the truth, and not sell it, is that who you are?

Fools get used like tools, seeking higher learning, must be equally important to breathing air, that's from one, to all.

Master the mind, body, feel not sad to the point that you volunteer to not stick to the script, rules, and important laws.

Those who lack currency tend to find themselves at crossroads, to either survive by any means necessary, or be patient, to get what they qualify themselves to accumulate, what will accommodate the lifestyle they live.

Cut no corners, take no short cuts, qualify self to get what is coming to self, simply from being at self-best, that which self was created to be, if you ever slip, or fall, get sharper like California pimp, mr. sharp game, and bounce back better than you was before, like iron mike tyson.

I'm listening to Jay-Z Memphis Bleek Snoop Dogg song, its called, "get ya mind right," "just put your mind to it, you can go real far."

With love for the dove above, with no breaks, when you stand out, you put yourself in a position to be a moving target.

Everything is lined up to be how it's meant to be, know what you getting into before you get in to it, it's all about budgeting, and maneuvering daily.

Self-incrimination is foolish behavior, life is based on what is meant to be, if a person isn't gone be right with you, social distance yourself from them, build a dream team, a boss player must be around what is in the longevity lanes.

I'm listening to Memphis Bleek song, it's called, "holla," "I'm focused now, the game ain't changed, its just taught different."

Truth is with the Most High, structure is mandatory, order is mandatory, and discipline is mandatory.

Stay out trap houses, always have a reason, purpose, and time limit for arrival, and departure.

Obedience creates peace, discipline creates a pathway leading to longevity, entertainment is not personal, its recreation.

Stay away from what is being promoted, if you ahead of the game of life, that mean you made it out the storm, simultaneously others is going directly into the heartless storm, ask hurricane Katrina victims, those that was in her pathway of unbearable unbelievable terror.

The game of life participants is getting out the storm, for those going into it, give them food for thought on their journey, and see them when they get out the storm, I know it's getting deeper then the pacific ocean thus far in this brilliantly written book.

Take heed to signs signals, warnings, the wrong people will alter your life, they will be sent by all that's wrong to infiltrate, provoking you to fall apart, only if you allow them to enter your lifestyle, and allow them to learn how to make you self-destruct.

When new arrivals arrive, it changes a normal routine, beware of those sent to destroy, master all that is possible to be mastered, it's always gone be somebody sent to attempt to knock a king off his throne.

Do what the Most High love, be as The I Am be to the best of your ability, do your best to be at your best, you can't be round hatred, you can't move forward if you stand still, nonsense will always forever cancel itself out.

Process of elimination, evil will divide to conquer to learn how this world work, study those who destroying this world, and remember weakness will never like strength.

Trickery is the devils wicked manipulation method, jail is the devil's playground, bait leads to traps, alcohol is the slob from the devil's mouth, women with polluted minds seems to be the devil's puppets.

Gentle giants move in silence, choices, options, kings understand kings, the second time around (when you turn 40 years old) is the best time around.

Everybody got a task in a king life, stay built to last when you roll solo, make no deals with the devil, stay true to the game, some people do what they taught, and some do what comes natural.

A specific queen is heaven sent, handpicked specifically for a king, stay out the dark playing, sneaking, creeping, a woman becomes a star when she boosts her man up, if you need to be first, put the right people first.

Cover all angles, discipline stops people from thinking what's wrong is right, the Mack lifestyle is a world within this world, anybody allowed in the family, must come in naked, pure, and ready to begin a new life.

I'm listening to Jay-Z song, it's called, "streets is watching," "waiting for you to break, making your first mistake."

Just like you pay a toll booth to enter a new city, it's the same to enter the Mack lifestyle, a fee to see, pay to play, come in naked, pure, reprogramming your computer (your brain), it all begins when you step on the Mack Moon.

Only those in your world will be seen, and known for that, anyone else is dealt with from a social distance, anyone carrying baggage with trails following them, is not welcome.

If a woman has a man she represents, she cannot be welcomed to the Mack moon, she gets dealt with from a distance.

Memorize greatness inside your heart, it will bring goodness from above on solid ground, always roll with the Most High program, and never think you bigger than life, respect & blessings to og Ron newt, mr. Bigger than big Bay Area San Francisco og Ron newt.

Always ask the Most High, to guide your feet, & speak out your mouth, keep off the trail towards dead end streets, give with what you receive, in order to get rewards back every time, what you put in is what you get out, those first will be last, because those last will be first.

Onyx pinky ring symbolize universal intelligence, higher learning, intelligent to brilliant, lion head Madeline symbolize strength, knowledge as power, lion head pinky ring says street king on all levels of life.

Always have something to say about the Most High in every conversation, for those who leave the kingdom, they must come back better then when they left.

Appreciate mistakes being made now, and corrected, life lessons learned, enlightenment is an award benefitable, with longevity involved as the reward.

Patience created, humble prolongs, understand what is required to be understood, stay low key under the radar, and your pathway will be accommodative, it also puts fear in the rear until it decide that its best to disappear.

Help when you can help, the humble rule the jungle, be focused on self, but aware of others in your vision, what's written in between lines is seen by the heaven sent wise third eye, (your computer, your brain, your mind, man, you know what um tum bout).

I'm listening to jay-z song, it's called, "where you from," "how real is this, stop using that hand held scale, you laughing ain't you."

No none sense is the diet, a king knows that those that cross you, have a sentence for the crime they committed to be placed under pimp arrest, master your mind, and body to graduate to greater heights.

Never live in the shadows of darkness, you are who you are, because this how life molded you to be, let no one get the best of you, for being at their worst, because that means you got caught slipping for being weak.

If they help you destroy it, they not gone help you build it, if you survive the game of life as a man, you become a king, know your mandatory options, and recognize what is automatic, is always gone be automatic.

What the Most High create to be automatic, its gone be just how He made it to be, patience created the nations, and game rain so boss players don't have to complain.

A king gone maintain seeking progress while eliminating stress, ducking foolishness, handcuff answers to upcoming possible questions, live, let live, stay alive, and bow down to the Most High.

The truth will set you free to shame evil wickedness, when it's time to learn, the opportunity will present itself to you properly, give undivided attention to all details, and memorize it's always a snake in the grass, even if it ain't no water around that area, Louisiana taught me that, kitori said, "it's snakes in the grass when it's water is near."

When a Mack stop being what a king is, he loses his way, then he start falling in traps, when you at your best, you get exactly that, from every direction, good, and bad.

It seems like it's illegal for indigenous people to give one another props, in the county of Milwaukee Wisconsin.

Over reacting shows weakness, self can't play both sides of the field, some people is not stupid, it's just not in their nature to be any other way, except who they was created to be.

Represent the Most High, do what the Most high love none stop, forever analyze all the players in the game of life at all times, be well aware of what you consciously need to be aware of.

Lion head chain represents all kings that walked the earth, past to present, do what the Most High love, with color diamonds as stars in the lion eyes representing truth beyond belief, and a color diamond as the third eye, symbolizing higher learning.

Converse not with those who have nothing to say to you mentally, so physically, spiritually, or financially figure yourself out to know thy self.

Be invited not self-invited, don't invite yourself, be invited, you got to be bold to have self-control, your first mistake can be your last mistake, let every move you make be precise, brilliantly thought out, it's a hidden message in all that transpire, only the brilliance can recognize that, capital game recognize capital game, weak minds can't say they know this, because this out their league, no fake it til you make it can walk on the mack moon, because it's out of their sight.

Some people shouldn't have privileges, just orders, city to city, state to state, contribute to everybody state one way or another helpfully, let everything fall into place, see, and not be seen.

Evil will give you illusions in exchange for your blessings, evil make slaves out of men, it's not who sell their soul, it's about who get it back, evil will create a problem, then arrive like superman, to save the day after secretly creating the problem.

Infiltrators is always lurking, stay away from those who feed off negative energy, The great I Am will always speak through indigenous soulful to the indigenous soulful, it's always best to speak on what you know about, not because you heard about it, yet because you studied it, and learned about it, & finally mastered it, I'm listening to j cole song, it's called, "middle child."

The wise will rise surprise, seek to be motivated by the Creator, speak loud silent, always remember what good who did what for you, let everything pay for itself.

You can't rise with the wrong crowd, your up rise will be postponed till you distance yourself from them, you will remain in quick sand, believe that, or let it alone, like minister Farrakhan be saying.

I'm listening to jay-z song, its called, "you only a customer," futuristic smith.

Never break yourself, eliminate self-destruction, manmade happiness lead to sadness, if things is hard, pray to be taught how to make it easy, anything of importance revolves around the indigenous soulful pyramid golden brown alpha omega.

In the concrete jungle, I'm a Mack, I reached a king level in the Mack lifestyle, which is why I'm a king named Mack, because it's not just a name, it's what I was born to do, believe that, or let it a lone.

So it is who I am, so it's not Mack joe, or mackin' joe, it is I King Mack, a Mack crowned king by the Most High, with forever prosperity, Lord Willing' like the Virginia clipse said, strictly for all the right reasons.

Always put elders first, also those worthy of being in high rank, stay away from where you not invited, once you in the door, do not point out no faults, see without saying what you see, master feelings, and emotions, mind, body, and memories.

Permission to continue to wake up from the Creator is appreciated very much so, seek not sadness, anger, or happiness, seek a relationship with the Creator, and complete your twenty fours of consistently talking to The Most High, to humble yourself.

I'm listening to jay-z too short song, it's called, "week ago," they made this during east coast west coast feud, too short caught a airplane to New York, something about Scarface didn't make the flight, nothing like that was expected to happen, too short just took the flight and made history.

Retired pinky ring street Kings will do community service consistently, to give back to the Most High, get old mentally before you get old physically, if you don't know how to play your part, you can not get in powerful positions, or you will get took out of powerful positions, capitol game is ancient global brilliance, those who never lived your lifestyle, they will not understand you, or the lifestyle you live, I'm listening to leroy hutson song, it's called, "when you smile," respect to wegonridetv, they was in hollywood hitting switches on new year's Eve, bumping that song, respect to pee wee kirkland, for his harlem worldwide community service.

Keep yourself silent like the night, study, analyze, if somebody life going in the direction yourself is going into, think, link up like Jamaicans say, endure the test of time, patience is why everything will work itself out, always put the Most High first.

Mack 10 song called, "take a hit," it just went off, now I'm listening to sway interview kristen davis, the manhattan madam is what she known as, her & remy ma cool, she spoke highly about remy ma.

LITTLE ROCK ARKANSAS
PLAYBOY JESSE

Introduction or foreword from my book

"Funny how we today abuse our authority when given to hinder, halt, usurp, and hold back black men women and children for less than sensible reasons in a somewhat ambiguous manner as if, they are uncertain, whether the harm they cause benefits or hinders themselves. As the slaves believed it takes more than a village it takes all. How many of us today would benefit from reading about our past or being in the presence of great leaders of all races. Instead of hood celebrities.

Rough cut.

THE GAME OF LIFE SCRIPTURES

15.

Playing the game of life, is knowing how to roll it, live to give, give to live, it's about unity, team work works, it's a proven fact, teams have won championships, everybody need everybody, cross country living, will explain what the game of life scriptures is all about.

I'm listening to Suga free song, it's called, "tmz," I'm in kneely North Carolina, and it's 40 degrees, Ia be back in Florida in three days for show, young bleed song, It's called, " I couldn't c' it," it just came on, " you think about it," now I'm listening to california pimpin Ken, gangsta brown family, he speaking on who was the best," "at one point in time everybody was the best, when you having so much money that you can't count it, you got to weigh it, you are the best," now the click song just came on, it's called, "money luv us," I'm watching bro. C. Freeman-el Esther: realm of the eastern star, peace to blessings to the elder, now back to this brilliantly written book.

PIMPOLOGY

Pimpology is the studying of where somebody else left off, hearing the wicked ways of getting paid, simultaneously surviving in the most righteous gentleman way possible.

Pimpology is making every move beneficial, also consistently staying futuristic, accumulating right now to accommodate pimpin' in time to come.

Pimpin' don't get involved in hear say, hoe say, they say, seeing is believing, hearing is spelt analyzing.

A pimp main objective in the game of life, is to master life situations, and not let no situation in life master pimpin'.

A pimp concern is his pimpin, that's the source to his existence, which consist of his kingdom, his business, his future, and what is long-term beneficial.

When a pimp start seeing himself in another state, city, country, or continent, it's time to go, fly, yacht, or highway, or subway, one way or another, it's time to go.

Pimpology is strictly for the Suga Free, last of the dinosaurs, the ism is sold, simply because the buyer of ism will cherish it, and put it to use, the game is sold, Because a lot of people don't know how to comprehend the game of life scriptures, so if they buy it, I would say they would understand it more, how that sounds, if you buy game, you will respect it better, a lot of chosen individuals is born with game, so if you given the unchosen individuals game, & they don't understand it, they gone have to pay for it, either way it go, just to get more help to figure out what type of game you gave them, so they can put it to use.

A pimp doesn't stand behind a woman, a pimp sits on a throne to rule in his pimpdom, he live for those who put him on top of the world.

Pimpin' is a way of living, it has a language only spoken by pimpin', and it can only be translated by pimpin'.

Pimpology is transitioning from player to coach, seeking the most valuable players to coach, which will be those born to be with him.

A pimp ain't got no day off, or time to lose, a pimp stays physically built, mentally balanced, and financially healthy.

A pimp knows it's not necessary to handcuff money routes, because a lineup is always on standby, and ready to sub in, can't hold somebody that don't want to be under your wings, sometimes people just got another purpose in life, & all the time it ain't serving your purpose, live & let live.

A pimp knows if he has to teach a rose how to be a rose, it's like force, you can't make somebody be somebody they weren't born to be.

Pimpology teaches to respect all pimps, down, or sitting on a throne, if possible, help out any pimp in need of a helping hand, to a pimp, that's considered to be standing tall through it all, lows to highs, keeping head above water, & lending a helping hand to a friend down on bended knees.

A pimp keep his pimpdom out his business, if a pimp give an inch to a rose, that which is not born to be his business, she will take a mile, and see his kindness as his weakness, strictly for her to attack him, every opportunity possible, that which she feels like it is being presented to her.

Pimpology teaches a pimp to study the ways of his pimpdom, and which direction to direct his pimpdom.

A pimp doesn't have time to hate, debate, or time waste, if something, or someone is not worth time, or effort, all will fall victim to becoming invisible to a pimp.

A pimp always got something to do, even when he doesn't have anything to do.

Everything a pimp do, it will be important to somebody somewhere, other than his pimpin self.

A pimp is the king on the chessboard, all the way inside the game of life, a pimp number one rule is to stick to the script, and play it full effortfully, how it goes to win, without a doubt, or question.

A pimp number two rule, strictly deal with the real, keep a grip so he won't slip, that's the pimpin truth in more ways than one.

A pimp never follow the enemy lead, only his right mind.

Pimpology teaches to prevent self-destruction, finding new ways every day to do so, trust, or bust, sink, or swim.

A pimp knows, when it is time to change how he plays his cards, strategically in order to win, he knows automatically its mandatory to do so.

A pimp full time job, is to stay on point, never fall off his square.

A pimp lets his game speak for itself, no need to brag, or stand in the spotlight, his ism has magnetism, no need to seek attention.

A pimp that seeks help to speak hatred on a pimp, is not a pimp, he is a fraud, an infiltrator stealing a pimp glory, he need to be placed under pimp arrest, and reprogrammed.

Pimpology teaches pimpin how to put a strain on weak game, that which will attempt to attack his pimpin, a pimp got to stay ready till his day is complete.

A pimp doesn't let a person, place, or thing make him, or break him, he self-made, self inspired, self motivated, self encouraged, and self-educated.

When a pimp need to update, upgrade, rebuild, he sits down without, or before being made to sit down.

A pimp ain't negotiating, or making deals, nor will he cross in other lanes,foolishly mixing business with pleasure.

A pimp's pimpdom's individuals, must be born to be dedicated, to keeping the pimp with all he need for his pimpdom, in order to properly lead his pimpdom, straight to longevity.

A pimp let every individual, show that they want to be down, simply by contributing to his bank account, to help him accomplish goals, that was set up for his pimp lifestyle, and pimpdom, that's mandatorily meant to be accomplished, by one king plus all.

Pimpin' is king, pimpdom is behind him every step the king takes, backing him all the way up, holding up his throne, he keeps his pimpdom out his business, his pimpdom is his intermediate family, strictly united for survival, and to handlelifev long term business, all live long day to night to day again.

Pimp, plus another pimp pimpin', a lot of the times don't add up to friendship, no late-night hangouts, strictly come up missions, don't tempt a pimp, or distract a mack, warren g song is called, "in the midnight hour," featuring Nate dogg, it just came on, a song like this will set up a scene with you, as you're theme music, to get the conversation started, speaking on any topic that requires attention.

A pimp personal preference is progress, prosperity, peace, currency, property, accommodations, consistency, dedication, cooperation, no stress, no trouble, or problems.

A pimp got to get right, stay right, all that before he takes flight.

A pimp is his own best friend, or worst enemy, a pimpdom know not to create problems, then want a reward for it.

A pimp pimpdom is safe, secure, setup to have what is wanted, needed, and what they should have, a pimp knows if he do what others do, he will become like them, so that's why It mandatory for him to keep it pimpin', all live long day to night to morning again, no breaks, or setbacks welcomed.

A pimp will not simp wimp for a price tag, a pimpdom must be wise, with good intentions, learning advanced intelligence, to better assist their lifetime king.

The average person has a problem telling themselves no, a pimp main aim is to master, mind, body, and controlling his spirit on all levels.

The pimpin' never get old, or played out, as long as he stays sharp, keeping his game tighter than the Virgin Islands, this book, showl is keeping it pimpin.

Pimpology, is knowing about the weather before it's about to change, a pimp speaks professional, intellectually, and brilliantly consistently naturally.

A pimp get paid for thinking, putting cash in his hand, is a form of the ultimate respecting to him.

A pimp never accepts offers, that which will bring the worst out of him, or his pimpdom.

A pimp knows its traps in the world, strategically setup to get the best out of him first, then everything else he got next, I mean straight drain him, sucking the life out of him, all the way til he Po, broke, and lonely.

Real pimpin is based around love, dedication, respect, & the Most High, with a time limit on everything being done, especially around people dedicated to habits, stay clear of drink talkers, take no breaks til it's time to retire, mandatory to aim consistently for the next level, leave when you get to big for a small town, it's time to depart to new places to cover more ground, which is unknown territory to you, never forget when the grass get low, the snakes will show, and if you put a rose in a garden, it will grow, great development will transpire in the correct environments.

Respect to author slim diamond book, "pimpknowledgy," also author mr. Fly from New York, his book Is called, "love, fantasy & money: the chronicles of a master pimp," also the grandmaster king Virgil fairley book is called, "from the inside out: forced In the game," which I read cover to cover, it's what some call a must read.

THE LAST MACK STANDING SCRIPTURES

11.

Step in smooth to lay It down thick, straight grinding like they do in Little Rock Arkansas, got to learn how to live, then learn how to earn, then learn how to make money work for you, then learn how to pull up shining brand new, like they say In Memphis, "this what game plus money do for you," if you learn how to direct traffic, Memphis know the business, on some project pat type stuff, It's all about getting life right, wealthy comfortable with longevity, and spirituality.

I want to say thank you to one, to all, thank you for reading my book with your undivided attention, this the full effort, I mean full effort I'm putting in this book, to make it complete, I'm listening to Jay-Z song called, "so ghetto," I'm still in ft. Pierce Florida, forts usually means war grounds, I'm sweating like I'm nervous, it's 77 degrees right now at night, this perfect weather for February, I'm rushing to get this book done for January, so forgive me for any incomplete sentences, I'm editing this complicated book myself, when you see the word me instead of the word my, I did it on purpose, back to the book, troy ave & fabolous song, it's called, "street life," it's playing right now.

PIMPOLOGY

Now check this out, people saying something to you, verbally, text, or written letter, you got to recognize, in order to put a spell on somebody, you got to use letters to spell a word, then group words up in a sentence to recite to ears listening, that's how you get cursed, or a spell put on you, but you ain't heard that from me, that's what Kim wayans said, she said on the classic tv show, "in living color,"

my mind be thinking millions of thoughts like this every hour, a group of world famous rap duo called south circle, their song is called, "all day everyday," it just came on in the delta 88, I made enough mistakes in life, simply to teach my royal family how to stay alive, & how to be comfortable for the rest of their life, peace & blessings to those I met, knew, or will meet, jay-z intro for tru life album, It just came on.

While I watched Tousha Dominique sexy hood rat walk directly towards the delta 88, just to come get in the delta 88, I had my last two dobb godfather hats in the back window, when her & baby ghetto got out the crowded ghetto fabulous gas station, I started thinking to myself; I got to talk to Uncle Sunny about my lifestyle, & this powerful Pimp Game I'm benefiting from, this king macklifestyle is seriously complicated if you not globally historically educated, with ancient wisdom, it will lead you up to self destruction.

When they was on their way back to the original gangster car, I was cell phone chopping up game with Big Money Sunny, speaking on how I'm feeling unbalanced, Pondering through my thoughts thinking about my parents, he said, "that's bound to happen sooner than later, Millon mackin."

He said, "Remember it's all about timing, if something, or somebody supposed to come into your life, they, or it will come, if something supposed to happen, its gone happen no matter what, what you put in is what you get out, what you do might get done to you, & sometimes people just need to feel certain people presents."

"People who been here for years, they can let you know what went on before you were born, certain thoughts shouldn't be spoken out loud, what you do shall be done to you, so treat people how you want to be treated."

I said, "If you don't mind, I'm going to come by your boss player palace for a little while," he said, "nephew you always invited, he spoke in Swahili, yale yangu ni yako," I said, "Give me like 20 minutes, me, and my lovely ladies will be pulling up, soon come mon," That's what Jamaican Richard would say.

I was driving while I was iPhone 10 cell phone talking, when I got off the Prime Co cell phone, I was watching Ms. Baby Ghetto, she reach to the alpine radio to play Suga Free song, its called, "Pimpin in the year 3000," I was thinking to myself whispering in the wind to the Most High, thank you for the ladies that's in my life, to those who will be in my life, and forgive us for making a way out of nowhere, the way we doing it.

I skip to south circle song, its called, "attitudes," & I turned it up a notch, or two, if you saw us, you would recognize my royal family will be certified players anywhere in the world, we play the music that complements the mood we in, and to celebrate us John Trevota style, straight staying alive, just like phill Collins, "I been waiting for this moment all my life."

By the time we were pulling up to the duplex building, we noticed Salena looking out her sister house burgundy curtain window, when Salena stepped in the name of love on the front porch, her elegant self, she was wearing a sexy red carpet, somewhat see threw pitch black Cannes Dior looking dress; she called it her sexy Azizi Johari playboy bunny dress, I told you my royal family is stars, straight loveable certified characters, straight stars in sunlight to moonlight, and I mean that.

I got out the antique delta currency mean green delta 88, I felt like mean green master p Mia x, "major players," it was like I pulled up to the Ken ivy 1997 players ball, I noticed rw brother p was driving pass in his Rivera on BRABUS 24" MONOBLOCK Z "PLATINUM EDITION" rims, he was banging Gucci mane song, it's called, "trap house."

Ms. Baby Ghetto took it upon herself to get in the back seat, I opened the trunk, I got out their Tiffany & Co. ring boxes, and then I got back in the mean green colored Delta 88, it was sitting on Forgiato Estremo rims.

I turned on Sade song, it's called, "Your Love is King," they all said, "hello," to each other, the saying is, threes company, I felt like John Ritter, you know Jack Tripper.

I said, "here's a 5ct Verragio Designer ring for Ms. Salena, here's a 2ct Oval Pave ring for Ms. Baby Ghetto, & here a 1.7ct Round Halo ring for our newest royal family member, the intelligent beautiful unique Ms. Tousha Dominique," I'm like silkk the shocker, "just be straight with me," if not I can, "charge it to the game," respect to all the no limit soldiers, welcome home to Mac Phillips.

They each gave me a Christopher George Latore Wallace Kimberly Denise Jones husband wife I do kiss, I said, "learn history, which is the language of the land, take heed to guidance, signs, signals, know when to speak, keep quiet, ignore, mistakes make us brilliant, & use your gifts to start, & finish your life."

"Let neither man nor woman separate what the Most High has brought together, & with a "say what you mean, & mean what you say voice tone," I said, "I love my royal family."

When I pulled off slower then two 57 year old turtles running to a Mongoose, they each were admiring their unexpected well deserved gifts, they were looking at me like I proposed to them at the Apollo Theater, in Harlem, on 253 West 125th street, peace to blessings to basketball giant Tyrone alimoe evans the cross country street ball king of your courts,?also welcome back to guy fisher the one time owner of Apollo theater, big time stuff right there, who else owned the Apollo theater.

I said, "it's a full-time job being alive, staying alive, saying no to yourself, fighting temptation, & avoiding distractions."

"I don't have to explain what I said, because my royal ladies understand what need to be understood, plus its self-explanatory to the royal family."

I said, "We going to relax in the Michigan lakefront penthouse condo, at 601 Lofts, with the 2.7-million-dollar expensive Lake Front view," y'all know, it's some million dollar mackin going on in this brilliant wrote, reality based, Mackology 2nd edition book.

They sat silent like the Great Sphinx of Giza, while waiting to eat the food for thought I fed them, I said, "interference comes to let you know to never get to comfortable, it's always somebody who want what you want, or trying to stop you from getting what you want, in this lifetime, some people will do the unbelievable to eliminate competition."

"Be careful what you ask for, never put too much on your Naomi Osaka Japanese Kobe Steak plate, trickery can end up making somebody miserable, forever to always, it will show when people get placed in a new position."

Beautiful nice Heather hunter height Salena said, "I can listen to you talk all night king mackin," meanwhile, Ms. Baby Ghetto, & tousha D., They was sleep in the back seats on the ostrich skin back seats, I said, "we here boss lady, wake the sleeping beauties up."

I reached in my outer space, pitch black rabbit fur coat, for my solid gold prime co cell phone, then I called Big Money Sunny, I said, "Unc Man, the King here with his Queens," he said, "I'm gone tell lapham park Bunchie, he working at the front desk, in the lobby, to buzz y'all in, Little ancient Pimpin."

I got my eyes on Rihanna and Chris Jenner, them some cold ladies, I'm listening to jay-z Rihanna song, its called, "run this town," she singing like a mug, her voice just complements the night life, like black rob said, "whoa," that's whoa.

She woke the beauty queens up, finally we all got out the green colored limousine, I said, "If the Cadillac North star light hit them rings right, it's gone look like a disco ball in Studio 54 outside," they all started smiling like they was American idol winners, from where we was standing by the Delta 88, we can hear the condo front door speakers, it was playing coo coo cal song, it's called, "mind is gone," now this how a condo welcome a royal family, we felt like we was going to our new home away from home in the boss player palace.

They was walking next to me glancing at the lake front on our right side, very proudly confidently smiling so hard, it was like somebody said, "it was raining hundred dollar bills," respect to north memphis project pat, I said, "before we go in here, y'all know the business, don't test the best, test the rest, speak slow, play defense, plus play offense when you walk, talk, arrive, & depart."

In less then a missy elliott minute man minute, after getting off the elevator, we was walking in his rich man penthouse; the girls went straight to the Lake Front view window, directly after greeting uncle big money Sunny, they wanted to see Milwaukee from over 150 feet in the sky, on the low, I did to, it looked good fifth teen floors high up in the clouds, perfect view to watch the u.s. bank building 4th of july lake front fireworks show.

While they was rushing to the window to see the scenery, Uncle Sunny had the Dynamikks Ultima home radio playing Suga free song, it's called, "circus music," featuring STL Chingy, what you know about that, he had it playing for us, uncle Sunny is more of a james Brown Willie Hutch type of music man, you know what um tum bout.

I came in wearing my rex rabbit, Mayfair mall nickavonni's clothing store $1500 fur coat, choking the goose neck bottle of Rose Moet Tousha D gave me, Uncle Sunny looked at me to say, "You know I love Rose Moet," I said, "if you got the glasses, we can sip, chill, & lean on the truth."

He grab the Tizo Versailles champagne flutes out his Sonoma bar corner cabinet, I popped the Moet open, like a Beverly Hills, urasawa miss America winning waitress, popped it open like she be doing, Uncle Sunny said, "tell them if they want something to eat, or drink, don't hesitate to get it," I said, "ladies one shot a piece of whatever y'all prefer, matter of fact, eat some of them cut up fresh fruits, in the william yeoward crystal bowl first, then drink, & all Newport 100's, california, or denver smoke signals activities will transpire on the luxurious balcony," simultaneously they all said, "ok Mackology," sounding like a singing group named swv, I love these ladies, they cool, respectful, and funny, my royal family lovely ladies, a round of applause for my royal family everybody, Brooklyn nets fabolous song called, "cold summer," just gangsta walked in my area, this video true classic for a lifetime, I heard somebody say, "timeless music."

I said, "cheers to more years Unc man," he said, "you doing progressively good, you prosperously maintaining drug free, sucker free, y'all down with each other.

Then c-bo the bald head nut, his song called, "getting to the money," featuring vallejo b-legit, it just came on, then uncle sunny said, "now listen, a wise man will put anything to good use, or turn nothing to something, or nobody into somebody, people who know more, will speak less, sometimes the people who always got something to say, they ain't got nothing to say at all."

I said, "That make sense to me, I agree with you Unc man, now if you feel the need to breakdown in fractions, this intelligent to brilliant Pimp game to me, please do so with a full effort."

He said, "person into making profit, life in the fast lane, the devil business, easy living, sipping, dipping, luxury living, counting dirty currency, the concrete jungle, business make me rich, to keep me rich, pimp or die, sex sell best in a five-star hotel, this game ain't for no lames, you can't complain, just spit more game, it's about selling sex to get paid in full, to retire early in life."

"This game ain't to be glorified, this a stepping stone, it's about progress without stress, it helps, it harm, it builds, it destroys, it's all about figuring out the hidden truth, it's about rising, and surprising."

"I learned how to Pimp anybody, by always staying near Killer Whales in the ocean, studying them when they was in motion, I looked, listened, learned, & waited till it was my turn, & time, to shine," then coo coo cal song called, "dedication," it came on.

"I told you when you were ten, when you get older, you will see more; you member I was on 6th street, now I'm in the penthouse suite, like Mr. Ken Ivy said, "from the lower class ghetto streets to millionaire executive suites," & keep in mind, presently all my royal family members, they all got luxury apartments, that's the game of life, that's how it's played professionally."

"They each come here to drop off a thousand, or more, to keep the king motivated, to take extremely great care of his royal family, own live behind schedule, because I stay updated, upgraded, I treat my ladies accurately according to how they living, to keep us on top of the game of life."

Uncle Sunny was wearing a rare chinchilla robe, with hornback lizard sandals, with matching godfather dobb socks, with a gucci t shirt, with Gucci shorts, extra boss player style, he always comfortable, he known as the ultimate soul survivalist.

Uncle Sunny started saying, "I learned to dress with classic Harlem Cotton Club dapper Dan style, how to impress who want me, need me, should have me, like me, love me, that's who matter to me, those pros that pay my lifestyle."

"I been Pimpin' sense I was four-foot-tall, I met Boss Pimps in the Warren G mid night hours, I been putting in work as long as I had a peach fuzz, straight independent in this Game of Life, from paying my dues."

"One breeze I had, many moons ago, like California say, I say breeze, because she came to leave," she said, "who you Pimpin' for, God, or the devil?"

"I was 19 or 21, she was 24, she had Penske Truck Rental driver miles on her, she ran through years like Laverne Hart from New Jack City, local Pimps, heartless drugs, family pains, teary eyed sadness, & she said that smith to me," he shook my hands & said, "ooh wee man, that's cold ain't it lil pimpin."

{beautiful lady from Ohio told me about lil baby the rapper, his video is called, "the bigger picture."}

"If I could, I would Sidney Poitier In the Heat of the Night, slap her right before she said all that to me, I can't, & won't forget that question as long as I live, and you know what, I got to admit, she was right in more ways then one, but I want to say to her saying that, "I'm pimpin to have me a bank roll, but it wouldn't be for the devil, it would be for God in who we trust, that's on the dollar bill," what's up to dollar bill in Brockton Massachusetts, and to all the cape Verde ladies in Massachusetts.

He said, "capital game recognize capital game, don't it man, that business lady put me up on game, ahead of game, she futuristic me didn't she man, space age pimping like 8ball & MJG, it started right then, and there," he walked to his radio, just to turn up Suga free song, it's called, "can't lie to yourself," we clinged glasses, and sipped to the game of life, looking at my royal family, while they was on the luxury balcony with Milwaukee famous downtown skyline in front of them, the scenery is flawless.

My royal family was on the luxury balcony, they was puffing on cigs in the summer breeze, each one was sipping a flute glass of remy xo, they was smiling, glancing at their New Orleans bling bling lil Wayne rings, then 8ball orange mound mjg song, it came on, it was called, "classic pimpin."

I'm watching Olympic basketball USA vs Nigeria July 12, 2021, Nigeria making USA work, black vs brown, In't seen no good basketball game In years, this nice.

THE LAST MACK
STANDING SCRIPTURES

12.

Step in smooth to lay It down thick, straight grinding like they do in Little Rock Arkansas, got to learn how to live, then learn how to earn, then learn how to make money work for you, then learn how to pull up shining brand new, like they say In Memphis, "this what game plus money do for you," if you learn how to direct traffic, Memphis know the business, on some project pat type stuff, It's all about getting life right, wealthy comfortable with longevity, and spirituality.

I'm in Jefferson Ohio at the present moment, "leaning back," like fat joe said, I'm watching the king of bankhead Georgia, king shawty lo, it's his video, it's called, "Dunn dunn," respect to a mane that did his time, and got out on top of his game, he kilt the music industry, respect to the king, that's shawty lo, he ten toes down wearing a crown, never heard him hate on nobody, or talk that kill an indigenous person type stuff, in order for him to sell records, that's a king worthy of wearing his crown, never will it be misunderstood, that this sending message to imitate his life actions, this what you call showing love, respect, admiration, them type of words Is the point being made, no misunderstandings, or misleading the flock astray, this book is not to be misinforming anybody, or saying what is misunderstood is guidance, this book is meant for those with advanced intelligence, with skills to interpret what is precisely being insinuated in this brilliant book, called, "the king business Mackology 2nd edition!

This book is a conversation, chopping up game, braking down the ism in fractions you call chapters, speaking is complicated if you not self educated, or highly educated, either way you being told that this book Is not instructions manuals, it's a conversation of life itself, from a philosophical philosopher perspective of what have been perceived from the indigenous people journey to wealthy with longevity involved permanently.

NEW YEAR EVE 11:00PM

Around this time in my lifestyle, I was all the way on point, like snoop dogg's Stacey adams, the problem was, my royal family was getting tired of the lifestyle we was living, from my perspective, we was all thinking different about life, to much was happening, my little cousin telly toes, he was 15 driving a two seater, drop top, like Miami convertible bert, then next thing I know, i was in a courtroom, I was watching his sentencing, he was doing 5 years in a juvenile detention center, for a bank move, my other cousin t money, he was doing time for the same bank move, with telly toes, d block got caught up in a Lexus, in Texas, with a few ounces of el chapo, jj havin bread, he got caught with 8 p diddys of kush cologne, wozzie the don, he got caught with lassie favorite dog food, he was serving an under cover a trick or treat candy, og aj got caught with some of that Frank Lucas, on some Frank Mathew, cross country, live off the fat of the land type stuff, og don was locked up for kingpin gangster living conspiracy charges, & a childhood friend named Jamaica, he was from the London Square get money click, he caught over ten years, karnell got caught out of state laying low, I was on my own, like young bleed, everybody was becoming prisoners of war in the game of life.

I found myself thinking, if I don't row my boat somewhere tonight, I probably was gone be playing myself in monopoly, it's a way to stay sharpening up your business skills, time how long it took to get all properties, in a genius way this is played, analyzed, Its basically a way to brainstorm about life chessboard moves, then I was thinking about where should a young boss player, where should a boss player be chilling til the new year popup, a place where no boss player hatred was applauded, a place money makers chill balling comfortably, you know what um tum bout, a place where, I don't have to be carrying a desert eagle like lucky, a place where I can chop up game while playing pool, then it hit me, the bosses lounge, it was right by Mario liquor store, its on north holton, across the street from the come steal something gas station, I was in the kia truck rolling, bumping big tymers song, its called, "pimp on," this was my theme song, if they make a movie about this book, this song gone come on when the movie start, I had all four windows half way down, with the front sun roof open, I had a champagne bottle of mailly grand cru extra brut, I had It in the back seat area, a custom made champagne bottle holder, I had my cup filled up with pimp juice, Milford Connecticut, mailly grand cru champagne, it was bubbling all in my plastic cup, I just left that liquor store on 3rd wright, I had a fresh jazz black band lit, my fox fur coat uncle juny gave me, with rubber band green backs in my inside pockets, I was wearing mean money green colored horn back lizards on my feet, with a 3x brand new black t shirt on, with gold diamond front two teeth, I was coming east on north Avenue, then Westside connection song, it's called, "connected for life," it came on, I took a sip of the boss player mailly grand cru champagne, parked the 88, got out to walk to the east side most known spot, and I slid like seals on ice, directly towards the bosses lounge, a specific place where certified hustlers, to original gangsters, to solid gold pimps, where they ball out at, it's a song called, "players night out," 8ball made it, that's the theme song for the bosses lounge.

While I was walking to the lounge, I saw a better spot to park across the street, it was a spot inside the gas station, I can ask north India to let me park for a little while, By the time I was parking at the pump, at the gas station on holton north Avenue, lil flip song, its called, "this the way we ball 3," it was banging out the kia truck, I had the push start button, I locked the doors inside the truck with the moc-control, then I saw an indigenous soulful gal getting out her pretty hot pink s-class benz, loud was the volume of the music she was playing, she was dancing in the gas station by her s-class benz, it was a pretty round brown stripper, she was dancing to the song, its called, "blow the whistle," her plates said california, own know who she is, but she look like she got something good going on where ever she going to, then I saw an indigenous elder, he was getting in his pitch black stankin Lancoln, he was smiling proudly, his license plates said california to, he look like Vallejo j. Diggs, he was walking strong, like he just cashed a $50,000 check, his nikavonni mink was dragging on the ground, all that was happening as he walked to his comfortable car, I aimed myself in the gas station, so I can pay for parking at the pump, I was on some Milwaukee type stuff, slid kaladeed a couple dubs, told him I will be moving the kia 2013 sorento truck in a few hours, he head nodded, then asked the customer behind me, "is that all they was buying," I pimp stick walked out the door to explore through the new year eves night, crossed the busy north Avenue lake front route street, it was an og puffing some hydro outside, he was BBQing in the back, it was fenced off in the yard, on the side of the club, it was directly on the side of the club, I said what up though to him, he said, "just got the best baby back ribs, bbq chicken, & catfish for you young money, come get something to eat, after you finish two pool games," I said, "alright I got you."

I can hear the music from inside, outside, it was bumping chamillionaire & paul wall song, it's called, "n luv wit my money," I grabbed the door knob to open the door, I was greeted by an East side Milwaukee original gangster, by the name of j ro, pounded him up, then security pet me down like qincheng prison guards, the DJ was on the Microphone, doing what's called milwaukree jaw jackin, it was dj tony neal, & homer blow, I thought his name was home of blow all this time, they was hyping the crowded club up, homer blow said, "whats up to my li player newphew, millon mackin," he said, "you right on time, they choosin tonight," then he blended alabama dirty boyz song, it Is called, "Rollin vogues," they put that song on for me, introduction into the bosses lounge, let's see how the night go, then I slid in the crowd unnoticed.

I squeezed through towards the tyesia pretty face bartender, last time I was here, she gave a player a Remy Hennessey hypnotic drink, its called gangsta juice, she said, "mack what you sippin tonight, mailly grand cru extra brut, or don perigon?"

I said, "surprise me boss lady," the music was banging hard, I looked back at the wall by the front door, to look at the new painting, it was the tiger drawing of king stuff, boss player stuff was going on inside the details of the picture, with Siberian manchurian tigers in suits.

Next thing I know, poppy g tapped me on the shoulder, he was like whats up bro, he was wearing that camron oh boy avirex coat, it was him, Willie, & Shawn wearing a king fur hat, Shawn just got out a little while before this day, he was wearing ice chain with all diamonds from the rainbow, they all was paid in full, straight early young money makers, Milwaukee produced basketball players, hustlers, gangsters, and pimps, you was one or the others, or you grew up like me, combined with all that going on from your upbringing, I stayed studying the game of life scriptures from childhood to adulthood.

I shook all their hands, then told them to meet me in VIP in ten minutes, I'm bout to sit down at a table for a little bit, they said cool, we there, I slid through the crowd fur coating, & champagne sipping, I asked j ro for a $100 table section, just til I leave, he shook my money in hand, pointed to a table in the spotlight, gave an indigenous gangster that was looking serious faced, the he coming your way head nod, he headed noded back to j ro, I pounded him again, then headed myself towards the table, pointed my glass to the table while looking at poppy g, Willie, & king shawn, they raised their glasses up to me, I know they was on business, so I cool smiled, then the og DJ, he put on too short song, it was called, "blow the whistle," second time I heard this song tonight, I stepped to the indigenous young gangster, money hand shook up with him, in a $50 way, security was serious tonight, he lifted up the velvet looking rope for me to walk to my seat, then he locked the rope back, I was getting ready to start sitting down, then I heard a voice say, "fur coat," it was Kim & shay from 6th hadley, I said, they cool, spoke that to the young gangster, he lifted up the rope, then they came & sat down, both of them was saying what up, we ain't seen you in years, I said, yeah it's been a while, y'all drink rose moet, I saw a sexy Tina Marie looking waitress walking pass, she was winking at me, I said, "a, come mere boss lady, I told her I need rose moet, & three goblet glasses, I put two hundred in her apron, she said, "I got you mack."

Then snoop dogg song, it's called, "ups & downs," it came on, it was 11:45 at this time, the og DJ said, I asked shay & Kim how they been, they spoke loud over the music saying, "we living," then they told me that Melvin, Tim, & Cory was locked up, I said, "I heard," I said it's ruff out here ain't it, the waitress came back smiling, I think she realized what I gave her, she gave nicole ari parker looking shay the rose moet, & she gave nia long looking Kim the glasses, & she gave me a paper receipt with her number on it.

Then poppy g, Willie, & king Shawn walked up, I nodded to the young gangster to let them pass the velvet rope, then they sat down with their gangster juice, i was feeling like Lenox from belly, then I introduced them to the two beauty queens, one pretty light skin, one pretty brown, then the og DJ, he said it's almost new years, he played trick daddy song, it's called, "in da wind," with ceelow green, then I said, "here's a toast to us all, we young not dumb, turning dreams to reality, the strong last long, the humble rule the jungle, & when game rain, laims complain, we tapped glasses indigenous soul folks people style, then we sipped the hard work pay off dranks in our cups, then my prime co cell rang, it was the royal family, I didn't want to answer yet, til big boi part went off on the trick daddy song, and I knew wh wast they was gone be telling me about, they was most likely gone be talking about changing their life.

Then pastor troy song, it's called, "ridin' big," it came on, I just pressed ignore, because I knew, I knew I had to make a plan for the new year, it had to be without the ladies I got, I was thinking about the money we stacked up, I was gone send them in the direction they deserve to be in, right before the Sumner end, I had capital game to proceed with, they put me where I'm at without a doubt, so I was ready to keep escalating to greater heights, recruit regroup, it's only the right thing to do, I was looking at Kim & shay enjoying themselves, then 50 cent song, it's called, "happy New Year," it came on, the crowd went crazy blowing horns, wearing happy New Year hats, even though I was starting a new plan, I was disappointed my ladies was leaving me, I still was happy with my hair long, & game strong, and all eyes watching knew it.

Happy New Year is what the og DJ said, then he dj kool herc spent the record around with one finger, & 50 cent song called, "happy New Year," it came back on, it was midnight, I poured shay & Kim up some moe rose moet, king Shawn, Willie, & poppy g had a bottle of Hennessey xo, & Remy xo on the table, with three ladies sitting on their legs, it was turning into a tupac shakur, calvin broadus, type of gangster party, it felt like Coolio said, "this the real gangster paradise," on some Las Vegas type stuff.

Then young jeezy song, it's called, "don't get caught," it came on, the young gangsters was bouncing their head, the ladies was choosing who they was leaving with, I poured the young goon up some rose moet, mixed with a glass of gangster juice, it was courtesy of poppy g.

At the same time, the dj said where all my East side players at, they all pop their fur collars, flick their bracelet, or diamond watch, or diamonds rings in the air, some had all that in the air, it's a celebration came on, then I noticed a boss player, eastside baller rapper, his name is young robo, he was in VIP next to me, he was surrounded by the east side, he said happy New year, it was his song the dj started playing, "celebration," and he threw up some hundreds, look like around $5000 easy, then the club went crazy, this was all 30 years old & younger crowd, it was unbelievable, look like a Lions gate movie, or hype Williams million dollar video.

Then the DJ said, "it's time to smoke like a castlewood fireplace chimney, the people in the crowd pulled out cabrini green to light up, I pulled a ounce of purple haze from Harlem, I pulled it out my pants pocket, I opened the bag, so I can pour it on the miranda acrylic backgammon glass table, it was all purple green buds, I pulled out three boxes of spice 1 mjg chocolate Phillies, I felt like I was a green Bay Packer, clethius hunt, I gave the goon gangster, a hand full of haze with three spice 1 chocolate phillies, then I rolled up two Phillies to leave with, then shay & Kim rolled up a Philly a piece, king Shawn, Willie, & poppy g let their new ladies roll up to, I passed haze to j ro with a philly, I saw that sexy waitress again, I told her come mere, I put haze on her tray with two Phillies, then I told her to roll one, then give the DJ one to roll, it was like snoop dogg, cheech, chong, & Willie Nelson was chilling in the club, if you didn't smoke, you still got Bob Marley lifted, on some dave chappelle, "I want to talk to samson," type stuff.

Drake song, it's called, "God's plan," it came on, I grabbed my Vic lighter to dry the fresh rolled philly, then i passed it in the crowd, to a young lady namedyalena k. the russian, then I put Hennessey xo in a shot glass, mixed it with Remy xo, with a splash of hynotic, gangster juice, i touched it with my clean fingernail finger tip, I did that to wet my philly, then it was done, purple haze chocolate philadelphia blunt, I call it the boss baller gangster blunt, with don in my glass, I lit it up, the club was on some, b real Dr greenthumbs, hotboxin with Mike Tyson type stuff, it was so smoky, it looked like we was standing in heaven front lobby, all the smoky Robinson mountain way up in the clouds, then nas & methodman song, it's called, "tales from the hood," it came on, I can tell the og DJ was relaxing now, he was laid back thinking, he was thinking about his gangster memories.

I took a Dizzy Wright, type of pull on the haze XO Philly, I did it like I was in Kingston with spragga benz, I was talking to the Most High about my lifestyle, I was thinking about wozzie the don, d block, jj havin bread, telly toes, & big cousin Chicago dino, I exhaled with a boat load of smoke dancing out my mouth, I felt like I was shaun lenox lewis, straight smoking good in the hood.

my royal family leaving me, yet I'm looking forward to a new royal family, you know what I'm tum bout, I sipped my don p, inhaled my Harlem world purple haze XO philly, exhaled it like I was kissing the sky, the club was puffing like they was in denver on 420, shay & Kim, they pulled on their haze in the prettiest woman way possible, then ace hood song, it's called, "hustle hard remix," it came on, the og DJ, he was back feeling gangster in the most, I made it this far way possible, in my do or die Chicago lifestyle.

I knew I spent around a thousand today, 28 grams of haze, boxes of chocolate Phillies from Greenfield smoke shop, yellow ribbon mailly grand cru extra brut, was waiting for me in the Kia truck, rose moet for Kim & shay, hundred for j ro vip section, 50 for goon gangster, 2 hundred for waitress, 50 for glass of don p, hit my mother with a hundred for her nails, sipped Remy xo with ray ray, & r&b singer lawyer tiara & dreena, and east side robbo just through 5 thousand up in the club, straight making it rain, he was on some given back to the community type stuff, I was looking in the club scoping the scenary, I saw a black chyna looking, nice height, thick lady, she was dancing stripper style with high heels on, with a matching knee high kim kardashian designed dress on, then I saw tiara friend, I call her rose Mary, she was sitting at the bar waving at me, I head nodded gold diamond teeth smiling, then I saw a Compton game looking gangster, he was throwing gang signs up at me, he was representing what block he from, I knew him from d block, block used to buy pounds of haze from him, I saw big Pete & fresh from lapham Park projects, with e Eric mika baby daddy with them, they all head nodded to me, I pointed my cup at them, I did that to show respect, then the og DJ put on the game song, it's called, "one blood," then I saw e Mike from Hamilton, he was with sunny from 4 5, I saw king center Bob behind them, then I saw king center laron & Charlotte at the bar, they was buying rose moet, Joey with the braces came in with Jason, Jason was fresh out prison, he was standing by gold mouth Jimmy, he just got out to, he put you in the mind of ceelow green, he stayed shining, jewleryed up from wrist, to fingers, to his neck, just boss balling, all the money makers was in attendance tonight, cash rule everything around me like wu tang said, that statement from staten island was in full effect.

Seeing all this, I knew I had to come out hard, like orange mound 8ball & mjg, that was the move this year, so I put my game face on, I was ready to excuse my current royal family now, so I can make space for my new royal family, own know about nobody else, but after growing up with who I grew up with, I knew I had to get wealthy in this lifetime, it's a reason I stay stepping my game up, all these young go getters would be looking at me sideways, if I didn't show my king macking currency increasing skills, I noticed a lady identical to flavor flav hoopz, I was tempted to pop my ps at her, but not tonight, I like to clock fat nots, & knock bad women when nobody looking, it's all part of that low key living under the radar, if what you do is unknown, who gone try to block you, or get what you aiming for, so I kept everybody thinking, all I did was, just get bread, I kept all from knowing how I get it, or from who I got it from, it's all game entertainment, low key under the radar.

Then troy ave & faboulous song, its called, "only life I know," it came on, I really wanted to get at shay & Kim in the most anxious way possible, these was the baddest women in Milwaukee, but I was taught that if a woman ain't living like you, don't tamper with them, tempt them, or put thoughts in their head, because when something hit the fan, they gone crack first under pressure, I needed women already in motion, with no strings attached to them, I looked in the crowd, I was seeing women reckless eyeballing, but I knew they was watching all us all night ballin, so I couldn't trust them, or who they might know, or run their mouth to about me, I had to catch my action in the act of paper chasing, you know what I'm tum bout, it's like those I grew up with, they don't understand the game of life, or know me, because I don't live like them, nor do they live like me, I need to be around risk takers, the do or die crowd, them who do what they do for bread & water, that's what isiah j.r. rider said, say no to wondering women, & bee's chasing hunny, I need women who got their hands on everything, abbreviations in full effect.

369

I'm playing with the hand I was dealt, I'm playing to win longevity style, one city ain't big enough, settling for whoever is unacceptable, um tum bout lifetime partners, I was starting to feel the don p, & XO haze philly taking control of me, it was time to go, I had to excuse myself, it was time to get on my new game plan, & do it in a mastermind, og gangster brown Oakland, general dubie Los Angeles type of way, that will set me up for a lifetime.

I hugged Kim & shay, pounded my London Square brothers up, Willie, poppy g, & king shawn, I inhaled my XO haze philly, the young gangster goon unlocked the velvet rope, then he dapped me up, I noticed he was wearing a custom made harlem dapper dan alfit, I squeezed the waitress knowing I wasn't gone call her, unless I saw her clocking dollars in a 5 star hotel, a place where sex sell best in the Midwest, kissed her neck in the most playboy maroy gentleman Chicago way possible, I reached inside my fur coat pocket, I was doing that to see how fat my green rubber band knot was, I didn't need a take home glass, only because I had mailly grand cru extra dry champagne, I had that sitting patiently in the Kia truck waiting on royalty, that was parked in the come steal something gas station, I left the haze on the glass table, I just remembered, it was for the night life, from me, grease palms they call it, lay it out nice for who around you, and it keeps violence from happening, jolly green giant left over, after I'm gone, I bought VIP seats, plus drinks, paid waitress, goon gangster, & og j ro, I left on, how you say a good note, welcome to Milwaukee night life, I was leaving to go on my all night flight.

I pounded j ro up, then I nodded to the sexy players club regina hall looking bartender, I nodded to the og dj, I inhaled the purple haze, then I passed it to og j ro, I walked out door with haze XO smoke stalking behind me, others in the club could see, that it was stalking me, until I closed the club door on it, I could still hear troy ave saying, "this the only life I know o o oh o o o," I aimed to cross the busy lake front route, on north Avenue street, so I could get to my Kia truck.

I was nikavonni's fured up, bank roll rubber banded back up, my boss player long hair blowing in the wind, my hornback lizards click clocking on the concrete jungle ground floor, traffic was to quiet, probably cause everybody somewhere happy New yearing, I still heard guns blasting in the air around me, I saw the lady by the gas station, she the one that everybody call crazy, but I know, that she just was acting like that, to pump fear in the young world she became old in, we eye contacted, & I gave her a dub, she smiled & said, "be safe," I said that as I slid in the Kia truck, she was smiling being her normal self, simply because nobody was looking, it's all game entertainment, & I appreciated the hidden truth revealing itself to me, as I was pouring my Mailly grand cru champagne up, I asked did she want some Connecticut champagne, she said, "on New Years night, yes I do young man," she said let me get a cup from kaladeed, I started the Kia up with the push start one button, with the truck keys in my pocket.

She came back out with ice in a large coffee cup, she had the top in her other hand, Milwaukee night life is game tight if you got game that recognize game, I mean really, who want everybody to know their business, I handed her the mailly champagne bottle, she said game recognize game, & when game rain, laims complain, I said you know the business like project pat said, she said, "I be watching you roll in & roll out, always slapping hands with money helping all us, you gone get your blessings baby, keep moving, you not like the others in the nightlife, the Most High got his yellow brick road under your feet, He love how you living your life, & you know, int lying, even if I was a character in your book, this to real to say, it's made up, or fake, your life is realer then real, it's just the truth like gucci mane said, you know everybody been lied to, it's like thinking, being real is about wasting time, sitting in prison, or wasting their life dying young, she gave me the most game back, I ever got for $20, and she said, "a life worth living is a life worth learning, enjoy your new year king."

I diamond teeth smiled at her, & said, "ia catch you later MS ma'am," that was her real name to me, you know the Giants told me her story, on how how she ended up on the streets, she caught a body & did her time, & this how she living now, she fighting her demons It looks like, I guess she dealing with the spirit of who she killed, it's real in the field.

I turned up mobb deep featuring lil kim song, it's called, "quiet storm remix," I put the Kia in drive, then I slid off like I was leaving An Oakland oeste bar parking lot, my music was banging out the sun roof, and half way down four windows, it was around 20 degrees, I sipped my cup of mailly grand cru champagne, took a pull on my Mississippi jazz band Louis Armstrong black e mild, then big Mike song, it's called, "havin thangs," it came on, it felt like big Mike was sitting next to me, in the passenger seat rapping his song, word for word, with pimp c in the back seat singing the chorus, smoking hydro til his chorus part came on.

I was on my way back in traffic, I was ready to major mack for huge faces, to pay for vacations in over the seas foreign places, my license plates said macking, it was king mack backwards, I was thinking about calling big money sunny, but I didn't want to interrupt him on his cross country, mr. Terry type 1970s pimpin, so I just drove to downtown Milwaukee, I went by the million dollar condo, I turned on bill withers song, its called, "grandma's hand," it made me want to call my grandma, but I didn't, because it was already late, I was young, wise, & having bread mastering the game of life, I been thinking about going to Miami for a day, just to chop up game with big money sunny, I knew that was gone be his last state, that he was gone hit, right before he make his way back to Wisconsin.

I was puffing my jazz black, I was still thinking about miami, I had this feeling that miami was gone be my new home, so I turned on og jt money song, it's called, "hustling," & it just hit me, I'm on the right track, og jt money was speaking to me through his music, directly to my ears, he was saying in so many words, in between his lines, that basically I was getting to big for Wisconsin, I knew from that point on, I finally built my self up to a giant level, boss player king status, huhn what, what you know about that, working hard reading every day, writing my way to genius thinking everyday, childhood to adulthood progress without stress, the game of life ingredients to a gourmet meal for a ten star recipe to surviving a good life.

THE LAST MACK STANDING SCRIPTURES

13.

Step in smooth, to lay It down thick, straight grinding like they do in Little Rock Arkansas, got to learn how to live, then learn how to earn, then learn how to make money work for you, then learn how to pull up shining brand new, like they say In Memphis, "this what game plus money do for you," if you learn how to direct traffic, Memphis know the business, on some project pat type stuff, It's all about getting life right, wealthy comfortable with longevity, and spirituality.

I'm in Indiana, just, "leaning back," Like og fat joe, chilling sipping Moscato in these corona days, champagne used to be in arm reach, now it's get what you see when you see it, it's easy money season I'm noticing, ball out time is after everything get back on track, thank you for reading, I'm Listening to Philly lyrical king, og beanie Siegel, his song is called, "mack b$tch," what's up to gilly the king, own know about y'all, but I'm having the best days of my life in 2020.

I'm editing this part of this book: the king business Mackology 2nd edition, while watching 1963 malcom x interview, when he was at Berkeley, I'm sipping rose moet, & I'm about to big pun featuring nas - jadakiss - Raekwon, "john blaze," some massachusetts, what's up to Mack 10 being the garbage man in the video, fat joe was doing a classic verse to, classic, classic song that will last a lifetime, peace & blessings to big pun, & those who responsible for making his life important.

Doug Williams just spoke on black college hall of fame, he the co founder of the black college football hall of fame, he is the senior advisor, Washington football team senior advisor Doug Williams.

BIG MONEY SUNNY

"The perfect storm," written by sebastian junger, was said to be an authorhouse best seller, also on August 3rd, 2000 Vince carter did the most important nba slam dunk contest performance, also I graduated out of an independent high school at this same time, it was named NSCS, I stepped on the stage to get my diploma boss playerish, I was wearing og aj pin stripe black grey suit pants, with a shiny silver silk long sleeve shirt, no tie, with my godfather dobb smoke grey hat to match, baby ghetto bought it for me, I was wearing pitch black Stacey Adams, and matching grey Dobbs socks, normal everyday wear for a young boss player, just dressed for success that's all, nothing major, or minor.

During this time Ms. Baby Ghetto got pregnant, she got pregnant by a luxury auto sales & service car salesman, he was from Lennon Wisconsin, I found out through a meeting we had during her pregnancy, that it was planned out to happen, just to get out of living the fast life, the lifestyle that she was living in my royal family, I usually have a meeting with my royal family on spiritual Sunday, I paid different aunties a few hundred to cook a big meal for us, rib eye steak, cheese broccoli, baked potatoes, smothered pork chop in gravy, buttered up corn on cob, lobster from maine, pumpkin pie made in mississippi, asparagus tips, sirloin steak tips, oysters from blue point Long Island, Asian calamari, with a few bottles of rose moet to sip on, specifically to drank on while we talk, directly after we all finish eating, real family stuff type conversation, we would speak on their feelings towards how we living, laugh about funny moments they experienced in making money for our family, as well as sadness caused by living this life, this meeting also was for them to call their mother, father, aunties, uncles, cousins, grand parents, real family orientated stuff took place on that day, I had movies from the 70s to 90s, playing on our dining room samsung 75 inch class frame qled ls03 tv, it was playing a video by the botany boyz featuring flip, it's called, "bloc boyz ride'n slabs 2nd version," but normally we watch movies from Pam Grier movies, all the way up to ice cube movies, also our surround sound music speakers, located in the living room, would be playing music from sade, to big TMyers, big l, to ol dirty bastard, al green, leroy hutson, to goldy from the land of funk album, to isley brothers, soul brother number 1, James Brown, Marvin Gaye, to scarface, do or die, crucial conflict, to Mary j. blidge, to suga free from pomona, I played their favorite songs, to my favorite songs, to the family member that cooked, their favorite songs, it was a real indigenous soulful spirituality Sunday with heavenly energy, in the royal family of king Mack house, in Mackwaukee mid west con son territory.

After baby g spoke on herself, wanting to be with the salesman, we decided she should build a future with him, because I wasn't interested in playing that baby mama, baby daddy laim game, that love triangle stuff, it just ain't for me at all, it just ain't part of my life line, plus she deserves to be happy, I loved the gal a lot, we built good memories together to last us a lifetime, she was dedicated to putting paper in my pocket, consistently up to this point, plus we was all young, no reason to stop her from having a second chance at a first class life, international red from San Francisco said that, keep in mind, a king named mack is all about love, peace, & happiness, I grew up on that al green Memphis music, Willie hutch, & Anita Baker nem, I felt good about her wanting to start a new life, everybody run their program differently, this just how I run mine, and it works out nice for me to this day.

Attractive Ms. Salena, well she ended up getting a high paying Pharmacists job opportunity, in Tulsa Oklahoma, her walton-raji's family tree been living there, generations after generations, way before black Wall Street started there, she always spoke on being in the medical field helping people, that's why she enjoyed making 9 - 5 money, she only worked real jobs, she called it beneficial community service, in my world, I always knew it was important, it's always important to know what my royal ladies wanted to do, to do in the second part of their life, the way we was living, it was consistently all about survival, due to the lack of jobs in our environment, which is what really brought us all together in the first place, you might think this funny, but all while we was living our lifestyle, I had her looking for jobs in the medical field, & I had her picking a college to go to, know your flock, it was always about thinking long term, I knew one day we would get older, which means we can't live this life forever, the objective was, it was to setup different directions for all to go into, all about timing, so every strategically made move was based on when the time was right, so I decided that she should jump on that move, so she can start a more positive, productive lifestyle, that she could be happy to retire from doing, plus we was tighter than the virgin islands, meaning if push came to shove, I could come to get her to look out for me, in her new lifestyle, mastermind moves got to made, never burning bridges, only building bridges, simply to last a lifetime, cover all angles, & connect game the indigenous soulful ancestors peoples way.

Now, watch this, that same hustler looking player, that I saw inside mPD Golden Chicken, he was nickel slick talking to Tousha Dominique, I thought he was a nephew of a Legendary retired Boss Pimp, by the name of King Gus, but he was cross country professional paid pimpin from Louisiana, I had plenty thoughts telling me that it was gone take place, I had these thoughts when I first saw them talking, I saw it all on her face, that she was in love with him, whatever he was spitting at her mind, she was deep in love with it, I had her long enough to know, to know when she was intrigued by what she was hearing, I know because that's how she was, when we first met each other, as time went from them two first meetings, I found out she was sneaking, paying him through western union, then eventually shooting out to Davenport Iowa, Chicago Illinois, & Detroit Michigan with him, I can't believe it, but she doing all this working her way up, to becoming his new main lady, & eventually his best money maker, ain't that something.

That's the last I heard of her, "cop & blow," like Johnny guitar Watson, his Texas song said that, stick & move, recruit, & regroup, but I always told my royal family during our spiritual Sunday meetings, that which transpired in our castle, "our lifestyle is all about progress."

I politely consistently during our family meetings, I none aggressively humbly said, "if you find somebody better than me, you get at him with no hesitation, because if you don't want to stay with me, you gone consistently cause unnecessary problems for me every chance you get, I studied my lifestyle enough to know, that this was accurate thinking on my part.

So when I graduated out of NSCS high school at age 19, when my mother earth moved us to Milwaukee from Chicago in 88, Milwaukee decided to keep me back in first grade because my reading wasn't good, which is why, my mother earth PUT thoughts in my long term memory bank, to read anything to everything, so this would never happen again, which led up to my learning global intelligence, this took me from intelligent to brilliant, before I became a teenager, like rakim said, all I could hear was the spirits in church saying, "look out world, here come the youngest pinky ring street king, in Milwaukee Wisconsin history, he about to put on a show, a show to write a book about, and make a movie about.

Summertime after I graduated, I was thinking about, beautiful Ellen O'Brien, she was my high school English teacher, she the reason I graduated, took me to her friends, they told me what I did wrong on final high school graduation test, then told me I passed, the royal treatment, wonderful lady right there in every way possible, she was really fascinated with my verbal communication skills, & how brilliantly I could read flawlessly pronouncing my words with no help, she also liked how I used fancy talking big words in my conversation, how complete I could use dictionary words in sentences, she didn't know I used to pick words from the Webster dictionary, a to z, I find words to write down the definitions of, them long letter words, to use in everyday sentences, to perfect my communication conversation skills, I was capitol game tight, early in my wonder years, when kids my age was having young fun, I was reading, & writing what to say, always according to who I Converse with, & when to say these words with good timing, how to say it.

I was watching gangster, to pimp movies, I would be analyzing to studying these classic movies like, "the mack," "the godfather," "mr. Lucky," "hoodlum," "belly," "baby face," "buck and the preacher," "brewster's millions," starring Richard Pryor, "bugsy," "cotton comes to harlem," "the good the bad the ugly," "harlem nights," "she done him wrong," "idlewild," "petty wheatstraw," I did this strategically, specifically to know how to play my game, run my program, also not to make mistakes they made, I was on my job everyday all day, they call it having an old soul, I call it born to know what to do, natural Instincts, you can self teach yourself, to play to win on all levels, anywhere, & everywhere in the world.

379

I attended summer school at north division, I had to get ready for culinary arts college courses at matc, I wore my Stacey adams, with cubic zirconiums tears in each my ears, I was calling myself mr. twankle at this time, cousin Trina used to smile when I said that, during this time after summer school class, I went to the bus stop to catch the center street bus, so I can get to hillside, I spotted a pretty light bright tight, & right for all night street lady in the distance, she was by a store flashing cars periodically, I got thoughts she was a street player, young just seeing huge faces, to pay for vacations in tropical places, dressed up in Stacey Adams for a reason, hidden in plain sight, all about the cash flowing to me for a lifetime, if you keep quiet, not one person will know who started the riot, respectfully as a gentleman, I walked over the way towards her, I gamed this little Christine Flores, better known as Christina Milian light skin looking young lady, her name was something that started with the letter j, sounds similar to Chicago onenita name.

On her first night to get us some currency, to start our new kingdom, she asked me to rename her, when she was ready to go get cash for us, to start our life together, I enjoyed her hypnotizing eyes so much so, I titled her Hazel, we were doing about 200 to 300 a night, then from 14th & McKinley, the Very seductive Ms. Lady joined the royal family, we decided to hit the mall to talk, we passed a store that caught her attention, clothes that cost nice Las Vegas high class call girl money, so, that was the conversation to join our minds together, this how you decide what direction to aim for together, then decide what parts to play, how to decide what is the long-term outcomes, it's always wealthy longevity, so we decided she should have nice things out of life, as a matter of fact, the best that life got to offer, and a friendship was formed, meeting each other due to being born into poverty environments.

Ms. Lady was a full time professional street lady, which I never knew when I used to see her in spots around the city, places teenagers was going into, mainly places with basketball courts, I member seeing her playing basketball, shooting the ball like, when a woman first learn how to shoot a basketball, real feminine, real seducing to males looking, back then, my game didn't recognize game, it's funny, because, I never revealed this part of my game that I played, not to nobody really, except those who had conversations about the game of life with royalty, I had to catch a ride with l dog, so he got a visual of what I was on, what exactly under the radar I had going on.

Young, "lady," she was cold, slash a part time exotic stripper, she got paid at this exotic Gentleman's Club, it was somewhere on the south side p waukee county, that's what the pinky ring street kings called it.

These two hands on everything ladies, they was them, "use what you got to get what you need ladies," harony hoe quotes type gals, they was in the midnight league, willing participants, how they got to this point, I would say poverty environments living conditions, for some reason, they got along right away, I mean instantaneously, I tell you what, it's always real comfortable good, when everything fall into place naturally, less hands on contact verbally, just to persuade things to fall in place, these unknowing each other pretty ladies, they got along unbelievably good together, when they first met each other, they were collecting about 400 to 500 a night, straight go getters, they full effortfully got down with the get down, they consistently was blending in with every city cash flow, every city we walk through, not ran through, no fear, just intelligence to brilliance behavior, it was like how fish will take to water, straight consistently accumulating fat bank rolls, I could tell from this point, they loved me unconditionally, just by how, we all enjoyed being in the lifestyle we was living, you know they say gangsters don't live to long, so I read between the lines, & I knew to pick a route that suit, & tie us all, retired pimp juju said, "you got to know your role in society," that's a wise man, with wise words spoken, again I say this sincerely, it all came out to be, we met for survival purposes, due to lack of jobs, depression in poverty lifestyles, that's what led us to make moves, to live how we needed to live, we just wasn't with living poor broke, or was ok with people our age, in middle upper class families with cars, & taking vacations, & living in houses our parents couldn't afford, that looked like backwards thinking to us, we had to fight back financially, it's getting real right about now, if this book ain't all game entertainment, I owe you a car of your choice, in your price range.

We stayed on the east side in the harambee area, in swahili, Harambee means pulling together, we was on condo avenue, near the big hill in the sky, it's where you can overlook the city, it's important to everybody on the 4th of July, it's where everybody in the city went to, just to get an overhead view of the fireworks, on the lake front, some people never heard of Milwaukee Wisconsin, not until the bucks drafted giannis sina ougko antetokounmpo, I think he from Greece, I think he got Nigeria parents, west africa upbringing, peace to blessings to his father, Milwaukee is an indigenous pyramid golden brown city, beautiful ladies, survival expert businessman, indigenous peoples make Milwaukee Milwaukee, if you don't believe what you reading, go vacate their for a month, you might not want to leave.

Me, lady, & hazel had the Boss Player palace, it was laid out with Kodak moment portraits, like Kobe Bryant, & his daughter, life size living room portrait, truly a masterpiece, and Ayzha Fine Arts Llc throughout the palace, they liked art pictures in frames in our palace, me & lady first time meeting, we went to the grand Avenue mall, she didn't want to go window shopping, but she did with me, the point was to see what she wanted to have, but couldn't have, due to lack of currency, she was sad facing because of this, so I said I want us to stick together to have more out of life, the look on her face hurt me, she couldn't buy clothes she wanted like rich girls, I felt it was messed up, I didn't know at that time, that lady was living fast to pay her rent, she was very pretty brown in every way possible, I really loved her after seeing her sad, I just felt like it was my job to never see her sad again, so we became friends before anything that day, just young figuring out how to survive, and how to get off the bottom, how to get out the bucket infested with tears, sadness, anger, & disappointment, where people is sad fighting, and killing each other due to lack of money, we just was tired of struggling, and being broke, wishing what we could have, people kids get tired of wishing on a star.

Our second spot to chill out, just so we could enjoy, being comfortable celebrating our days being alive moving together, it was in the Grand Avenue Mall downtown apartments, our neighbor was young yellie, she a big time lady in the medical field, our apartment, it had our priceless pictures of Kodak memorable moments on all the walls, from the front door, in the bathroom, to inside both the bedrooms, it was our place to count currency, stash currency, and have our, "watching new movie nights," together, we would chill out on days, when any of the new movies came out, and relax together, while watching it on a Sony vpl projector screen.

Inside our harambee, swahili definition is, "pulling together," north Avenue eastside house, we also had pictures of delightful wonderful street ladies, those who came to pay like they weigh, & out of nowhere, they eventually left like a breeze, like a breeze in Phoenix Arizona day time.

We had three nice size bedrooms, all three master bedrooms was coordinated with pumpkin orange, to Avon lady colored soap lavender, look like memphis purple candy paint, but we all slept together in the master's master bedroom, it was located upstairs surprisingly, for some reason on them Seattle long rainy type nights, we was starting to have in harambee, they would talk my ears off, until they one by one started nodding off, & finally got sleepy, then they would lean over, one after the other, to Queen Califia, 1850, California kiss me goodnight, straight San Francisco brothel street lady style.

When they finally got deep into their snoring sleep, I would walk downstairs, specifically to go to the Thermador refrigerator, just so i can get the cool, chilling, Armand de Brignac, or Richard Baccarat Cognac Hennessey to poe me up an ounce to sip on In my Lycurgus cglass cup, then I sat in my favorite, Ostrich skin leather tan, "love, New Jersey, lazy boy seat," & I would look at the breezes photos, that was inside the Mayotte Bamboo picture frames, that was all surrounding me, these was midnight ladies, those that which who came to leave, and usually I would do this until about 1a.m., or 2:30a.m.

Then I Staggered Lee upstairs, Barney Gumble drunk, with disappointment on my mind, simply because my amateur pimping, It was not making all, who come to royal family want to stay forever, now this what game recognize game mean.

You know it's well known, that a Most high, hand picked king, he will sincerely consistently love those, that which who first rolled with his lifestyle, in the times when he was fresh, I mean those who first put bread in his hand proudly, they will never be forgotten in his lifetime, they always pop up in his conversation every year, usually on holidays, especially new years Eve.

It's understandable, for those who got paid properly by queens, to think about the First Ladies of their Royal family, it's like a innocent kid first girlfriend thoughts, that pop up while he, "going back down memory lane, i had to slide that in for Minnie riperton, respect to her for making that song.

A great way to describe this unbelievable feeling, it would be to say, it's like the love you have for your first born, it's a feeling somewhat

383

indescribable, it's a memory that always speaks to you, it speak to you when you listen to a soulful song, a song like luther vandross song, it's called, "creep."

Its like the Mumar Gaddafi love, that he had for his virgin female bodyguards, it's that type of unbreakable relationship, seriously, I mean it was deeper then the ocean floor, I had these lovely street ladies all before I learned how to cook me something good to eat.

These the type of make something good happen ladies, that made a prince mackadon, grow Into a fat Mackin' King mack, these ladies paid me properly, consistently, proudly, that's the most important one, that definition of proudly, and they laid on my chest the best, they brought something to the table, & looked forward to relaxing with royalty, they took care of home, & looked forward to being up under my wings, i mean these was real ladies in every way possible, when I think about them now, I hear one of Maxwell's undying songs, it's called, "accession don't ever wonder," & twista featuring lil kim, their song is called, "do wrong."

(Chicago the place to be, the place to see, the money to make, the place to be rich, the people you can meet, the life you can live to give, & give to live, it is what it is, it tis what it is, it is, it tis Chicago)

I need to say blessings to love, to these lovely unique ladies wherever they at right now, they stayed Player with me every chance they had, and most importantly, appreciation to light bright tight right for all night mack'$ hazel, also known as my Hazel eyed queen bee, she the first to pay royalty, with wet wet money, if I could, I would put her on billboards waving, to say welcome to your state, appearing on every highway state line.

Respect to all ladies that tangled up with me, that played their part wonderfully beneficially for us, in a way the pimp God said, "you can't be allowed to imagine," keep in mind, these is different time frames, some years I had one, or two, or three ladies on my team, to Phill jackson coach, all this in one year, or more, & without sex as my main focus, really though, talking is like walking, when you master your communication skills.

These was just ladies down with a king in one way, or another, & this can be for whatever reason, it's a new breed of women in the world today, with strange confused mentalities, boss players, and king pimps would say, "they just don't make em like they used to, now, the ladies raised up by grandma, they can show other women how to treat a real Indigenous king, a king you will see every year, wearing nikovanni's fur coats.

With all that being said, humbly I'm thankful for who stay year after mysterious year, I call it a trust worthy relationship, hate it, or love it, reality is lived on infinity levels, & simultaneously in unlimited directions, now let's get back to this enjoyable, love for money attracting ladies with a king story, this the book of the century, it's giving you ingredients to what makes a king reign supreme, a whole lifetime, I'm in pine bluff Arkansas, I'm editing this part of the king business, that's right, Mackology second edition, pimp c got a song called, "down 4 mine," it just came on in a, "sweet james story," type way.

I really amour {French} these two-hard hustling, mack town, Milwaukee born street ladies, they keep feeding me bread, like Detroit boss hogg instructions say, they tell me who trying to knock them, they tell me if they want more girls on our team, this what transpire after one black rose leave, or if they just want it to be us three surviving day to night, that's right together.

I put all my amateur pimpin' in these two ladies, consistently 24 hours a day, 365 days a year, we done already been to Pender County N.C., St. John's County Florida, we hit them jack pots, we go for longevity dough, also we do this for us, to create memorable moments, every hour on top of the hour, straight professionally living, a life waiting to be put in the AMC, Harlem, Earving, Magic Johnson theater.

El Salvador Transfiguration Bank Holiday August 4th, 2000, also Robert Lee Maupin Iceberg Slim birthday, around 8 a.m., I drove my Onyx colored, pitch black, 98 North Star Cadillac, directly to Big Money Sunny mansion, it was on Lake Drive, on every August 4th around this time of the day, we would pimpishly pay our respect, to Uncle Sunny's uncle Iceberg Slim, respect, and prosperity to his progressing, cool children, that live up to their father wishes, with him smiling at them, for succeeding in this world successfully.

This a real capital game brilliantly written book, I know this a book, but reality is, your game gone recognize my game, my title, my ism, my honesty, my knowledge, my wisdom, my full effort that I put into my royal family, just to escalate to the next level in society, how it's setup, my sadness loneliness, my aim to never be poe broke, or lonely again, was all our main objective, sad to say, but reality is exactly what was just said, believe it or not, look around at what people do for money, I just told you why they do it, you heard it here first, "but you ain't hear that from me," is what Kim wayans said repeatedly.

I never used, abused, or confused the ladies in my lifestyle, make show your mother love what you say about me, I played this life Capital game tight right with mistakes, I been all over the country collecting currency legally, if it was Lord Willing, I would be still tight with all my lifetime ladies, that I laid my eyes on, kissed respectfully, hugged up because they was sad, or mad, or glad, and spiritually I touched them with words speaking on the Most High, letting them know, that they not dealing with a society they can't handle, and master mind living it.

I'm listening to too short album, "chase the cat," it's a song called, "looking for a baller," featuring Milwaukee county Mr. ken Ivy, now look what just came on, OutKast song, it's called, "spottieottiedopaliscious," it's 84 degrees here in Orlando Florida, all up in February, no lie, it's heaven on earth in florida, ask anybody from key west, a beautiful young lady, she told me it's necessary to have two jobs out here in florida.

Uncle Sunny, & I, we rolled to Iceberg Slim grave site, just to leave a $20 bill for each year after he was born, inside an A9 Invitation envelope, we placed it directly under an Uncle Nearest, Green 1856 Jack Daniel bottle, directly by his grave site, respectfully, with no intentions to seem disrespectful to his children, or loved ones.

After we left, inside Big Money Sunny pitch black mirror tent Mercedes Benz E-Class, we did all this under the influence of Ace of Spade champagne, courtesy of Mr. Billionaire, Shawn Brooklyn Carter, Marcy Project, respect to Memphis Bleek, we would drive off smoother than a breeze, on waves in the Pacific Ocean, to speak heavy on how to stay on top, inside this game of life that we voluntarily participate in, due to influences by low paying jobs, that we refused to slave for, just to merry go round back to being poor.

He said, he just heard on the California grape vine, king Derrick Avery moved to Las Vegas Nevada, specifically strategically to stack up on real estate currency," it's always necessary to see what other international moves pinky ring street kings is benefiting from, steel sharpen steel is what the basic instructions before leaving earth be saying," to who read it.

He also heard, king Ken ivy was dipping, & dabbing with the entertainment industry, these all boss players moves they both made, Ken ivy did this from New York, Texas, new orleans, to California, from the ghetto streets, to doing business inside executive suites, twista said, "legit ballin."

I said, "my life alright, but I think I want longevity involved in my pimping, I know its Johnny Guitar Watson, cop & blow, but, I get attached to the hand that feed me, having lifetime partners seem more consistent to me, more then kicking women to the curb, simply because they woe out, Int on that, I treat the game how it supposed to treat me royally, finders keepers, keep everybody if they stay voluntarily, if it's important for it to happen that way.

He said, "seduction transpire to use people, tears can be a form of trickery, smiles in your face can turn into knifes in the back, your partner got to be your reflection, to prevent people from infiltrating your system, or what's good you got going on, for yourself."

"It's a way to hit everybody where it hurt, people can only take so much, before they give up, temptation come in all shapes, & sizes, people will be desperate, & be fake to keep somebody paying attention to them."

I said, "I see your point, but I talk smoother then a Coleman Hawkins, "gigolo," jazz band song, I spit capital game fluently to a point, that it becomes delicious nutritious food for thought, which will be considered fantastically fabulous, to whoever ears is listening."

I am who I am, but in't beneath a leaf, or above a flying dove."

"It's good to be confident, but too much confidence will bring problems, never brag, or boast, one person will introduce another person into something they knew nothing about, every time life needs to humble that person."

"Always have a team to play with, everybody got a task, or purpose in your life, kids can't be adults, or treated like something they not, they can't grow up faster than life allow."

"Stay in control of every situation you be in, or put in, when you lose control, that's when you end up being scared, or hurt, never aim intentionally to impress, or compete with anybody, be yourself at all times, if somebody accept you for who you are, they worth dealing with."

"The youngest person in the group, is a combination of everybody around them, never give up, never concentrate on what can make you self-destruct, don't hold a grudge, or dwell in the past."

As we glided to our destination, Big Money Sunny played Rick James's song, it's called, "Cold Blooded," Smokey Robinson got a song, it's called, "Quiet Storm," Marvin Gaye song called, "Inner City Blues," Isaac Hayes song called, "The Look of Love," & when all these songs went off, we were pulling up at his Lake Front mansion, I mean to me, to see this every time was amazing to me, that he lived like this, motivation, inspiring, proof living life to the fullest is possible, in Milwaukee, & any other city indigenous soulful pyramid golden brown people is being blocked out of real bread In.

He said, "I got to pick up, "Diamond," from Mitchell International Airport," she just came back to Milwaukee from Jim Green Dallas Texas, she was picking up several Mouawad 1001 Nights Diamond Purses, straight full of Benjamin Banneker's huge face green backs, peace & blessings to Indigenous people in Philadelphia.

Her mission was to buy a small house in Freedman's Town Oak Cliff Texas, for us, & unintentionally she knocked some youngster for one of his midnight roses, they was at Mikki's Soulfood Café, I guess the gul was impressed by, "Diamond's," wardrobe, her, Seattle Washington "red chair salon," hairstyle, and wanted to be down with whatever Diamond had going on, have you ever heard such a statement so well put, troy ave got a song called, "do me no favors."

He a cross country trophy winning professional paid pimp, she told me he was known as Ivory P, peace to blessings to his loved ones, had to throw him in the book respectfully, after I heard somebody stopped his clock from ticking, peace to blessings to a texas Indigenous king, she knocked him for his Iceland born snow bunny, her hands on everything name was, Kenyette C, this what you call chopping up good game that recognize game.

Uncle Sunny said, "don't forget what I said, put it in your long-term memory bank, I'll call you when the time is right, to check on your nephew, I'm gone with the wind, like an indigenous brown abraham lincoln penny, it's just business as usual."

I said, "ok Unc man," boss player association style is, how I shook his hand, then I snuck in my Antarctica snow white 1994 Cadillac, I got in it like Special Agent Robert Lamphere was watching me.

Then I gently started up my, King Mack name on my license plates Cadillac, discreetly turned on Jay-z's song, it's called, "Soon You'll Understand," then I called my royal family house phone, the communication, it was setup like charlie did his angels, my royal ladies of the night, they put it on speaker phone, it was like they was Charlie's angles.

I said, "y'all be on y'all best behavior, hit the Marquette campus ground area, then handle street business after that, do all that in that intelligent to brilliant order, always watch each other back, and everybody make show everybody come back home the same way y'all left, it's time to shine, wu tang said it best, "cash rule everything around me."

They said, "we will Millon mackin," I said, "who you with?"

Just like I was Legendary Chicago born Bernie Mac, the royal family said, "the one, & only King Mack Millon dollar," I smiled so hard my teeth almost cracked, if you knew these ladies, or had the combination, the feeling you wake up with Is like winning $20,000 in Potawatomi casino five minutes after you got there, ain't that something to feel good about, that feeling um tum bout.

I said, "no drugs, thugs, arguing with each other, think together, aim for high numbers, and talk beneficial, and if need be, get currency in advance, before y'all use hips lips and fingertips ladies," I said in the most gentleman sporting way possible, respect to james brown, peace & blessings, had to throw that in there, to show respect to all indigenous kings on earth.

Then I said, "Hazel, I know about your mother my boss lady, don't let that alter you while you out here on business, we can speak on that, when we all have our royal family meeting on spiritual Sunday, Its mandatory to be 100 percent focused when you away from me, survival is number one goal, to accomplish when we leave home, take this with you today, when it comes to drugs, or alcohol, don't get mad at that person, because the drugs & alcohol is in control of that person, they not a hundred percent themselves, so no anger or being mad will help them, only wisdom, knowledge, respect love and patience, respect to Blytheville Arkansas temper the don, he well loved & respected in that town, two indigenous soulful pyramid golden brown people in the petro shopping center, they spoke very high about him, respect.

On the strength it's not them in control, it's the drug, or alcohol in control, and worldwide almost everybody living a double life, and its two sides to everybody living from kids to adults."

"The eyes don't lie, some people burn up bridges, so other people can't go where they went, some adapt to their surroundings, others get lost in the role they playing, which leads up to them losing their identity, which will eventually have them lost in character, so recognize this a business, and our personal life is inside our castle.

"The aim is to be where your kind is, that's what I done came to realize in this lifetime, it's more comfortable being around people who that can relate to you, as well as you relate to them, it's called find your kind.

My beauty queen unique lovely ladies said, "we gone take heed to what drip off your lip," I said, "call me at the right time ladies, I will see my boss ladies later."

Routinely, I honked the custom made car horn twice simultaneously, I did this while I was driving off on to my next destination, see they remember that, & think about what I say to them, I'm always on their mind, Identical to how ja rule always being on time, I'm never invisible, I'm always sitting on a throne in their head, it doesn't matter if I'm not in their face speaking, they gone hear the horn that I always beep at them, & my voice chopping up game with them, it's gone ring in their head, each, & every time It need to block off what my opponents say to them, meanwhile in the luxury automobile, I turned up the song, it's called, "magic man," made by Robert winters and fall.

Michael Jackson, Ron Newt, smooth criminal style, I was driving off, slower then Thomas the Giant tortoises from Britain, slower than he can run fast, I drove off Uncle Sunny sixty seven foot driveway, straight on to wealthy mansion luxury living lake drive, into the night life with the eye of the tiger, I always kept in my mind, like I did with my first royal family, that I was gone put these new ladies, directly in a position to live a life they always wanted to live, ms. lady wanted to become a lawyer straight out of Harvard, she always said she needed to do her life like omarosa mabigault newman, or in a higher intelligence position, like Condoleezza rice, and

I knew hazel just wanted to be my queen all her life, no matter what happens next, from prison to us finding a longevity route on our journey to get wealthy doing real estate, or writing million dollar books that will happy life us, to show we lived this life for a good purpose, making things happen, living a life worth living.

My ladies was getting in their 1994 mahogany bowling ball paint colored Cadillac brougham, it was off white, with mahogany trimming exterior type stuff going on, the inside was pretty hot pink, ostrich seats, with silver nikavonni rabbit fur coat rugs, and everything else was wood grain indigenous brown, to represent the natives of America ancient times, the original copper complexion of America Indigenous people, oh and the license plates said trf, the royal family, they was on their way to get paid in full, just like Eric b. & rakim.

For some mysterious pimp reason, I was feeling like this night was gone change everything, in my game of life, to the point it would bring us closer, closer all together, or split us up, when these type feelings pushed me around, I would read proverbs from the basic instructions before leaving earth, or ancient Egyptian proverbs written by Dr Maura ashby, somehow these two books would relax me, comfort me, uplift me, similar to listening to eryhka badu singing to me, It just seemed like these was the top ways, for me to stay motivated, encouraged, inspired, specifically during uneasy moments, for some spiritual everything happens for a reason.

I just member listening to songs like, "orange moon," by erykah badu, Smokey Robinson, "quiet storm," or Latoya Williams song called, "Jimmy bones," or her song called, "it feels so good," straight soul music that kiss you all over, inside to outside spiritually respectfully, like puffing on california smoke signals, spice 1 song called, "187 he wrote," just came on, just left mississippi, a place I call, "is you my cousin state," everybody look like they could be from my grandma side of her Mississippi family tree, so everybody seem like, is you my cousin, indigenous soul folks up north need to step down south, so everybody can get some southern ism from Indigenous soulful people down south, they living life with doors open for all indigenous, spice 1 just said, "I'm thinking about the baby, and I'm leaving on that note," intelligent to brilliant hidden in plain sight, say this, how you living is how you learning, "very good children," is what the teacher used to say.

Everything you touch turn to gold, the meaning of that statement is: you got game that spit game, your name spit game, & your game speak for itself, without you saying a word or two or three, your game spit game when you say nothing, now that's a master of the game, It also means you got sober skills that turns nothing to something, & turning crumbs to bricks.

Here's a Chattanooga Tennessee story to remember, two Indigenous people was outside a roach motel in Chattanooga mountain area, then across the four street lanes, facing the highway entrance, It was a suspicious gas station average height European young man, he was leaving the gas station, then he headed towards the direction towards the roach motel, it appears the European man made it to the street near the roach motel, he climbed over railing in grass, then went down the dip down the hill, like a scary movie with ghost, he was walking up hill towards roach motel, simultaneously as he been walking towards roach motel, all while the two Indigenous people was standing smoking black mild jazz band, it was rain snow falling down, mountains weather, so the European was walking towards the indigenous people, the indigenous man was watching this European from the gas station, up to him walking in there space, the European had no shoes on, just muddy socks, no coat, his hair appeared to be frozen, with ice sickles on tips of his hair, he was shivering as rain snow ran from his hair to down his face, to drip off his chin, the indigenous man was saying, "what's going on with you," in a concerned, this don't make any sense, type of way, the Indigenous woman said, "is you alright, where is your shoes, the European man said, "I lost my girlfriend In the woods, the Indigenous people said, "where is your shoes at, he said, "in the woods," the indigenous people said, "why Is your nose bleeding?"

He ignored the questions, & said, "I need to find my girlfriend in the woods," he was looking freezing, his hair was wet with ice sickles, indigenous people said, "why did you leave her in the woods?"

He ignored all questions, his nose was cricket bleeding, he asked Indigenous people to use their phone to call the last person she was with, then indigenous people said they will call police, he rejected that offer, then he walked off towards other hotel in the rain snow, with no shoes on, then he left that hotel, walking towards the woods, with a sad lonely look on his face, when the indigenous woman saw him walk towards the

392

woods, it looked like a movie scene, & the first thing that popped up In her head, was this: tell the b$tch in the woods I said this, she owed somebody some money, they fount him in the woods with no shoes on, no coat, his girlfriend ran deep in the woods, & the fellas she owed currency to, they grabbed the European man, one grabbed his collar, reached his arm back to give him a Popeye the sailor, pow, zonk, one of them Batman punches, before he got punched in the nose, the fella the money was owed to, he said, "tell your b$tch In the woods I said this," pow, right in the nose, then It started snow raining mix, then the European man managed to get away running towards suspicious gas station, the fellas that was owed the money, they ran towards the way the European's girlfriend ran deep inside the woods to hide in, this was when the Indigenous man spotted the European man, he was leaving suspicious gas station near upper hill woods entrance.

THE GAME OF LIFE SCRIPTURES

16.

Playing the game of life, is knowing how to roll it, live to give, give to live, it's about unity, team work works, it's a proven fact, teams have won championships, everybody need everybody, cross country living will explain precisely what the game of life scriptures is all about.

I'm In kingman Arizona, it's where rock mountain foundations Is In full effect, I enjoy arizona sceneries, & red rock pileups, look like statues was dynamited, & left piled on top of each other, it's some where to visit, arizona, phoenix, Tuscon, flagstaff, arizona is a need to see, especially riding on interstate 10, from california to arizona, san Diego, interstate 10 got something to show you, hollywood, los Angeles staple center area, kobe Bryant, & daughter pictures posterized in downtown los Angeles, staple center, dispensary is where the stars go, interstate ten gone take you to see the unbelievable goodness greatness, memorable moments happen on interstate 10, east to west, & everything in between.

Now let me say this, right now, book editing is going on, I'm listening to the last mack standing music, international red from san Francisco is talking, then boss player music plays in between his breaks, I'm sipping Don pérignon at the moment, with some og taxachusetts smoke signals in the air, three rubber bands, I'm in peaceful 60 degrees weather, all in January, I'm In super 8 Lounging like ll, massage chair in room, I thank you for reading my words to the wise, I'm listening to d-shot, e-40 brother, his song Is called, "true world wide players," your game is my game, my game is your game, is what he say, appreciation to the Most High for the pathway I been on, from birth to earth, up to this present moment, Im watching diamond league track & field, never watched stuff like this, this is interesting watching the running, & shot put, long jump, I think this Is cool, & Its people from all nationalities competing peacefully hugging each other.

Milwaukee to Arizona boss player Hillside Dexter told me, "women fear when you say pimp," but why hate the word, it can be good like any other title, if you say baby sitter, it can be good, or bad, depending how you look at it, my childhood babysitter let me do as I please with her, why, own know why, was she told, was she curious, she turned me into a ladies man first, I been studying women to master them every sense, this the game of life, all types of situations transpire, and ain't nothing you can do about it, ain't no rewind button, if I could have self taught myself before I started to make mistakes, would have been able to count my mistakes on one hand right now.

BOSS PLAYER ASSOCIATION

Women with hatred in them, they subject to feel the need to provoke a man to think evil, behave evil, or self-destruct to prove to her he is not weak, and he is above, and beyond failure, ain't that something that most men fall victim to, childhood to adulthood, is you a victim or king, or queen playing to win with the mane you choose.

Only queens will be handpicked for kings, a king has his third eye watching at all times, those who live learning in the dark, they shall be avoided by scary women, and for those who live in truth, they subjected to being hated by those living in lies.

Every pinch of life has a lesson to be studied to learn, it's mandatory to roll with the Most High, you can't base your life around currency, because if it leave, then you done, one track mind is limited in a isolated way, evil will drain you of all your strength, to keep you weak, and vulnerable, so you cannot escape the programmed world of illusions, got to mandatorily stay on point like a german Shepherd, or that's it, you out of here literally, in more ways then one., When you got stuff to do, you don't have time to waste, so every move made, is strategically planned out to make what needs to happen that needs to happen.

Bears hibernate till its time to come back on the scene, its best to receive, then to be a quarter back for some, because being responsible for a team, for some that's an overload, it is a heavy load to carry, speaking when spoken to, it is better to listen, then be known as he who talks to much.

Time effort and energy, dedication and a sought-out destinations, it is a way to bring action verbally, or physically to welcome good, or bad, and or run good action away, and bad problems away.

If you not watching everything moving, you will miss out on what's going on in front of you, things will be set up right in front of your eyes, strategically against you, to see if game recognize game.

Timing is everything, expect the unexpected, business is business, balance is required hourly, the best solid ism will have no strings attached to it, it usually comes when you hit rock bottom, then you get revitalized, and then you bounce back better than ever.

I'm listening to 8ball & MJG song, it's called, "Memphis city blues," now, the one singing the chorus part, will have you feeling like you got the Memphis city blues, you will feel it in your bones, "and everybody we know, who use to play in them streets, oh man oh man."

Keep everybody in your lifetime, in line on point, never reveal your hand to your opponent, doing the Most High things is what makes you a king, doing what the Most High love makes you a king.

Smiles arrive for heaven-sent gifts, that which will be coming soon, only when you acknowledge its purpose in life, foolishness is not important, nor will it ever be, no matter what you tell yourself.

Those who is fortunate, will help those less fortunate, the wise will help the unwise, stay on your square at all times indigenous soul people

The truth is stranger then fiction, in this lifetime, some people miss out on information, only because they rather learn on their own, instead of letting those who paid their dues, teach them what they trying to figure out.

Black is a hidden way of saying indigenous copper complexion individuals, sometimes people need to talk, to hear what they got to say to themselves.

THE LAST MACK
STANDING SCRIPTURES

13.

Step in smooth to lay It down thick, straight grinding like they do in Little Rock Arkansas, got to learn how to live, then learn how to earn, then learn how to make money work for you, then learn how to pull up shining brand new, like they say In Memphis, "this what game plus money do for you," if you learn how to direct traffic, Memphis know the business, on some project pat type stuff, It's all about getting life right, wealthy comfortable with longevity, and spirituality.

I'm listening to busta rhymes, Ron brownz song called, "Arab money," cant nobody do it like we do it, from the beginning to the present moment, it take skillful minds to create something from the ground up.

I'm listening to the black mafia, that's right, above the law song, it's called, "call it what you want," featuring money b, Tupac, cold 187, and my main man kmg, rap session in the coldest way, "now clear the smoke, I like to clock big gs and hang out all night," Pomona Suga Free, sugar Shane Mosley, Pomona pimpin young, these ones be cut from the cloth, "like bam, I'm like damn, drinking coffee straight waiting to talk see, a simp might hesitate to check you but I want, I can never be a customer, money money b it's a pimp thang."

In dover delaware on the beach area, watching georgia baby giant Chris, he picked up a horseshoe crab, they come once a year on shore, on some dinosaur ancient times to now routine, ended the night with rose moet, & Hennessey xo, red roof hotel, underground railroad state.

I'm 30 minutes from the bean, Boston Massachuetes, taxachuetes, I'm watching classic Raekwon battle Ghostface Killah, this a highlight in the new year, I'm bout to edit this chapter, blow some Worcester smoke signals, like Wampanoag peace makers of ancient times did, do, doing.

This book is created with messages, like secret passageways through wealthy people mansions, enjoy what you read, read what you enjoy, I wrote this book happy, I didn't take these routes through life, just reading this book is heavy on the mind, so imagine living this lifestyle, it's most definitely a heavy load to carry, peace to blessings to sir Phoenix, also known as king martell Rogers, peace & blessings now to whenever, forever, always, keep evil away from the god, king Cappadonna said, "set the black peoples free, wtc," wait a minute, Raekwon the chef song just got cooked up, "dart school," let all worldwide masters of the game play, y'all got to spend the globe like Eddie Murphy, go where it stop, cover all angles, connect game, worldwide pick a spot.

SIR PREACHER THE GENTLEMEN OF LEISURE

When I drove off from Uncle Sunny lake front luxurious mansion, I decided to go down the hill directly towards the famous summer time Milwaukee lake front Bradford beach, then ride pass Bradford beach towards the art museum, this where a scene from the Transformer movie was filmed.

Next, I went back up to Wisconsin Avenue pass the 4th of July U.S. Bank building, located directly across the street from Northwestern Bank, with that waterfall in front of it, & the great spirits instantly told me to park.

I pulled over safely like a west african New York city cab driver, the stylistics song called, "children of the night, it was playing on my Rogue Acoustics Audio system, I turned the lac off before I slid out the lac, pimp stick walked to the waterfall to sit down near it, & to pimpishly make a call to check on my royal family, checking on them every two hours during night fall is what you call mandatory royal duties.

It took ten minutes to see what they had to let me know, I never attempt to pull all their attention off what they got going on, on the strength I know they will go into a daze hearing my words, so I speak long short to them, paragraphs in sentences, real brief yet straight to the point, so as I ended my conference call, with all my beautiful game tight boss ladies, I was looking around me, similar to hall of famer Brett Favre's home surveillance camera.

In the midnight hour, out my left eye, I spotted a man walking with a big daddy Brooklyn kane, as he got closer near me, he put me in the mind of Saint Louis Missouri born, the Legendary Redd Foxx, the way he was walking towards my area, it was talking to me, it was telling me, that he had something to tell me, all about what I don't know about the game of life, on this wealthy journey to longevity, becoming deeper in the lifestyle, similar to the last mack standing, that which needs to be known for boss player reasons, to help me escalate to greater heights in the game of life, he look like he drank more rose moet then puff daddy, & Damon dash combined, during his golden years.

He was pimp stick walking literally, in the most loudest, quietest way, to himself he was singing James brown song, it's called, "Funky Good Time," then he took a long short sip of his White Lightening energy drank, also known in other places as grandpa moonshine, grandpa cough syrup, he never stumbled, or missed a step, he was drinking thinking, focused on not disappointing James brown, it was like he knew that James the godfather of soul brown was somewhere listening to him sing his song, every word for word, and sound effecting the beat to the song at the same time, it was like I was watching a one man band, coming directly towards me on a red, brown, blue carpet, I was anxious to see, exactly how this whole scene was gone transpire.

He saw me looking at him, all the while I was putting my smart phone, cell phone, in my Jj havin bread pitch black waist line rabbit fur coat pocket, then he started singing Curtis Mayfield song, it's called, "Little Child Running Wild," Its stunning & amazing, by his timing with his accurate song selection, felt like I was at Fred in the wheelchair 70s party, it felt like I was in a lion gate movie, I sat their like general dubie, the king of Los Angeles, a straight king sitting on his throne appearance, I had the waterfall dancing behind me, out of nowhere six grey brown pigeons, they flew in a circle over the waterfall, then they all landed on the edge of the waterfall wall, then I saw a brown rabbit stiff In the grass by the 38 year old tree, it was like they came to watch the show.

He never smiled once while singing, "father gone, mother gone, so alone," then he started singing al green song, it's called, "jesus is waiting," he was singing, " Jesus is waiting, thank you thank you thank you," I just sat their like a Martin Luther King statue, in every state in the country, straight stiff, I was thinking to myself, how much this game of life entertained me, with educational messages from the mouths, of characters you wish you could meet, from individuals you made yourself avoid talking to, it was like the night life was revealing to me, precisely what is hidden in daylight, in plain sight, Its like when brad Pitt saw the statue move to look at him In his movie, "interview with a vampire."

He said, "staying updated, upgraded, to be aware of what is, what could be, or what was, simply to pinpoint your faults, your areas that require improvement."

"You never know how much you got until its gone, when a person become bigger than life, something will happen to bring them back down to earth."

I said, "what made you say all that?," he said, "you need to hear what you need to hear young pimp."

I said, "what you see, when you see me?"

He said, "real players got a magnetism that attract people to them, it's a good vibration we release super naturally without trying to, it's not what you see, it's what you feel, and what you sent to, who you sent it to, where you sent to."

I might be drinking, but I'm thinking, even if I'm drunk, you know what um tum bout, I been on my toes my first day from birth to earth, I see you smiling, you like that young money, get to the top intelligent to brilliant proper prosperous progressive way possible, go city to city, state to state, then continent to continent, do it like Jim Kelly did it with his Afro, true boss player indeed, he said, "man you come straight out a comic book."

I'm still focused, like an Atlanta Hawk eye in the sky when looking at a songbird, it's time to get bread fat, so all indigenous can eat like nfl Rodney Pete, I mean that respectfully, ain't nothing.

I said, "sense you on the top shelf, let me drain some original game out your brain," he said, "shoot your shot while I'm standing still, because a moving target, is hard to catch, and if that was a secret, it ain't nan one now."

I noticed a 1967 Rolls-Royce Phantom V State driving pass, somebody driving was throwing the boss player sign up at me, it was Mr. East side stripper store owner Terry, with Money green Bentley driving Latham park Dalon, they probably was late night chopping up game, about tax paying lifestyle businesses, look like they just rolling through the city, most likely on an all night flight, they was bumping al green song, its called, "simply beautiful," you know they was at the top of their game playing that, riding like that, all I heard was, "when you get right down to it," al green cold, I know that much, I threw my hand up to say, peace and respect to Indigenous soul survivors, age & experience just strolling & patrolling, chopping up boss game, in downtown Mackwaukee.

I said, "I know everything happen for a reason sir, but tell me how the grass grow, the sun shine, how good game rain, and why lames complain."

He said, "two clicks, "it don't cost nothing, to be nothing,"Stanley Jeferson most famous quote, know your limit kid, when to go, or stop, at no time should anybody with game be a fool, every state is for your personal preference, party people with long money Is in Miami, when you reach the boss player level you take your game to Las Vegas, now if you into selling clothes for high prices, you setup shop in Harlem, make show you bring jobs for the community, that's how you play to win, indigenous soulful peoples got what It takes to get back on their throne, kings & queen, now if you Into billionaires business, then you hit Chicago with top of the line game, now if you fat in the mattresses, then you hit California, let your game sell for millions of dollars, they got it to spend, it's like a bid, throw the high prices out, bait for the whales looking to eat.

Don't ever never be forcing something to work, it's about choice, not force, over doing something is like asking for trouble, its somebody above everybody, and everybody got a story to tell, write a book that's never been heard before."

I said, "feel my cup up with Moet Chandon," he said, "all I got is White Lighten," then he said, "now a person can do wrong for so long, let your countenance be your guide, put fear in the rear, then switch to fifth gear, it's always options hiding in plain sight, you can't help anybody, until they decide to choose to change, excuses is weak game, good game is effective with longevity included."

I said, "now explain to me, how you progress with no day off, no rest," he said, "two clicks, then he made two click noises."

Another car strolled through, it was og aj, the original gangster was rolling on three wheels, in a sky blue colored cutlass, he was bumping b.g. Song, it's called, "get your shine on," he gave me an og head nod, just to let me know he was checking on me, he was in an ohio cutlass thang, boss riding high, boss balling as usual, just dipping in the warren g midnight hour, I head nodded back, just to let him know I'm straight, like uncle Sunny's mansion gate.

After that, the older soulful indigenous red foxx looking man, he said, "you can't do better until you know better, you got to have a mentor in your life style, life brings gifts along with a curse, good verse evil, righteous verse bad, past verse present, family verse outcast, love verse hate, you can't play both sides of the field, & test come in all shapes, plus sizes."

I said, "I been macknificently coaching with good players on my team, but a breeze come to leave, but contenders, & winners, stay planted in this garden of eden, I call Macklifestyle," now you can obviously tell, that the battle of the minds respectfully just started, it's serious like optimis prime verse magatron, it's that serious, it's like seeing optimis prime fighting magatron in the sky right now, on some geico commercial type stuff.

He said, "good point, "but separate real from fake, who wants what's temporary, who wants to be a slave to money, on a pathway leading to death," he George foreman hit me hard with that one, on some Muhammad Ali word play type stuff, life long memorable malcom x interviews.

He said, "it's about knowing what to believe, what to expect, what to white out, what to let go, what to keep, what to say, and what to keep low."

Then a pretty happy hot pink Porsche drove by, it was pat & chase waving at me, they was listening to Anita Baker song, it's called, "angel," this was a memorable night, I waved back, thinking big Bryant probably gone drive pass in a pitch black Range Rover.

I started back talking to the legendary red foxx looking Indigenous soulful man, I said, "it's my pleasure chopping up game with you sir," he said, "real people meet to help each other greet success, be the best, live the best, and do our best."

I said, "punk $2 problems be creeping up on me when I sleep, I always aim to always dismiss the nonsense, and bring forth the realness."

He said, "if you know what the problem is, you can create, or find the solution to it, understand opposites attract, truth meets lies, real meets fake, and like Shaq said, "I got skills that will separate me from half steppers, I got skills to make mills, & pay bills."

"Certain specific people will rise, or fall, yet they will always end up where they belong, by way of strength where weakness used to be, and control where idle behavior once overwhelmed."

"You got to give up specific certain things, just to get what's waiting for you, know what to do next, it's up to us to do it by way of choice, and decisions."

He said, "this what the untrained mind don't know that which it should know, which is once you figure somebody out, then you can deal with them on the level they on," (Ted Jones famous quote).

I said, "what you mean?" he said, "my name Sir Preacher," by the way, I said, "I'm Mack Millon," he said, "that's a strong name to live up to," then he said, "put Mr. in front of it, and you good to go."

Then he said, "if somebody answer a question with a question, it's a good chance they avoiding answering your question, or they trying to figure out how to out think you, or they creating an answer, that will be a lie so good you change subjects."

He said, "you see young money, questions is the door way to see where people head at, test them with statements, to see how they respond to you by way of facial expressions, body language, voice tone, and what they say."

I said, "people try to get in your head by selling you dreams, now you can buy dreams, or you can sell dreams, either way it's gone happen one way, or another."

All while we was talking, time was Central Park walking past fast, that waterfall behind us was dancing, to the beat of the wind blowing, it had multi colors of lights underneath it, flickering from the touch of water splashing on them, the six pigeons was silent as the night, looking at everything moving like a trump tower surveillance camera, acting like they was hearing our conversation, then a teenager boy, with a teenager girl, they skateboarded pass the waterfall, they jumped in the air to skate down the handrail, down the steps back into the midnight hours.

I said, "what you put in is what you get out, simply by playing to win, with the cards you was dealt from birth to earth."

He said, "knowledge is power, wisdom helps you pick which choices to choose, that which will bring progress directly to your lifestyle."

"It's all about quick thinking, outsmarting your opponent, so you won't be getting used, confused, or abused, mentally physically or financially, either you gone play, or you gone be getting played.

He said, "also the element of surprise is when you don't tell your left hand, what your right hand is gone do next, be prepared not scared, expect the unexpected, always have more than two options, "one is so close to none," like Don Juan said, and I always said, "two is so close to one."

Then Sir Preacher said, "I got a walking bank roll to catch, but first, this your last lesson, pain slash suffering, first to deal with problems, mean to find a solution, then step two is dig deeper, for another solution just in case the first one don't work, it's all about your back up plan, family."

Me, & liquor been fighting for about 5 years now, easy living setup this main event boxing match, like mike tyson roy jones jr. Fight, this a big time fight, just knocked liquor out, I deal with it when I choose to, not when it make me, control is mandatory behavior every second, now watch this, I got shot bottles of bacardi in a cranberry bottle, do something when you doing something, jazz band playing, og kush songs in missouri with me, I'm listening to big Mike, the Louisiana Texas soulful indigenous intelligent to brilliant man, the song is called, "finish the job, now that explains it all, ain't no breaks if you wake up, now you can avoid your purpose, but you gone have to make up for time lost, um tum bout doing two jobs at once, heavy load, so finish what you start now, don't wait, it's time to earn your turn, & time to shine, ain't no little light, Indigenous soul people is stars daylight to moonlight, you know what it is, back to this brilliant book, Mackology 2nd edition.

Sir preacher the gentleman of leisure said, "until the next round, stay cool, move smooth all round the world, city to city, state to state, country to country, continent to continent, & stay down for your hard earned crown king, peace and Pimpin' like California gangsta brown say," then he pimp stick walked off with his Brooklyn big daddy Kane, directly into the midnight hours, Milwaukee night life stay in motion like the Pacific, and Atlantic Ocean, pay for a visit, get some game that's sold not told to who ain't gone put it to use, this the game of life with no breaks, no matter what who say what, that's what it is, the game of life is soulful Indigenous, call it how you see it, that's worldwide, if you don't believe me, be a Harlem globe trotter.

I'm in hardeeville South Carolina, Its where the Indigenous soulful women of this land, the ladies talk like the indigenous ladies of New Orleans, I'm listening to Baton Rouge Legend, its young bleed song, it's called, "on my own," I'm on my own, strong, built to last like cormega,, The Most High blesses the child that hold his own, this a cold song by young bleed.

I'm in Polk city Florida, I'm watching the 2020 nba dunk contest, it's February here with 81 degrees, they putting on a show in Chicago, dr j seems impressed by what he see, Aaron Gordon reverse between the legs jackknife backwards dunk, never seen that before, is what Kenny Smith said, dwhite howard full spread out 360, got Scottie pippen smiling in the crowd, Giannis Sina Ougko Antetokounmpo recording everybody, Pat Connaughton jumped over giannis, and slapped backboard dunk, Derrick Jones jr did reverse tornado through the legs, Aaron Gordon got spike lee anticipating his dunk, over the head of chance the rapper, it's a reverse 360, with common smiling so hard his teeth almost cracked, Shaquille raised eyebrow surprised, Derrick Jones jr between legs over two people, Aaron Gordon over chance the rapper reverse 360, Derrick Jones jr off the backboard between the legs over somebody, Arron Gordon over somebody 360 off side of backboard, it got dr j standing up in amazement, Derrick Jones jr off side of backboard between legs windmill, this the best I done seen, all in Chicago, it's gone be so much money being made there for all February.

2pac video called, do for love," video just came on, it's winter, I'm in missouri with a hoodie on, don't even have to wear my coat, three rubber bands, two cell phones, can smoke or don't smoke, og kush decisions, I'm gone finish this cranberry bacardi, then whisper in the wind, then sleep good, dreams to reality.

THE GAME OF LIFE SCRIPTURES

14.

Playing the game of life, is knowing how to roll it, live to give, give to live, it's about unity, team work works, it's a proven fact teams have won championships, everybody need everybody, cross country living, it will explain what the game of life scriptures is all about.

Respect to the king of the crop, because his game don't stop, you got to aim for millions not thousands, you got to conquer continents not blocks, some play their game with their muscles, some play their game with their brain, "who do you think you are," like John legend said.

I'm listening to a California soul singer, maybe you heard of him, he came out cold on the city bus, with a soda, he was singing hard, tyreese, his song is called, "lately," straight boss player music, when you riding in Seattle on a rainy night, straight picking up bread, here to there boss ballin, tyreese gone talk to your audience.

It's something gigantic, when they have a street named after you, in every state, dr. Martin Luther king jr., in every major indigenous soulful city, will tang just got their own street a li while ago, James brown got his own street to in Augusta Georgia, malcom x got his own street in Lincoln Nebraska, I saw that on hood2hood part 3.

G – CODE

How many peach white owls, how many optimoes, how many Garcia Vegas, how many el productos, how many cigarillos, how many swishers sweets, how many snoop dogg ez rolls gin juice, how many strawberry Phillies, how many Crystal ball cigars in tubes, I'm listening to spice 1 mjg song, it's called, "chocolate Phillies," featuring MJG, this when only ballers could afford dro, purple haze to the Midwest was coming around once, or twice a year on holidays, sticks and stims was Midwest green, this when original gangsters, king pimps, and boss players was telling everybody to stay up, and one, you know what, don't stop the show, throwback realness right there, first heard that one right there In the late 90's.

G-Code is abiding by rules, & laws paved in the mind of a born to be gangster, that's floating all over the universe.

Being a gentleman at all time, never seeking violence, or have cruel intentions, to be a menace to society.

A gangster is not an extra in a movie, he the star of the show, most likely, he directing traffic, and conducting what is going on, in the atmosphere he assigned to.

Now, I'm listening to south circle song, it's called, "attitude," og Ted, t hops, he introduced me to this song, it's so treal like king pimp c chad butler said, be what you want to be, the og's played their favorite songs for me when I took gangster rides with them, they felt good showing me how g's ride, game all over the board was being passed on to me, in my childhood to my adulthood, very early.

A gangster know it's traps set up specifically for him, just to knock him off his square, simply to get him caught up in somebody else problems, but he stay on point, is what ogs told me, & side step all that, young jeezy said, "it's only one rule, don't get caught."

I'm listening to Georgia born mr young jeezy, his song is called, "don't get caught," it don't get no more realer then that, right there, like Oakland gangsta brown, the king In front of divine brown, he said, "they job was to catch me, my job was to get away," that's so gangsta, ogs said, "don't be throwing rocks at the penitentiary, have you heard the words the bird sings in the sky, look listen, and learn, nature is the true boss player, study the animal kingdom," respect to Telly toes, he figuring out how to get his time reduced, they hit him with 27 off top, with the plea deal being 20 years, he took it to trial, and they hit him with 27, then they said, "he wasn't remorseful laughing in court," in reality, everybody in authority, was talking like people do, making jokes passing time, they said he got to register as a sex offender, because underage kids was present during his accused home invasion criminal act, you like me, that don't apply to sex offender definition, do it?

welcome to the game of life scriptures, see in the system we born in forcefully, we learn to master everything as we advance ourselves year after year, but we isolated, playing the local game, instead of the global game, it's how the up level folks out do the competition, keep the strong living weak, until they start doing desperate stuff to survive, only because they know they deserve better, then what is in arm reach, far as the perspectives in the fox eyes can see.

I'm listening to spice 1 song, it's called, "faces of a desperate man," it's all falling into place now, ain't it man, like Chicago say, peep game, or be a fool for the wicked wise to use, & confuse you.

A gangster don't interfere, or mislead, he advise in his community services, & he say may one, & all do as they desire to do, to uplift themselves to advance to higher learning.

A gangster knows 304's is under pimp business, so he stick to the original g code, & stay out of that line of pimp business.

A gangster know to stay built like a mountain, unmovable, he know to live, let live, set up today for tomorrow, straight longevity style, indigenous peoples know what I'm tum bout.

A gangster know what he say, also what he do, It can be used against him, in the world he live in, it's setup to the point, what he put in, is what he get out.

A gangster is about being intelligent to brilliant, a fool with no rules will lose, so he seek to advance his intelligence level with higher learning.

Juvenile to Mac minister, they was the first to speak on the g code on the air waves, that I first heard, respect to these giants, oh spice 1 made a song called, "g code," to, so to these three representatives, I say salute to original gangsters, respect them, G-Code explains in more ways then one, nonsense will cancel itself out, a gangster studies life, to live it twice, as nice.

A gangster main objective is to set things up now, so he don't have to worry about setbacks later, he is all about building an longevity lifetime empire.

A gangster is out of sight, out of mind, he speak with conscious awareness, with respect for all those that know what he tum bout, indigenously speaking, you like that right, step in smooth, and lay it down thick.

Now a gangster can get chose by a madam, & he will let her pimp, slash run the girls, he will benefit, but not run her business, he will stick to what he born to do, the objective is, rise above what bottom pathways you on, play the spiritual master mind game, you know what um tum bout.

A gangster like to collect huge face hundreds, fifties, & twenties its a childhood habit he grew up with, you know the business, like Memphis say, indigenous peoples just like having big bills, & usually their favorite color is happy green, they love to ball like pimp c said, it's in their nature to be kings, king living on some Mansa Musa central Africa ancient type stuff, you know what um tum bout.

If a gangster slip, g-code 675, it says its mandatory for him to, "bounce back," like New Orleans juvenile, & mystikal said, it's his only mother loving option, you know what um tum bout.

A gangster that got put, or pushed down off his throne in gangster heaven, will uplift himself, so he can qualify to get back in gangster heaven, in the smiles of the Most High blessings, amun ra shining sun, we all dedicated to being in the Most High smiles, gangsters live to please the Most High, believe that, or, "let it alone," like Minister Farrakhan said!

I'm listening to tela black haven song, it's called, "success," a real ice cold song, now this book is for the people made by the people, he said, "I don't want to be living this way, I rather be set making money, because success is a way of life," we let these people throw us off course, really though, all the way off course.

G-Code 781, it says, respect every pinch of existence, past, present, to future, also those who play to win, a gangster knows money don't make the gangster, the gangster makes money work for him, in every way possible.

G-Code 329, it says, if a gangster gone survive, he got to go to the source that created his bloodline, peep how they conduct traffic, & control the population.

G-Code 286, It says never let nobody check a gangster pockets, directly, physically, verbally, mentally, or indirectly physically, verbally, or mentally.

G-Code 122, it says, creating a clear view is a world wide perspective, it's a mandatory action that has to transpire on all levels, not being simple minded, but more so open minded.

Gangsters is town leaders, protectors of the weak, innocent, they put in positions of power, simply by the Most High.

G-Code 81, it says, hard work pays off, no good deed goes unnoticed, what you put in is what you get out.

A gangster has been known to turn nothing into something, also sacrifice wants for what is needed, not wants sacrificed for what is needed, & enjoy rewards for self discipline.

G-Code 7234, it says, avoid letting something, or somebody put self in a conversation, that which will has a bad outcome.

When a gangster get put on pause, he uses that time wisely, to get back right.

A gangster lifestyle builds a legacy of triumph, Based around defeat, victory & longevity.

Gangsters know about the weather before its about to change, watch who watch you, & stay ahead of the opposers.

G-Code 684, it says, stepping stones, one thing leads up to something better, get in where you fit in, and build a future.

A gangster is polite, respectful, consciously aware, protective of what he love, he doesn't hate, discriminate, & he sticks to the G-Code at all times.

I'm watching e-40 & too $hort ep 75 all the smoke full episode, if everybody had their own shows from the 70's to present moment, it would be more of us on top, & out of incarceration.

THE LAST MACK STANDING SCRIPTURES

15.

Step in smooth to lay It down thick, straight grinding like they do in Little Rock Arkansas, got to learn how to live, then learn how to earn, then learn how to make money work for you, then learn how to pull up shining brand new, like they say In Memphis, "this what game plus money do for you," if you learn how to direct traffic, Memphis know the business, on some project pat type stuff, It's all about getting life right, wealthy, comfortable with longevity, & spirituality.

I'm in Amarillo Texas right now, I'm finishing up the editing part of this unbelievable, amazingly, once in a lifetime book of the century, I want to take this time to say, my life has been sad, lonely, happy, I enjoy everybody being happy worldwide, women I met, I rather we all stayed friends, I really don't have control of them leaving the royal family, everything happens for a reason, if everything kept blowing up great for me, from 1996 to now, I don't think I would have wrote this book, due to not having time, also from traveling, collecting cash, doing international business, sometimes we have to be put on pause, just so we can serve our true purpose in life, to the Most High, I appreciate the fact I was kept out of the direction I was going into, who knows how devastating the outcome could have been, I seen others who lived this Macklifestyle self destruct, fall victim to short life spans, and even killed by weapons of mass destruction.

To the ladies that came to leave, I say this to them respectfully, thank you for your time, energy, contributions, also effort, I hope they got what they needed from me, I learned from each one of them individually, in ways I will keep to myself, life is mysterious, in ways one person can not understand alone, brains United will figure out what is really going on together, thank you for reaching my boss player status book, I have never had peers, friends, or foes, just a life being lived, learned with me, and my Creator, respect, prosperity, progress to you, yours mine, and all ours, I'm listening to, too short featuring snoop dogg, the song is called, "respect the pimpin," and it sounds like my theme song, to float around Milwaukee, straight blasting it respectfully for all ears to hear, in the lake front area, In the summer time.

Complied by Dr. Muata ashby, "Egyptian proverbs," from the author of Egyptian yoga, quote from, "Egyptian proverbs," "the cosmos Is like a book, anyone who learns the language can read the knowledge and history of humanity."

I'm In wells Maine sight seeing like a tourist, Woods everywhere, I'm watching drink champs with Philadelphia cassidy, Philadelphia dj drama, & Michael Blackmon, can't really hear what's been said, it's loud around me at the moment.

I'm in hazel Arkansas leaning back, "Blues city cafe," was recommended by shorty, Richard, met him in Memphis ten, he been to Wisconsin, he said, "it's cool, but just to cold," he said, "he originally from Mississippi," I met him by, "central bbq,," the famous Memphis restaurant, its by the, "Lorain hotel," Its where Martin Luther king got killed, it's real close to, "Beal street," inside Memphis downtown.

ONE & GONE

On the 358th day of the year, which is December 24th, on this day, I was humbly reading a magazine, it's called, "All Game Entertainment," it had an article about a man named Marcus Prinz von Anhalt, a brilliant businessman, playboy, he was known as one of the largest, most visible owners of brothels in Germany, with over twenty brothels in Germany, a better way to phrase that is by saying it was reported that he had over twenty brothels, & night clubs, negative is a perspective, as well as positive is a perspective, it's your choice, of how you see what you see, from your perspective.

The article reads to me, saying It is said, "that he like to refer to himself as Prinz Germany," I also came across another article, in the, "All Game Entertainment," magazine, it was speaking heavily on human trafficking, but it didn't interest me to much, because my mind started thinking about, on two separate occasions, two experienced pimps, one from Louisiana, the other from the Midwest, both offered to buy the woman I was with, on each occasion, those was the first, and last time a person offered to buy a woman from me, I said a little something each time, but no transaction was made, those was my first introduction to cross country professional paid pimpin, in a way, it was saying the pimpin spirits had considered me one of their own, in more ways then one, my Milwaukee godfather said, "son, you the chosen one," that, amongst other statements, it seems to echo in my head, from state to state, city to city, randomly.

I remember sir Sunny was chopping up game with me, we was leaning back, we was by the lake front one day, the wind was river dancing on the waves, the sun was sitting on cloud 9, the seagulls, to ducks, they was eating bread an older man in dickie shorts, he was throwing bread out his 2020 Maserati ghibli door, as both his feet laid on the ground, inside cobra snakeskin sandals, he was playing bob marley song, it's called, "natural mystic," i was feeling reggae vibrations all around us on the lake front, it felt like we was in Kingston Jamaica, with Christopher Michael dudus coke, puffing on indica strains, like Hindu Kush, with Buju Banton, at the, "mi hungry now," restaurant.

As all this transpired, Uncle Sunny tapped my shoulder, as I starred at the twelve Snow White seagulls, they was gliding pass, Uncle Sunny said, "corruption among law enforcements officials, is one of the reasons why small penalties exist, that's why it keeps going on."

Then Sir Sunny said, "see, you rookie pimps, y'all don't be knowing that you suppose to dig Mariana Trench deep in the life style you live," then the sounds of bass beating hard from five Chevys, sounding like a stampede of African bush elephants coming towards me, it was a box Chevy, then I noticed a Chevy impala, it was pulling up into Bradford beach parking lot, the box Chevy in front, was money green with a pink top, sitting on 22 inch, customized pink forged aluminum wheels, it had TVs in the head rest, and a tv in the steering wheel, the hustler in the front seat driving, he was bumping camron song, it's called, "killa cam," this day, it was like a movie scene on Lake Michigan right now, in Milwaukee Wisconsin, like lavell Crawford from Saint Louis said, "take a ride down by the lake."

Then Uncle Sunny tapped my shoulder again, Just to say, "let me run down the world of pimping to you, Mackology, some people buy women with wedding rings, some supply women for services, some sell women dreams, to set them up to sell high price sex for them, because sex sell best in all five star hotels, because in those places, everybody minds their business, all of it, which is specifically exchanging a woman for just her beauty, or services, all of which lives inside the world of Pimpology, it's the highest form of living on earth, just like a king mysteriously living on lake drive, to everybody who find that out, it's surprising for some sad reason."

As I looked towards the 76 foot, 2020 offshore, fiberglass, $2,490,000 San Diego, California, motor-yacht, It was floating on the lake towards downtown Milwaukee, I then saw a 1971 Chevrolet Caprice colored pitch black all over, with mean green interior, sitting on forgiato 24 inch wheels, it was slowly entering Bradford beach parking lot, in the longest way possible, the driver was an og named funny, he was from 6th Hadley in

426

Milwaukee, peace & blessings to him, he was bumping dr. Dre song, its called, "Deeez nuuuts," it's from the classic, "chronic," album.

Uncle Sunny tapped me again, as we stood in front of the boulders, the boulders was stopping the waves on Lake Michigan from coming on shore, the same spot I almost dropped young Yellie at, that happen when I was walking to a spot, to see the fireworks on 4th of July, near summer fest grounds, it was by the us bank building, the tallest building in Milwaukee, Uncle Sunny said, "It was a disputed boss pimp overseas, supposedly he got caught for human trafficking, the ski mask police escorted him to prison, with ski mask on, clutching automatic army guns in their hands, whatever his life was, he was considered dangerous, and a giant in his lifestyle."

I looked down to my pants, to make show, my pants was pulled up properly, then I looked up to see, two pecan colored, Marquita Rivera looking ladies, they was walking inside Susan Rosen Diamond purple bikinis, directly behind three Dominican Republic golden brown miss universe Yaritza miguelina reyes ramíerz looking ladies, wearing Red Hot Fantasy swimsuit bikinis, then a tear drop, crystal benson clear, silver Bugatti veyron pulled up, with ken ivy in the passenger seat, & father John Devine, the king of the land, he was driving with platinum fangs in his mouth, with his two lovely ladies pushing a Mercedes Benz maybach exelero, they was driving right behind him, the ladies was bumping trina song, Its called, "the baddest b*tch," John Devine was playing The Godfather of soul, Augusta Georgia born James Brown, it was his world famous song, it's called, "doing it to death," it was very low loud, it was so him, & ken ivy, they could hear what they was chopping up game about, the whole parking lot got silent, staring directly at them four, all while pulling into the parking lot, even the sheriff, he was looking in amazement, he was scratching his chin, oh yeah, he was impressed by all of this happening in one day.

I tapped Uncle Sunny to say, "this everlasting pimp game, it seem to be deeper than the Kola super deep Borehole, also it seems like a setup to trap yourself in themidst of aegypius monachus type vultures, aegypius monachus type vultures, who will feed off downing you, so people will look up to them, some call it politics."

Uncle Sunny then said, "if it's a secret, it ain't nan one now," then he said, "madams bought women to, all over the green water globe, reflecting on the gal beauty, the price will either sky rocket, or fall below sea level, you know what um tum bout."

Then he said, "some lady named Big Sister Ping, supposedly sold women for over 16 years, all this supposedly happened before she got caught supposedly, and in 1452, none Christians was titled slaves, we call that bully ball where I'm from," then I saw the car I been waiting to buy, for around 38 years, it just pulled up, it was a burgundy outside, mean green interior, 1956 rolls Royce silver wraith, touring limousine, with mr. Jim dandy the supreme hustler, gambler, business man of the century In wisc history, he was sitting in the back seat, wearing a Harlem dapper dan tailor made suit, with a black & white movie godfather dobb, derby type hat on, it was his oldest son driving, and other son sitting in the passenger seat, they was wearing holsters, with two mean green colored, TITANIUM GOLD desert eagles on both their sides, they was bumping war song, it's called, "the world is a ghetto."

Once again uncle Sunny tapped me to say, "The state George Washington Carver was born in, that's right soulful Indigenous young man, Missouri was admitted to the Union as a slave state in 1820, and the first written record of a whore, it was in London, It was right after the Romans carved it in stone, in 1058, after they left London."

"Now to me young nephew, a prostitute is a certified trouble maker, that is if she not tamed, or under the right man control, or raised by the right big mama," yes it does make a huge difference, between a mom, & a big moma upraising, for a gal.

I was once told by an soulful pyramid golden black indigenous woman, she said, "Green Bay Is about ponani, & politics," it was also once said, an Appleton madam once told me, "a prostitute is a man conqueror, a bold, cold hearted outlaw, who controls sex in this world,"

out of nowhere I heard Lil boosie song called, "smoking on purple," blasting out a 1939 Lincoln, sunshine, special presidential limousine, jj havin bread, he was driving, Belinda's son Leon, he was in the passenger seat, he was smoking og kush, hillside pooder, he was in the back seat smoking lil boosie, webbie, Baton Rouge, Lousisana's purple haze, with cj nick puffing on hydro, & nunu Antwon, he was smoking on that, Indiana's bin laden, they was smiling with smoke running out the car, pass the windows, it was giving the charger driving sheriff, a little contact,

428

so much so, the sheriff walked to the hot dog line, to order food to eat, the contact smell was that strong, lil boosie said, "smoking on purple, eas your mind," It was said, "he did like any officer of the law would do," & was ready eat anything he saw.

Uncle Sunny said, "to be honest, a man such as myself, gone, "tell it like it is," (respect to Aaron Neville), words spoken In midnight breeze, blowing in dragon Arizona, it was said by a Midwest boss player, near a truck stop, "the thing," a pimp is very necessary, as long as a sex hungry woman exist."

My Google Pixel 4 Verizon Wireless phone began to rang, It was my e-40, "ring it," ringtone, iPhone 12 was vibrating to, it was Amanda Cunningham, I messaged her text me, then my Louis Armstrong Mack the knife ringtone flew to my ear, as we stood near our money green North Star Cadillac, then that flashback memory faded away, as my cell phone continued to rang on my second first phone.

When I came out that memory, back down to earth, I heard In the background, Uncle Sunny was playing Ill Al Skratch song, it's called, "I'll take her," it's gently bumping loud from the Seat-craft Sienna Home theater speakers.

I pressed answer on my cell phone, then I said, "hello," it was my boss lady Hazel, she was frantically anxious talking loud, like a true queen, respectfully, she said, "baby, don't be mad at me royalty, your favorite ms.Lady paid Stoney from New York, he used to play ball with you at the king center, & she told me, she was on her way to Atomic Tattoo Parlor, to get his name tattooed on her."

Hazel said, "I kept my eyes on the street were Pirelli tires, & all type of expensive cars meet, to greet me with huge faces, to take us on vacations, in tropical places."

I heard Ill Al Skratch song, it is called, "where my homies," it was banging hard, playing loud in her background, she said, "I'm talking loud, because D block the local hustler at the stop light, he was in his cutlass supreme, he was banging his alpine speakers, at the stop light downtown, he was on that Texas, Yungstar, "knocking pictures off the wall," type stuff, in the Milwaukee nightlife, the midnight league.

I said, "make your way to Uncle Sunny's Lake Front luxurious mansion on lake drive, to give me what you got, (for a pork chop, that popped up in my head, it was hustler in Miami on yukmouth, "United ghettos of America" dvd), & show me who your lifetime partner is unique delicate attractive loyal before betrayal boss lady hazel."

She said, "can I catch a cab Mackology?"

"I'm at the Hilton hotel, Its downtown," I said, "thata work," she said, "ok, thank you baby daddy, I'm on my, "Suga free, Pomona way."

I started thinking about west division Carolyn, for some reason, I met her Chicago Lisa Ray Tina Marie looking self outside the west division high school, she was being player for joining me on the first day, of us meeting, to help us stay paid In full, she was one of them ladies worth keeping, but you know the wrong woman, she always gone come get in the way of success with the solid women like Carolyn, that type of wrong woman, she will arrive when survival mode is in full effect, I pressed end on the Stuart Hughes iPhone 4s Elite Gold cell phone, then fixed royalty green, white, black, diamond, white gold, $2000 faith Ann pinky ring, looked at Uncle Sunny, then I said, "one & gone," he said, "I already know nephew, cop and blow, like an older Mississippi pimp, he told me, "one 304, she don't stop the show," I said, "another breeze coming to leave," Sir Sunny said, "one so close to none, two a do, three a keep you happy, four gone open the traveling door, five will most definitely keep you alive, & six, or more is a gift, & curse."

I said, "business as usual," then Uncle Sunny said, "don't let this game beat you, or defeat you," in the background, New Orleans juvenile song, it's called, "lil daddy," It came on, right on time.

Another 20 minutes blew by, it blew by faster than ten years, in Waupun Prison, respect to the giant, mr. Martell Rogers, the iPhone 11 began to rang, it was light skin, born to sin win, hard hustling', Laura London looking Hazel, I said, "what's going on boss lady."

Then, built to last like lil kim Hazel said, "come get your winning, mega bucks lottery ticket, my one, & only king Mack," then I said, "cut all that out hazel, until I put my hand in your pocket," she said, "I love you to playboy," then we hung up, she got to understand, I just, "lost one," like Jay-Z, so I had my game face on tight, with major love for her, in a way you will never know..

I went to the multi million dollar mansion front stainless steel lassen pivot door, the door was literally 7 feet tall, when I opened the fancy front door, she had Big Bird yellow on, Chicago Taylor made style, from the top of her cleavage, to the bottom of her Stuart WeitzmanRita Hayworth high heels,, she shined brighter than the sun rising in A Gullah morning, in South Carolina, if you from, or been to Charleston South Carolina, you know what um tum bout, in the background, in the mansion, you could hear t.p. From Massachusetts song, it was playing, it was called, "all I know," I first heard this song, It was on the cross country pimping part four dvd, respect to Chicago born, Michael Maroy, mr too real for tv.

She said, "heymillon mackin," with a nice-looking fat envelope in her hand, I said, "come here Queen Bee," she Julie Newmar, Lee Meriwether, Eartha Kitt, Michelle Pfeiffer, Halle Berry, Anne Hathaway cat walked to me.

I noticed she was sober as a Judge Judy, on a Sunday night in Bora Bora, with Memphis judge joe brown playing monopoly, I also noticed her glowing like Fernando Jorge, Gravity Diamond ear rings on Nina Simone at Sidney Opera House, I said this to perfect Hazel, "with me is where you belong," she said, "I made around 18 tonight, Mackology."

I said, "enter enter," like the Colombian man told Tony Montana, when he was going to pick up the two keys, he was doing it for, "bad business handling," Omar, as she sexy Jennifer Jackson, playboy bunny walked in, tru life, "freestyle intro," song was coming on, with Jay-Z saying, "allow me to introduce y'all to,tru life.

I thought to myself, I got to do something mind boggling right now, so I said, "take your Christian Louis Vuitton Crystal Queen Embellished Sandals off, its FursNewYork, Mahogany Mink carpet, all around the first floor boss lady hazel," smiling I said, "you know better pretty lady," she said, "sandals, excuse me daddy, but, these is Saint Laurent optimism sandals," then she started smiling to, I loved that about her, she will put you in your place, if you treat her incorrect, especially, after she worked hard for her royal family, all night to.

She smiled saying, "hush up," like she was from Mobile Alabama, then She said, "baby listen to me, I tried to talk Lady into not leaving our royal family, but when she said, "the royal family can kiss her where they gone miss her," I snapped out fast, In't gone say what I said, but I did say, "you gone be where you at ms. Lady, until you come back home."

I smiled serious looking like Denzel Washington in, "training day," with that same mustache beard, the same lining, then I said, "what happened boss lady Hazel?"

431

She said, "I knew I had to put some pep in my go getter, money making step, add some tens on my 5s, with some 20s on my tens, 50s on my 20s, & hundreds on my 50s," I said in my head, "this my lifetime partner, what more can a boss player ask for on Christmas, you know what um tum bout, this a wife on the next level, & for that reason, I crown her queen."

I said, "you priceless Hazel, until you start living worthless," she said, "I know three is company, four is a crowd, so if you want me to recruit players to play with, to win with us, I will make it happen Millon mackin, my royalty, my first my last king."

I turned into Gucci Mane, Mr. Radric Delantic Davis, I said, "hold that thought," go lay on that, FursNewYork, Mahogany, Tracy Diana Ross Mink rug, Directly in front of the Aqueon Fireplace all the way in back of the mansion, & tell my Uncle Sunny how much you love my pimping."

She, Tyra Banks, Ivanka Trump, Naomi Campbell, cat walked to the Aqueon fireplace, it was somewhat near Sir Sunny, she spoke saying, "hey Uncle Sunny," in a sweet Phylicia Rashad voice tone, with a young, Keshia Knight Pulliam, Rudy Huxtable innocent look on her face.

Sir Sunny said, "Privetstvuyu, {Russian}, baby girl," with a deep growling voice like Mufasa, or Barry Eugene White, or James Earl Jones bass deep voice tone, he was sitting in his custom made gold onyx king chair hand made in Jamaica Queens by somebody that dapper dan introduced him to..

Uncle Sunny said, "I see you stuck with your king named Mack," Hazel smiled ear to ear, then she said, "oui j'ai fait, {French}," as I walked towards her, she said, "if I don't, who will?," I was diamond gold teeth smiling, she was Atlana hawk eye, she starring at me, she was smiling with her Houston Texas condo bedroom eyes.

I stared so deep in her pretty tiara Ashleigh hazel eyes, I saw the Macula in her left eye, then I said, "you belong with the strong," with a crooked sideways slanted smile on my face, Jay-z song called, "all I need," started beating in the background.

Beautiful lakesha Miller, Deirdra funches looking Hazel, she said, "I love you to baby, but the money is extra," then I said, "speak on it, speak on it boss lady," next she said, "it come to leave, but I'm here to stay Millon mackin," I said, "like a breeze," she said, "I'm here to stay as long as I live, with no question of am I supposed to leave, I belong with you, and that's written in my book of life, mack daddy."

My Uncle Sunny said, "from Mackarony, to Holy Matrimony," Kenny Red from deep East Oakland, probably smiling laughing, or saying, "Int say it like that," then uncle big money Sunny said, "y'all got a glow, around y'all so real, I'm gone put a life size portrait of you two on the dining room extended wide wall, it's located inside this mansion, on the first floor, near the hall of game, (respect to sir earl Stevens), so y'all can join the hall of fame, & Capital game, soul survivors."

Then Sir Sunny said, "one left, now y'all can gone had to the top, progress without stress, with all y'all 8 hours of rest, every day of y'all life, and set everything up around you two, with those, who come to join y'all, for the rest of their live long life," then in the background, young jeezy song, Its called, "my hood," it just came on now, I mean, Its right on time.

Humble like Hawaii pimpin' Juny J.B. Buns, Uncle Sunny said, I got to go collect currency, checks, check on my Royal Family, & my property, so y'all enjoy the castle, if y'all here when I get back, we can play 2k20," he started pimp laughing, he was saying, "I'm just playing, I'a catch y'all on the next round, & remember a king ain't complete without a queen, & a queen ain't complete without her king, may the Most High, allow all to recognize who they belong with."

Then too short song called, "good life," it snapped on, it was beating hard, Northern California Oakland style all in the background, it was a bowl of Cabrini greens, it was on the kitchen borbonese table, seem like it was waiting to be rolled up, inhaled, then exhaled, straight enjoyed Rastafarian bob marley style, Jamaicans all over the world, they know what um tum bout.

Uncle Sunny said, "it's all types of Moet Chandon in the Moet closet, all flavors of cognac Hennessy's inside the Hennessy closet, all type of global foods inside the stainless-steel French Door refrigerator, with the worlds best water bottles, from iceberg water, to acqua do cristallo tributo a modigliani."

Then too short song called, "how does it feel," it came on within a blink of an eye, I enjoyed the bass dropping, it had mastermind lyrics for days, straight representing the real from Oakland, to Milwaukee, to Chicago, to Wilmington Delaware, to Memphis, to Miami, to New York City, to Dallas, Houston, Phoenix, Fargo North Dakota, Savannah Georgia, to all over the country, believe that, you know what um tum bout soulful indigenous individuals.

Then Uncle Sunny said, "Your Royalty room, you already know it's located on the second floor of the boss player palace customized mansion, I told Dandy'lion, she was the middle aged, Norwegian maid, I told her, y'all was coming home tonight, so she took it upon herself, upon herself, to hook y'all royalty room up, specifically for y'all earlier, to enjoy y'all night, & I paid for her, plus her husband, plus their six kids vacation in Kerala India, for four days, and three nights."

"I am not expecting uninvited visitors, so don't pay attention to, the Carlon RC3510D door bell, if you hear it, "ring ding donggggg," like dr. Dre song said, my six-member family of 4 year old Romanian pit bulls, they most definitely roaming inside the antique fence on our royal estate, they all know to guard their Royal Family Estate, because this their home to, believe that, at the same time, be on red alert, stay on point, be well aware of everything going on around y'all.

I said, "yes Sir Uncle Boss Player," then Uncle Sunny said, "y'all enjoy, & figure out why I wanted y'all to stay here, and why y'all chose to stay super glued to each other, while most who live this lifestyle, they all split up from each other, cracked under pressure, turned on each other, let drugs infiltrate their business, & kingdom, but you two managed to overcome obstacles, not only that, you two figured out, one way, or another, how to stay down with each other, & this outcome at this present moment, this the reward, this the stay down til you come up benefits."

Then Uncle Sunny grabbed his Idelwild, Big Boi, Brown, Black Fox Fur coat, he grabbed it from inside his twenty-foot-long, solid gold pyramid brown walk in closet, which is located next to the Yao Ming tall, front, fancy, castle, double doors, then a famous group called badwayz, their song is called, "g-2000," It came on banging out the speakers loud, it was talking about, "gangsters live, gangsters ride, its hard to survive, either do or die, in this gangster life, gangsta gangsta gangsta, to all my true gangstas."

Uncle Sunny slid out the door, in no rush at all, comfortable, he reached inside his Idelwild, brown Black, Fox Fur coat pocket, to pull out his antique, Convergent Smartphone BlackBerry, next he slowly, carefully, punched codes in his antique mansion NCB Shelter alarm system, that he calls his Caucasian Ovcharka security system.

Finally, Uncle Sunny went to his hand full of car's garage, he Ludwig van Beethoven, piano tapped in the SABRE Shed garage alarm system

434

code, next he cautiously handpicked the car he preferred, for the profitable mission he was on, at this particular present moment.

He decided to pick the 1998, Russia Wolf Snow White colored North Star Cadillac, with gold interior, when he started the 1998 Cadillac up, Too Short's song, It called, "Pimp Me," it Gangsta Mack style walked out the speakers, he changed it to his favorite song, it's called, "hood been good," made by shawty lo & king Georgia kool Ace.

Then he spoke a name into his TAG Heuer Connected Modular, then his TAG Heuer Connected Modular repeated the name, next it dialed that person number Bluetooth style, then that person picked up.

Sir Sunny said, "what you know good Lola?"

Lola said, "we hit the finish line, the trophy worth 5 triple ogs, what's ours is your Sir Sunny, you need not to forget that," they communicated in a way nobody else would, or could interpret, Uncle big money Sunny has a top secret style conversation communication that James Bond would never be-able to figure out.

Sir Sunny said, "in 15 minutes, I'm going to call somebody, just to see how much a Milwaukee Coach & Carriage LLC ride cost, to go to the Lake front from the downtown area, just for us tonight," then too short song, it's called, "I've been watching you," featuring parliament funkadelic, & about face, It just came on inside his alpine radio.

Then Lola said, "even if it cost 45 triple ogs, I will work hard to get it so you can pay for it daddy."

Then Lola said, "ok, your wish is my command," then Sir Sunny said, "make it happen, proceed to progress with the Midwest best," then he ended the phone call right then, and there, he spoke paragraph style in sentences, he mastered the art of saying a novel worth of words, in as less words as possible like the new book called, "Mackology 2nd edition," written by a king named Mack.

Sir Sunny put the somewhat customary luxury automobile in reverse, simultaneously while reaching towards the Pioneer cd player to play Louis Armstrong's song, it's called,"What a Wonderful World," he was a Louisiana laid back type king pimp, he the type to tell a lady, " I'm not here to entertain you like a tv, if you need entertainment, play your favorite song, go to the wringley brothers circus, we here to survive, so don't get confused on how man to woman deal with each other in my world baby."

Sir Sunny opened a text message, that he got texted right before he started changing the Compact Disc to the next song.

The text message said, "bench players ready to get out the game, to throw in the towel, to see if it's enough to be allowed to get some sleep daddy."

He pulled out in the middle of the street in slow motion, he slowly smashed down on the breaks, pushed a 24k gold button, then the driver side window went down, next he kissed the sky, and said, "if this how my Royal Family is going to continue to be, I pray to the Most High, we float pass the rope, to get to the truth, to retire before 2022."

Then too short song, it's called, "California girls," it straight came on nice, low beating, respectfully out his clarion cm3013wl subwoofer speakers, I heard it from inside the castle, it was saying, "tell me I'm not dreaming.," he said wait a minute, then skipped to too short song, It's called, "don't act like that," it said, "I was raised to cope with life, and make my own choices in life," then like an ancient giant Madagascar turtle, he very fast in the slowest way possible, he shot up the streets, the dogs on the royal estate, they knew it was him, so they all howled, to say be safe to their master, with love for the hand that feed them, that's in more ways then one, like lil Wayne said, "y'all ain't ready, y'all ain't ready," then the speakers in the yards, with the dogs, it said, "cut the music up please," it was lil Wayne song, it's called, "oh no," it kept the dogs on red alert, bobbing their head, as they walked the estate, each neighbor was payed weekly to not be bothered by the sounds of the music, the big payoff, if that music from the boss player palace was dancing second line style from the royal estate to all over the neighborhood, the music could be heard loud, clearly, in a ten mile radius.

Learning the importance of communication through verbally, physically, mentally, spiritually is the expression of love.

Florida got a severe storm stalking them, respect blessings peace to the elements around them, I al wanted to say deep at the bottom of the map the indigenous soulful peoples got dress that look like the palm trees, believe that.

THE LAST MACK
STANDING SCRIPTURES

16.

Step in smooth to lay It down thick, straight grinding like they do in Little Rock Arkansas, got to learn how to live, then learn how to earn, then learn how to make money work for you, then learn how to pull up shining brand new, like they say In Memphis, "this what game plus money do for you," if you learn how to direct traffic, Memphis know the business, on some project pat type stuff, It's all about getting life right, wealthy, comfortable with longevity, and spirituality.

I'm listening to, sir too short song, it's called, "triple x," It says, "he came to play the game."

To know who I am, I would say, "I'm just working on getting back on my throne, I got distracted to walk out of bounds, now the step by step process will include getting back on the pathway I was born to be on."

I'm leaning back in hazen Arkansas watching the pure rain drops as they drop out the water colored clouds, I'm sitting in a chair from 1981, it's downtown Julie brown, bugs be out here, fat flies, giant mosquitoes, trees in wooded areas everywhere, I'm listening to baby drew song, it's called, "weakness," it's making right now feel like I'm at back in Milwaukee, it's setting up the meditation mood, Massachusetts smoke signals in full effect.

I'm in Arkansas watching the George Floyd trial, I'm listening to snoop dogg song, it's called, "Intrology," blowing Massachusetts smoke signals in the most peaceful indigenous way possible, now twista song came on, it's called, "It feels so good," who can a real one chop up major game with?

I'm back In Milwaukee leaning back, freezing In the first week of April at the lake front, Im editing this chapter watching, "quietroom," f.d.s. #184 - rafer Alston, then watching #182 - booger smith, earlier I watched, "drink champs," cam'ron episode, with that being said, let me get back to this miraculous chapter .

THE HISTORY IN ALL CAPITAL LETTERS

I'm listening to Derrick "Gary Indiana" note, his song is called, "fast livin," it's a classic timeless tune for the past, present, & future.

Uncle Sunny was blowing with the Lake Michigan cool Milwaukee breeze, he was on a trail of a fat rat, that means his money route, simultaneously all in front of me was the unbelievable Victoria secret swimsuit looking model, named Hazel, she threw her black widow eyes on me, then she said, "baby I need you to join me near this Aqueon Stevie wonder Fireplace."

With my hillside walnut Keith sweat vs. Bobby brown frog eyes, I started looking directly at her, with a tremendous amount of respectful love in my Chickasaw eyes, then I said, "pull that Boston slash Salem Rockers chair near you, and My macknificent self will join you very shortly, boss, Pequot lady."

Moe quitier than Cherokee tuch-ee walking through the night In Central Park New York City, more quitter than a Latosha colored shar pei In a Beverly Hills mansion eating, I guided my boss player status self to the Shoshone champagne Moet closet, real Annapolis Maryland orchid praying mantis quiet, in my horn-back money green colored lizard shoes, I thought to myself, I should take these lizards off my Major mackin feet right now, to chill chill, so I placed my horn back hundred dollar bill green lizard shoes, I made the decision to place my lizards by the manute bol Turalei

Sudan African custom made onyx galaxy black Dawes roll administration mansion tall front door.

I decided to compliment us with the September 4th, 1957, Columbus Ohio Don Perigon, February 4th, 1981 rose flavored Williams apess Pequot champagne, then too short song called, "that's right," it creeped into the airwaves in the background, it's mandatory for that to happen, just to compliment the mood we was in precisely correctly in the most spectacular way possible at that crispus attucks Wampanoag present moment.

My next decision, it was to grab two Elegant Baccara Champagne Flutes from out the mahogany George bonga Pierre bonga ojibwe ogibwayquay bonga cabinet, that which I magnificently did with no hesitation, it was located directly above the orange mound candy color coated kitchen Vessel billy bowlegs iii cofehapkee Seminole sink.

After that move was made with precise Olivia ward bush-banks montaukett movements, I walked like an ancient Nubian king, an ancient Floridian king from calusa, confident like Dr. John Bayne going through Heaven's front gate, directly towards my loyalty before betrayal boss lady, the scenery was setup picture perfect, and the energy in the room was heartwarming like taking a Leica 0-series no. 122 Picture of two Caribbean flamingos flying In the sun setting direction, it was in a mysterious way you wouldn't believe, it was nice like getting a luxurious mansion built from the ground up in Baton Rouge Louisiana, just to sell for double the price that it's worth, or getting it built directly in your favorite city in your favorite state, boss player association be on that professional type living.

I said, "Here's your Las Vegas Gautier Cognac, 1762 eaux-de-vie, distilled from Grande Champagne grapes, Crystal Champagne Elegant Baccara Flute glass, you became my number one lady in my royal family, voluntarily you was dedicated to putting in work to make that happen, to qualify yourself to be put in that position on my throne," she said, "sit back King Mack, and let me open this rose Moët simply so I can feel up our cuca Fresca premium artisanal cachaça crystal Champaign glasses, with Evangaline Jada Pret 2021 morning made Rose Moet, so together as one, we can celebrate our togetherness in this unbelievable memorable moment," then too short song called, "get that cheese," it came on in the background, it was saying, "I'm the player of year, I bought a mansion for my mother."

I leaned back respectfully, then I said, "You my rib, my reflection, my heart in your chest, you my reason for breathing," as she opened the Carmen Barbara hardy lisa Rogers Rose Moet, she started getting overwhelmed with joy, and five Edith crystal clear tears appeared in both her eyes.

441

She dropped all ten tears on the Japanese macaque colored Mink Rug, it was laying in a seductive way, directly in front of the antique Aqueon fireplace, we was creating a movie scene type memory only a hype Williams, or only a lion gate film can show you, then proudly she started politely pouring Lil April Rose Moet in my glass first, she was wiping some Trina Theresa nene tears off her lovely face, she was titling the tiara Rogers tyeishia keke Danielle Rose Moet, like rapping superstar nore said, "French waiters be doing."

Still slightly crying happy auntie reese bay sister tears, It was like she been waiting for this moment all her life, she poured Rose Moet in her crystal Champaign glass second, & after she did that, she looked at me with big red cartoon colored hearts in her eyes, and handed me the Rose Moet bottle, then too short song called, "female players," it came on, then she said, "I been working hard all my life to get to this point with you my king."

I gently sat the Rose Moet on my right side, directly on top of the mahogany forgers coffee table, I then with my undivided attention, I looked deep in my beautiful queen Hazel's Hazel eyes, directly at her soul, then I said, "bring your south beach sexy self to me, so you can toast with King Mack," then too short song called, "she loves her," it stomped out the speaker, keep in my mind, this a king book right here, it's not made for minors in the minor league, this a major league players book, for those who can understand what is required to be understood not misunderstood, and not attempt to reenact the lifestyle of this book, simply for negative gain, peace & blessings to all over the world we call earth, make the earth your turf like they be saying on the west coast.

Picture perfect jada Pinkett looking Hazel started slowly walking on her knees to Royalty, and on her knees she stood in between my Royal legs proudly, she was slowly dropping Birta Abiba Þórhallsdóttir Iceland, I mean Nulle Josephsen Greenland cold water clear tears of joy again, my royal soft clean fingernail hand reached out to wipe her waterfall clear tears away, she said, "king mack don't wipe my tears away, my tears show my love for you, my truth, my honesty to you, its like you giving me roses subliminally, I will lay them in the Milwaukee River alive fresh, I won't keep them because they will die, but as they lay in the Milwaukee River forever in my eyes, symbolizing your love for me, which will last forever, lasting all eternity, never dying," I said, "boss lady, you cold like heaven in the winter time, you somebody every man dream about."

As king & queen, we lifted our Elegant Baccara Chrystal Champagne glasses in the sky, higher than a FedEx airplane leaving Mitchell international airport In Milwaukee Wisconsin.

Hazel had that Alice Jubert teary eyed look on her face, while she was black, Chinese, Jeanette lee widow professional pool tournament staring at me, she blinked twice, then she said, "Can I kiss your million dollar lips sir Mack?"

I said, "Lick your lips first like a black Polynesian Magic City stripper looking at $10,000 in all hundred dollar bills, right after Bankhead king, Shawty lo made it rain.

She seductively in the most attractive way possible, she leaned close to Royalty, gently smashing her head into my magnificent face, punching her K.D. Aubert type lips into royalty lips, she did it sexier than a creole Lynn Whitfield New Orleans kiss from Martin Lawrence movie, Its called, "thin line between love & hate."

It lasted thirty six love me long time seconds, I magnificently, Phoenicianly rubbed her Regla Torres Herrera Olympic gold medal winning volleyball type thighs, & then I said, "You taste like love and happiness," I was on some April 13th 1946, Forrest city Arkansa, Albert Leornes Greene type stuff.

I was on that Atlanta king Kool Ace type stuff, She said, "All Mack, really?" with six tears in her eyes, she had that Angela Devi look on her face staring at me, I said, "we gone toast to us, we was united to get comfortable wealthy on the first day we met boss lady."

"We saw people come, stay, play, pay, and leave, but we stuck together like we were Chang Bunker and Eng Bunker Siamese twins, born to stay together forever In this wisdom knowledge is powerful lifetime."

I said, "I appreciate you dealing with Royalty, bowing down to a king with a crown, paying the fee to see what I can show you, then crowning me your million dollar dollars dollars king, and staying down with royalty until you was crowned queen, I really appreciate that in more ways then one."

She said, "I love you to Mack, you taught me with your thoughts, you turned me from a young lady Into a professional Femi Otedola Oprah

Winfrey business woman, from a broke down alcoholic sad female into a built up happy Philippa of Hainault queen of England, I was broken when I met you, and you built me back up Millon mackin."

I said, "This exactly what the heads of a Royal Family requires, we served our purpose in each other life with no hateful jealousy, we both played our part full effortfully consistently, achieved, & retrieved satisfaction by qualifying ourselves to get all that was coming to us."

She started dropping Ethel Waters academy award winning tears of joy again, It was like she just found out she indigenous to North America, she wiped two tears away from her beautiful Jorja Alice Smith looking face, then she said, "I want to say also, I put my trust in the Most High, & after that, two golden banana brown Queen Liliuokalani looking angels guided me to you, like Sade said in her, "kiss of life," song."

While all this was transpiring, simultaneously I grabbed the brand new surface pro x radio remote, simply to turn on Sade classic song, Its called, "No ordinary love," strictly to compliment this memorable moment, her & I naturally creating spiritually, with lovely energy dancing in the air we was breathing in, and exhaling half baked out.

We made a classic I choose you max julien, annazette chase type of eye contact, she said, "Here's to us baby for better ways, & better days," then we taped glasses, sipped our hard work paid off trust, and love for the dove above Don periogn champagne.

Then we looked at the Aqueon fireplace, finding ourselves being hypnotized by the roasting birch firewood by the crackling sounds It was making, & simultaneously it was proudly warming us both up, it seemed like the large birch logs was burning like it was happy to see us together, the full lit moon was shining on us through the luxurious mansion, right through the crystal clear nate Robinson height windows.

At the same time, I noticed myself melting out my seat, dripping directly to the floor next to queen hazel, directly in front of the Aqueon fireplace, we both felt our guardian angels looking at us, & smiling at each other.

I was sitting down peacefully, while she laid her head on my thirty inch vertical jumping legs, out of nowhere, My hillside walnut 803 west galena brown eyes started noticing her smiling, she was smiling happily saying, "we made it through the poverty storm Royalty," I said, "yeah, now we got to switch lanes to a bigger better lifestyle," she said, "I agree baby, you my leader, I follow you, just don't let me down, or disappoint me Millon mackin."

In my Apple computer complicated brilliant mind, humbly I said to myself, "she priceless until she start living worthless," then I spoke verbally in the most nzinga mbande articulate way possible, I said, "Trust, or bust, sink, or swim, we gone turn our new Nokia 1100 cell phones off, & figure out our next route boss lady, siamotainously while we enjoying this unique night together, in the most spectacular unique memorable way possible.

She said, "That's exactly what I'm gone do with you king," I said, "Now we got around forty thousand worth of currency here in cash, not to mention what is on all these debit cards, that's lined up on this 17th century Japanese lacquer, Alessandro de' Medici complexion colored chest, all of which we made during our journey to get wealthy, simultaneously while we was looking for the green colored brick road leading up to abram petrovich gannibal imperial longevity."

She sipped her august 3rd love potion in the Blanche Bruce expensive senator glass, then she said, "I'm glad we met when we met, I remember you approached me coordinated great in baby sky blue, when you was coming to me, out of nowhere my mind said, "this who you need to succeed successfully with juanita," I said, "what's gone happen gone happen, but east side Uncle Frank all that, it's time for you to be naked, so you can walk comfortable to my Vicente Guerrero first black presidential king room, you royalty qualified to be a cross country, boss, number one lady."

Too short song called, "dirty love," It stepped In smooth, to lay it down thick in our background, the bass was vibrating throughout the yasuke king castle, we was born to live in this boss player palace, I know our phones was getting calls back to back, but I kept both expensive cell phones off, so we can focus on each other, and put our undivided attention on exactly what we was speaking on, as we did what we do.

I stood up on my square like kwame Anthony appiah, straight Mary Frances berry strong, looking like I was Stephen l. Carter on my way to the lifestyle of being wealthy for life, then she stood up next to me, she was none aggressively Pushing her little Patricia hill Collins neck under my polar bear size strong arm, then we cartoon style tip toed to the luxurious mansion custom made stairway, it was like we was superglued to each other, perfectly side by side, with her seductive nakedness, to me she was teasing the mansion shiny walls, we walked one step at a time, directly up the ta-nehisi Coates complexion colored steps, to make our way towards our lonely kimberlé w. Crenshaw royalty room.

When we walked in the pyramid golden brown Angela Davis royalty room, her eyes opened wide like Galagos eyes, or African grass owl eyes, & on the African Forktail Catfish saltwater bed, it was another twenty three thousand dollars worth of currency, literally on top of the Don Perigion colored Mulberry silk Henry Louis gates, jr. sheets, with a joy degruy royal a900 whirlpool bathtub, the inside of the bathtub was hand painted mean green, all the way to the boss player association outside of It was hand painted mean green.

The currency was in brand new Annette Gordon-reed Graphene rubber bands, I put it in sets of 5s, 10s, 20s, 50s, & 100s, I was being lazy not feeling like counting it all at that time, while I was Angela p. Harris rubber banning it, in the background was j diggs song, It was called, "counting money," it started getting louder as she walked towards the whirlpool, the queen boss lady was sommer ziggy naked, it was like she was in Hugh Hefner playboy mansion on movie night.

She excitedly, in a satisfied ephraim Isaac voice tone, she said, "is This all ours Millon mackin, my king, I did everything I did for us with a Edmond j. Keller full effort, you don't understand mackology, even when I was mad sad jealous with hate, I still put you first, you will never know how hard it is for a woman to not be jealous, or how much it takes for a woman to love, and not hate a man she love."

I was finishing my last swig from my Randall l. Kennedy champagne glass, simultaneously I was listening to her Rhonda vonshay sharpe sentimental talk, with my undivided attention, then I licked john h. Mcwhorter type lips before I said, "Let's live like ancient ancestors soulful indigenous knowledge king, & ancient indigenous ancestor soulful wisdom queen, with Claude. M. Steele good intentions to recruit a new royal family, we gone buy property, great pieces of the land, from Beverley daniel Tatum Wisconsin to cornel west Florida, also make some investments in the William j wilson money market, and probably get into the semi truck industry boss lady."

446

She looked at me like Nicole Natalie Austin did when she first met Tracey Lauren marrow, then she said to royalty, "What's next Mackology? a trip to Rita Pierson Hawaii, or carlotta walls lanier Jamaica, a weekend at the Charlotte forten grimke Chicago trump tower, or a few days on Kelly Miller necker island private resort?"

She was being so Fanny Jackson coppin sincere, Inez Beverly prosser smiling so hard, her teeth almost cracked, like it was a Mary McLeod Bethune Massachusetts, to septima poinsette Clark Maine, dr. Jeanne l. Noble lobster tail, then I said, "We gone do whatever our minds make happen for us to do, "ain't no limit," like master p said, but not at this marva Collins present moment, boss lady, first let's sit in the Marble mean green hand painted Dr. Edmund Gordon Whirlpool, check this out baby boss lady, look at what is written on the Charles Hamilton Houston floor mat, that's directly in front of the whirlpool, it says, "Welcome King & Queen."

I'm listening to Texas giants, the world famous Southside playaz, the classic everlasting song is called, "swang down," peace to blessings to dj screw, king fat pat, king hawk, & mr 3-2, respect to them from king Mack, peace to blessings to Mac Dre the California thizz founder, the name of his song playing right now is, "miss you."

Just been informed by John letzing and Andrew Berkeley that Juneteenth matters everywhere in the world.

I turned the brand new aethiopes whirlpool on for her, I did It as she began to step in the brand new ivory bangle lady whirlpool, she was obviously doing it to Sit her sexy happy self down nakedly, while she was sitting inside the brand new mean green marble beachy head woman whirlpool, the warm mansion water was racing out the Emma dabiri whirlpool holes, faster than nascar driver Wendell Scott drive, plus the air pressure was pumping harder than bass in Lil Webbie hummer, it was pushing water all over her unique body for royalty, I can tell by her facial expressions, that the air pressure was gently provoking her to get excited, I said, "Its lifetime rewards for zeinab badawi winners like you, that which look like how you look, you paid your dues, you proved you need me to be your king boss lady, you never turned on me, you never let your emotions stop you from putting us on top of the kush kingdom ladder, women came to leave, but you dedicated yourself to staying super glued to me, no matter

447

what your sexy highly intelligent self had to go through, and you the perfect definition of a top of the line street lady, on all levels a woman can be at her best on, which is the definition of a perfect woman on all levels.

She was leaning back in the Richard Leakey whirlpool fixing her bold beautiful dark lovely just for me hair, seems to me, she was making show she was Axum picture perfect, that's right, yeah for me, I leaned towards her young active attractive Daytona beach wet breast, she was in the water licking her College professor Nerrisa reaves type lips, you know Mackology, before I knew it, I was leaning towards her, My plan was to kiss her once, with a boat load of love in my body for her, when I pulled back off her Birmingham Alabama perfect condoleezza rice type lips, She started to cry in slow motion zoë saldaña, It was like she was Oscar award winning Hattie McDaniel, once again she lavinya stennett smiled so hard, her teeth almost cracked, while she was crying in the most Angela Bassett beautiful way possible, I changed the Marantz Black Super Audio CD Player music in the background, I decided to bump the best Smokey Robinson song ever created, you already know what it's called, "Quiet Storm," it was perfect to play at this John blanke trumpeter present moment.

The Marantz Black Super Audio CD Player, it had Dynamikkus Ultima speakers, which was connected to all parts of the queen Charlotte British mansion, including all the William wilberforce bathrooms, so whatever I decide to play, it would echo all over the multi-million-dollar antique Lake Michigan David matthews mansion, this was the perfect mansion to have a bbq,,or new years everything Charles Wooten celebration.

I just remembered what uncle Sir Sunny called this guy Bailey Roy Hackett Paul Stephenson Rosa park land I'm on, The Royal Family Estate, a place where hate don't exist, a place where capital game rain supreme, a place where truth swims in the air, at the same time, good spiritual energy marches on it, and the meanest loyal Perro de Presa Canario guard dogs you ever will see in your life, they was all around this estate, own member how many at the moment, my mind on something else, I know they was protecting all in the phillis Wheatley mansion from being bothered, even a little bit wasn't gone be happening, one look at these guard dogs, it can make Shaquille O'Neal get forehead sweating nervous, I mean, we straight safer then prince Akeem Joffer in zamunda.

She stood up in the hand painted mean tqueray bottle green colored marble Mary seacole whirlpool, she soaking wet like Traci Bingham running on bay watch beach, she got out the whirlpool looking sexy like 1998 Mya, I saw water dripping off her, I was smiling before it hit the floor mat in front of the Fanny Eaton whirlpool, humbly with gold diamond teeth like c-murder, ceelow green,& crime boss, I said to her, "Go take a Caribbean Bl luxury steam shower, in our Congo solid gold Evelyn dove bathroom, boss lady, it's the frameless glass door, with green diamonds inside the Emtek Windsor Crystal Dummy Lilian Bader door knob."

At this particular Joan armatrading time, I had one leg on the floor, one leg on the queen angelfish saltwater olive Morris bed, I was laying down pimpishly, I was floating on the waves it created, & guess what, you already know, like Texas say, I was counting currency, she dried herself off on the king queen Margaret busby publishing expensive Britain floor mat, she was drying off with a hermès dry towel, then she walked to me, It was like she was Lavita Raynor in the movie belly, she stood up in between my pimp stick walking legs to say, "baby, Little Kim nasty girl with Too $hort kiss me," as we kissed, her Luke warm tears dripped down her taral hicks perfect cheek bones, dropping down to her Tera Patrick porno star type breast, and my eyes was smiling excitedly as all this transpired."

I said, "get to that DreamLine Shen Engima-X Diane Abbott shower," I smiled like a 1993 Fritsch Middle school boy, standing in the Milwaukee Bucks cheerleaders locker room, while the ladies was getting undressed to take a shower, directly after the bucks won the 1971 nba championship.

She malorie Blackman smiled back at me with one of them Louisiana Chyna white light skin lady smiles, all while nakedly making her way to our Royal bedroom Caribbean bl luxury steam shower area, while She was doing all that, I was putting the huge faces in the Gucci Signature dr. Shirley Thompson suitcase, the Gucci zadie smith suitcase was a gift from Uncle Sunny, he splashed this Katherine Johnson suitcase in my face for me, when I got to the six-digit area in my making money stage in this lifetime.

She was looking like San San from the movie shottas as she walked to the DreamLine Enigma-X Lonnie bunch shower, she opened the green diamond door knob frameless glass Nadia valentine shower door, Just to place her nscs Evelyn sexy Latino looking self in the shower, while she was turning the expensive shower on, she was fixing the Philippe starck shower head to her personal preference, I was sipping octavia butler Don Periogòn, I was putting the green backs in the Gucci Signature Mae jemison suitcase neatly, professionally in a lined up order like the movies, at the same time, Smokey Robinson explained what Quiet Storm meant to him in the background to both of us, then erykah badu bob marley song, it's called, "in love with you," it Caribbean island danced out the speakers, it did this as I lit three Duke Of Gloucester Fu Dog Jar candles inside the royal Shirley Chisholm bedroom, simply for her to relax with, after she get out the shower.

My mind was having flashbacks of my cross country boss player adventures, sounds like an up all night cartoon waiting to happen, so I decided to stroll through the multi-million-dollar antique Fannie Lou hamer mansion, while she enjoyed her millionaire ruby bridges shower, she was singing lovely spiritual erykah badu part in the bob marley song.

As I pimp stick walked through the boss player status lyda d. Newman mansion, I realized Sir Sunny grew up in a sophisticated madam c.j. Walker family, a sophisticated family of intellectual wisdom pimps, and intelligent to brilliant hypnotizing seductive unbelievably attractive madams, all the way from the 1700's, all the way up to the Claudette Colvin present moment, it amazed me how they lasted this long, robert Abbott generation after Alvin Ailey generation, not to mention these Richard Allen pictures was still in good condition, from these old maya angelou Kodak paper photographic pictures, to the updated Polaroid Ella baker photos, it just intrigued me while I was looking at these James Baldwin photos, I wasn't trying to visualize what was going on, how their normal day transpired morning to bed time, it just was fascinating how a lifestyle could last 300 years, and Jean-Michel basquiat counting.

All I can remember uncle Sunny saying is, "he inherited a lifetime of Royal Benjamin o. Davis sr. Family wealth, which included this antique Frederick Douglass mansion from my dr. Charles drew fathers w.e.b. Du bois father, as we both know, my father, the giant from Fargo North Dakota, is doing federal time, with the above the law black Superman, "big meech."

As I stood in the antique 17th century duke ellington mansion 1800 square foot living room, by the Swarovski Crystal Aretha Franklin Fireplace,

I was looking at hand drawn pictures of king pimps posing together, by what looks like a horse & carriage, it was a five foot tall, five foot wall, hand drawn picture, in a stainless steel jemison Hendrix picture frame.

I took a sip of my 1996 zora neale Hurston dom perignon rose gold methuselah champagne, then I decided to walk through the antique Jesse Jackson mansion halls, outside the 1800 square foot Michael Jackson living room, on both sides of the walls of me, It was family portraits of his father's, father's, brother's, cousin's, auntie's, mother's, & sisters in Kodak Quincy Jones moments, straight prison picture posing, (respect to baby drew song, "posing like picture on a wall,"), one photo was a madam named Nola, she was posing with what looks like seven women that worked for her, they wore them Luxurious bustle dresses, looking like Henrietta lacks evening gowns, you can tell it was evening by the sun setting behind all of them, it was a black & white daguerreotype Toni Morrison photograph, for some reason that photo grabbed me, and kissed my eyes with a hypnotic hypnotizing unique appearance, in all my years, I never seen anything like this before.

Each one of these Barack Obama picture frames showed a picture of a sophisticated pimp, or intellectual madam, also the working ladies of the night that reeled the money in from miles around, their madam cj walker houses at the time, some jack Johnson vehicles they drove, it was also updated pictures, yet these antique priceless old daguerreotype photographs, they really demanded my attention in more ways then one, it also had at the bottom of each photograph, the year of their start in their game of life lifestyles, their retirement Jesse Owens finish, their game of life Gordon parks chosen names, & birthdays, this really was fascinating & intriguing to me in more Harriet Tubman ways then one.

As I fillmore slim pimp sticked walked through these Green Bay packers Wisconsin Lambeau long football field halls, of generational pimp history, my giant kind heart, it was beating like a senior drummer in a southern booker t. Washington Alabama State college marching band, and I heard queen hazel calling my name as she came down the custom made ida b. Wells staircase, her voice was a Minnie Julia riperton Rudolph Chicago Illinois accent type voice tone, it was echoing through the halls licking the inside of my ears, to let me know she was being sent to me by her august Wilson guardian angel.

JOURNEY WEALTHY LONGEVITY SCRIPTURES

13.

Everywhere you go, be on the prowl to see if that city got benefits for you on the business tip, vehicles, homes, a new crew, or new members bringing something to the table, showing a down for life mentality, simply to be in the royal family, to help the royal family get wealthy on the journey to longevity.

PIECES TO THE PUZZLE

"Meek is a humble person, they have a certain peace, so what I get is a spiritual aspect. The meek and humble, God will take care of in the end. They would inherit the earth, and live in peace." C. Hardy

I'm watching lovely sade video, It called, "nothing can come between us," seem like musicians had dance moves to explain the songs they was performing.

to know the game of life, is identical to saying that you working on mastering the game of life in the most indigenous ancestry soulful people way possible.

I'm in Edwardsville Illinois sipping kernel brut champagne.

It took 39 years & counting to write this brilliant book Properly, I'm back in Wisconsin, Lacrosse to be precise.

I'm leaning back boss playerish, looking at this city from my 4th floor room in the historic lacrosse Wisconsin charmant hotel, it's the end of February, I got green green on my mind, with intentions to put it on my menu soon.

Respect to the game of life, I edited this book me self, royalty way, royalty indigenous soulful style of talking, me, regular Hennessy, h20, green tea, & a jazz band is hanging together right now.

I enjoyed reading this intriguing book as I was editing it, I tell you what, life is nice if you play it right, people gone argue just to forgive each other without even knowing that's exactly what is waiting to transpire.

I put music I listened to, inside this unbelievable book, on the strength, so you can see what I was listening to, as I was editing this historical book, appliances I used in this special book, names I slid in this book, United States cities I was in through out this unbelievable book, vehicles I wrote in this fabulous fantastic book, along with vehicle parts, clothing got wrote in this brilliant book, including shoes, animal kingdom individuals I wrote in this intellectual book, hotels to motels I wrote inside this global book, words I wrote in this simply remarkable book, words I compensated from the Mack Moon.

I put a full effort in this unique amazing simply remarkable book, described as stupendously spectacular, I appreciate you for reading my ism, knowing knowledge is what really creates power.

Og aj says, "this book Is for the boss players cross country, the international hustlers, & the the 1950s 1960s 1970s 1980s gangster pimps.

Buttercup Johnson said during his interview on Mack 10 news network, "this book is brilliant in more ways then one for all to read, it's a hidden treasure in plain sight, if you didn't read it yet, you gone always feel like something is missing in your life."

King coleon was on Bill Cosby cable network channel giving a lecture about indigenous soulful unity, he said this, "if you knew better you would do better, Mackology 2nd edition can help you with that."

I'm still in half moon New York upstate finalizing royalty once in a lifetime book, I just finished watching "chicken and watermelon podcast with three New Orleans giants, new episodes every week live from holy grove New Orleans Louisiana.

THE LAST MACK
STANDING SCRIPTURES

17.

Step in smooth to lay It down thick, straight grinding like they do in Little Rock Arkansas, got to learn how to live, then learn how to earn, then learn how to make money work for you, then learn how to pull up shining brand new, like they say In Memphis, "this what game plus money do for you," if you learn how to direct traffic, Memphis know the business, on some project pat type stuff, It's all about getting life right wealthy, comfortable with longevity, and spirituality.

I'm headed to the north west coast, leaning back with that Gary Payton, & Pakistan, a king once said, "it take a lot out you from you when you going to the top of your game," that Eightball just came on, the classic song, "all 4 nuthin', so then what happens next?, if you ask a Missouri born pastor, he gone say, "if you knew how to work your magic, would you do it for everything available, I mean the journey to get wealthy with longevity, to grab hold control dominate conquer, to have all that in arm reach, what is it all for, what is the reward, currency luxury best life got to offer in arm reach, & then what, always expect the unexpected, I'm listening to Eightball classic song, it's called, "drama in my life," with Chicago psycho drama, respect to blessings to doc in the hospital right now, it's traps around every corner, always remember it's the bottom that's builds everything up for those on the top, & they get crumbs off the table, Morris day classic song just came on, Its ca, "gigolos get lonely."

I'm watching hezakya newz network, it's showing 1968 special report: Howard university rebellion, this network is the business in ways important can't come close to describing correctly.

EXPECT THE UNEXPECTED

That same night, hazel was laid out million dollar chilling in the wealthiest way possible, she relaxing like she was in lofoten island Norway somewhere with fireplace action, & jaccuzi access, I was scrapping the streets pimpishly investigating Milwaukee professionaly, I ended up parking by 27th wells, directly by the corner store, I was bumping project pat song, it's called, "gorilla pimpin," this a boss player association song, but I don't beat on my chest never ever, I turned the car off, got out player pimpish, then I hit the sidewalk nice & smooth style(rap group).

I was focused like an Atlanta hawk eye in the sky, I was thinking about recruiting & regrouping, the show don't stop because three gone, life goes on, the world still spinning, I'm still alive with a will to make something happen, so as I walked the sidewalk towards the corner store, behind the corner store was a big stupid big mean green dumpster.

Keep this in mind, it was Miami raining fat rain drops, it felt like angles was throwing rain drops all around me, throwing the rain at me hard as they can, faster then bob gibson hall of fame MLB pitcher pitches, then as I passed the jolly green dumpster in the rain storm, I heard what sounds like an innocent infant baby crying, I said please Father not me, the cry got louder as I got closer to the jolly green dumpster, I said Father not me, I knew I was in for something major tonight, something more important then knocking off a money maker lady with her hands on everything, I just got myself prepared not scared, just ready to expect the unexpected.

This mind boggling sound of sadness crying was coming from the jolly green dumpster, if indigenous people hear any sounds of sadness crying, or somebody saying help, we can't say no, or ignore it, because it hunts us for not being godbody, a green grey rim Cadillac was subbing hard, it was earth quaking 27th street, the Caddillac was bumping project pat, juicy j, la chat, & DJ Paul, "chicken head," song, um tum bout banging hard, call the police disturbing the peace, banging hard, neighborhood watch looking out the apartment building window hard, they was balling out of control, but for some reason, I still heard the sounds of now an infant baby crying, then an all night flight ambulance was going up 26th wells, towards 25th, I still heard the sounds of an infant baby crying, so I said, "ain't no avoiding this baby crying sound banging on my Congo ear drums," so I step to the dumpster, it was like I threw a 90 pack sack of $20 each worth of ready rocks in the dumpster, after being chased by chief Arthur Jones himself.

I said oh boy, because I heard the baby loud & clear Now, I was thinking, who in this particular city had thought about putting a baby in this jolly green dumpster tonight, I felt like I was being setup, what would you do, what would you be thinking before you looked in this dumpster, what would you expect, so I took a deep breath, the clouds above was just pouring buckets of rain on me, & the jolly green dumpster, so I said, "let's get this innocent infant baby out the jolly green dumpster before it get drowned out by the family of pure rain drops," I said, when I find this Infant inconsiderate mother, she gone get slapped up real nice, I'm gone slap her three times before she try to get mad, she straight out of order, I know own know why she did it, but the baby didn't ask to be here, so I'm rolling with the baby all the way, all the way on this one.

Then I heard detrict in that wagon, he had a flipping paint job on dubs, consistently he was banging project pat song, It's called, "keep it hood," I knew it was him because this his area, plus he bump that song hard after midnight every night, then I looked in the jolly green dumpster, I was on my Gloria daughter tippy toes, to my surprise, the baby was right on top of the random pile of garbage, on top of several cardboard ruffled up flat box, this birth to earth sad eyes innocent infant baby was looking at me screaming louder then an angry chimpanzee, I think I was setup, my cell phone Was ringing vibrating, it was queen hazel ringtone, I said she not gone believe this, but I bet she gone be like, "baby can we keep the baby, I said, "oh boy," (respect to Cam'ron), as I reached to pick the Inn infant baby up, the baby had A hunny bun plastic wrapper on it, a banana peel on its forehead, just some odd stuff going on, don't ask me why, own know yet.

The baby was fresh out the womb bloody, so I know it had to be a young girl, she probably was trying to get rid of an infant innocent baby

463

she just gave birth to, the umbilical cord was still in the innocent baby stomach, with the other end ruggedly cut off, you like me, what in the world going on right now, I got a fresh clean Michigan fox fur on, so I know this fur is gone be through with tonight real soon, I can tell my Michigan fox fur coat didn't want to deal with none of this, what dry cleaners can clean a bloody Michigan fox fur In Milwaukee, who gone clean a bloody Michigan fox fur, all this in one night, the funny part is, In't even surprised, or nervous, this all part of currency increasers community service if you getting consistent bread, this community service responsibility come with it, always expect the unexpected, no lie, so I'm doing what you would do, I picked the innocent infant baby up, & started falling in love with the sad eyes crying delicate baby, own some, "da last don," movie investigator scene, "all these kids is like my own."

Then the pure rain drops stopped falling, then Terrance from carver park, his Memphis brother Timmy, Memphis Timmy pulled up with his his little brother, he said, "mack Maine what's up," he was banging oj da juiceman song, it's called, "I'm getting money," it was straight banging hard, player was blowing kush out the driver side window, Gucci mane style, just balling like a b$tch, on some yo gotti Memphis hustler players night out 8ball type stuff, I said, "man, I just got a baby out the dumpster," he said, "you lying," then he turned his music down, see we get it how we live, but we still godbody, he said, "you got to take the baby to the hospital mack," I said, "I'm on my way now bra," he said, "hit me up tomorrow, to let me know what happen," he turned up his subs, he was playing Gucci mane song, it's called, "freaky gurl," I said, "perfect song Timmy," my Michigan fox fur coat got a bloody baby on it, I slid in the antique classic car, I was putting the innocent Infant sad eyes bloody umbilical cord baby on my passenger seat, inside my Michigan fox fur coat, so it can warm up, then I zoomed to the nearest closest hospital on teutiona, & highland, I turned on Florida plies song, Its called, "meet me at the Orlando Miami Ritz carlton hotel," then my right mind, my soulful spirit told me to put on Sade song, it's called, "kiss of life," then when it went off, i played her other undying song, Its called, "lover's rock," looking at this baby infant innocent girl made me think about Bessie Coleman, I was thinking with the motivation, perfect upbringing, this little gal can make history with the life she live.

JOURNEY WEALTHY LONGEVITY SCRIPTURES

15.

Everywhere you go, be on the prowl to see if that city got benefits for you on the business tip, vehicles, homes, a new crew, or new members bringing something to the table, showing a down for life mentality, simply to be in the royal family, to help the royal family get wealthy on the journey to longevity.

Respect to the ward brothers from Oakland, I'm in Gary Indiana with Rose Moet, remy Martin, and a Jazz black band, I'm listening to mjg classic song, It's called, "Memphis 10," featuring dj Paul, lil wyte, frayser boy, I just left Memphis ten, I saw where dr. Martin Luther king jr. got shot down at, inside the Lorraine hotel, it just happen, I never thought about Memphis being the place Martin Luther king jr. got kilt, I ran into the Lorraine hotel looking for indigenous Memphis soul restaurant, to get me something to eat, 8-Ball & mjg Classic song just came on, it's called, "pimps," indigenous soulful peoples everywhere go visit historical deep meaning Memphis, I felt right at home in the city of making easy money, you know the rest if game recognizes game.

I pray to the sir c pimp god, that my mackin be straight, peace & blessings to us all, keep evil away from us all Most High.

Royalty Had to say this, the Harlem globetrotters created generational wealth, I think that was a generational wealth creation one way, or another, respect to the, "savoy big five players: tommy brookings, tootz Wright, Lester Johnson, south side of Chicago, Byron long, kid Oliver, Inman Jackson, runt pullins, & their substitute Abe saperstein, Reese goose tatum is the star in daylight, he played for the Indianapolis clowns baseball team, they was famous for hijinks on the Baseball diamond, sweet Georgia brown, Marcus Haynes was the best dribbler in history, nay sweetwater Clifton was the best athlete of all time, at the same time this started, "indigenous brown cultural renaissance was a seed growing fast brilliantly, it was the definition of geniuses Is at work.

The Original in crowd has been taught that they should fit In with those who want to be like them, reprogrammed to think backwards, k-dee video just came on, it's called, "the freshest mc in the world."

ROUND TABLE MEETING

Self counseling in the form of being in a placed called Mound Key Florida, Estero Bay, King Calusa island, the point is to self check self, for the foolishness transpiring from self own doings.

"Good evening ladies & gentleman, this is king Larry Lane, I'm from, "the Mack," the movie, I like to welcome with open arms, all y'all, (respect to timbaland & magoo), to the main event of this brilliant book, you show got it together this day," then mr. Michael buffer said, "let's get ready to humblllllllllle."

With permission from King Calusa, a royal meeting was demanded, he commanded King Mack to have a sit down with Mack Millon, to create global unity, to strengthen the turtle island indigenous soulful spirituality people, they all spreaded out globally, just look around wherever you at in the world.

Inside the kings royal court was thousands of ancient indigenous soulful spiritual people, they was glowing, gathered with the Most High assigned, wise knowledgeable kings, and wisdom queens, everybody together in one place from all over the globe, a gathering like the million man march.

The King Calusa sat on his pyramid solid gold throne, with his mysterious royal family over looking the meeting, with Cassowaries walking around the king, strategically protecting him, it was like They was blue nose pit bulls, born bred raised in Jasper carrot, Birmingham Alabama.

Sandra Cross was singing her song called, "African King," as she sang, you could, if you was there, you would feel the blessings from the Most High, that was surrounding the kings island, positive energy appeared dancing in the air like ruby throated hummingbirds, all the indigenous ancient people breathed in, simultaneously, all these friendly strong spiritual soul people sat peacefully, sit back relax, & open mindedly watch how this unique brilliant meaningful story goes.

A deep Michael McCary bass voice appeared, it appeared throughout the kings island echoing, it sounded like It was saying, "all rise for the honorable King Mack Millon, he sits on a Kemet solid gold created throne, ten inches directly above the marble floor on kings Calusa island."

He sits proudly in the center of the royal Barrington levy jamaica black roses, In the happy Jackson Mississippi fried green tomatoes st Augustine colored green grass, they also somehow in the water grass, they was circle surrounded by mean green colored Atlantic alligators, and a tremendous amount of amazon born crocodiles, indigenous spectacular kings, & simply remarkable dark lovey bold beautiful queens, they all sat down in kings Calusa royal chairs, with other stupendously Chicago Scorpio pimpish indigenous soulful willie Lloyd Larry Hoover gangster people, including worldwide indigenous spiritual soulful children, all was proudly anticipating the long awaited start of this long time coming unity indigenous spiritual soulful peoples meeting.

The deep Michael McCary base voice appeared, simultaneously it was all around the island, it was like the sound of thunder was saying, "to all ears listening, let all eyes watching, acknowledge a master mind crowned king by the Most High, a wisdom righteous good intentions king, an indigenous miraculous man, amongst all indigenous extraordinary gentleman, the pinky ring street king, the one and only, globally don magic Juan Chicago upbringing King Mack."

The deep Barry white bass voice, it was continuing to speak King Calusa approved words in existence, the philosophical voice was saying, "blessings from one to all, from the thoughts of the king Calusa, love is life, & you can say together, life is love, respect to all indigenous spiritual soul people all over our world, all is from our Most High."

All the indigenous spiritual highly educated soul people, they closed their eyes while swaying to the song, it's being sang by queen Sandra Cross, simultaneously, all was feeling the words of the deep bass voice whispering in the wind, the deep James earl jones arkabutla Mississippi bass voice, it was speaking strongly directly precisely to all soulful indigenous spiritual ears listening.

Once again, the deep Paul Robeson bass voice spoke saying, "all be seated my ancient bloodline spiritual indigenous soul people," then the lovely heaven sent wisdom queen Sandra Cross, her voice slowly got low, lower, lower, until silence grabbed everybody attention by the collar.

Then king Calusa tapped his crocodile Belvedere sandals twice, he did that with his eyes closed, and then queen Dezarie started singing her song, it's called,"Most High."

When she started singing, it proudly loudly danced in the air waves, strategically it was touching the ear drums of all indigenous soul people throughout the solar system, I mean everybody listening started getting in the amen ra spirit, it felt like reverend b.w. Smith was preaching a sermon, the Most High spirit fingers tapped them all on the shoulders.

All fantastic ancient bloodline indigenous soul people, respectfully, prayerfully bowed their heads, holding ancient bloodline indigenous hand in hand, on the king Calusa island, one to all was sharing their love for the Most High, with their thoughts that can be bought, & the energy their spiritual released.

The everlasting love from the Most High, a large percentage of it brought Jamaican spiritual Rastafarian warmth to all indigenous righteous soul people globally, from that moment to forever in the air, queen wisdom Dezarie, her wonderful beautiful voice sang to the Most High, her spirit was saying, "calling to the Most High, praise to Him."

As queen Dezarie voice slowly faded into the silence, it was blending in with the delta 88 colored Atlantic alligators swimming sounds, specifically being made from the Atlantic alligators consistently swimming around the kings island, king Calusa opened his eyes, identical to how a lion awakens from its slumber right before the kemet sun rises, strong proudly, then the spiritual indigenous soul people released hands from each other hands, acknowledging the prayer that which was said to transpire this particular meeting, that boss player prayer had to been accepted by the Most High this specific day, tears of joy crawled down the indigenous spiritual kush pyramid golden brown women copper colored sun blackened faces.

From his throne high in the rain cloud sky, his throne was shining hard at this time like untouched earth crust deep diamonds, it was blowing kisses at the clouds as it sparkled glistening, King Calusa spoke fearlessly saying, "to all you intelligent international brilliant indigenous soul people, from the past present to the future, "let all ears listening be thankful to our Most High every hour, on top of every hour, always to forever, to all our past present future's Most High Creator, I ask You to put my truth, & prayers on all, to every pinch of existence, now to forever, past present, future."

Appearing like a cool breeze above the waves on Lake Michigan, was king Gregory Isaacs singing his classic song, it's called, "Temptation," from the album Inna Rub a Dub style.

Then the Cassowaries guarding the ancient indigenous king, they started moving to the beat as Jamaican King Gregory sang, his wise parable message went from soulful ear to spiritual ear, it was really touching their spirits, from the king island to all Caribbean islands worldwide, to all other islands worldwide, to all over the globe, to the ears of all indigenous Intellectual soul people ears, even the def unable to hear soul people, even they heard his message through their spirit vibrations.

The deep 1949 Greg brown bass voice appeared again, It was saying, "from the thoughts of king Calusa to all ears listening, peace be on to the ancient ancestors from the beginning to now, peace be to the great spirits from the beginning to nowadays, peace to blessings to mut nature from beginning to now, peace to blessings to the elements, peace to blessings to above belove inside outside, & beyond."

King Gregory Issacs voice got lower, lower, then the Christión twins started singing their song called, "Full of Smoke," it started dancing New Orleans horse Toni in the air ways, the twenty dollar bill green colored Atlantic alligators, Deinosuchus Montana Dinosaur stomped out the water, just to lay on the edge of the kings island, so when these incredible indigenous soul people started singing more songs, they can enjoy it while they let amen ra sun rays rub their back for them, I mean if you know how to play this game of life professionally, brilliantly, magnificently you play this game of life to win, serve your purpose, get down with the get down, know the meaning of life, y'all remember jay-z nem said, "what's the meaning," I say respect to all the indigenous spiritual soulful peoples who kept It Pimpin' for decades in their lifetime, like Don magic Juan said, "It's a deadly game If you don't play it right."

Suddenly the soul people started to recognize that king Calusa was looking Marcus Garvey humbly, Philip Emeagwali smiling, dropping queen nzingha tears of joy, from seeing this long awaited meeting, amongst all indigenous turtle island soul people, he pointed at king Gregory isaacs to come sit on his throne with him, true player move right their, Gregory Isaacs Is a solid man to chop up game with.

The king Calusa stood up on his throne high in the sky, with Unique Cassowaries watching everything moving near him, straight protecting your highness, he looked in the crowd of the indigenous Soul people, directly at queen chief warhorse, then he said my queen, speak your words to us wisdom daughter.

The queen said, "peace be on to my king Calusa, peace be on all us indigenous soul people of North America turtle island, blessings respectfully to our Most High, peace to the elements, peace to above to beyond, peace to below to beyond, peace to the inside to beyond, peace to outside to beyond, peace to the animal kingdom, peace to Amen Ra, peace to Mut Nature, love is life life is love."

The reason being for this session is to have a one on one meeting with mr. Mack Millon, also known as Millon mackin'.

Silence in the royal kingdom walked around dancing like boogaloo shrimp on the kings island key mound Florida, the deep thunder voice said, "sitting in the deep dark green Atlantic alligator Gaga recliner chair, is mr. Mack Millon."

Once again, the king stood up to say, "if you gone roll with me, let's ride," then New Orleans rebirth brass band started playing their song, it's called, "rebirth grove," and the audience got silent at first, they looked at king Calusa tapping His crocodile sandals, and the indigenous extraordinary soul people got up slow, then their spirits felt the love in the air, then they started dancing indigenous soul people New Orleans style.

The rebirth brass band finished hyping the crowd spirits up, the King Calusa nodded at king Mack to start the round table conversation, then king Mack said, "we don't need no liquor nor champagne," let bilal sing his song called, "soul sista," then king bilal started saying, "thank you king Mack, thank you Most High, thank you king Calusa, this song is dedicated to all strong like a mountain indigenous soul people," and he closed his eyes, then the instrumental soul people started playing their instruments, then bilal started to sing, then a crew of 40 great egret, & great blue heron flew over everybody on the island.

King Mack started saying, "Mack Millon dollars, you in the major leagues now like Mamie peanut Johnson, you been to 43 states helping all people, your knowledge is polished, I want you to step in smooth to lay down thick, from now on, i told you already royalty, learn how to earn your turn to shine, your queen gone come to you, simply because you been working hard, "with your whole life," like Tousha be saying, to set everything up for your kingdom, your blessings will come to you, to help you build your kingdom, respect the Most High day to night, I know it's been a ruff ride like dmx song said, but listen to this, "Childhood is first twenty years on earth, then it takes twenty more years to learn how to be an adult, then at age 40 you will become a full grown spiritual soulful indigenous wealthy adult, and then you will start, "living luxury," like Memphis og double d said."

Then I thought to my myself, "Give visuals with words, I member Uncle Geno said, "everything in life, it's written in the book of life already," then I thought about Michael v roberts gave a secular sermon at new birth in Atlana, i member how much inspired me to setup retirement by age 40, so royalty can focus completely on spirituality.

I said, "Pimpology was in the air I inhaled all my life, but it wasn't the air I breathed in consistently, Am I a pimp pretending to be a Mack, or am I going against the grain, knowing pimpin is part of my unavoidable history, and future, am I wrong, will the pimpin in the air royalty inhale, will the pimp spirits hate me for this, will I be facing pimp arrest."

King Mack said, "Stay updated upgraded, Those who talk like they know, and those who talk what they heard will confuse you, Your life is the gun, you the only bullet, make it count."

Royalty said, " it's about Choice not force, because pressure will bust pipes, Get everybody perspective From childhood to adulthood, some kids had imaginary friends, but pimpin has always been my friend, even when I was alone sad mad, pimpin always been their to lift me up, and motivate me to progress without stress, that's how it be in a city with economic disparity In Milwaukee."

King Mack said, "If a woman ain't got my game in her, I can't deal with her, or have her around me neither, near, or far, she got to be dealt with like everybody else, identical to the treatment they gets issued out, I can't interact with those who don't hold the title I hold, or live the lifestyle I live, because confusion creates chaos."

King Mack said, "let's chop up game according to what you learned city to city, state to state, straight cross country living, international like uncle Juny J.B. buns."

Suga free stood up with his perm long hair blowing in the wind, boss player long hair blowing in the wind on the king calusa island, he started rapping his song called, "if you stay ready."

While Pomona Suga Free was pimp rapping in the background, about being prepared for anything that comes next, Mack Millon said, "if you ain't put no food in the zline 48" professional gas burner, don't expect something to come out for you to eat, a whole crew that's born to be with the king a lifetime will reveal themselves, why look for who should be looking for you, respect is mandatory, important effort is not put in those outside the royal family, & memorize laughter is the key to living a full long life."

Then queens bridge Nas stood up to perform his worldwide classic song, it's called, "street dreams," he said, "street dreams are made of these, everybody is looking for something."

King Mack said, "Texas is big time, up north seem thirsty for not getting proper ingredients to feel complete, down South is spacious, and everything is plentiful all across the country, If your movement rotate state to state that is."

Mr. Mack Millon said, "got to stay on top of everything, throw some food on the floor, then wait to see who a rat."

King Mack said, "can't let nobody profit off me more then I profit off me, rule number one, when it comes to business that is, I'm not looking to recruit, let the Most High hand pick individuals for me, those who belong with me permanently, they fit right in with me, just like my Havana joe hustler shoes, wu tang call them shoes wallabees on the east coast, y'all know what um tum bout, I know mine when I see mine, people globally gone fake hate, I decline bad offers, I disregard bad opportunities, never get lost in character."

Lil Wayne New Orleans style, he stood strong, ready to beat down hurricane Katrina with his eyes closed the whole time, in his mind he was staring fearlessly in the eyes of hurricane Katrina, and he said, "cut the music up please," out of nowhere, Mary j bridge stood up, it was like a true spiritual indigenous New York City soul woman, just to say, "oh nawl

nawl, oh nawl nawl, oh nawl nawl, oh nawl nawl, oh nawl nawl," then lil Wayne started rapping his song, it's called, "oh no," then the deep dark brown skinned, indigenous Lousisana soul people stood up, with their eyes closed holding hands in hands, praying for everybody that hurricane Katrina ended their life, you know it's getting real, in the crowd king Calusa noticed tommie Smith, & John Carlos, just from putting up a fist for black power, on October 1968 in Mexico City.

Then project pat from Memphis stood up to rap his song, it's called, "take the charge," it was saying, "she a ghetto type broad, catching me with the dope, & she gone take the charge," then Angie stone starting singing, "the closer I get to you, the more you make me see, by giving me all you got, your pimpin has captured me, " while I'm finalizing this brilliant chapter, I'm watching dr. Ivan van sertima lecture on African presence In early Asia.

King Mack said, "we all gone get caught in traps set up for us to fall into," then New Orleans juvenile said, "it's all about bouncing back," King Mack said, "over coming, then master the world you live in, or it will master you, stay updated upgraded."

Orange mound Tennessee 8ball & MJG stood up to perform their classic song, it's called, "space age pimpin," then Mack Millon said, "getting ready for this next week this week, getting ready for next month this month, getting ready for next year this year, staying sober to build your kingdom."

D shot, Too Short, & spice 1 from northern California, they stood up to do their classic song, it's called, "true world wide playaz," then king Mack said, "ahead not behind, ahead of opponents, not being stood on, thinking first, out thinking those competing with you, making competition wish they was your competition."

Then Memphis three 6 mafia stood up to perform their classic song, it's called, "gold shine," then Mack Millon said, "we all from a tree taller then Hyperion trees, depending on what land you born on, but all branches grow differently, producing certain unique fruits, with specific necessities to grow stronger hourly, to get full, each branch requires specific yes, and declines specific nos."

Then snoop from the land of Long Beach, with Newark New Jersey brick city red man stood up, to perform their song called, "what u looking

4," then king Mack said, "all in Memphis, I was reading, writing, gambling, it's real live players full of life in Memphis, love, longevity, same for Mack's, gangsters, pimps, hustlers, we all specialize in knowledge about what we born to focus on, y'all know what um tum bout."

Then Eric b. Walked up to his custom made turn tables, he was on a mission to show djs from long Island to worldwide, how to mix like dj jam master j, then rakim said, "In't no joke," then they performed their everlasting song, Its called, "I ain't no joke," then flavor flav started dancing by them, the intelligent to brilliant indigenous soul people, from the 70s, 80s, & 90s, they got up doing their flavor flav dance, simultaneously flavor flav was dancing his dance to this beat, with a Duc D'Orleans Breguet Sympathique clock on his neck, with green diamonds all over it, then Mack Millon said, "my spirit name is Royalty, my business name is on my birth certification card, relax when you major mackin, big pimpin, original gangster living, boss playing, king hustling for longevity, stress don't bring out the best in you."

Then Brooklyn Jay-z, & Marcy projects Memphis Bleek stood up to do their classic song, it's called, "coming of age," dame dash from Harlem world, he was standing up with them sipping expensive Africa 'Gout de Diamants' champagne, you can't buy It in North America, then Mack Millon said, "some of us gone live to help other unique indigenous soul people, some of us gone build our kingdom, or empire, I went to Texas to get my mind right, then left to go back up north, just to see the difference in everyday life, from people, to weather, to energy, create your own good vibrations, turn weakness to strength, rebuild longevity routes everyday, everyday brings new battles, keep your knowledge polished, game got to be Virgin Island tight, like Tim Duncan, global intelligence is very relevant, stay on your pyramid gold brick road, the more you learn to chill, the more your bread will increase, get all that is coming to you, never down play yourself, be surrounded by indigenous spiritual soulful powerful energy."

Once again snoop from Long Beach stood up with butch cassidy from southern California, just to do their song, it's called, "so gangsta," then king Mack said, "I was all in Mississippi with skinny long tall trees, welcoming weather, good energy type sceneries, all at once, recognize life is set up, it's all written like Milwaukee geno said, no worries, sit back to enjoy the show, and get ready for the main event."

A helicopter was flying over head full of peeping toms taking pictures, then Lousisana juvenile, he stood up with Soulja slim, bg & big moe to perform the song called, "solja rag," then Mack Millon said, "appreciation to the Most High, I woke up in Alabama with great intentions to keep it throwback pimpin like Fillmore Slim, I understand Florida where I was headed next, that's right, let good situations find you, stop looking, plundering for trouble, focus on whats in front you(country grammar, you like that right, what state talk like that) whoaday whoaday whoaday is what homer blow said at king Derrick Avery 1st annual players ball In Milwaukee Wisconsin.

Then Brooklyn Jay-z, with Chicago Kanye West, & Rihanna from the Barbados, they all stood up to do their indigenous powerful global song, its called, "run this town," Rihanna cold, her voice can get the saddest king hyped up, her indigenous singing making me feel like I'm in chocolate city Dover Delaware, then Mack Millon said, "never use abuse confuse hate debate time waste, a black brown rose don't belong in the dark hidden, what is, belong with what it is, know the difference between this, keep self preserved in full effect hourly, Most High what will you do for me, that you ain't did for me already, what can top what has been happening so far."

Then queens bridge havoc & prodigy stood up to do their song, it's called, "get away," then Mack Millon said, "I love Memphis, stay in the sun to get your shine on, stay hydrated updated upgraded, ahead of what's going on that which is seen the most, which is the worlds most wanted," (currency).

Then westside Chicago twista, & Memphis jazze phae stood up to do their song, it's called, still feels so good," then king Mack said, "a wild horse will scream, kick, then run away, just being out of control, if you not on point, it will get you caught up in a world of trouble, so it's best to stay away from untamed wild horses."

Then Vallejo d shot, & e-40 stood up to perform their classic song, Its called, "keep Pimpin," then king Mack said, "if a dog sense fear, it will feed off it, possibly attack, or just growl loud, bite you when it want to, just to keep you in fear of it, so it can keep you under its control, so it's best to put fear in the rear, keep the throne with one seat for the king, with seats below the throne, for a chosen few," then Felix Mitchell stood up to wave at his Oakland player partners, respect to mr. Mitchell son, & community activist mr. Lil d Darrel reed.

Big pat from Memphis stood up like anna Illinois giant to do his song, it's called, "cocaine," then Mack Millon said, "don't support bad vibrations, nor glorify encouraging negativity, those who survived the game of life, some made songs, or told you the business, because they survived hard times, just to tell you how bad it was, not to do as they did, but to take better long term routes, & others wrote books to come from other angles, yet also with the same purpose of intentions like sir j. Prince book called, "the art & science of respect."

Then bankhead Georgia, king shawty lo stood up tall, like Colossi of Memnon, to do his famous classic song, it's called, "that's shawty lo," then king Mack said, "I was all in Georgia drunk, but Georgia took care of me, I love my indigenous soul people in Georgia, for real for real, they got love strong in Georgia, I chopped up game with them, g invited me to mobile Alabama Mardi Gras this year, couldn't make it, had to get bread, timing is everything, if you not working mentally physically spiritually financially, you don't belong in the royal family, I got mad love for Georgia, in every city, they treat me like family, believe that, if you aiming to have fun, do it with who on what you on, everything is based on mathematics ray virgil fairley said, I was so tow up, easily they could have violated, but they didn't, I got love for Georgia indigenous Cherokee soulful people, what's up to Georgia.

Then Chicago born ludacris with Texas born Jamie foxx with Georgia field mobb, they all stood up together, like they was in the 1963 march on Washington, straight smiling together, to do their song, "Georgia," then Mack Millon said, "distractions is specks flying in the eye, who is who, anybody can be a distraction, except certain people, like those who may be wise knowledgeable indigenous soul people.

What's up to Savannah camaflauz, (forgive if I spelt his name wrong), I'm in Gary Indiana, if you straight with the Most High, Gary Indiana will show you a bunch of smiling face love."

Stooges brass band stood up talking first, with New Orleans accents saying, "an indigenous can't find no weed," then started performing their classic song performance with the instruments, the song Is called, "weed drought," once again New Orleans indigenous soul people stood up to dance 1960 New Orleans jazz club second line style.

Then King Mack said, " black people is our universal name, the person with experience has the right to teach, preach, simply because it's mandatory to do so for the Most High reasons."

Then Mack Millon said, "a preacher preaches, a teacher teaches, a wise man shares his wisdom, adapt to the Most High, don't adapt to a kind of a man who knows not that he is self destructing the world, that which is yours, also those who look identical to you, it's all about raising your game, your ism, your way of existing to a whole nother level."

Then King Mack said, "opportunities come to those who will share it with others, you must cover your wake up with truth, your mid day with truth, before you sleep with truth, by way of reading higher learning, mixed with self empowerment, by way of body building, writing to the Most High, thank you Most High for all, or nothing, anything, and everything."

Bay Area Andre nickatina stood up with Vallejo Dubee, they did their song called, "fly like a bird," then Mack Millon said, "successful everything only, strong last long, built to last, no limit like New Orleans master Percy Miller, receive power every hour, day to night, eyes don't lie, look listen learn, earned turn time to shine, stay in it to the finish, lifestyle has got to be defined as stupendous."

B-legit stood up with sir Todd Shaw to perform their classic song, it's called, "so international," then king Mack said, "the master mind is back in business, batteries not included, the king has done great up to this point, allowance to take it to the next level, this level has been granted by the Most High, professionalism is in existence, it consistently still is transpiring, another royalty level has been reached July seventh twenty twenty one in upstate half moon New York, a place where everything is advanced."

B-legit stayed standing after too short sat down, then levitti stood up to do the California night song, It's called, "city to city," then Mack Millon said, everybody got to walk their path, hopefully wisdom Is with you on the pathway you on, time to enjoy self happiness enjoyments, mind self business, king intellectual New game, secluded lifestyle, isolated intelligence, confidential brilliance, classified wisdom, low key under radar with polished knowledge, staying out of sight out of mind," then Figueroa pretty pimpin Dino stood up suited up in true blue, from tip top of hat, to the point of his Mauri alligator shoes to take a bow to all eyes watching greatness.

B-legit stayed standing while livitte sat down, then kurupt stood up to perform the summer song called, "check it out," with Earl Stevens, then Mack Millon said, "ask the Most High to teach you how to read what you reading, dig down deep in it, helping hands for those on top of their game, on some Gina Davis type stuff, just adapting with the decades, putting pimpin' in the trunk til it's time to release the Mack with in, king intellectual new game, back to the original ism, that ism is in him which birthed the present moment progress to transpire."

King Mack said, "The indigenous soul people have been told they lost, in all actuality, all pyramid golden brown indigenous soulful peoples is native to the land they born in, with no connection to their nationality with another continent, with respect that is written."

B-legit stayed standing alone, giant rock in Mojave's desert landers California bolder strong, to perform his song called, "destiny," then Mack Millon said, "back to the basics that created the foundation, that was created for solid people to build on, original game is what every brain need to contain, everything is being pulled out storage, it was kept away for safe keeping, simply for the right time to set everything off right, gate keepers is polishing it off right now, just so the true amen ra sun light can shine bright properly all year around.

B-legit started doing his next song called, "it's in the game," then king Mack said, "Your elders only see you in the light they trained you to be in, certain things said, and thought will anchor a person, or keep that person stuck on stupid, not knowing they straight standing still In quick sand in Maine, learn from other people life experience, don't count your eggs til they hatch, like Georgia Big Boi said, qualified contestants will be blessed with game, and a new name, everything today is combined creating confusion & misunderstandings, do background checks, and read resumes, a lot is known, but only a select few can confirm its true, customize your lifestyle, write your history, its still a lot of individuals putting real game on their shoulders, and taking it with them everywhere they go, years to build, but seconds can destroy it, play the game in a way described as simply remarkable, can't let the game beat you, when you don't give up, you don't see your progress until you reach your throne, control

480

your powers like laxer cyclops, business, and personal contracts is what you put in full effect."

Zap & roger stood up to perform their timeless unforgettable classic 1986 song, it's called, "computer love," then Mack Millon said, "Toast to those who can't toast with us today right now, indigenous soul people appreciate everybody who played their part in our bloodline existence, those who was, is, will be contributing one way, or another, also we thank them all, whom ever they might be, for helping this day transpire, because our success was not created alone, peace and our blessings be upon them all Most High." (Harlem alamoe the black widow the truth.

When Mack Millon stopped talking, Zapp did the next classic song, its called, "more bounce to the ounce," ask your elders to translate what the song mean, then king Mack said, "Throw your prayers in the air, whisper in the wind, & let it go everywhere, let the sun shine while you water the grass, that mean reach the youth & preach the truth, a sign of intelligence is shown when thinking before reacting transpire, Pay all your dues then retire, You want me on top, or not, Power is in the hand of those who know what to do with it, Learn disrespectful words spoken against you in other languages, so you know if it's being said around you, keep eyes open to see bigger better deals, Watch everybody like a black mamba snake out of grass, learn how to use your powers properly righteously, every sleeping giant needs the precise environment to grow properly, Use negativity to inspire positivity, If I follow, or believe you, display proof why I should, or prove to me I should follow your lead, show, & prove, Missouri born show me state."

Xzibit, j ro, & tash stood up with the green eyed bandit to perform their song, it's called, "allkaholik," then king Mack said, "when you get bigger than your boss, it will be time to go, help right the wrong for those who look like you, even level out the playing field, strippers is mistaught, introduce yourself to who you want to be your customers, like a job interview, if you need to get paid in full, what was important last year ain't important this year, that's how the story goes, like Texas crime boss said, money brings money, brilliance is intelligence in a court of law, it is about what you can prove, pray for knowledge to get necessities, trickery is in the air everywhere, everywhere has its form of everything, if you need to do something, you got to be ready to do it, get to know a person before you think you know a person, in prayers ask to be taught how to make something happen, brake the most complicated situation down to simplicity, learn how to fill up empty spaces, with the most valuable information."

The west side connection stood up to gangster rap their most memorable song, it's called, "gangstas make the world go round," then Mack Millon said, "the right environment will setup retirement, easy women, is who you turn the wise pimpin on for y'all longevity purposes, where you from is getting you ready for the world, accusations pride and prejudice is floating in plain sight, my people spend days to nights speaking on our denied history, while other nationalities spend time plotting to take over the world, that which is bad intentions over do everything to let you know bad intentions is transpiring, being real is making progress with what you choose, or what choose you, words is miss used about you behind you, because of hate jealousy, let everybody know what time it is with you, if they misunderstand your lifestyle that Is."

The Long Beach California dynamic duo, warren g & Nate dogg stood up to perform their song, its called, "I need a light," then King Mack said, "One is the key number, because it leads up to more, it also lead up to a million, everything starts with the copper colored number one, Opinion: gangsters run things boss status with no hands on, pimps control minds & the bodies follows, hustlers is hands on everything, which is where I believe a pimp lady gets the name abbreviation hoe from, that which Is abbreviated explaining the meaning of hands on everything, back to hustlers, which is the road runners like the mailman, being here there to everywhere suppling what is in beneficial demand, that which can be from A to Z, name it, price tag it, in one hand out another, selling books, selling albums, selling game, price tag it, a boss player plays everybody that cross their path talking about currency, for the main purpose to keep their self with a consistent income of cash flow, which to them is never personal, it's strictly business, a mack crowned king by the Most High for studying all walks of life, discovering that all that needs to be done in life is to get the Royal treatment, by studying analyzing reading writing, self preservation, help to get help is natural law, which falls into the thinking process, that which will explains why you should stick to the scripture, given from the words of the Most High, it's known by all, that good game is laid in all

482

soul survivors minds, be as little Gods in reflection of the Most High, knowing mistakes will be made, like saint Louis natives said, "just do as much good as possible, & life will take care of you on all levels, no wants, no needs, no reason to step on toes burning bridges, don't be sad mad or glad, just sit back relax and enjoy the show.

The dogg pound stood up barking out their California Christmas classic song, it's called, "Santa clause goes straight to the ghetto," then Mack Millon said, "Ame' Rican soul people, land of rich soil, What you do that release your power is your gift, soul people Develop your style around your people, The Bible is indigenous soul people history book, if it's read right, because it proves in everyday life who talks none stop about the Father mother most high Creator, and practicing ways to be right all day everyday."

Nate dogg stood up alone, while the dogg pound sat down, he soulfully sang his magical song, it's called, "one more day," tears from loved ones fell down their face happily, with their eyes closed while he whispered in the wind loud, then King Mack said, "keeping it Pimpin' is putting game in your brain every brain need to contain, Crying is getting rid of something that is creating weakness inside you, bad energy, crying It out your existence, Watch those that don't study, & study those that study, Everything is based on rhythm and melody, & the sun people can catch the rhythm and melodies, it's about figuring out the patterns in life, Everybody got their moments when their light shines unstoppably bright, incredibly."

Oakland California Keak Da Sneak with frank sticks, & Killa klump, they stood up to do their hood to hood, Bay Area song, it's called, "nigga rah," then King Mack said, "in Tampa Florida, a thought popped up on my mind, bullet in the gun, born to live this way, As the soul people circulate the earth, it will be creating balance with those they meet, & those they know, One impact two, two impact three, three impact four, it's time to start pressing Play on songs that be popping throwback pimping in the strip clubs, Soul people got a language spoken in the English language with words, or sign language, If you need something, do something good to make it happen, Connect the dots, Blessed to have a happy privilege, You don't outsmart me, I outsmarted you, Everything comes back around full circle, Good has to out weigh bad, Unlearn one track mind thinking immediately."

Inglewood California Mack 10 stood up to read from his hustler manual, also to perform a song called, "take a hit," then Mack Millon said, "I member I was in New Jersey talking to Florida, about longevity, It's a full time job staying alive, I was On the east coast bumping that west coast, that's what you call unity, Drinking Moët in New Jersey, playing nipsey hussle, respect to the giant wilt chamberlain boss player, Keeping it real to a dead end is pointless, keeping it real staying down ignorant is foolish, keeping it real helping indigenous soul people to progress, making show they elevate is the nipsey hussle way, my opinion, If the ones saying they keeping it real is in Hawaii pushing a Lamborghini, while me & you still on the block, we missing the point of what keeping it real is, it's not being broke, or bragging about smoking weed, then asking for money to pay your phone bill, you missing the point of keeping it real, when you go for broke to keep it real, you missing the message, is you keeping it real, or standing still faking like you keeping it real?"

Rick James stood up looking like 1985 rick James, then snoop dogg stood up Lbc style, to do his boss players song, it's called, "player's way," then Mack Millon said, "Prime time hustlers hit the highway, the Triplets pimp cities used to be Milwaukee, Minniapolis, & Chicago, How you think will open doors, or close doors, I member spending the weekend in the Appalachian mountains, waking up looking at mountains, sleeping inside the mountains like it wasn't nothing feeling like ancient America giants, Stay away from what will change your character, Everything everybody say is important, a woman can have sex without playing both sides of the field, but her bouncing around can cause conflict from her feelings, in no way is that acceptable, or allowed, The Most High deals with each generation differently, with different task to perform to do The most high will, as He will it to be done, Each state has specific types of ancestors, or great spirits you can talk to about specific stuff."

California stood up puffing mean green hydroponics during a famous song, it's called, "I got 5 on it remix," it was the luniz, dru down, richie rich, e-40, shock g, & spice 1, then King Mack said, "Don't put yourself, or someone else in a position, you, or they don't, or shouldn't be in, No more still in the hood situations, it's like this now with me saying I can get you where I'm at, you can see how it feels to get out to, Soul people got their own clever word play in every city, & style to communicate it to whom ever, it's called a language inside any language."

"The old fashioned way," west coast song, soul sista Latoiya Williams, music genius Soopafly, coldest p spita Suga Free, & tha eastsidaz stood up to do their memorable song, it's called, "I don't know," then Mack Millon said, "Play the game correctly, when you get the chance to tell strippers to keep it player with boss players, & seductive with customers, a boss player gone always do, or say something to separate himself from everybody else, so you can recognize who he is, ask her, do she want a trick, or treat, a trick is a customer, a treat is a night to remember with a boss player, winter time is the playoffs in the Midwest, the worst joke is when your uber driver say, "I'm glad that light was green."

C-bo stood up in steel toes, to do his west coast famous song, Its called, "the autopsy," then mr. Mack Millon said, "Master this world, read write exercise, teach yourself, preach to yourself, master the life you live to perfection, study your city you from, learn all about it from ancient times to present moment, to peep the changes, the truth of those indigenous spiritual soulful natives of that land, the mardi gras is in New Orleans, all the way to mobile Alabama, master this world, don't let life blow by you, study every day, know everything you allowed to find out, to the point everything becomes simple, Code of silence is speaking without speaking, I member telling a boss lady she was very attractive, but if you don't figure out how to master money, you gone forever be without it, money is a tool, it's mandatory you shoot for jobs that pay bankroll fat, if your city not paying you right, then you got to pick a new city that will pay you properly royally," you know what getting paid royalties mean right, that means figuring out how to have your own business."

West coast legend c-bo did his next song, it's called, "ghetto flight," the island got 2:30am Arkansas church silent, then Mack Millon said, "A partner that share their life with you completely, putting to use your advice, gaining joy from putting to use the huddled up information you gave them, is powerful in a major way, Mackology is not based around sex, it's based around powerful knowledgeable ancient wisdom, who can become the ultimate overcoming obstacles rising above, and beyond, being the definition of a soul survivor, with none stop respect for a lioness with impressive behavior."

E-40 & the click stood up to perform their favorite song, its called, "money luv us," then King Mack said, "Everything is about making the connection with a long term currency route, Warren g, xzibit, Nate dogg, bigg snoop dogg, they all got up to perform, "the game don't wait remix."

"Learn what happens, why, where, Mistakes makes us great believe that, America policies keeps the foolishness transpiring for old reasons, that millions of peoples say, "it's pointless now," Some risks it all just to get on top of the world, Game brings a boss player to the point where extraordinarily talking becomes natural, as well as brilliantly thinking consistently, A place where women are more manly is where she been around men dominating in her lifestyle, that dominate everyday life, or that city is dominated by men everyday, a real Star on Mother Earth, shine & stand out every second, All willing Participants have to bring something to the table, When time move fast, it means it's getting you somewhere fast for a reason, Play Ritual songs that speak to the soul, Spiritual healing ceremonies to heal the mind, Spiritual awakening is how you start the new year off on New Year's Eve at 11:59p.m., Over indulgence in moderation, not repeatedly, Life after death is being born again, in a way the average will not be able to interpret."

Dj quik stood up with 2nd II none, & Peter gunz to do that their classic song, it's called, "so many wayz," then Mack Millon said, "it's always a blessing to meet solid people on solid ground, for all the righteous spiritual reasons, Pimpology is black magic, which means his knowledge is power, Don't have a fear of flying ever in your live long life, always play the reverse game when necessary, People think I be bragging, or showing off because they haven't figured it out, that they supposed to be doing what I'm doing, & more in their own way & style, Power is in the darkness, & if you feed the brown to blackness, it becomes a power known as unbelievable, Robert jelly Shawn Carter best of both worlds type stuff."

Vallejo E-40 stood up to perform this song called, "mustard & mayonnaise," then King Mack said, "Control your environment, Never allow a fool to have a position of power in your lifestyle, Good human qualifications is mandatory, Rerouting through life playing human chess, is retirement mandatory, Statements is like keys that keep unlocking doors to different parts of the mind, The word nigga is a fool to people, and easy prey to spot if you don't know that, I'm a mack, respected, and feared, you should see how people look at me, especially now I got these crocodiles from Philadelphia on my feet, they study me like I'm a teacher, and they in my class, Doing my job means I'm doing this for fat bank rolls of currency, State to state, country to country, continent to continent, continent visiting creates a king, If what you want is more important than your Creator lined up for you to do, you through, what direction is your life going into?, Your knowledge will make your presence felt, We have to know who we are, to know what direction our life is going into, now that's the game of life like that classic song, black haven Memphis Tennessee tela made, Its called, "tired of ballin," I want to say blessings to indigenous soulful spiritual people, past present future, appreciation to the most High for allowing royalty to reach another king boss player level," respect to zaila avant-garde the 2021 spelling bee from Louisiana.

Virginia beach brothers, the clipse, they stood up with E-40 to do their brilliant song, it's called, "quarterbackin'," then Mack Millon said, "stay on the Top floor, to over see everything, as a true born over seer wake up to make transpire, Don't reveal truth to lies never, Keep all inside information inside the bank vaults, If you know rules & laws, always leave without fear, because you understand the ways of the world, The less is somehow making the supposed strong adjust to them, instead of the less building their way up to the mark Felix strong status mentally, strengthening up yourself to the strength to be on their level, the strong is going backwards adjusting to the weak, I'm not into conversation battles, mind wrestling like Arkansas Greg said in Missouri, who can out talk who, or say better than what I said, I got other things to do then mind wrestle, what's up to giant Greg from Alabama, he used to call me black."

E-40 stood up alone, bold like Bruce Leroy to perform his song, it's called, "ballaholic," then Mack Millon said, "If I give you my game, who, & how you gone give it to the next person, or people, I can't give you my game if you not in my kingdom, because your king is responsible for you, that's what you supposed to know if money the direction you going into, In summer school I wore Stacey Adams with two tears in my ears, & was addressed as Mr twankle in north division, When you tight with your Creator, there will be nothing else mattering, You got to be welcomed by the ancient ancestors everywhere you end up next, & great spirits welcoming you to new land, on the low they own these mother lands, &

they allow people to come, & go, The physical realm is below the spiritual existence, In't showing off, you just so happened to be at the right place, at the right time, is what you tell people that's looking at a star, When coming to a new land, you ask for permission to enter peacefully, say thank you for being allowed in new land that belongs to the ancient ancestors, and great spirits."

E-40 did his next million & one classic songs, it's called, "rules & regulations," then King Mack said, "Cooking an egg don't make you a chef, with that being said, assume the position you qualified to be in, Start from the ground floor, I was handpicked to be in the position I'm in young amateur player, Part of the downfall of an ancient people is being guilty by association, through bloodline, now if you can interpret that, you on top of your game, weakness is subject to be infiltrated, & all members will be targeted and pinpointed, You can't be taught by those people living a lie in a world of fantasy lifestyles, recognize What you got taught, & learned is different than what I was taught, & learned, Ask to be taught, not freely given, that which is earned is rewarded, A life based around drugs is not beneficial some will tell you."

Tash from California, with Raekwon from staten island New York, they stood up to perform their song, it's called, "rap life," what's up to shyheim from Staten Island New York, then mack millon said, "know how to interpret visuals as well as verbals, my ism is for my royal family, you can not talk yourself into what you want to happen, if it does not need to happen, get rid of all stubborn ways, learn how to listen, in order to break away from a curse, you have to stop doing what created the curse upon yourself, keep trouble makers out your business, the humble rules the jungle, beware of those who play both sides of the field, they live for nothing in life, nor anybody in it."

50 cent stood up with Troy ave, & young buck to perform their classic song, it's called, "drug money," then King mack said, "study one to all, feed off what drips off the Most High lips, these thoughts came upon me during my visit to Seneca south Carolina, gulf of Mississippi soulful spiritual indigenous peoples naturally give everyone spiritual healing, mankind lives their lifestyle according to how the Suns live their life, but until they realize their purpose is to help the Suns to serve their purpose, mankind doings will not serve its purpose."

488

Mack millon said, "learn from the Most High truth beyond belief, in order to live life how it is supposed to be lived, feel what you doing, shoot straight shots verbally, precise movements, everything is obtainable, only if traps, and mistakes is avoided consistently, feed the soul soul food, feed the mind delicious nutritious food for thought."

King mack said, "set everything up to accumulate what will accommodate, everything will be done according to what is going on."

Mack millon said, "triumph, conquered obstacles, stood tall through it all, not looking while being watched, also studied, also mimicked, as well as followed, sense when did we get limited to blocks.

King mack said, "now they will see who the rightful king is, and how they played themselves, not figuring out how the game of life is meant to be mastered, time waited for no one before."

Mack millon said, "read yourself into a higher position in life, when you get caught in a trap, people will move on in life, like buffalo seeking food, so when you get out the trap, you focus on your purpose in life from that point on, also what got you out the trap you was in, everyone who finds out how to live comfortable, reads to succeed."

King mack said, "we done fought the fought to reclaim our throne, what you see is what you get, the waves creates the motion in the ocean, keep game that can recognize game, get to what you got to do, focus on the Most High, mind your business, stay out what don't concern you, work your way up the food chain."

Mack millon said, "words spoken correctly can create power, speech, dialogue, improving conversation to be sharp, masterfully."

King mack said, "it's always eyes watching, ears listening, master mind creating a masterpiece, a life worth living, a dream to reality, doing what was thought to be impossible, the magic show lifestyle, everybody thought it was over, it's just getting started.

THE LAST MACK STANDING SCRIPTURES

18.

Step in smooth to lay It down thick, straight grinding like they do in Little Rock Arkansas, got to learn how to live, then learn how to earn, then learn how to make money work for you, then learn how to pull up shining brand new, like they say In Memphis, "this what game, plus money, this what it do for you," if you learn how to direct traffic, Memphis know the business, on some project pat type stuff, It's all about getting life right, wealthy comfortable with longevity, and spirituality.

Respect to Zulu sky in the year 1670, respect to cheikh anta diop & his book, "precolonial black African," Respect to Lincoln Nebraska malcom x, respect to Huey p. Newton, respect to Ron newt from the Bay Area, respect to filmore slim The Godfather of the game of life, Respect to saint Maurice celestial saint of Germany, respect to Venus of willen dorf statue, respect to jean baptiste bernadotte from Sweden, respect to Benjamin Banneker, respect to Livingston the African missionary, respect to Austria Grimaldi people, respect to Beethoven & Joseph Haydn,Haydn, respect to Jose vasconcelos.

I'm out here in the snake mound state, I can see the clouds bringing rain, look like snow clouds, I never been a place geese run the city, they on the grass sitting on baby eggs, they on top of buildings flying off the building to the sidewalks like they keeping it gangster, Its cold in middle April, I'm leaning back like I'm from Michigan chilling with snoop dogg, bout to eat some afra restaurant food, that's the name, "afra," I'm watching the Ice-t movie, it's called, "surviving the game."

Peace & blessings to black rob from Buffalo New York, the creater of whoa, trial ended for George Floyd court trial for his life taker, the life taker was convicted, I'm in Savannah Georgia just leaning back with no liquor involved, OutKast made a song called, "just me and you, your cousin, and your moma to, just got a call from the other day, … facial expression looking silly, I skipped a line or two," classic classic song right there, Indigenous soulful spiritual people in Georgia is always prepared to give that southern hospitality.

THE MEMOIRS OF A GREAT GRANDFATHER

I'm watching lil Pimpin' dpg video, it's called, "square biz."

Own want to know trouble, or meet trouble, present self in the greatest fashion, when you at the top of your game, to stop nonsense from approaching self incorrectly, study your family tree, decorate your characteristic traits with ancient wisdom, establish yourself as important in this lifetime, customize your lifestyle, work your way up to first class.

I member waking up in South Carolina with intentions to eat in the most right way possible, bout to head up north on the east coast, hitting top states like I was on a rap tour with supreme lyricist king dmx, the original new York Indigenous soulful spiritual giant, rapping royalty.

In a small town a giant will stand out, but still look small, best to travel the globe til it's time to retire, acknowledge it's always somebody who will feel the need to reveal the game's being played In your city, stick together to leave safely, and come back home alive.

Watch those watching you, then get so far up away out their reach, they start to forget you was near them, to a point, you become a man, a myth, a legend, true accommodation accumulators will stick, & move like Muhammad ali, amateurs stay planted in their radius, day to night, their whole life.

Bourbon street is a world by itself, in daytime, costumes, liquor, drugs, crowded people partying, just like Las Vegas, everybody suspicious, this type of atmosphere is for those who aim to escape the stress of everyday life, It's also strictly business for those who survive in these areas, if you will be where people drink, don't drink, if they doing drugs, don't do drugs, acknowledge entertainment Is a distraction, as night fall, more situations transpire In the shadows, darkness in the nightlife will bring forth prowlers, queenbridge braveheart nas, the musical genius business man, he got a mysterious classic song called, "thief's theme."

Everyday is about living a life worth living, your lifetime is all about what you did, do, & done, Oakland rap legend too $hort has a song called, "longevity."

I remember waking up in Pennsylvania, I was feeling like new federal note currency, fresh out of the District of Columbia, all before the sun rose up, then I woke up in the big apple, I was looking at mountains in the background, feeling truly blessed to live how I live, my thoughts is in order, life is balanced for me now, "lights camera action," like mr cheeks said.

Everything is not meant to be got by you, everything Is for everybody, just enjoy the show, acknowledge everyday to night is already written to transpire the way it's written to transpire, your life story was written when you came from birth to earth, everything available to be got is obtainable.

Major league players started off in the minor leagues, paid their dues, earned their turn, to time, to shine, be true to what you say, at all times.

I remember waking up in Indiana, I was just thinking about how I survived in the ocean of sharks everywhere I went, I'm thinking about why I haven't bought a lakefront mansion near you yet.

Acknowledge that everybody do not want to hear about your blessings, unless they ask about it, I woke up in west memphis feeling cool, yet pressured from champagne bubbles from the night before, understand it's mandatory to speak when spoken to.

If you know how dangerous you can be, If you become provoked, stay away from situations that will push you to the edge, set life up so you can stay far away from dangerous outcomes.

I remember waking up In Virginia, realizing Its gone be days when currency will be raining on you, I was at the foot hill of the mountains, ordering food, & setting up business for the next week, I was very relaxed in Virginia mountain range.

Allow me to speak on chocolate city Milwaukee Wisconsin briefly, Milwaukee is a world within a world, just like the city you from, everybody play the hands they was dealt to win with, or they cheat, or quit, in Milwaukee, money making is just a hobby for some, and mandatory behavior for others.

Everybody look, & talk like indigenous soulful spiritual peoples in the state they from, as well as dress code, original spiritual soulful indigenous people be enjoying survival progressive prosperity, while surviving in these days of our lives, respect to bone thugs n harmony.

Let me say this through my perspective, Chicago is known as a pimp city, hear say, In Milwaukee money making is just a hobby, California is fun In the sun, Florida get wet & wild, New York is the concrete jungle, Detroit is gangsta heaven, Gary Indiana is gangsta island, Las Vegas Is gangsta paradise, it was spoke on in that song coolio created, in Memphis making easy money pimpin hoes in style is historical, Texas Is land of giants, Mississippi & Tennessee Is the motherlands, Missouri is the show me state.

To all I say, "get down with the right get down, protect each other, love each other, be thy brothers, & sisters keeper, it's time to meet your destiny properly."

I remember seeing a Harley motorcycle rider rolling hard, one hand steering In the rain, on some gangster type stuff in Pennsylvania, in the mountains, I rolled city to city, state to state, straight sight seeing like a tourist, grinding, & sweet spot finding, just left Dover Delaware, they had a classic Jeep vehicle show, I'm just ducking trouble, I wasn't ignoring people calling me, it's mandatory to put first things first, I sit alone sometime like the sun when it's rising, i like to enjoy myself in the king castle with the door open, with a floor mat saying welcome one to all, it's identical to a king living in the mountain, when he be ignoring his phone ringing, all calls from those who thought he was finished, that's all it is.

No distractions when the pharaoh building pyramids, respect the inside to outside, above to below, respect positions, titles, hard work, dedication, perfect being a communication conversationist, the king stay occupied, never give up, enjoy the show.

Strategically make your moves, lead by example, if you got to explain your game, I see that as a way of allowing infiltrators the opportunities to destroy a kingdom, stay strong to last long, huddle up with kings, & Queens, don't hesitate when it come to the point to be great, giants live a private lifestyle, out of sight, out of mind, low key under the radar.

Recognize what you need to know later, right now, master what is in arm reach, & leave the rest up to the Most High, when something is meant to happen, guess what, it changes your gps to your new route to your new direction, Qualify thyself to be on the next level, keep the taste for hate, & fake out your lifestyle, it's some people having shootouts, while others is getting paid for being in vehicle shows, ain't that something.

Appreciate love to hate, knowing both will make you great, categorize what people say to you at all times, competition be wishing to be my competition, because I stay working hard, to self empower self all live life long day, to night, no breaks, no time off, steady at it, no slow poking, or half stepping, full speed ahead, full effortfully, read the best of the best books, learn from the best teachers, each book in your lifestyle, also each teacher will specialize in specific lessons, lessons necessary to teach your lifestyle.

When you adjust to other people, you become like them In different ways, never get comfortable in a position you do not want to be in, or need to be In, put the Most High first, everything will be everything like baby drew told you, when a person realizes they can not get something for nothing, they start to think about other ways to get it, watch for people that pretend to be down with you, when their main objective is to dig deep in your pockets, or simply to destroy your kingdom, that which took you a lifetime to build.

It's time for you to get everything all the way up now, properly that is, present yourself from this point on, with the proper performance on all levels, when you start thinking these thoughts, it will symbolize self reaching masterful levels, which also creates wealthy intentions in your daily routine, all the way to the dreams you dream, dreams you will turn to reality.

After careful analysts of the game of life, you will realize that It is best to be quite, be where it is quite, stay out of sight, out of mind, a more meaningful way to phrase that is to say, "stay busy being occupied with progressive behavior, humble your personal personality, with gentleman characteristics traits influencing your every move.

Reflecting on being raised up by giants on earth, it helped me see life from the ground up, understanding life Is lived based on survival, survival is based on upbringing, and upbringing Is based on income in the household, which Is what really formulates the child development.

Interpret what Everybody Insinuate, decode the code language select chosen explosions is taught to speak naturally, see the unseen, see what some was not taught to see naturally, that which Is hidden in plain sight, train your perspective to recognize what you visualize in every way acceptable.

The truth is hidden in plain perspective everywhere you find yourself to be, in this lifetime, you either prey, or predator, just know how to be right with ever one you be in a day, or night with, this the game of life, by now you should, "know the business," like project pat said, straight learned in Memphis is how he found that out, either you know what is required to be understood, or you quick sand in Maine stuck, straight getting ran over, due to the fact you lack ancient ancestry soulful spiritual wisdom, and you lack ancient indigenous soulful spiritual ancestors knowledge.

Revenge is a weakness possessed by lazy spirits, turn weakness to strength everyday to the night, ol' dirty bastard said, "devil water,", to this day it remains to be undefeated, you know what um tum bout don't you, and forever liars is born to lie, with no stopping that from happening, no matter what you do, or say, believe that.

As you become a king In your late 30s, as you do, so does your kingdom do, who you develop into, they develop into, if they dedicated to being with you, your results Is shared with their results as you become one with your kingdom, and they become one with their king.

Now check this out, some gone love you while others hate you in your lifetime, at the same time, all will be Impressed by your lifetime performance, keep your basketball bouncing, you know what um tum bout, mark the calendar every time a new boss player level is reached, its Identical to climbing up to the top of mountain Kilimanjaro, if you decide to change, everything will be setup to change around you, and with you.

As a king myself, you a prince mackadon In the beginning rounds, then you become king Mack as you graduate to being crowned king by the most high, indigenous spiritual soulful pyramid golden brown people is kings & queens, got to get back on their throne, it's their birth right, while some want to be dressing up to fit the description of royalty, North America turtle island land of soul people, indigenous soul people is naturally born that way, look at the beginning to now, even if we was prisoners of war, we still remain royalty, and not one person erasing books of proof of that, destroying our ancestors statue monuments, it will not change the facts of life, If I gave you millions of bad days, you still gone be the king you born to be, if I stop you from having millions of green backs, you still gone be a king, ain't no stopping what supposed to happen, hey grandson, I remember I was in tifton Georgia when I finally realized this, see you got to be getting that solar power to embrace this, the heat gone light you up, the sun gone build you up, it's gone giant you in every way possible, you better get ready, because it's about to go down in every way possible, and up in every way possible simultaneously.

JOURNEY WEALTHY LONGEVITY SCRIPTURES

15.

Everywhere you go, be on the prowl to see if that city got benefits for you on the business tip, vehicles, homes, a new crew, or new members bringing something to the table, showing a down for life mentality, simply to be in the royal family, to help the royal family get wealthy on the journey to longevity.

I'm hearing New York has legalized the jolly green giant recreational activities, I always enjoy New York soulful spiritual indigenous people, they full of powerful knowledge, & supreme wisdom, found out the Statue of Liberty is in New Jersey, best view is in Jersey city, peace & blessings to dmx and black rob, true New York giants.

CROSS COUNTRY LIVING

Respect to these states I been to: Deleware, some Indigenous soulful people,, I mean those who was planted in this soil from the beginning of time, they showed mad love to me, of course Georgia showed mad love, my people big Chris the baby giant in Macon Georgia, my people Mr. Jessie from Arkansas, oh yeah, uncle dirty from pine bluff Arkansas, & tj & his brother Marcus, Arizona was straight to, the man from Texas listened to me playing kid frost while he fixed his vehicle in Phoenix, met bra there from San Diego Californian in Phoenix, he put me up on California game, in Las Vegas, two elders was solid with me on how Vegas rotate, bra from Michigan in Vegas showed love, bra from Nebraska in Vegas showed love, the ladies in Denver put me up on Colorado game, chopped up game with Mississippi bra in Denver, chopped up game with two Louisiana born hustlers In Colorado, chopped up game with them, bra from Texas In Colorado, chopped it up with bra from Louisiana in Denver about how Denver looked to him, said he got hired before he moved to Colorado by denver job, chopped it up with elder Jamaican in Florida about Florida in Florida, met li bra from Miami, chopped up game with him in Georgia, chilled in Maine, gave a Wisconsin lady a phone call with somebody from Maine to meet somebody from Maine, chopped up game in Massachusetts with a man from Jacksonville Florida, he showed me a side of Massachusetts that I never heard about, that I can see in up close & personal, of course Wisconsin, Chicago grew me up fast, I saw what a real gangster be about, did the paw of Judah with Jamaican in Georgia, Jamaican in Ohio heard me playing Gregory issac, he said it made him feel at home in this indigenous soul people country, chopped it up with a bad Miami Gardens lady, she was on top of her game majorly In Miami Gardens Florida, first time in Miami Gardens, I saw the four wheeler crew, they was driving in a motor cycle four wheeler parade, straight down the street, I was sitting at the stop light watching this transpire, that was boss status to me, I'm in Montana at the moment, just chopped it up brief with a Native American, specifically on the changes the Most High letting happen with mut nature, native Americans say Great Spirit, native bra said, "the earth correcting itself right now," I said the same thing, "it's balancing itself back out, to put order back on earth," Texas was good to me to, I got showed plenty love their, respect, brother Ben chopped It up with me on the George Floyd situation In Texas, we all agreed on a few things about that situation, how it came to current solutions for this country, nothing bad was said, we just spoke progress without stress, Bra Nem put me on the Texas game, Louisville was real nice, In North Carolina, everybody, all races was happy nice respectfully, just left Jacksonville Florida beach, it was jellyfish washed up on shore by the tide, saw birds i never saw before, I was In dover Delaware on the bay shore area sand, I saw horseshoe crabs, never expected to see that, went to Memphis & ran into the hotel Martin Luther king jr. life was took at, I didn't like the feeling I felt at that hotel, also stopped in Niagara Falls to get a glimpse of Niagara Falls, I never saw that much water in one place going everywhere was possible, i never get to close to the edge to view It, been there twice already, you can see Canada on the other side of the waterfall, It's a sight to see, I got to get that passport, down here in Savannah Georgia on the fourth floor over looking area I'm In, sun beaming nice down here, hotel room look like a penthouse suite, for under $200, look like I paid $500 a night, Washington state & California got best snoop dogg this country got to offer my opinion, Washington state was the greenest state I ever seen, waterfalls everywhere, I was told in snoqualamie falls Washington that it don't snow on this side of the mountain In winter time, it mostly rains in winter, that was the opposite of what I thought, I went to Roswell New Mexico, the theme of the city was aliens, aliens was holding up a donut in front of dunking donuts, New Mexico was clean, & palm trees everywhere, it's plenty more to say, but I supposed to been done with this book, so I'm gone save it for Mackology 3rd Edition, whenever I edited a chapter, I usually put in the place I'm visiting, I been to every United state except Oregon, the best place I been so far is got to be Florida, water & heat, California was real nice to with that mountain in the background, I enjoyed the staples Lakers stadium scenery, I saw the Kobe Bryant paintings on walls, Denver is real nice to for snoop dogg refreshments, I'm almost done with editing the last chapters in this magnificent book, I really appreciate you reading what you enjoy, and enjoying what you read, I'm bout to leave this best hotel I ever been In, I'm In Savannah Georgia at the home2home hotel, feel like Im right at home, whoever designed this hotel, is a hotel genius.

I'm still in upstate New York In a place call Saratoga half moon, it's plazas everywhere, went to one fresh market, never saw Saint louis ribs in market before already cooked, this super market got everything even a bar area In a super market by the alcohol section, all the cakes pies sweets you can think of, all types of nationalities everywhere, New York got the best of the best on all levels possible, I'm watching mortal Kim at 2021 movie, & meet the blacks 2, this what is helping finalize last chapters, I appreciate one to all for enjoying what you read, & reading what you enjoy, not one place in the country is the same, not one city town village state, everywhere has Its Own style, what better place to finalize this brilliant book: the king business Mackology 2nd edition, in New York the advanced state in the country.

THE GAME OF LIFE
SCRIPTURES

15.

Playing the game of life, is knowing how to roll it, live to give, give to live, it's about unity, team work works, it's a proven fact, teams have won championships, everybody need everybody, cross country living will explain exactly precisely specifically what the game of life scriptures is all about.

Respect to formal chief Angela green, I just left Georgia 80 degrees, now I'm in Latin Virginia, In the blue ridge mountain 30 degrees, always expect the unexpected.

A LETTER TO THE ANCIENT ANCESTORS

Peace & blessings to the ancient ancestors from the beginning of existence up to the present moment, peace & blessings to the great spirits from the beginning Of time to the present moment, peace & blessings to the elements, peace & blessings to above & beyond, below & beyond, inside & beyond, outside & beyond, "connect game, connect game," like w.c. Said, & cover all angles, all indigenous spiritual soulful peoples all over the world is thankful, for those who created their family tree, from every continent on this planet, respect to the first on every continent to create civilization, respect, unity, happiness, the first Indigenous spiritual soulful golden brown people on every continent for starting civilizations on their land, respect to those who started communication for generations to teach others with, symbolism to describe what was first scenes created, memories, the indigenous spiritual soulful ones who created the first statues of powerful kings & queens, the first indigenous spiritual soulful ones who built the first kingdoms, the first empires, the first schools, the first indigenous spiritual soulful ones who wrote the first basic instructions before leaving earth, the first indigenous spiritual soulful ones who wrote scriptures, the first indigenous spiritual soulful ones who created pathways to follow on leading towards longevity, the first indigenous spiritual soulful leaders of the first Indigenous spiritual soulful tribes.

Peace & blessings to North America turtle, Canada, South America, Mexico, the Caribbean islands, Tanzania, Australia indigenous spiritual ancient ancestors from day one to the present moment, all their tribe names, their kingdom names, their empire names, their civilizations names, peace & blessings for all contributions to help the present moment indigenous spiritual peoples all over the world. (Peace & blessings to the the 1990s number one small forward, Arkansas born Scottie pippen, to him & his family tree, peace & blessings to his son, respect to the Arkansas indigenous spiritual soulful peoples).

It's a thing called reality, it's also a thing called fantasy, it's a saying that was made, "the truth is stranger than fiction, the pyramid golden brown Indigenous spiritual soulful people been told myths is true, the reality is, who is the Indigenous spiritual people on every continent, first things first, number one is first, the first number one thing to know Is the truth is stranger than fiction, simply because of not knowing how to read between the lines, see with the third eye, knowledge is powerful, turn weakness to strength, If you got a throne your birth right assigned you to, then that mean reclaim your throne, wake up the sleeping giants, appreciation to all the ancient indigenous soulful spiritual ancestors from the beginning to the present moment, to all them that left clues for us that lead to our family jewels & treasure chest, game recognizing game Is the ism the ancestors pass down generations to generations, peep game, if you don't know, bow wow said, "you better ask somebody, like Lil Kim the queen b once said, "we keep It going man, we keep it going man," classic song called, "whoa," respect to black rob the New York giant, peace & blessings, Lil Kim said, "my players stack figures, In the club we sipping Don p, me & my team we trying to own casinos," that's knowledge power paid dues real gangsters & ain't got to prove it," now she along with others, has kept what notorious big built up, now that's a New York giant move, supreme player ism he grew to develop, simply from passed down inherited game, from generations to generations, from the ancient ancestors to the present moment indigenous soulful spiritual golden brown ancestors that passed it to the future, he said, "throw your hangs up if you a player," now that's indigenous spiritual respect, love, & game recognizes the real city to city, just so they know, we all cool with each other, network, connect game & cover all angles, then puff daddy laid his knowledge on that whole building of his empire, it all created kings & queens, they all that took this empire serious, & figured out how to get crowned, & how to reclaim their throne imposters sit on by way of thievery, qualifying themselves to be In powerful positions is mandatory, if you falsely sit on a throne you don't supposed to be sitting on, you gone eventually be escorted by the game of life away from a position you not qualified to fit in, it's certain requirements required to have to get crowned king, notorious big song called, "one more chance," it's simply remarkable, boss player association approved this message, all capital letters in game, gorgeous adult mackin excellent, let's take a moment to pause for the cause, peace to blessings to shock g, respect to a solid indigenous musical genius, mr. Humpty hump, & Aretha Franklin, peace to blessings.

JOURNEY WEALTHY LONGEVITY SCRIPTURES

16.

Everywhere you go, be on the prowl to see if that city got benefits for you on the business tip, vehicles, homes, a new crew, or new members bringing something to the table, showing a down for life mentality, simply to be in the royal family, to help the royal family get wealthy on the journey to longevity.

LEANING BACK STATE TO STATE

I'm In Cleveland Ohio, it's nice out here as far as the eyes can see, If I knew members from bone thugs n harmony, I would ask them to tell me what is a good investment In Cleveland, just always looking for opportunities to progress beneficially financially, also I would ask about indigenous spiritual soulful peoples history, in this land of the Cleveland indigenous spiritual ancestor soulful peoples, the many shades of ancient indigenous soulful spiritual pyramid golden brown peoples from the land of Ohio, to know other indigenous spiritual soulful ancestors peoples story, it's identical to finding missing pieces to the puzzle that completes the game of life scriptures, knowledge is powerful, every indigenous spiritual soulful people state history, It's a missing piece to put together the game of life puzzle, so the full picture can be seen, then like bizzy bone said, "heavens movie," you will see what life is all about from every indigenous spiritual soulful people state perspective, knowing what each other knows, creates growth & development.

I'm in Phoenix Arizona leaning back enjoying the west coast soulful heat, just left Utah sightseeing around the mountain sceneries, then before that, royalty was visiting commerce city Colorado shaking hands with shaggy & scooby, they was just eating tall sandwiches laughing loud, before I got to soulful people Arizona, I was sightseeing In Las Vegas on the strip perimeter, royalty looking forward to hitting the Los angles area this week, seem like it's taking major time to finish this fine piece of literature, a modern day ancient book, few chapters left to go, to all who purchased this brilliant book, solve the mysteriousness Inside these pages, if I could, I would thank you a thousand times for reading what I wrote, just listened to an North Carolina indigenous spiritual soulful elder, he told me Arizona running out of houses, all the snow birds is flying these ways to leave the lands of snow, make sense to me, I speak for many northern indigenous spiritual soulful peoples, everybody tired of the freezing weather conditions, sun people going back to where they can enjoy living at, amen ra.

JOURNEY WEALTHY LONGEVITY SCRIPTURES

19.

Everywhere you go, be on the prowl to see if that city got benefits for you on the business tip, vehicles, homes, a new crew, or new members bringing something to the table, showing a down for life mentality, simply to be in the royal family, to help the royal family get wealthy on the journey to longevity.

BE GREAT IN YOUR MEMOIRS

Communication is not always verbal, it comes in many forms, & tonight, it's through symbols called words, so we really talking to each other through our minds, If you ahead of what's going on, you can see everything before it get to you, it's like when Bruce Leroy caught the bullet in his teeth, & saw it before it happened, Your eyes is to see Like the Georgia hawk eye in the sky, & ears to hear like king corleon guard dogs, & your third eye, if it's open, it knows all, & sees all, It's always good to show people what you saying with how you group your words up, so it will be seen exactly how you saying what you saying, that's what indigenous spiritual soulful peoples say, "can you see what Royalty saying."

I got the chance to leave how I left, I did as much reading as I could, to figure out as much hidden truth as I could, so I can figure out how to make doors open for royalty, it's like being in prison with a life sentence, so if you read, read the right books, gathering information, put it together, you can learn how to get released from prison, it's identical to being free, if you learn the magic words from gathering information, all of sudden, you will see things changing, then doors will open, then you will either go through the traveling door, or say next time, & stay where you at, some people call it a fear of flying, but those who take that chance to see what happens behind door number one, they usually take off from there, & then they be gone on their way to the top of the Kilimanjaro mountain, strategically exploring what they never seen before, that which they never knew existed, nor could they ever get close to what they assumed was out of arm reach, & once you get that taste of something new, it just triggers something in you, & then you take off like a speeding desert eagle bullet, never ever looking back like a Smithsonian museum ancient North America statue, because it's so much to see in one lifetime, so many Indigenous spiritual soulful people to meet, a tremendous amount of currency to j-stack up, with countless meaningful things to king Mack make happen.

home in a state you from is like being in the adx Florence facility, nobody leaves, nobody gets ahead in life, because in order to start living life to the fullest meaningfully with a Most High purpose, you got to see what is going on in the world you exist in, up close & personal hands on experience, and then you realize why you exist, why you still alive, what you aiming for, & what is coming to you, you can settle now with what you been allowed to have, or get what's coming to you.

It's players, & haters everywhere you end up next, you either one, or the other, you either the solution, or the problem, if your peoples is in another state, meaning it can be family, cousin, or big bra, one, or the other, we connected through birth rights on some royal family king type stuff.

If you need something on your journey to get wealthy with longevity, whisper in the wind to speak it In existence, and work your way up to qualifying yourself to be satisfied, and then that's when you get what you need from every place on Mother Earth, A name is given according to what a person is known for, On the low, the 1990's projects indigenous soulful peoples lived in worldwide was known for creating professional intelligent to brilliant intellectual thinkers, some of the world's most successful indigenous spiritual soulful peoples was, "raised in the projects," ask project pat.

When a rich man lose his bread, he soon comes to realize he just a normal person like everybody else, & money don't make him no better.

Wise gentlemen of leisure sidewalk talked, (respect to Suga free & his dark side, Pomona Pimpin' young), like this, "Brake her down like a quarter pound, reprogram her, born again her, put you in her, remember If you not with her, & somebody else is in her face, what they say will be obsolete if you a gorgeous adult mackin excellent, now that's some Cleveland good game, respect to the og.

Power is in the touch of words when it comes directly from an unique mind with polished knowledge, it's absolutely Mandatory to speak with precautions, the 70s created King pimps, the 80s created wealthy gangstas, the 90s created prime time hustlers.

so now check this with me, I grew up with my mother being a retired Chicago gangster, she relocated to Milwaukee to be born again as a lpn, she had me on an army base in Missouri, I grew up with little to no contact from father, he was over seas in the army doing America duties in places like Germany, so I was raised up under the basketball lifestyle, then due to lack of motivational family support, the idea of nba slowly but shortly faded away, indigenous soulful spiritual people was talking about me going to the nba, but I had that street ism in my blood from birth to earth, so I saw women as my way to the rolls Royce with a 18 color viewing choice, with a multi million dollar mansion on the lake front near you preferably, I picked the mansion I saw for sell as my goal to accomplish around 16 years old, and it was in my arm reach, very strong Michael v. Roberts possibility to me having it before the year 2000 popped up, but I got distracted, then that cash money record company "millionaire dream," i was looking to turn that to reality, it got farther away from me like the first time your grandfather turned one years old, I then met my pinky ring street king Godfather, a well known legendary Wisconsin Mississippi born pimp, then that boost the ism in me stronger to a boss player association status, and consistently year after years, women always housed me, I made my own money add up, and that attracted them to royalty, then that led up to royalty becoming a king named Mack, and I'm in it to the finish in the Mack lifestyle I perfect, but I learned how to control my ism, which has got me living like this, right back where I started with the "millionaire dream," in arm reach, Royalty was renting out a downstairs duplex two years ago, left it all to write this millionaire priceless book, so I have no place to call home, no car to drive to a lake, or ocean front near you, all the women in my kingdom throughout the years I been building my kingdom gave up, they threw in the towel, so for a woman to roll with me now, it's gone be hard to help me build my empire again, and own believe that pressure is what a woman should deal with, so I'm getting my empire built up as we speak, so who chooses to join my kingdom, so the chosen few can blend in comfortable, A king has Got to have the mind to read to succeed with a royal family equipped with an understanding about how to get paid in full, also well aware of how to qualify to sit on the throne with royalty as lifetime partners, with no attentions to saying no to anything royalty say, everything is yes, full cooperation, dedication to participating In uprising royalty royal family kingdom, and Dreams will be turned to reality, It's a full time job to be with a king, no breaks, no cracking under pressure, not never, Missouri is the show me state, a woman got to show royalty she down for a lifetime, because this is a, "wonderful world," ask Louis Armstrong, such a brilliant man, he very present In New Orleans, respect to all my indigenous spiritual soulful New Orleans peoples.

ain't no room for if, maybe, I think I can type stuff, everything got to be automatic, Being with a king is like being born again, and the only thing that matters is, helping him build his kingdom, to keep his kingdom strong for a lifetime, Prove to yourself you need a king, by getting things ready for your king, being wise with knowledge, without being mad about doing exactly that for the king, not stepping on his toes, and always thinking of full effort ways of making everything happen for him, and still maintaining what is going on around you simultaneously, to all it is written In the sky to recognize This a professional lifestyle, which means, any woman who chooses to get in this lifestyle with a king, the queen has to make things happen everyday all day, (respect to south circle the dynamic duo) with big time results, not getting stressed out, just handling everything with no hesitation, never ever ever, (respect to Chris tucker the Georgia legendary comedian), cracking under pressure, as I reflect on what needs to happen next, i come to TVs conclusion, it's Time to get things started tonight to forever, if a potential queen decides she needs to be down with royalty, Its mandatory to know that Royalty eat steak for breakfast, Royalty drink Don perion in royalty spare time, ace of spade in Savannah Georgia, & Las Vegas, and smoke purple when listening to Lil boosie & Webbie song, it's called "smoking on purple," that's almost a $1000 when Royalty straight relaxing in one day.

A king mandatory requirement Is a wisdom queen, she has to be able to provide royalty with a luxurious mansion, or extravagant extraordinary house, expensive car keys, and her own yearly income, ancient wisdom to solve show stopping problems, polished ancient soulful pyramid golden brown knowledge to improvise, Yeah it's like breathing new fresh air in your lungs, It's in your face now, let's see what you can do with it, & I usually don't reveal this classified confidentiality, but if you're persistent, I will show you what the king Mack lifestyle is all about, Easier said then done, because actions speak louder then words, This can be the first day of the rest of your life, read my brilliant book first, front to end, Dealing with a king for a lifetime is like figuring out how to get to mars, and surviving a year with no help.

Some people have not got touched by the truth yet, All indigenous powers combined Is Pimpology, gangsterism, spirituality ancient ancestral wisdom, polished knowledge, gangsters is the indigenous spiritual soulful warriors, king pimps is the wisdom spiritual teachers, indigenous spiritual second language is capital GAME, a hidden language within the most famous worldwide language, all hatred should clear the way, and let the boss players play, respect to negro leaugues hall of famer Dave Winfield.

It was once said by a unknown brilliant 1981 madam from New Hampshire, "ladies of the night will come back as birds to explore the world they once breathed air in," when you need to make Certain specific situation complete, Ask everybody in your conversation to tell you what is the most important Information they survived in their lifestyle lifetime to tell you.

If you not contributing to the royal family, you only will get dealt with for specific reasons, at this moment of finalizing this brilliant book, I'm watching Bobby hemmitt lecture on dreamland gateway to other worlds.

If your intelligence offends someone you in a conversation with, then you have to have a time limit with them, What can you tell somebody who knows everything, Pyramid golden brown gone last long strong, light skin gone stay down, and be under control, Study your friends and enemies, Tropical lands is spiritual healing energy destinations for all indigenous spiritual soulful pyramid golden brown peoples.

Indigenous spiritual pyramid golden brown people have to share spirituality with each other all over the galaxy, past present to future.

It's something important and special about being from Milwaukee, Chicago, Mississippi, Harlem, Memphis, Detroit, Memphis, Louisville, Dallas, Los angles, Oakland, they all the same, they first permanent cousins,Your spirit will go where it needs healing and energy In this lifetime, in this lifestyle.

Indigenous spiritual pyramid golden brown peoples will Put others first, and will never be last In this lifetime, in this lifestyle, Grandma said, "money talks."

Certified females is qualified to be a king queen, with no need to reprogram her Apple computer, or train her, or tame her, they straight game tight, seasoned, no babysitting, because she fully grown mentally not numerically, I mean straight down with a king, with intentions to put him on top of the world, a lifetime partner with a genius thinking process, Real go getters is hitting them jackpot spots in this year to every year, certain places is paying hard, and we bulls eyeing specifically precisely exact location.

It's about keeping up with the times, getting down properly, precisely, Hitting them places with precision, people ready to get generational wealth, these types of women gone roll for a lifetime, respect to the land of giants sir Demetrius big meech flenory.

In this lifetime, In this lifestyle, It's about what the real said, "stay up," and staying up mean money routing consistently, play no contact sports, Uriah Rennie The most known unknown referee said, "no harm no foul."

If your complexion is pitch black In North America, you African American, if you pyramid golden brown Brown you indigenous anywhere in the galaxy.

West coast react off your reaction, Any person, places, or things named used in this book, is only to help promote the best that life has to offer, in an Easter so called holiday movie, the Burning bush represents the sun people, Moses got dark when he was with the burning bush, it was saying indigenous spiritual soulful people know the creator from birth to earth, You can't lie about the truth, only temporarily hide it in plain sight.

Some people put the right words together for personal gain, Power overcomes weakness, In't never signed royalty signature on that, "setup to loose contract."

Every piece is needed to complete, and create the game of life puzzle, Never volunteer information to those who don't need it, Never should one live isolated, Breath life in the King with actions and words.

Pyramid golden brown indigenous soulful spiritual peoples in the south is getting rich from rapping, sports, everything, so they heavy in the south straight living it up, most definitely being respected, because money and Power talk, don't get lost in character in a role you play year after year, know how to keep your mind in its natural state of being.

The energy between a king & queen grows stronger when love meets love, and when love see hate coming to hurt it, love will be gone with the wind before it's feelings get hurt, who better for you then me, and who better for me then you is what love says to loving energy, what's important to you is important to me, which Is unified unity, back like I never left, let not your foolishness overwhelm your right mind intelligence, order will organize cooperation, if we both stand straight up, we can stay up, find the mathematical routes, the numeric route pattern, no matter where you at in life, the most important thing is that you still here existing with purpose, & meaning.

What applies to one, applies to all, the soul is not glowing inside entertainment today, You can't do something to make what you want to believe is the truth, it still will not be true, you want to stomp the baby mouse, but then when you see the Chicago New York City super rat, then you want to run scared, the hunter was talking about, "it ain't no fun when the rabbit got the gun," then they started laughing at what they was watching, if you can't see what is hidden in plain sight, you will miss out on life opportunities.

if today in Harlem there was a meeting with Malcom x, John henrik Clarke, Marcus Garvey, w. E. B. Du bois, dr. Martin Luther king jr., Huey p newton, there would be immediate changes being made amongst the indigenous spiritual soulful peoples all over the world.

the strong have become weak because their relationship with the Most High has been broken, due to alcohol, & drugs, etc.

Doors is made to open & close, it will always be a door ready to open for those seeking to find their pathway In life, which will be paved with marble, granite, & gold, I'm leaning back checking out bhightv interview Memphis la chat speak on what everybody been waiting for her to speak on.

Royalty has Got to get more in to doing adult business on tv, such as the global stock market, it was information in Colorado about South America, Columbia will be selling grass to Colorado legally, if you been playing the game backwards, it's time to set it straight, When it come to passing information, it's the fastest way to travel, the power to reach each other, that which will create knowledge amongst all the world, which will show routes, better routes to take to get to our accomplished goals destination.

Mandatory advice says, "just stay on the live it up stage, and information fount out daily through brilliant books, plus what you already found out through your life experiences you lived to talk about, that's power developing to create strength where weakness was.

Speak on giants from your home town land when you out of town, if you a giant, your game gone speak for it self, let it be known about the giants from your home town land, speak of their triumph, their distractions, their blessings, let them get their shine on with people you meet in your lifetime, it's all for the game of life scriptures, during your journey to wealthy longevity, let your historical statements being spoken on in time to come for all to learn from.

Know what you doing, why you doing it, what you aiming to get, income outcome, is it for business, pleasure, personal enjoyment, the experience, is it to make you feel better, purpose and meaning is very important forever for the mind, the mind has to know what is going on at all times near, or far, so no confusion will be caused in time to come, sex is a spiritual ritual misunderstood, & energy building process for men with woman, king with queen, it's either done to keep hold of someone for foolish reasons, or to consistently build an undying connection amongst king & queen, life is based on a need to know bases, know what tools to use to get every job done, & solve any to every problem.

Years ago I asked my elder pimp people recovering from heroine, "how do you win in the game of life," he said, "you don't," an indigenous soulful spiritual man in Saint Louis told me, "do as much good as you can, while you can," a Saint Louis lady told me, "her circle only deal with natural law."

Is you from a land that says, "no matter what you do, it ain't never enough?," get gone.

It's a dangerous competition going on specifically on the ground level poverty floor, Geniuses grouped together systematically subliminally taught to hate, kill, & stop each Other from uprising.

Voting incorrectly only puts them people higher above indigenous peoples, it's best to assume positions of power to replace chaos with order, masters of the universe is the best way to describe this action, The mind will randomly think wonderful, and terrible thoughts simultaneously.

Dominate those aiming to self destruct you through your own mind, strengthening the brain with the worlds best written information available, and take advantage of ways available to mark henry Olympian style all your muscles muscles.

Get where you going in your lifetime sooner than later, then be where you at brilliantly with your self created brilliance.

People fear what is great in this world, with love, or hate, Build an incredible unbreakable relationship with the Most High.

How you go for what you know, if you don't know what you going for, Everybody feeling out of place, because out of place stuff is going on, Make moves when nobody pays attention,

Kids that never played with each other, but was allowed to meet up in adulthood, is what has been happening worldwide.

It's not necessary to have everybody in the business, that means, a floater is bouncing around ear to ear speaking on everybody, to everybody, If you not leading crowds, that mean stay out the crowds, You got people that pattern their life after people in every way possible, it's mandatory to Stay out the middle sections, either go all the way up, or stay down till you come up as some boss players mentioned to royalty, never forget you Can't be nice to mean.

I'm listening to Louisiana big mike song, Its called, all a dream, I'm in California, about a Bay Area pimpin" hour away from Los angles, I'm about to be sightseeing in Los angles for macknificent reasons,

A West Virginia elder once said, "the best thing about being in prison, is you know everybody there is out to get you, but being free in society, you don't know who to watch," Don't play with anybody without their permission, "wise words to live by," is what the California pimp said, then he said in a deep earthquake in Valdiviaway voice tone, I mean it was getting serious when he spoke, " I been where I'm going already," a memory about a young notorious big kango wearing young upcoming king, he was Walking down the most known unknown Milwaukee street, an indigenous soulful man was washing his boss player car, at this time he was playing the new Playboy Todd Shaw album called, "you nasty,", I asked to sit and listen while he was playing it with the windows down, so this the type situations that made me royalty, everybody got to be able to handle what you hear, A new face in the place Is bout that huge faces tropical places sightseeing, it's a mandatory movement by certain unique individuals, its mandatory to look listen learn first before going left or right, that's what the indigenous soulful spiritual men used to say for royalty to remember.

Where games is being played, money is being made, If I could have raised myself up, everything would be way different in the most beneficial way possible, the Indigenous spiritual soulful man standing by the corner with a, "buck and the preacher," elder cane, he said, "Real pimpin, genius divine brown hands on everything, and tricks all meet because they all looking for each other, that's one way or another," everyday it's always gone be One who don't know, and one who do know, not one person breathing air can make sense out of nonesense, If they lack a tremendous amount of powerful knowledge, That's all part of life, you have to grow mentally to know what's really going on, indigenous soulful peoples is the only group on Mother Earth, where every man is a king, and every woman is a queen.

From birth to earth, you been being taught how to live your life, today Good game is knowledge, its power under control of the beholder, and anything that will throw it off will be avoided, which includes alcohol, drugs, etc.

It's not the money that changes you, it's the people around you that change you, Where I'm from we learn a woman who speaks negatively of others, or mistreat those down on their blessings, she is not to be trusted, because if we fall short, she will kick us while we down on the sidewalk dirty grounds to, in the Midwest land of the snow, we study everybody walking talking, and learn from all down falls being made by all breathing air, who is wise, and who will turn their back on us, so we taught to only deal with solid Individuals that will treat all living life good, no matter if they mad, or if a person trapped in a direction they got lost in, like that man sleeping on the bench near you, "that was heart breaking to me," Is what the elder indigenous soulful speaking woman said, "to see somebody speak to him terribly while he lost in his lifetime, all because, you know he didn't volunteer to be in the state of mind he in, so we put ourselves in his shoes, and say what if that was me getting treated that way."

where Royalty from, indigenous soulful spiritual peoples feel others pain, and help, or pray for them, because indigenous spiritual soulful peoples would need the same treatment, to be helped consistently til they hit the top of the food chain, or Mississippi preaching prayed for, that's why I chilled with Arizona Niagara Falls sunny, I saw him alone playing the guitar, so it was mandatory to see if he was alright, listening to him not let him be looked at as if he was nothing, we do things Godbody in the Midwest is what the elders is saying, "the only way you can learn from the game of life scriptures is If you In the game of life, & the last Mack standing.

In the air it was once said, "don't lean on another boss player game, because your game will imitate his, but just like everybody taught you how to talk your language you speak, most indigenous soulful spiritual peoples speak a language In a language, everybody got information for you to complete the puzzle that complete your game of life, and to all those amateurs who aim to know everything on their own, it's possible they will lack information from every direction, they don't allow themselves to go in to study, and which is where they will learn from lessons other people lifestyle taught them, this is the hall of game e-40 tum bout, which is how you learn how to master life with everybody help, because everybody past present and future makes the world what it is, wise words spoken by King Mack million dollars.

You got to deal with willing participants, & born raised taught participants In the game of life, and the games they attempt to play, simultaneously still being you, some exist while others live, some live to die while others is dying to live, in other words, some is figuring out how to stay alive forever, while others is living to die, seek ancient powerful knowledge wisdom, seek not people, because they will be sent to you after you seek knowledge wisdom, just like good music, it will come to you wherever you at, whom ever you boss playerly be, to show you that it was meant to be yours, it will introduce itself to you, timing is everything, let everything fall into place, kids intelligence is not the same as adults brilliance, you gone be where you at til you get where you going, everybody got their definition of words spoken in every language.

I'm listening to too short song, it's called, "triple x."

It's more beneficial to be superglued to the truth, so those who role with lies will have to continue being at the bottom of the food chain, because they get short term benefits, but if they stop siding with crooked people on the top level of positions in the game of life top, they will realize they missing out on the finer things in life, while those they side with is on vacations on islands, just laughing at them.

It's not the money that changes you in every way possible, then again it Is, it's like letting evil juice touch your tongue, ol' dirty bastard call it "devil water," it's the people around you that can help change you, You don't change the game of life, you perfect the game of life scriptures, If the king consistently lead by example, that behavior, that memory is a seed planted in the minds, it's offense and defense for all indigenous soulful spiritual peoples, simply Because one good deed deserves another, it's the blessings accumulation way, it kills hate faster then a whale shark will eat a seal, it also will create love respect, & dedication to greatness.

THE GAME OF LIFE SCRIPTURES

18.

Playing the game of life, is knowing how to roll it, live to give, give to live, it's about unity, team work works, it's a proven fact, teams have won championships, everybody need everybody, cross country living will explain what the game of life scriptures is all about.

HISTORIC STATEMENTS SPOKEN

Busta Rhymes: understanding Is best part, it's reflection of knowledge and wisdom

A California Native American told me, "I thought everybody was getting along," introduced himself to royalty, then he told me to listen to boosie & webbie song called, "bet ya."

Willing participants want to participate in the game of life, but they don't respect the game of scriptures that has been written.

King Mack million

Pimps and willing participants be competing for these millennium women, everything backwards, instead of qualifying to be chose, these individuals is playing the game of life breaking all the natural laws in the game of life scriptures, they just trying to dion sanders everything, that means Intercept everything moving, stars like Michael Jordan just played to win every time He was in the playoffs, big Bryan always said, "nephew you in the playoffs year after year," & j ro said, " you not down," as I stood sitting on my car I bought, I was talking about taking my game I built up to relocate toNew York, & California, I did that, & saw how it go while living cross country month to month consistently, I saw this through my eyes on the journey to get wealthy with a longevity perspective .

Mr. Mack Millon

"It don't cost nothing to be nothing, & don't let nobody throw your game off."

Stanley stack Jefferson

"Never lose your identity."

Biggie

Most known unknown throwback king pimp said, "one business lady don't stop the show," he saw me in my longterm lifestyle, the game of life speaks through us to us."

Unknown Milwaukee boss pimp

"What we need to do to create the abundant life, we need to be about the business of buying, & owning hotels."

Michael v roberts

"Back in the day, gangsters knew how to do karate, they would jump in the air, & kick your whole face off."

Sam love, jr

"It's 90 percent business, &10 percent talent."

Master p

"I'm a normal guy, with an extraordinary job."

Shannon sharpe

"Knowing I can control somebody with my mouth piece, & effect them in a game."

Gary Payton.

"Own like to talk about the shit they talk to me about."

Crunchy black

"Columbus never came to United States of America, or north and South America, he came as close as El Salvador."

Dr. Yosef Ben-jochannan

"It's easier to roll shit down hill, then it is to push a ball of shit up hill."

Iowa worker just like everybody else

"If you gonna be broke, don't be tired to."

Iowa father

"Ain't nothing about to change in America for indigenous peoples, no matter which one of them haters win."

Utp skip

"We out here working on it, that's the reason we out here now."

Beats by the pound

"It's more like an addiction to most of them."

Nate "boone" craft

"What I used to do is watch the big players, riding down the street when I was in high school looking out the windows, so that created a fascination in me, because ah very seldom did you see a black man riding in a brand new Cadillac, dressing real sharp, wearing big diamonds, you know ah looking like a celebrity riding through the town."

The grand master ray virgil fairley

"We had some rough days you know what I mean, and ah some hungry days, but once I found out about how to get some money, then I went out on my own at 13."

Diamond d

"It's the story of growing up In poverty you know yeah."
Fertado brothers

"It's easy for me to hurt somebody then kill somebody."
John alite

"You becoming a part of a team now you know, we was as much of a family as we could be."
Brian glaze Gibbs

"You know it's next to a miracle getting this many of our people together."
Malcolm x

"Just being surrounded by death, you know coming up in that town you know, just common to die young, everybody do die young, we was planning It in our minds, and I came up fast, so I said I'm gone try something different."
Bryan birdman Williams

"You know growing up In New York the point guard game is big, so I tried to be like Kenny Anderson."
Lamar Odom

"Sense Irv gotti & Dame dash has been out the game, the game has not been the same."
Drink champs nore

"Everything happens when it supposed to, Just look at it as preparation, for when you get to where you're supposed to be in life."
Lovely Amanda

"That braud was in heaven, you know she was in heaven, cause she with her man, her man is a motherf$@ker, now I get to be with him, this is why I'm h@eing."

Rosebudd with two d's for
double dose of this pimping
Hollywood

"Pimpin' started like this here, first is was the hooker getting money, but didn't know what to do with it, til the guy came along the point showed them where, let me manage your money, let me manage your money, they was managing their own money, you know, but they didn't know what to do with It, then they had to get the pimp, he was for protection."

Fillmore slim San Francisco

"A lot of those brothers used to be riding In town man, with those really nice carriages, that they wasn't driving for masta, that they wasn't their carriages, you understand me, masta, they was their carriages you understand me, & they was dressed in those nice outfits, nobody really paid them that much attention."

Danny brown Los angles

"I come from the ghetto you know, ah it was something I always wanted to do, I wanted an easy job, my mom passed away when I was 18 years old, & I ran Into a friend of mine, you know & everythang, & you know I was hanging out on the corner, so you know he come like rescue me, and ah gimme the game, about what this Ism was about, so I stayed down & dirty, here I am, today."

Kenny red Deep east Oakland

"In this underworld thing we call the game, you have your pimps players your Mack's, & all this other stuff."

Jade Carson city Nevada

"The street game is the black man game."

Sir captain Mississippi

"I wanted to be in the best suit, best shoes an ah you know the best cologne, and ah you know it was all image, you know If you look like a million bucks, you have more opportunities to attract a million bucks, then if you don't."

Gorgeous Dre Seattle

"I mean I mean it was just like something that ah was blessed upon me, this is the west side the best side."

Bishop Don magic Juan Chicago

"When they see me they get away you know what um saying, It's like Um the one they moma warned them about, I mean I'm not notorious you know, um charm know what Um saying, charm man right, I mean a name like that how notorious can I be."

Charm Hawaii

"Understand me, If he talking about he pimpin', We ain't making nem do a damn thing, we just Introducing them into this sh$t, & making sure they do this sh$t right, you understand me, so we can be professional and live like maf$ckin' king."

R.p. Peace & blessings to his
family tree New York City

"You got to have visionnnn."

Roger Robinson peace and
blessings to his family tree
Seattle Washington

"Now some of you guys might be surprised at what Im about to say, and say, who Is this lame that says he knows the game, and where did he learn to play, so gather around, and I'll run It down, and unravel my pedigree."

Iceberg slim peace & blessings to his family tree
Chicago

"The game will be good to you if you be good to the game, you know."

Fillmore slim New Orleans

"Rules regulations guidelines, before you pimp you got to be a man."

Gorgeous Dre Global

"So If you present yourself a certain way, you have to be consistently that way, that's how you get judged, you know."

Mel Taylor Peace & blessings to his family tree

"I'm telling you baby It might look easy, but you gone have to work some, to get to this status baby, see you at the top."

Bishop Don magic Juan Hollywood

"We discussed having a lot of money, and defying the system, ahm, and not having bosses, us being together and having an empire."

Danny brown Los angles

544

"I always was taught, "I always was taught that, if you ain't making no money, you couldn't be out here on these streets, um if you was gone be out In these streets, you was gone make money, you was gone support your family."

Curtis "Wall Street" Carroll Oakland

"You got to be born first, to obtain knowledge."

Suten seti Detroit Michigan

"History is a clock that people use to tell their political cultural time of day, it is also a compass people use, to find themselves on the map of human geography, history tells a people where they been, what they have been, where they are, what they are, Most important, history tells a people, where they still must go, what they still must be, relationship of history with the people is the same as a relationship of a mother, to her child."

Dr. John henrik Clarke Union springs
Alabama

"Think we auta wash white, but we aint gonna."

Bill Cosby Philadelphia

"Countering the conspiracy to destroy black boys."

Dr. Jawanza kunjufu Chicago

"It's gone get heated as It has before."

Blair Underwood Tacoma Washington

"Instill in our own peoples to stand on our own feet."

Malcolm x Lincoln Nebraska

"Black people in America seem to be generally unaware that they had a history, and that they where told they achieved nothing."

Dr. Chancellor Williams Bennetsville
South Carolina

"You have to have such a strong belief in yourself that you can quiet out all the outside noise."

Jay-z Brooklyn

"I got the right to live my life the way I want to live It, I mean being rich & black mean something man don't you know that, being poor & black don't mean sh$t, we living in different times you & I, I mean when we where young kids, there was no heroes, we got all sorts of heroes now, there's kids out there now that look up to me.

Max julien Washington, D.C.

"As he darts down the road, he looks back at his own home town, he didn't know where he was going, he didn't know what he was doing, but he was going to a world of trouble, a world of misunderstanding, a world of dog, a world of wh$res, a world of hypocrites, a world of gamble, a world of dope smokers, a world of prostitutes, he was going into a mean world, but he didn't know where he was going, you understand me, he didn't know where he was going, he was going into a world that was going to destroy him, but he didn't know where he was going, so many of us today doing these things to ourselves, because we don't know what we are doing, you understand me, & if we stop & think about ourselves sometimes, everything would be alright, you understand me, we going to jump off the bay bridge worrying about this man, worrying about that man, because we don't know who we are, we don't know where we going, & we don't know what we was here for, you understand me, good god almighty, oh look at this boy with his big money, oh he own the crap table now, he shooting his dice, he don't have sense enough to know his money not gone last doing these wrong things, doing these worldly things, gambling & drinking, It's an end to these things, one of these days, one of these hours, it's gone run out, but one of these days, you gone have to make up your mind to change your ways, I can see this young man, oh good god, I can see this young man as he made up in his mind, ta start back home, his money run out, his friends walked off & left him, his his buddies walked off & left him, his girlfriends quit him, he lost all he had."

Oakland preacher the Mack

"That's the only way to get something done man, you got to get out, & do it yourself if you want to accomplish something."

Roger e. Mosley Los angles

"I was riding down on the streets you know, checking on my game ah, I ran into a nice little ol thing, you wouldn't believe it man, ah she's a beauty, well you know how these little ol Mack's are around here, they don't have their sh$t In order you know & ah, I ran down & caught this little thing, & ah knocked her over you know, so I went & stashed that away you know, all man sh$t you know how I am, um gone run my thang you know, it's all about the money game with me, I do mine from frisco to Maine, you know how that is, oh most definitely got to do a little grooming first."

Frank d. ward Oakland California peace
& blessings to his family tree

"Well actually um, it all started In Michigan, you know um, Just having a dream, believing, believing in myself, believing In my skills, believing in my talent, & also surrounding myself with the right team, had to surround myself with the right people, & everything took flight."

Floyd mayweather jr.
Grand Rapids Michigan

"Our lives is about peakes & valleys, I like challenges, when people say we can't do It, it makes us work harder."
Shaquille O'Neil Newark New Jersey

"True thugs care about the whole family, the daughter, the moma, the daddy, everybody."

Tupac shakur New York City

"What I do I do for anybody."

Shock g Peace & blessings to
his family tree Brooklyn

"If you don't like the show, hall it."

Redd foxx Saint Louis Missouri

"What It did was free them, that's god work."
Paul Mooney Shreveport Louisiana

"I had to wait 40 minutes for my grits, this generation had to wait five minutes, they want stuff instantly now, they can't even wait to die, that's why they kill each other."
Paul Mooney Shreveport Louisiana

"Forever physical law there is a mental & physical counterpart everything in nature enjoys the sun, baths in the sun, bask in the sun, the sun gives light life and energy to everything in the universe, some flowers turn with the sun, which ever direction the sun is in that you find the plant leaning in that direction turning in that direction."
Dr. Khalid Muhammad Houston Texas

"If you keep your day good It go good."
Preacher Milwaukee

"When game recognizes game it connect the pieces to the puzzle, then cover all angles."
Boss player association Ancient indigenous

"What can we do to put us both on top from this point on, because it seem like that's what we both aiming for, you want to stay a queen I want to stay a king, so we can figure something out, it's about that time now, just think about it, Choices and options, short term long term, set up for life outcomes."
Big money sunny Milwaukee

"This world is setup as a joke, & everybody Is laughing at everybody."
Global

"California is the place to make everything go right to the top."
Ancient indigenous

"Minor setback for a major come back."
                              Mack breed Cross country

"Stay in motion til lightening strike, then you get what's coming to you."
                              Cj Milwaukee

"Player where you playing at, chopping that game at, where you sipping champagne at, where they know your name at.
                              Rappin 4 tay Bay Area

"Recognize who keep you in motion, who got your back, who down with you."
                              Mr. Mack Millon

"If you don't control your mind, something else will."
                              Missouri

"Control your mind & thoughts and put everything in order it need to be done, and do a process of elimination, and put time energy focus on best option, and learn to enjoy the option you pick."
                              Mack dulo Cross country

"Keep a grip so you won't slip on the game, ain't no break, full speed ahead."
                              Boss player association

"The goal In life is spiritual enlightenment."
                              Ancient indigenous

"I just can't seem to get my foot on the ground."

Eightball & mjg Tennessee

"A boss player build with bricks around him."

Boss player association

"Make the mind think, & don't force behavior."

Ancient indigenous

"Didn't have time for that, he was busy getting it out."

Shock g

"It's just a players world, you get the money the power the girl."

Goldy Oakland in the land of funk

"They have been playing the same divide and conquer game the whole time."

Kastonius prime

"Man what make her so better than you, you forgot about yourself dude, this what you working for."

Suga free Pomona

"Turned around her baby daddy grabbed her by the throat saying what you playing foe, I said man gone somewhere, he said what player, I said man I'm just saying though."

Suga free pomona

"It's mandatory I fall in season."

Pomona Pimpin young

"I'm so fly a replaced feather In The Godfather with a whole bird."

Pomona Pimpin young

"It's people all over the country saying why you move out there, I'm trying to move out there."

Too $hort Oakland California

"I got such a mixture of races that's why I can't fight anybody on race."

Rev Ike

"As far as the surveillance I welcome you understand anybody feel like they want to waste their time watching me you understand."

Eddie Jackson Detroit

"If I tell you that then you would know my business."

Eddie Jackson Detroit

"The expectation sort of controls everything after that."

Pee wee Kirkland Harlem

"Sometimes it takes somebody old enough to raise your level of countenance in every level of life it is."

Pee wee Kirkland

"Isn't it fun to be like everybody fresh on me, I don't understand how that's not fun to people."

Dame dash Harlem

"The way our logic was it was alwayss math."

Dame dash

"You know what I'm a man of god, and I realize you don't have to fear no man but god, that's it,"

Master p

"I felt that way I shared those thoughts with many some believed some didn't."

Sir j prince houston

"I'm just trying to diversify my portfolio."

Sir j prince

"Feed your brain and your nervous system, giving you balance."

Bro c. Freeman-el

"Without information you can't form a plan."

Bro Otis larib

"We take the Greek name and Latin names out the myths and we call them fairytales."

Dr. Laila afrika

"Today I give thanks to the most high, and our ancestors whom shoulders we stand on, if we stand tall, it's because we stand on the shoulders of our ancestors."

Bro. Otim larib

JOURNEY WEALTHY LONGEVITY SCRIPTURES

19.

Everywhere you go, be on the prowl to see if that city got benefits for you on the business tip, vehicles, homes, a new crew, or new members bringing something to the table, showing a down for life mentality, simply to be in the royal family, to help the royal family get wealthy on the journey to longevity.

WAKE UP THE SLEEPING GIANTS

Leon, Dottie, big Greg, dmx, shock g, Louis Armstrong, Marvin Gaye, malcom x, dr Martin Luther king jr., pimp c, Tupac, biggie smalls, Aretha Franklin, og double d, stack bundles, r.p., frank ward, king boo, jj havin bread, cj nick, Ed lee, e.l., jimmy Rogers, Eva, jean Rogers, glo, uncle Floyd, uncle joe, pooter, auntie Reese, bay sister, aunt a., aunt d., bob marley, king bean, pimp god, Jim dandy, skinny rob, quita, big Ed, Soulja slim, Nate dogg, bb king, Mac Dre.

Martha, cowboy boots, senio sister, Ron newt, general dubie, Marcus Garvey, the jacka, George Floyd, ezell Ford jr., Jamal Clark, philando castile, dreason "Sean" reed, breonna Taylor, ahmaud arbery, botham Jean, Trayvon martin, Michael brown, Michelle Shirley, redel Jones, Kenny watkins, stephon Clark, laquan McDonald, Tamil rice, Eric garner.

Curtis, UNCLE MALCHIA HE WAS A UNCLE I LOOK UP TO HE WAS FROM SHANKLEVILLE TX BURKEVILLE TX, Bianca, Bowie, Heem, Retta, JAM, Martez, Syville, Kyle, ShoWout, JACAri, Rahkei, Meechie, major, Mookie, Tezo, Braxton, Josiah Sheehan, Laron Pace, Meezy, and Rasheed, Annshica Davis, Annie Bess Davis, Viola Nellums,Katherine Holloway, Jeremy Holden, Jeremy Aka Kool Aid, Freddie Davis and Willie Nellums, Shaun Pearson aka Knott Head.

My cousins Black Rue, his sister Tiffany, died back to back two weeks apart young, my auntie lost both her children in one month, Strapp and slim, lil d dorlett son.

JOURNEY WEALTHY LONGEVITY SCRIPTURES

20.

Everywhere you go, be on the prowl to see if that city got benefits for you on the business tip, vehicles, homes, a new crew, or new members bringing something to the table, showing a down for life mentality, simply to be in the royal family, to help the royal family get wealthy on the journey to longevity.

CLASSIC UNFORGETTABLE MOVIES

Ray virgil fairly story: my life over the top

Larry fishburne: deep cover

Mack 10: It ain't easy

Fat joe: thicker than water

Outkast: idlewild

Master p: Im bout it, I got the hook up, I got the hook up 2, hot Boyz, repo

Ice cube: the players club, all about the Benjamins, trespass, Friday, next Friday, janky promoters, Friday after next, barbershop

Richard Pryor: see no evil hear no evil, Harlem nights, brewsters millions, stir crazy, the wiz, uptown Saturday night, car wash, bustin loose

Dmx: exit wounds, never die alone, belly, backstage

Ron O'Neil: superfly

Pam grier: foxy brown, Jackie brown, Coffy, Friday foster, escape from l.a., bucktown, bones, original gangstas.

Mack 10 & Fat joe: blood thicker than water

E-40 obstacles

Big ballin Florida movie

Black Caesar

The Mack

Willie dynamite

Pimps up hoes down

American pimp

Menace to society

New jack city

Caught up

Baby face

Buck town

Buck & the preacher

Skin game

Cabin in the sky

Cocaine cowboys 2

Cotton comes to Harlem

Dj screw: soldiers United for cash

Half baked

Up In smoke

Harlem nights

Heart breakers

Baby face

Hood2hood and three versions

I'm gonna get you sucka

Candy tangerine man

Pretty baby

Mon homme

King of kings

King of New York

The ladies man

The law and the lady

Money trucks

Mr. Lucky

Nina Simone what happened

The wiz

Up from the streets: New Orleans

Tradition is a temple

Tony roberts: wired, I'm different

Three 6 mafia: choices both versions

Snoop: Da game is sold not told, the wash, jimmy bones, soul plane

Mike Epps: School dance

Samson and Delilah

Scarface

Rhyme and reason

Rudy ray Moore: pettey wheatstraw, dolimite

A rage in Harlem

Leaving Las Vegas

Too $hort: Pimpin inc

Pimp c: pimpalation

Gangsta brown all his documentaries

Michael Maria all his documentaries

Master players ball

Mil town connected dvd

Hidden colors all versions

Eddie Murphy: Coming to America: vampire in Brooklyn, Beverly Hills cop all three, golden child

Chris rock all his movies

Thursday

3 strikes

Get on up

He got game

Tupac all his movies

Blue chips

Sunset park

Booger: Soul In the hole

And1 street ball all versions

Cookout

More than a game

Freddy got fingered

Baseketball, orgazmo

Martin Lawrence all his movies

South central

Damon dash all his movies

Blue hill avenue

Lil boosie webbie Ghetto stories

House party all three versions

Sugar hill

High school high

Fresh

Cooley high, jd's revenge

Shottas

Hot boyz, baller blockin

Jason lyric

The wayans family all their movies

Get rich or die trying

The players club

Superfly

Dead presidents

New Jersey drive

In too deep

Foolish

Tha eastsidaz

Tales from the hood

How high

Atl

Jay-z: streetz iz watchin, fade to black

Who's the man

Across 110th street

Trespass

Pimpology uncut

Really really pimpin in da south

Mortal kombat 2021

Meet the blacks 2

The cash money store: before anything

Panther

Killa season

A social media movie

Trouble man

Trick baby

Loyalty & respect cashville

The spot Gucci mane

JOURNEY WEALTHY LONGEVITY SCRIPTURES

21.

Everywhere you go, be on the prowl to see if that city got benefits for you on the business tip, vehicles, homes, a new crew, or new members bringing something to the table, showing a down for life mentality, simply to be in the royal family, to help the royal family get wealthy on the journey to longevity.

CLASSIC UNFORGETTABLE SONGS

Al green: for the good times, tired of being alone, look what you done for me, you ought to be with me, simply beautiful, love and happiness, call me, Jesus is waiting, I'm still in love with you, let's stay together

Silk tha shocker: just be straight me, if I don't gotta, who can I trust, you ain't gotta lie to kick It, pop lockin, give me the world, the shocker, mama alwayss told me, the day I was made, my car

E-40: keep pimpin, choices, bootsie, rappers ball, dusted & disgusted, da bumble, quarterbackin, ghetto celebrity, record haters, l.i.q., flashin, 43, earl that's yo life,

Missy Elliot, friendly skies, best friend, bite my style, beep me 911

Aaliyah: at your best, one in a million, 4 page letter, hot like fire, rock the boat

Swv: rain

The stylistics: children of the night

Fiend: corner store, waiting on god, I know what it's like

Nas: project windows

Typ: let's get it together, pinky ring

Mac Dre: feeling myself, Cali bear

Gangsta brown Intro hunnid racks

Og Fillmore slim outro

Mac minister all his ministry

Country boy clique: millennium muzic

Quint black: pimpin tools

Sir Charles sugar ray: running

Kool aceah: choosin

Goldy: in the land of funk,

Too short: longevity

Alphonso Mays: sex love and romance

Dirty boyz: hit the flo

Eightball and mjg: reason for rhymes, pimps

Rappin 4 tay: playa where you playing at, do you wanna ride, ain't no playa

Do or die: Pimpology

Baby drew: gold fangaz

Coo coo cal: mind is gone, penny for your thoughts

Louis Armstrong: Mack the knife

Stooges brass band: weed drout

Too short: respect the pimpin

Big mike: bourbans and lacs, all a dream, makin moves, unfinished business

Bob Marley: natural mystic

Gregory isaacs: temptation, lead me into temptation featuring sly Dunbar

Sister Nancy: bam bam

Nipsey hussle: victory lap, grinding all my life

Country boy clique: powder whole album

Jay-z: you only a customer

Sam sneed: lady heroine, you better recognize

Dj quik: jus lyke Compton

Gucci mane: lemonade, hold that thought

Dry down: can you feel me

E-40: undstandz me

50 cent: first date

Big mike: finish the job

Yung wun: tear it up

Troy ave: New York City

Father Dom: same ol song

Jay-z: dead presidents, the city is mine

Ill al skratch: I'll take her

Raekwon: frozen

Latoiya Williams: it feelz good

Utp og skip: playas & pimps

Shaquille O'Neal: can't stop the reign

Baby drew: hand that rock the cradle

Eric sermon: I'm hot, come thru, music

Tru life: bag for it

Moneybagg yo: In da air

Bb king: the thrill is gone

Knoc turn'al: the way I am

Tela: playboy, can't stop me

Yarbough & peoples: dont stop the music

Marvin Gaye: don't mess with mr. T

Kid frost: la raza

Tego Calderón: chillin, pà que retozen

Sade: king of sorrow

Sam Cooke: change is gone come

Master p: best hustler

The last mr. Bigg: traffic king

South circle: attitudes

Suga free: like what, can't lie to yourself

Outkast: Decatur psalms

Stevie wonder: that girl, as

Pimpin young: I wanna be

Super cat: dolly my baby

Swizz beatz, bigger business

Syleena Johnson: I am your woman

T.p. All I know

Tash: rap life, g's iz g's

Zapp: computer love, more bounce to the ounce

Z-ro: 25 lighters

Youngbloodz: 87 fleetwood, 85

Gangsta black : keep It real

Young jeezy: jeezy the snowman, don't get caught

Young buck: you ain't going nowhere, walk with me

Young bleed: keep it real, better than the last time, confedi, my own whole album

Baby drew: pimp tight

Xzibit: been a long time, alkoholik

Dog: Big pimpin

Wyclef jean: low income

Wu tang clan: reunited, it't yourz

Rza: Holocaust

Woozie: white or brown

Willie hutch: I choose you, sunshine lady, the Mack soundtrack

Lil keke: chunk up Duce

William devaughn: be thankful

Westside connection: gangstas make the world go round

Warren g: I need a light, get u down, pyt, walk these streets, in the midn-nite hour

War: the world is a ghetto

B-legit: g.a.m.e.

Glasses Malone: certified

Snoop dogg: just a baby boy

Dmx: grand finale

Aaliyah: one in a million

Busta rhymes: cocaine

Howlin' wolf: smokestack lightnin

Dru down: the game, playa fo real

Nate dogg: Santa Claus goes straight to the ghetto

Paul wall: smooth Operator

Flipmode squad: everybody on the line outside

Nate dogg: one more day

Keak da sneak: nigga rah

Dr. Dre: been there done that

Aaliyah: hot like fire

Mack10: take a hit

50 cent: when it rains it pours

Musical youth: pass the Dutchie

Jon b.: they know

Mo b. Dick: that thing Is on

C-loc: who's who

K-ci & jojo: life

Earth wind & fire: reasons

Anita baker: angel

Kane & able: gangstafied both versions

C-murder: like a jungle

Coleman Hawkins: stardust

Sandra cross: African king

Faith evans: can't believe

Above the law: call it what you want

Barrington levy: under mi sensi

Celly cell: it's going down

Maze: slwe are one

Mista f.a.b. Super sic wit it

Po' boy: bound 2 happen

Twista: front porch

Devin the dude: that dude

Twista: fire, holding down the game,

Still feel good, pimp on

James brown: like it is like it was

Jay-z: family feud

Shawty lo: dunn dunn

Too short: blow the whistle

Usher: superstar

Silkk the shocker: my car

Young bleed: keep it real

Baby drew: weakness

Andre nickatina: jungle

Project pat: keep it hood

Soulja slim: street life

Mr. Magic: that's me

Country boy clique: we dere

Gucci mane: 16 fever

Trick daddy: back In the day

Andre nickatina: cocaine

ChristOn: full of smoke

South side playaz: swang down

Derrick note:: u ain't Pimpin

JOURNEY WEALTHY LONGEVITY SCRIPTURES

22.

Everywhere you go, be on the prowl to see if that city got benefits for you on the business tip, vehicles, homes, a new crew, or new members bringing something to the table, showing a down for life mentality, simply to be in the royal family, to help the royal family get wealthy on the journey to longevity.

GLOBAL BEST SELLING AUTHORS

1. Michael v. Roberts: action has no season
2. J. prince: the art & science of respect a memoir by James prince
3. Wainworth m. Hall: a roar in Harlem based on true events, also he known as unique Mecca audio former Harlem ny kingpin
4. Pimpin ken ivy: pimpology the 48 laws of the game, the art of human chess a study guide to winning
5. Don magic Juan: from pimp stick to pulpit it's magic the life story of Don Juan
6. Dd Sullivan: the kingpins of the pimps
7. Iceberg slim: pimp the story of my life, trick baby
8. Alfred bilbo gholson: the pimp bible the sweet science of sin
9. Richard milner: black players the secret world of black pimps
10. Burt McKinley jr.: black Inventors of America
11. Maya Angelou: mother: a cradle to hold me
12. James Baldwin: notes of a native son
13. Phillis Wheatley peters: being brought Africa to America
14. Mickey royal: the pimp game
15. John Dickson: rosebudd the American pimp
16. Kenneth hunter: Pimpology: the street life of a real life pimp
17. Donald goines: whoreson
18. Thomas an Johnson and Dominic Jordan: pimp to paradise
19. Howard mcClearin lee: from pimp to prison to preacher
20. James prince: the art & science of respect
21. Rick Ross: hurricanes
22. Mayme Johnson: Harlem godfather
23. Seth ferranti: the supreme team
24. Willie lynch: the Willie lynch letter

25. Carter Godwin Woodson: the miseducation of the negro
26. George g. M James: stolen legacy
27. Kaba Hiawatha kamene: Shabaka's stone
28. Chancellor Williams: destruction of black civilization
29. Clyde the glide: Clyde drexler
30. Koran or al-Quran
31. Veda
32. Holy Bible
33. Ptahhotep: the instructions of ptah-hotep
34. Mfundishi jhutyms salim: mentchu-hotep and the spirit of the medjay
35. Elijah Muhammad: message to the Blackman in America
36. Dante fortson: the 48 laws of black empowerment
37. Sujan k. Dass: black people invented everything
38. Anu m'bantu: the black kings of Europe
39. Ice-t: Ice: a memoir of gangster life and redemption
40. Albert "prodigy" Johnson: my Infam life
41. Darlene Ortiz: definition of down
42. Mike Epps: unsuccessful thug
43. Brad "Scarface" Jordan: diary of a madman
44. Chuck d: fight the power
45. Mara shalhoup: bmf
46. Rakim: sweat the technique
47. 50 cent: from pieces to weight
48. Mike Tyson: undisputed truth
49. Luther Campbell: the book of Luke
50. Rick Ross: freeway Rick Ross
51. Julia Beverly: sweet jones
52. Tayannah lee mcquillar: Tupac shakur
53. Rick James: glow
54. Eugene weems: the marathon continues
55. Lamont "u-god" Hawkins: raw
56. Stanley tookie Williams: blue rage black redemption
57. T. Rogers:? The fifty most asked questions about gangs
58. Dmx: e.a.r.l.
59. Charlamagne tha god: black privilege
60. Gucci mane: the Gucci mane guide to greatness
61. Ivan van sertima: they came before Columbus

62. Ron chepesiuk: black Caesar
63. Leroy Barnes: mr. Untouchable
64. Sean Patrick griffin: black brothers inc.
65. Azie faison: game over
66. Jermaine Atkins: Zoe pound mafia
67. Cesar pina: flipping keys
68. Frank Lucas: original gangster
69. C-murder: bound by loyalty
70. Kevin chiles: the crack era
71. Sean branch: money, murder, and mayhem
72. Shomari wills: black fortunes
73. Brian Gibbs: the Brian "Gibbs" glaze story
74. Reginald f. Lewis: why should white guys have all the life?
75. Carol Jenkins: black titan
76. Herman Russell: building Atlanta
77. Shane white: prince of darkness
78. Elizabeth dowling Taylor: the original black elite
79. J.a. Rogers: the five negro presidents
80. Tricia martineau Wagner: black cowboys of the old west
81. Hannibal b. Johnson: Tulsa's historic greenwood district
82. George c Fraser: success runs in our race
83. David f. Krugler: 1919 the year of the racial violence
84. Art t. Burton: black gun, silver star
85. Dennis kimbro: think and grow rich
86. Mehrsa baradaran: the color of money
87. Raymond John: rise and grind
88. Reggie whittaker: as a black man thinketh
89. John henrik Clarke: my life in search of Africa
90. Michael v roberts: actions have no time
91. James p. Beckwourth: the life and adventures of James p. Beckwourth
92. Chancellor Williams: destruction of black civilization
93. The philosophical philosopher presents street life philosophy Mackology 1st edition written by royalty
94. The philosophical philosopher presents the king business Mackology 2nd written by a king named Mack
95. The philosophical philosopher presents Mackology 3rd edition coming 2022

JOURNEY WEALTHY LONGEVITY SCRIPTURES

23.

Everywhere you go, be on the prowl to see if that city got benefits for you on the business tip, vehicles, homes, a new crew, or new members bringing something to the table, showing a down for life mentality, simply to be in the royal family, to help the royal family get wealthy on the journey to longevity.

I'm watching sir David Attenborough: a life on our planet on Netflix, I just left mount pleasant, I'm headed to cedar falls Iowa to finish more chapters at the end of this unbelievable book Mackology 2nd edition, I just left George Floyd Minniapolis Minnesota, I was in the mall of America in Bloomington Minnesota, I was in the mirror maze, it was serious In there, I also saw the sea life aquarium, them sharks will follow you in there, & I was in game works, that was the business to, Minniapolis felt like home to me, I was In Salt Lake City Utah where the queen bee saw an owl, she just saw a wolf creeping through the night In mount pleasant Wisconsin, explore your world, find out why home is where the heart is, enjoy the rest of the book sir or madam.

All the respect in the world to him & his loved ones, I bought this cd when it first came out, "return to the 36 chambers," "the baddest hip hop man across the world", ol' dirty bastard, peace to his so for keeping his father alive, I'm listening to this album on my way to Iowa leaving Wisconsin, somebody said, "great minds think alike."

TOP PLACES TO BE

1. Dover Delaware: I saw ancient horseshoe crabs on bay here, me & Macon Georgia Chris.
2. Brockton Massachuetes: met a true giant by the name of dollar dollar bill y'all, his people showed me some areas there, mad love for Brockton indigenous peoples, they like that Hennessy privilege & west coast music.
3. Savannah Georgia: bought my first jay-z $300 champagne there, palm trees all over, saw tybee Isl to, dj played Ill al scratch songs for me.
4. Orlando Florida: everything about Orlando is right on time, the palm trees, the all year around weather, Shaquille O'Neal made this city what it is today in every way possible, the most enjoyable street is orange blossom trail.
5. Fargo North Dakota
6. Ontario California
7. Las Vegas Nevada: north Las Vegas is the place to be, lucky club hotel casino is the spot to lean back.
8. Niagara Falls New York: the scenery is flawless
9. Hollywood California
10. Milwaukee Wisconsin
11. Chicago Illinois
12. Saint Louis Missouri
13. Detroit Michigan
14. Dallas Texas
15. Houston Texas
16. Los angles California: saw Kobe Bryant murals out there, the traffic is exactly how it look on tv, & movies.

17. Snoqualmie Washington: just real peaceful, real green looking place to be.
18. Idaho falls Idaho
19. Gary Indiana: goldmine for anybody playing monopoly in real life.
20. Manhattan New York
21. Charlotte North Carolina
22. Charleston South Carolina
23. Minniapolis Minnesota: I pissed in every alley twice: uncle Robert king greedy, the name Is saying, "like you a greedy ass figga, straight from buelah Mississippi.
24. Boston Massachuetes
25. Worcester Massachusetts
26. Jersey city New Jersey
27. Philadelphia Pennsylvania
28. Jacksonville Florida
29. Tampa Florida
30. Tallahassee Florida
31. Miami Florida
32. Olive branch Mississippi: feel like home
33. Memphis Tennessee: feel like home, I was on my way to get bbq, I randomly ran into the Lorraine motel, where he was laid down to Rest In Peace, no good feelings in the air near that motel.
34. Nashville Tennessee
35. Chattanooga Tennessee
36. Cleveland Ohio
37. Columbus Ohio
38. Seattle Washington
39. Las cruces New Mexico
40. Buffalo New York
41. Denver Colorado
42. Aurora Colorado
43. Des Moines Iowa
44. Louisville Kentucky
45. Cincinnati Ohio
46. Mobile Alabama

47. Montgomery Alabama: I saw where Martin Luther king jr. nem was marching on highway.
48. Augusta Georgia: I saw hothead street that's named after James brown.
49. Tucson Arizona
50. Little Rock Arkansas: banging in Little Rock made me think it was terrible, my incounters with indigenous people was peaceful.
51. New Orleans Louisiana: very very clean, didn't look like a hurricane was there, utp skip was chilling upside watermelon & chicken restaurant, I was treated like family there, ain't no where like It.
52. Baton Rouge Louisiana
53. Salt Lake City Utah

THE GAME OF LIFE SCRIPTURES

19.

Playing the game of life, is knowing how to roll it, live to give, give to live, it's about unity, team work works, it's a proven fact, teams have won championships, everybody need everybody, cross country living will explain what the game of life scriptures is all about.

I'm leaning back with Duce & hypnotic editing this chapter, I'm watching drink champs episode with fat joe & og pistol Pete the giant.

I'm in New York watching Paul muni movie, it's called, "angel on my shoulder," unforgettable movie right here, I'm bout to re-edit this chapter.

Left Philadelphia earlier today, old head in the food truck said, "mind your business in Philly, & watch who you be around to avoid trouble in Philly, but all in all, it's straight in Philly.

UNFORGETTABLE INDIGENOUS PEOPLE

1. Michael v Roberts: billionaire mogul
2. Michael Jackson gary Indiana
3. Malcom x Lincoln Nebraska
4. Martin Luther king jr. Atlanta Georgia
5. George Floyd Fayetteville Nc
6. Trayvon martin Miami Florida
7. Emmett till Chicago Illinois
8. Yelitsa Jean-Charles Detroit
9. Russel Simmons hollins queens ny
10. Earl dmx Simmons Yonkers ny
11. Frank matthews Durham nc
12. Pee wee Kirkland Harlem ny
13. Dr. Patricia bath Harlem ny
14. Loretta Ford Saint Louis Missouri
15. Lewis Howard latimer Chelsea ma
16. Alex: Joe, Djay, Jaylen, Devin and Darin
17. Og aj
18. Big Bryan
19. Funny
20. Big pun
21. David steward
22. Fat joe
23. Ike Atkinson
24. Michael lee-chin
25. Run dmc
26. Chancellor Williams
27. Shyne

28. Ivan van sertima
29. Jimmy Hamilton graduated at 17
30. Runoko rashidi
31. Smithy
32. Preach Mac
33. Amos n. Wilson
34. Mona
35. Frances cress welsing
36. Cash money brothers records family
37. Notorious big Craig Mack
38. Murder inc records family
39. Tela suave house family
40. Typ dj screw family lil flip the whole screwed up click family
41. Roc a fella records family
42. Freeway Ricky Ross Rick Ross rapper
43. Convertible Burt
44. Hollywood division pimpin
45. Don Juan pimp family Chicago Scorpio king James king Burt king boo jojo bilbo June bug 4 j Twista crucial conflict do or die
46. Nas jungle brave hearts 50 cent az foxy brown Ill nana Capone n noreaga mc Shan queens bridge history
47. Rap a lot Lil j prince whole crew
48. Rappin 4 tay suga free Mac Dre Mac minister e-40 suga t d shot b legit
49. Lil Bruce Andre nickatina j. Diggs
50. Norbert rillieux
51. Too short father dom goldy kool aceah mc breed Tupac shock g money b Fillmore slim gangsta brown Mac breed hook the crook
52. Cheikn anta diop
53. Yosef Ben jochannan
54. D block
55. James Pierson beckwourth "bloody arm Virginia"
56. Dollar bill
57. Lewis Howard latimer
58. George Washington carver
59. jt money
60. rayful Edmond guy fisher

61. Utp skip
62. Spice 1
63. Mr. Kurt
64. Benjamin Banneker
65. Dino martell Rogers Jamaica karnell
66. Sarah Boone craven
67. Otis frank Boykin
68. Jim dandy
69. George Edward alcorn jr.
70. Andrew Jackson beard
71. Pimpin snooky pimpin ken
72. The entire cast of Friday 1 2 & 3 & the soundtrack for all three movies.
73. The entire cast of let's do it again & uptown Saturday night.
74. David n. Crosthwait jr.
75. Henry Blair
76. Miriam Benjamin
77. Majrjorie Joyner
78. Lloyd hall
79. Lewis temple
80. George Robert carruthers
81. Benjamin thornton Montgomery
82. Thomas l. Jennings
83. Alfred l. Cralle
84. Phillip b. Downing
85. Janet Rita Emerson bashen
86. Richard Bowie spikes
87. Granville tailer woods
88. Emmett w. Chappell
89. Frederick McKinley Jones
90. Jan Ernst matzeliger
91. Alexander miles
92. Garrett Augustus Morgan sr.
93. Lonnie George Johnson
94. Madam c.j. Walker
95. Alielia walker
96. Booker t Washington

97. Ida bell wells Barnett
98. Frederick Douglas
99. Carter Godwin Woodson
100. Olivia America Davidson
101. Sojourner truth
102. Alonzo Franklin herdon
103. 101.Carole Merritt
104. Andrew young
105. Sarah e. Goode
106. Alice h. Parker
107. Mark e. Dean
108. Leonard c. Bailey
109. Samuel Raymond scottron
110. Valerie l. Thomas
111. Mary Beatrice Davidson Kenner
112. John lee love
113. Ellen Elgin
114. Joseph Richard winters
115. Gerald Lawson
116. Jose vasconcelos
117. The Grimaldi
118. King kundur

THE GAME OF LIFE SCRIPTURES

20.

Playing the game of life, is knowing how to roll it, live to give, give to live, it's about unity, team work works, it's a proven fact, teams have won championships, everybody need everybody, cross country living, will explain what the game of life scriptures is all about.

I'm on the border line of Ohio & West Virginia, it took a while to finish this brilliant book of the century, I had to edit it with a tremendous amount of full effort, often surrounded by smoke signals from all over the country, or bubbles from imported champagne, Im sober as a retired Louisville pimp in South Africa cooking chitterlings, I decided what to take out this brilliant book, & what to leave in, I'm watching on Netflix, a four part series called, "high on the hog."

I hopped you enjoyed the book of the century, I think we all have purpose plus meaning In the game of life, if anything is out of your reach, believe it's in the palms of the most High, thank you a king Mack Millon times for your undivided attention, this last chapter is pieces I didn't get to squeeze In the chapters before this chapter, plus songs i crown very important in more ways then one to royalty.

Respect to Jalen Tyrese Johnson from Wisconsin hitting that nba accomplished goal, that's ho real players do It from Wisconsin.

THE KING BUSINESS MACKOLOGY 2ND EDITION SOUL TRACK LIST

Fiend: corner store

Stan: he would change how he lived if he could turn back hands of time, he didn't get a chance to pick how he wanted to live, at 13 he got paid from girl and it was off to the races, no break no day off.

Marvin Gaye: dont mess with mr. T

Playing the piano in the middle of time square, with a penguin Standing in a bucket of freezing cold Alaska water, right next to me, & I'm smoking a jazz black from denver Colorado, simultaneously drinking a plastic cup of New Orleans Hennessy xo, simultaneously wearing a Versace suit, with amazon cayman gator sandals on, with Michael Jordan socks on pulled up to my knees, with a Saint Louis creole woman tap dancing on top of the piano, she doing this as I try to play a p an e song.

Stooges brass band: weed drought

They lived that life so I didn't have to,

Pimp is a character, a mack is reality,

East coast & south deal with reality, Midwest & west coast create characters,

Get back on the throne together indigenous peoples, Trickery, intimidation, liquor, sex, kindness, is all weapons to catch a person off guard, Smokey moma says, "make it enough," that's what we gone do, Y'all got to plug with your people around the country, Rise above your nature, to adapt and maintain righteousnessly.

Father dom: same old song

You only got a problem if you don't know you have a problem, Maintain like a single mother in 1988, Some play, some win, Appreciation for haves, and have nots, To be a god, you have to be god body, It take one to know one, once a pimp, always a pimp, It's about direction, & guidance, Mack 10 hustler hand book says, "get in get out," Don't connect our spirits, if you being wrong with royalty.

Lil' keke: slab holiday(featuring crys wall)

Kingpin hustler boss player king pimp music, recognize who being touched by the spirit,You clean up the mess you made by not making a mess, Big meech had a billboard just like billy the kid, as well as bank robbers from the past in certain parts of this country, not to mention Bonnie and Clyde car, is in a museum with over one hundred bullet holes in it, Some people history started as nomads, drifters, scavengers, so it's normal for their off spring to do the same as they did, Know what each person is doing with their life, to know how to deal with them, or not deal with them at all, Incase their day to night is to make trouble, or be a distraction, or to help you progress with full effort assistance from that person, When you can avoid temptation & stay away from distractions, that means you focused,

Africa is made of many nations, which means the world, when it was one land mass, it was combined with many nations, meaning: when dynasties was in greatness, it was because a combination of many nations joined as one to create greatness, What you go through, will automatically be what makes you great, that is if you don't fall victim to it, or let it defeat you.

Eightball & m.j.g.: reason for rhyme

Always get yours off top, anything else is extra, business is never personal, what Is personal is never business.

Frank ocean: voodoo

Women was my friends, I didn't need man friends to not trust,or watch, or be jealous of me, women I can build with them, and tame them, see, hustlers need backup, because they on the front line, gangsters is a family structure, pimps & ballers is solo artist, leaning more towards teaming up with a group of women type thing, one stop shop, all is needed is in a huddle of women,that pertains to some not all.

Lil' keke: 4 doors and coupes

Bra from the Bronx said, " we got everybody here."

Lil' keke: I'm a g

Milwaukee cool, but it's a prison town, simply because it's in a prison state, so be prepared for that type of atmosphere when you cross state line, i got to put the fat meat in this book, you know everybody like to eat to be full, so that's how I got to serve it up, I got to serve it right, you know I'm also a survivor of the Chicago 80s, and Milwaukee 90s, like shyne said, "that's gangster," Int saying I'm gangster, but game recognizes game, and I learned how to mingle with women, survive with women, get wealthy with a royal family, and maintain that way with longevity embedded in my long term memory bank, for a lifetime, with a solid circle around royalty, see, put yourself in royalty crocodile shoes that was Purchased In Philadelphia, royalty pulled up to the front door, see game got to recognize game because it's mandatory in this lifetime, I mean, to be on point, it mean you on some John travolta type stuff, you staying alive strong, built to last, building yourself to last long strong, um tum bout staying afloat, living your style everyday, no breaks, I mean it's a full time job staying alive, it's a 24 hour procedure watching everything moving like Bill gates surveillance cameras, it's real in the world, from the front of time beginning to the present moment, royalty appreciate what Was learned, and stopped from doing, living a major lifestyle, this lifestyle I'm living is low key under the radar, it's like shooter said in Cincinnati kid, "I only play for percentage," nothing major, far as eyes can see, I been where I'm going, see, I be into global learning the ancient kingdom way, I'm tum bout, boss player counsel, a x female gangster, plus a boss retired pimp born again boss player as my counsel members, see you got to know I know the business, I'm just a modest fella, a great motivational speaker story teller, I can inspire the youth to focus on retirement before turning 30 years old, I mean it's golden child's existing from ancient times up to now, they shine in the day, and they shine at night, I mean, it look like heaven spotlight beaming out the clouds directly on them.

R. Kelly & jay-z: best of both worlds

One Feather in the head dres symbolizes matt, and Matt is what it is, the world was under one umbrella, the new world idea came to leave the past in the past, and recreate what was perfect into new ways which caused chaos in the world ever sense, from the beginning was passed down original teachings of higher learning to the original generations from the beginning to present moment, so much so it lives in normal conversations amongst indigenous people worldwide every live long day, some aware and some unaware that they keeping the original teachings in everyday circulation amongst all ears listening.

Too $hort: that's why

A new boss player level reached in January 21 2022, I think everybody be chilling, waiting to see what their next move gone be, Truth be spoken, truth be heard, so let it be written, so let it be done.

Little John: in the ghetto

Blues city cafe in Memphis Tennessee was recommended by shorty, also known as Richard in Memphis, he said, "he been to Wisconsin," he then said, "it's cool but just to cold," & he originally from Mississippi, royalty met him by world famous central bbq, it's located by the Lorain hotel, it's the hotel where Martin Luther king got killed, it's close to Beal street by Memphis downtown area.

Tha dogg pound: New York, New York

Everything gone come back around full circle.

Young bleed: I couldn't c' it

"Ain't nobody here except a bunch of us Mack's, mackin on the microphone for money," like king jb stomp down said, it's from the baileys sprinkled heavy on the Mac sauce album, I mean look at this what I say, I mean literally, now if I can be invisible in plain sight, huge face stack, major mackin when I talk, how I walk I speak to game that recognize game, so it's all us who see the invisible in plain sight, those letting their game speak for them, it's boss players status living, I mean interacting simultaneously adapting updated upgraded, in it to the finish, being stupendous fantastic and fabulous, living to learn, learning how to live simultaneously, I mean all that at once, I mean with a dream team turning dreams to reality, bout to press play soon I'm on pause at the moment under construction like tiara said, I mean making room for improvement spring cleaning process of elimination, with intentions to rise and surprise, then wake up to grind, royalty don't stop or take breaks, even when sleeping the brain building game, with wisdom knowledge creating more power, when you see royalty walking built up like a gorilla glue, strong confident ahead handling business, read to succeed is routine in leisure time, straight watching the history from start to present moment, see living life is all good with game that recognize game, dedicated to being the greatest on top, it's only right, you got to get to & do it.

Yungstar: gots to be everything

It ain't close to over, matter of fact it's just getting started, I mean sound the alarm everywhere in the world, ring that Liberty bell in Philadelphia, Because it's time to get down with the get down, to get up & stay up, I done seen top individuals at their best, and it's time for imitation of life to transpire, exactly, with all their skills in one spot making what was speculated to be a mission impossible into a mission possible, & goal accomplished.

Young jeezy: don't get caught

My game 90s all the way down to the early 1900s, straight solid individual with respect for all I meet next, See this game of life is nice if you play it right, just keep a grip so you want slip, if you can't take your money in rubber bands with you, you going to the wrong place, I mean, be around the next levels individuals, see int got the game for those who aim to keep me down, or keep royalty standing still, see, it's more real then jack and Jill going down the hill, we going up the hill to see how it feel to live correctly, like it was meant to be.

Turk: it's in me

The philosophical philosopher presents the king business Mackology 2nd edition written by king Mack Millon dollars, million mackin is the name given by Chicago frank nitty.

T.p.: all I know

Make show who around you don't make currency more important then you.

Suga free & Pomona Pimpin' young: the players ball

Is people using the law as a tool to keep order in society, or is it being used as a weapon to demand people pay for those holding the law in their hands personal lifestyle.

Soulja slim: from what i was told

Like young guns said, "mount up," then if need be, you got to get your crew ready to play their part to help everybody get right.

Soulja slim: wootay

They leading us to quick sand every step we take when we wake up, got to rise above on the pathway of longevity, it's just about love & everything the Most High gave us at birth, can't live without love from above & beyond, we subject to go crazy without it, we need that love to be in us strong, you got to know that, the Most High is first in every race is the natural thought indigenous people born with, now I might have to give king pimpin up to California, they got fresh money pouring like rain everyday, & the scenery to go with all that, game recognize game, California is also by the ocean, that's more money attractive, all game supposed to recognize game in this book right here right now, respect to Ohio katt willams, this book is the business, I got the energy from all indigenous people all this country, I cross paths with indigenous peoples all over this country, now it's known by us all that indigenous need each other energy, that's why we always in groups, most title these groups gangs, it's just us what we call chillin like money In the freezer, game recognize game, you know people love memories, now you shouldn't say this to any old body, but when I'm stepping my game up, I say I'm working on my pimpin, & that's not what you know as modern day pimpology, you can tell who is an indigenous person, what type of indigenous person they been around, according to how they move, & talk, game recognize game, I mean the pimpin came from love, it grow because of love, no hate in the orginal pimpin, its love that produce real pimpin not hate, that's a lack of love that produce hate, what some of us have time for to figure out, the rest of us don't have time to figure out.

Utp skip: pimps/players

Sadness don't be with my people, we stepping back into love, which you call the sunlight, & if you visiting new land to you, ask the indigenous people how they living in their land, and they gone respect that in you, from you showing concern, & love, now even if the elders, or youth got caught up in the game of life, we still treat them like family, that's how you supposed play it, that's written in the game of life scriptures, always feel the need to step your game up, if you been introduced by love from your guardians, then you know what love is, what it mean, & how to touch somebody with it, it's mandatory worldwide for game to recognize game, absolutely no lame thinking process, or behavior is ever going to be acceptable on any land boss players play on, cross country kings is laying down old laws of the land, that which put indigenous people first, but you know the basic instructions before leaving earth say, "those last, will be first," game recognize game.

Suga free: suga free

Everything happens for the right reason at the right time.

Gucci mane: hold that thought

Ended up in north Kansas City Missouri in a super 8, & hotel cab didn't give me a ride to the sto, so I pulled off to go on champagne jazz black run, royalty noticed treatment received was identical to person on America's most wanted, funny style stuff like California say, then royalty hit a gas station noticing face turned up by gas station person, asked him where I'm at, he told me north Kansas City Missouri, then royalty checked him for frowning his face up at a king, then dipped, ungrateful faces don't know all money green, & when your store ain't making money add up, then they be nice with indigenous peoples, that's what you call a boat load of laim behavior, It transpires exactly like that in certain places around the country, not everywhere though, royalty just left Hollywood, same faces but it was ok, but still laim to the Game, so I just pop the cork screw, fire it up like busts rhymes, & push play on the last mack Standing all game entertainment music, & then focus on the business in my arm reach, so I stand under the green light spotlight as the cars, to trucks roll pass, I enjoy the peaceful game that rain drops hitting the ground, & then royalty realize why it's mandatory to play to win, like Mac Dre said, "it's raining game," as the wind blow, the rain passes me quietly, I hear a latoiya Williams song come on, & instantly the bugs fly in between the rain drops, I realize who is who, & how to side step them if need be, & continue to stay on my pathway, moments like this, remind royalty of upstate New York with wozzzie don, chopping up game, sipping rose Moet, with the retired army vet from South Carolina, I can still hear international red speaking all the way from San Francisco saying, "if you got twenty years in the game, you a boss player," I also notice the new generation don't realize the world they live in, it's all fantasy, they made to believe it's real, this is known because the the Most High is not first in their life, which stops them from living in the real world, most indigenous peoples will call it the game of life, and it's a sad sight to see those who indigenous but their game don't recognize game, it's a sad sight to see when game don't recognize game.

Sade: is it a crime

You got to like what you write.

Sade: never as good as the first time

Got to make show you not living in a fantasy world, because when you see nonsense, you will know it's a game being played, and the cereal once said, "tricks are for kids."

Red café: heart & soul

This ain't for show & tell purposes, this for the realest reasons Royalty play the royal game the way Royalty built it to be played, update it upgrade it every day, week, month, & year after 24 years, presently always customize the way you move, it's mandatory in this lifetime, & watch for traps, issues, & problems, don't be in the crowd, lean back, play the background, analyze, aim for the throne on the Kilimanjaro top, and if you want need to play the game of life with royalty, then follow my lead, and we gone figure it out to master the art of living life, see, most people believe life is one way, which is how some set it up to be played, & at the same time, it's consistently being played on all levels, now what you think about that.

Rakim: the mystery

Mike Jones said, "it fake grinding to be a king," Pimp c said, "take that monkey sh$t off you embarrassing us," Rich boy said, "you say I talk slow and rhyme funny but int thinking about nothing but the big money."

2pac: drunk freestyle

So you telling me my words can't reach your mind, or your heart, that mean you stuck on what you feel, & think is right, & that means what I'm saying is being blocked out.

2pac: my block (original 1995)

We more into music that make us comfortable with hitting the top of the food chain, serving our purpose in life living meaningful, music that's chopping up game with royalty, you know what um tum bout.

8ball & mjg: in the wind

10/29/20 Another boss player level has been reached through confirmation of chopping up game, & braking it down in fractions, to devise a new updated upgraded plan, to continue playing to win living life to the fullest, boss player from Georgia from Dayton Ohio, just told me Ohio players singing group just got a street named after them, he said they was still in the streets, & they got took out by the street life, he also told me the young players from mount vernon in Columbus Ohio showed him love first time seeing him, they told him if he have any issues let them know, I memb in Milwaukee Wisconsin I saw an indigenous man stealing a pizza out the freezer, & the foreigners told him get out, so I paid for it, I bought two for him matter of fact, a young player saw this, & told me outside the gas station if I need anything hit him up.

Andre nickatina: btch (upside down)

Never hate me, or be jealous, or envy me, or compete with me, you a woman, I'm a man, so we can never be against each other, or want to be each other, we both in positions that we can not put ourselves in simultaneously, you can be a queen, I can't be a queen, I can be a king, you can't be a king, & we both have to know our roles in this world, that's how you eliminate confusion and chaos.

I'm watching the Scarface dinner scene

To understand somebody, you got to know their perspective on life.

Big mike: finish the job

No reason to settle, you living so the only option is live it to the fullest, that's why royalty be how Royalty be, why keep playing around, its people out here living it up on a regular basis consistently, I been to one island in my life, Hawaii my major next move, so Im aiming at that right now, that's why I'm out here like this, own like this driving like this, it's a serious business, I'm like all man y'all ain't gone help out at all, so I got to dig in my pockets, so if I'm running my own business, & I see how it go this far, so I'm aiming to get more businesses started.

C-murder: been a long time

Touched by the Sun, so in the youth, movements is sometimes made incorrectly consistently, but living life in the fast lane on point all the way, but consistently making moves incorrectly, so then you keep on with the motion in the ocean, get the keys to what you need access to, it's all the game of life is, it's movements made strategically everyday consistently.

Choclair: let's ride

When you out of your home town, away from the land you indigenous to, & the people show you love, show it back, & invite them to your city.

Crucial conflict: when the playas live

When you dealing with the best, that amateur stuff gone feel out of place, & awkward when it see giants.

Pomona Pimpin young: I wanna be

Remembering black Wall Street Tulsa ok

Az: sugar hill

Reached another boss player level June 28th, 2021

Suga free: don't be thinking with yo $i@? Boy

Find out who will sell your information, The wise players get jobs with less work as possible, with more pay, with intentions to make more money greet them, then you get ones that compete to convince people to give up their money to them, so they can make money off other people's money.

Mike live Las Vegas pomopimpin young interview

Indigenous soulful spiritual people got to stay from out of bounds, looking for trouble, being curious like a cat, sit back focus on what you got in arm reach, use your tools, your Most High gifts you born with.

"The best way to heal it is get away from it."

Pomona Pimpin young

Pomona Pimpin young: I wanna go home featuring Pomona drey

Some don't want positive energy because the negative is more appealing more attractive the positive don't look like it's worth having.

Dangerous crew 1994 billyjam/hip hop slam interview pt 1

Every lane you going into to, get paid in full, find out who is the known mastermind in that lane, study them like Kobe studied Michael Jordan, that's how men, and women learn how to master the life they live, you then hit the top, and begin to meet, or get introduced to the people behind the scenes that's really running the show.

K-dee: hittin' corners 1994 official video

We get put in positions we qualified to be in, that which means you priceless until you start living worthless, all week indigenous spiritual soulful people been saying, "know your worth."

Bigsyke from Inglewood Interviewed by califaces

Sometimes it's necessary to hibernate to relax, isolate to sharpen up skills with proper tools in the correct environment, with energy that will rekindle old flames to build self strength back up, to see why self motivated to get back on the throne..

"It's all about longevity."

Big syke Inglewood

Bro. C. Freeman-el i self law am master

"You're ancient ancestors inheritance for you, hidden knowledge, sacred knowledge."

Bro. C. Freeman-el

California is the place to be all year around, it don't take no breaks, or day off.

Newtral groundz show interview mr. Marcelo from magnolia projects New Orleans Louisiana

Money be coming, but you got to know where to put it.

Music words and weather.

When delivering your introduction, game supposed to be involved, letting it be known game of life is how you play it, with all game dedication intelligent to brilliant thinking.

They king living in California, Texas, Georgia, and Florida.

N'focus media tv interview utp wacko

Put your bid in, to create options, and let the rest do something for itself.

For those with their hands on everything, getting better acquainted with who will invest in you, beneficially preferably, let all that happen naturally, because if you have to make it happen, it might be putting up a fight the whole time.

Customize the energy around you.

"I enjoy playing the game, because I play fair, I've always played fair, thats why I believe That I have reached the level of this game that I have reached, for playing fair.

Bishop Don magic Juan westside Chicago

Respect to sha'carri richardson for running 10.75 seconds breaking 100 m record at the national collegiate athletic association championships, born in fall Texas, 25 year old soulful Olympian.

THE GAME OF LIFE SCRIPTURES

21.

Playing the game of life, is knowing how to roll it, live to give, give to live, it's about unity, team work works, it's a proven fact, teams have won championships, everybody need everybody, cross country living will explain what the game of life scriptures is all about.

I'm listening to fabolous song, it's called, "cold summer."

STANLEY STACK JEFFERSON
STAY DOWN

James brown: it's a mans world

With a cup of Moët Chandon rose, he says, "Here's to life, and success son."

All yeah keep It moving.

What is your purpose In life?

"My purpose in life is living life as long as I can, & having as much money as I can."

Where you born and raised at?

James brown: super bad

"I was born in Mississippi, I raised in Milwaukee Wisconsin."

What was your introduction to the game of life?

"My Introduction to the game was um being around older players, listening, not opening my mouth, open my mind listening."

Your title that paid you the most?

"Pimpin'"

Who was giants in your lifestyle?

"Rob Robertson, giants in pimpin'?, or giants in general? Well being a player um my uncle big k, my uncle best friend big 50, peewee Ferguson, Jim dandy, running bear."

The greatest boss players you knew, and know now?

"Greatest boss player that I knew, was my uncle big k."

Now, number one thing you learned?

"I would say survival."

What's your favorite city and why?

"I would say my favorite city, is um Milwaukee, this where my roots come from."

The most Important person past or present?

"God"

What's your favorite person you ever had in life?

"My mother."

Number one rule in the game of life?

"Staying safe."

Wisest statement you can say? What's the best game you can give somebody?

"Mine your own business, stay safe."

What is life about?

"Living"

What is the most money you ever had in arm reach?

"40 $50,00."

The most dangerous day in your life?

"When a hater tried to kill me."

Worst mistake you ever made?

"Fu$?ing with drugs."

What would you do with a million dollars?

"Live rich."

What's the biggest accomplishment? Biggest thing you ever did?

James brown: payback

"That can be a few thangs you know, I would say, living the age that I am."

Who is god?

"A spirit."

Why was church important?

"Because I want to hear the word,"

Who your favorite person to make money with?

"Self"

What is the biggest rule you broke?

"Using drugs"

Do everything happen for a reason?

"Yes"

Why is family staying close important?

"Because that's who I been with all my life."

Who do you think about the most?

"I think about my parents."

Was you born in the game of life?

"I was born in the game."

What Is what was the most important thing to you?

"My family"

Who game you respect the most?

"My uncle my uncle big k."

Why is music important?

"Because it soothes me."

What Is the game of life?

"Survival"

What Is a king and queen?

"A king to me is ah ruler, a queen is somebody that sticks by her man."

What Is a gangster?

"Somebody who don't take no sh!t."

What Is a pimp?

"Somebody that collect h.ands o.n e.verything money.

James brown: down and out in New York City

What is a player?

"Somebody that do mix it up."

If you know then what you know now what would you say to your younger self?

"Not making mistakes that I did."

What's your message to the youth?

"Be the best that you can."

Who is indigenous to the land, to this country?

"I say Black folks."

What Is the best business move to make right now?

"Reality"

What do you want to see?

"I want to see the world."

Who do you want to see?

"I would say I want to see god."

What do you pray about?

"I pray about that he woke my family up, I pray that the world be a better place."

Why was everybody poor around you?

"Because they wanted to be."

What creates crime?

"People"

What you blessed to do?

"Live"

What is your purpose in life?

"Ta have a bunch of money, me & my family, live a long life.

What do you want to say to me?

"I want to say That you grown a lot, and I think I know that you on you on your way to be bigger,

What do money do?

"Money makes me happy, money makes me get some things I don't have."

Who was the best student in the game of life you taught?

"I would say my godson."

Talk about moma father grandma granddaddy.

"My mother Is the most wonderfulest thing in my life, my father is the best father I knowed that's in my life, my grandmother was a wonderful woman, my grandfather was a wonderful man."

Tell your kids something important.

"Dont be a fool, be careful in life."

What would you change? Would you change anything in your life?

James brown: sporting life

"Yes, the way that I'm living life now."

Is your game tight?

"Not tight as it should be."

How do you get your game tight?

"By correcting the things that I did that was loose."

Is you at the top of your game?

"No"

James brown: soul power

How do you play to win?

"Stay on top of my game"

James brown: dirty harri

What Is going on in the world right now?

"Ahhh lot of hate."

What Is your name how you get it?

"My name I got my name stack how I earn that name stack by stacking my money and having money."

James brown: the boss

What do you want to title your chapter?

"Stay down"

"That was good enough?"

That was straight

"You gone put that…."

James brown: blind man can see

streetlifephilosophy the 2019 book exclusive be the first to read it before everybody start buying it, amazon kindle books, google books, barnes and nobles authorhouse books. This book is like reading lyrics of your favorite album song or watching the number one movie of 2019, with your eyes reading the script before the movie come to the movie theater. A life worth living is a life worth learning read to suceed.

Lightning Source UK Ltd.
Milton Keynes UK
UKHW012020040821
388278UK00001B/47